CompTIA®

AutoOps+

STUDY GUIDE

EXAM AT0-001

CompTIA®

AutoOps+

STUDY GUIDE

EXAM AT0-001

BRANDON RICH

SYBEX
A Wiley Brand

Published by John Wiley & Sons, Inc., Hoboken, New Jersey.

For general information on our other products and services, please contact our Customer Care Department within the United States at (800) 762-2974, outside the United States at (317) 572- 3993. For product technical support, you can find answers to frequently asked questions or reach us via live chat at `https://sybexsupport.wiley.com`

Wiley also publishes its books in a variety of electronic formats. Some content that appears in print may not be available in electronic formats. For more information about Wiley products, visit our web site at `www.wiley.com`

Library of Congress Cataloging-in-Publication Data has been applied for:

Paperback ISBN: 9781394406067
ePDF ISBN: 9781394406081
ePub ISBN: 9781394406074

Cover design: Wiley
Cover Image: Jeremy Woodhouse/Getty Images

Typesetting: Set in 9.5/12 SabonLTStd by Lumina Datamatics
Printed and bound by CPI Group (UK) Ltd, Croydon, CR0 4YY
C9781394406067_270726

Acknowledgments

It takes a team to create a book like this. As always, I'm indebted to Carole Jelen for making connections and helping navigate all the ins and outs of the publishing process. I'd also like to thank the team at Wiley for helping bring this book to life, especially Krysta Winsheimer, project manager, for keeping things moving and answering my many questions, and to Ashirvad Moses and Pete Gaughan for their many contributions along the way. Thanks to Annie Melnick for jumping in mid-stream during a changing of the guard and making it a smooth transition. Thank you to Elizabeth Welch for copyediting my questionable prose and to Jajneswar Chhotaray for turning it all into the real finished product you're reading now. Finally, thanks to Kenyon Brown for the opportunity to tackle this new certification. Enjoy your retirement!

About the Author

Brandon Rich serves as Director of AI Enablement at the University of Notre Dame, where he leads institutional efforts to translate ever-evolving AI capabilities into responsible, scalable, and innovative practice. His career has spanned web and mobile application development, application and integration architecture, API development and design, enterprise architecture, and cloud architecture. He is the author of *AWS Certified Developer Study Guide: Associate (DVA-C02) Exam* (Sybex Study Guide) 2nd Edition and numerous LinkedIn Learning courses, including the Complete Guide to AWS Software Deployment, AWS: Storage and Data Management, and Advanced AWS CloudFormation for Enterprise.

His current work focuses on AI literacy, strategy, and production implementations, helping academic and administrative units move from experimentation to sustainable impact. He is the founder of the Notre Dame AI Forum, an annual conference convening higher ed AI strategists and technologists, co-founder of the Internet2 AI Innovation Accelerator, and creator of the Higher Ed AI Collaboration Hub, a community of peers sharing experiences as they deliver campus AI solutions that serve the mission of higher education.

Contents at a Glance

Contents

Introduction

Why learn to automate IT operations? The answer is simple: Automation has moved from a competitive edge to a baseline expectation in modern infrastructure roles. Whether you work in cloud, systems, or network administration, the ability to write scripts, build pipelines, and deploy configurations at scale is now central to how teams operate. Organizations that automate routine tasks ship changes faster, recover from failures more reliably, and manage larger environments with smaller teams. By mastering the skills covered in this book, you will be equipped to take on more complex responsibilities, contribute to DevOps and platform engineering workflows, and position yourself for roles that command greater scope and compensation.

CompTIA developed AutoOps+ as part of its Expansion Series, targeting IT professionals who want to validate their automation and operational scripting skills. The certification is designed for candidates with approximately two to three years of experience in a core IT infrastructure role, such as systems, cloud, or network administration. Recommended prerequisite certifications include Network+, Linux+, Cloud+, and Server+. The exam certifies that a candidate has the knowledge and skills required to use coding and scripting techniques to automate enterprise workflows, apply infrastructure-as-code and configuration management practices, build and troubleshoot continuous integration pipelines, and implement continuous delivery strategies while adhering to security best practices.

The purpose of this book is to help you pass the CompTIA AutoOps+ exam (AT0-001). The exam is organized into four domains: Automation Coding Concepts (31%), System Configuration (25%), Continuous Integration (24%), and Continuous Delivery (20%). This book covers all four domains, from working on the command line and writing scripts, through source control and infrastructure-as-code, to building CI/CD pipelines and operationalizing services. You will come away with the hands-on knowledge needed to pass the exam and, more importantly, to apply automation practices confidently in real production environments. Even after you have earned your AutoOps+ certification, this book will remain a practical reference for the tools and patterns you use every day.

NOTE Don't just study the questions and answers! The questions on the actual exam will be different from the practice questions included in this book. The exam is designed to test your knowledge of a concept or objective, so use this book to learn the objectives behind the questions.

The AutoOps+ Exam

AutoOps+ is CompTIA's vendor-neutral certification for IT professionals who automate infrastructure operations across cloud, hybrid, and on-premises environments. It validates practical skills across four domains: scripting and automation code, system configuration at scale, continuous integration pipelines, and continuous delivery practices. Candidates are expected to bring two to three years of hands-on infrastructure experience, and the exam assumes familiarity with core CompTIA credentials such as Network+, Linux+, Cloud+, or Server+.

Why Become AutoOps+ Certified?

There are several compelling reasons to earn your AutoOps+ certification:

It validates in-demand automation skills. As organizations accelerate their adoption of cloud infrastructure and DevOps practices, the ability to automate operations is increasingly a requirement rather than a differentiator. AutoOps+ gives employers an objective measure of a candidate's ability to write scripts, manage infrastructure-as-code, build CI/CD pipelines, and operate systems reliably at scale. Earning the certification demonstrates that you have moved beyond manual administration and are ready to work at the pace modern infrastructure demands.

It opens doors to higher-value roles. AutoOps+ is designed for IT professionals with two to three years of experience who want to formalize and credential their automation skills. Roles such as automation engineer, cloud operations specialist, site reliability engineer, and DevOps analyst all draw on the competencies the exam covers. Certified professionals bring verifiable skills to teams that are actively reducing manual effort and building the pipelines that keep modern applications running.

It accelerates your career in DevOps and platform engineering. The skills AutoOps+ certifies sit at the intersection of traditional IT operations and modern software delivery. Engineers who can automate infrastructure provisioning, enforce configuration at scale, and build reliable delivery pipelines are essential to any organization running workloads in cloud or hybrid environments. Earning AutoOps+ certification signals that you can bridge that gap, making you a stronger candidate for leadership and architecture roles that require both operational depth and engineering fluency.

It complements your existing CompTIA certifications. AutoOps+ is part of CompTIA's Expansion Series, which is built on top of core infrastructure certifications. CompTIA recommends Network+, Linux+, Cloud+, or Server+ as background for candidates sitting the exam. If you already hold one or more of those credentials, AutoOps+ is the natural next step: It takes the foundational knowledge those exams establish and extends it into the automation and continuous delivery practices that infrastructure teams apply every day.

It demonstrates operational readiness to employers. Hiring managers and engineering leads increasingly look for candidates who can demonstrate practical automation skills, not just describe them. AutoOps+ provides an independent, vendor-neutral benchmark that signals you are capable of building and maintaining the pipelines, scripts, and configuration management systems that real production environments depend on. In a field where the tools evolve quickly, a CompTIA certification shows that your skills have been validated against a current, industry-developed standard.

Study Guide Features

This study guide uses several common elements to help you prepare. These include the following:

Summaries The Summary section of each chapter briefly explains the chapter, allowing you to easily understand what it covers.

Exam Essentials The Exam Essentials focus on major exam topics and critical knowledge that you should take into the test. The Exam Essentials focus on the exam objectives provided by CompTIA.

Chapter Review Questions A set of questions at the end of each chapter will help you assess your knowledge and if you are ready to take the exam based on your knowledge of that chapter's topics.

WARNING

The review questions, assessment test, and other testing elements included in this book are *not* derived from the actual exam questions, so don't memorize the answers to these questions and assume that doing so will enable you to pass the exam. You should learn the underlying topic, as described in the text of the book. This will let you answer the questions provided with this book *and* pass the exam. Learning the underlying topic is also the approach that will serve you best in the workplace—the ultimate goal of a certification.

Interactive Online Learning Environment and TestBank

Studying the material in the *AutoOps+ Study Guide* is an important part of preparing for the AutoOps+ certification exam, but we provide additional tools to help you prepare. The online TestBank will help you understand the types of questions that will appear on the certification exam.

- The Practice Tests in the TestBank include all the questions in each chapter as well as the questions from the Assessment Test. *In addition*, there is a practice exam with 65 questions. You can use these tests to evaluate your understanding and identify areas that may require additional study.

- The Flashcards in the TestBank will push the limits of what you should know for the certification exam. There are 100 questions provided in digital format. Each flashcard has one question and one correct answer.
- The online Glossary is a searchable list of key terms introduced in this exam guide that you should know for the AutoOps+ certification exam.

To start using these to study for the AutoOps+ exam, go to `www.wiley.com/go/sybextestprep` and register your book to receive your unique PIN. Once you have the PIN, return to `www.wiley.com/go/sybextestprep`, find your book, and click Register or Login and follow the link to register a new account or add this book to an existing account.

> NOTE: Like all exams, the AutoOps+ certification from CompTIA is updated periodically and may eventually be retired or replaced. At some point after CompTIA is no longer offering this exam, the old editions of our books and online tools will be retired. If you have purchased this book after the exam was retired, or are attempting to register in the Sybex online learning environment after the exam was retired, please know that we make no guarantees that this exam's online Sybex tools will be available once the exam is no longer available.

AutoOps+ Objectives

The CompTIA AutoOps+ Official Study Guide has been written to cover every AutoOps+ exam objective at a level appropriate to its exam weighting. The following table provides a breakdown of this book's exam coverage, showing you the weight of each domain and the chapters where each objective is covered:

Subject Area	**% of Exam**
1.0 Automation Coding Concepts	31%
2.0 System Configuration	25%
3.0 Continuous Integration	24%
4.0 Continuous Delivery	20%
Total	100%

Exam Objective	Chapter(s)
1.0 Automation Coding Concepts	
1.1 Given a scenario, use code to support automation.	1, 2, 3, 4, 5, 6, 7, 8 9, 10
1.2 Given a scenario, use source control techniques to version code.	3, 10
1.3 Explain concepts related to infrastructure-as-code (IaC).	4, 5, 9
1.4 Given a scenario, troubleshoot common issues with the code life cycle.	2, 3, 4, 5, 9
2.0 System Configuration	1, 2
2.1 Given a scenario, use configuration management techniques to deploy a solution.	5, 7, 9
2.2 Compare and contrast basic approaches to automation.	1, 2, 4, 5, 6, 8
2.3 Given a scenario, interact with Representational State Transfer–compliant (RESTful) systems to perform create, read, update, and delete (CRUD) operations.	2, 6
2.4 Given a scenario, troubleshoot common issues with system configuration.	5, 6, 10
3.0 Continuous Integration	
3.1 Explain environmental factors related to continuous integration (CI) management.	7, 9
3.2 Explain workflow management concepts in CI.	8, 9, 10
3.3 Given a scenario, analyze configurations to manage basic automation pipelines.	6, 9, 10
4.0 Continuous Delivery (CD)	
4.1 Given a scenario, implement techniques of continuous delivery (CD).	10
4.2 Explain concepts related to application service levels.	6, 11
4.3 Compare and contrast different methods to secure a connection to providers.	7

Assessment Test

1. An engineer runs a command to list running processes and wants to save the output to a file while still seeing it on screen. Which command accomplishes this?

   A. `ps aux > processes.txt`

   B. `ps aux | tee processes.txt`

   C. `ps aux >> processes.txt`

   D. `ps aux 2> processes.txt`

2. A log file contains thousands of entries. An engineer needs to extract only the lines containing the string `"WARN"` and display the last 20 matching lines. Which command is most efficient?

   A. `grep "WARN" app.log | tail -20`

   B. `tail -20 app.log | grep "WARN"`

   C. `sed -n '/WARN/p' app.log | head -20`

   D. `awk '/WARN/ {print}' app.log > warn.log`

3. A Bash script runs a database backup command and then immediately runs a cleanup routine regardless of whether the backup succeeded. A colleague points out that this is dangerous. What mechanism should the script use to run cleanup only when the backup succeeds?

   A. Check the value of `$?` after the backup command and branch conditionally.

   B. Use the `trap` command to catch any signals emitted by the backup command.

   C. Run both commands on the same line separated by a semicolon.

   D. Set the `-e` flag so the script exits immediately on any error.

4. A Bash script defines a variable inside a function. After the function returns, the script attempts to print the variable but gets an empty result. What is the most likely explanation?

   A. Bash functions cannot define variables.

   B. The variable was declared with `local`, limiting its scope to the function body.

   C. Bash automatically deletes variables when a function completes.

   D. The variable must be `export`ed before it can be used outside the function.

5. A Python automation script must handle the case where an HTTP request fails due to a network timeout. The script should log the error and continue to the next item rather than crashing. Which construct accomplishes this?

   A. A `try/except` block that catches the exception, logs it, and continues the loop

   B. A conditional `if` statement checking the response status code before making the request

   C. Setting a global error handler that silently ignores all exceptions

   D. Using `assert` to validate the response and terminate early on failure

6. A development team wants all feature work to be isolated from the main branch and reviewed before merging, but they do not want to maintain separate long-lived release branches. Which branching strategy best fits their needs?

   A. Gitflow, with dedicated develop, release, and hotfix branches

   B. Trunk-based development with direct commits to main

   C. Feature branching, where each piece of work lives in its own short-lived branch and merges via pull request

   D. Release branching, where a new branch is cut from `main` for every release

7. A library is currently at version 2.4.1. A developer adds a new optional parameter to an existing public function without removing or changing its current behavior. How should the version number change?

   A. Increment to 3.0.0: adding parameters is always a major change.

   B. Increment to 2.5.0: new backward-compatible functionality increments the minor version.

   C. Increment to 2.4.2: any code change increments the patch version.

   D. No version change is needed since the existing behavior is unchanged.

8. An engineer writes a script that executes the following: create a virtual network, then create a subnet, then create a virtual machine, in that sequence. A colleague suggests using an IaC tool with a declarative template instead. What is the primary advantage of the declarative approach?

   A. Declarative templates execute faster because they skip steps the environment already has.

   B. Declarative templates describe the desired end state; the tool determines how to achieve it, including handling dependencies and drift.

   C. Declarative tools are simpler to write because they require no knowledge of the provider API.

   D. Declarative templates can be written in any programming language, unlike imperative scripts.

9. After deploying a web server using an IaC template, an operations engineer notices the application is misbehaving. Investigation reveals a developer SSH'd into the instance and manually changed an nginx configuration file three days ago. Which IaC principle, if enforced, would have prevented this situation?

   A. Idempotency; running the template again would have overwritten the manual change.

   B. Immutability; servers should be replaced rather than modified in place, making post-deployment SSH changes impossible by design.

   C. Parameterization; environment-specific values should be externalized to prevent manual overrides.

   D. Modularity; breaking templates into smaller modules limits the blast radius of manual changes.

10. A configuration management system runs nightly and reports that three web servers have a configuration file that differs from the template defined in source control. The report shows these servers are noncompliant. What term describes this condition?

    A. Configuration entropy

    B. Configuration drift

    C. State divergence

    D. Environment skew

11. A company needs to apply an emergency security patch to 300 servers immediately after a vulnerability is published. The patch must be applied within the hour. Which configuration management delivery model is best suited to this requirement?

    A. Pull model, because agents check in on their own schedule and will pick up the change automatically

    B. Pull model, because agents are more secure than push-based systems

    C. Push model, because the central system initiates delivery and can target all systems immediately

    D. Push model, because push-based systems do not require an installed agent on each host

12. An automation script needs to create a new user account in a web application. The application's API documentation says to send the user's details to `/api/users` and a new resource will be created with a server-generated ID. Which HTTP method should the script use?

    A. `GET`: to retrieve the list of users and check if the account exists first

    B. `PUT`: to create or replace the resource at a specific URL

    C. `POST`: to submit data and create a new resource with a server-assigned identifier

    D. `PATCH`: to partially update the users collection with the new entry

13. An automation engineer is designing a script that makes multiple sequential calls to a REST API. After the first call authenticates, the engineer plans to skip sending the `Authorization header` on subsequent calls, assuming the server remembers the session. Why will this approach fail?

    A. HTTP headers are cached after the first request, so the header is still sent automatically.

    B. REST APIs use stateless communication; each request must be self-contained with all required authentication information.

    C. The server will accept the requests but log a warning about the missing header.

    D. Authentication headers are only required for `POST` and `DELETE` requests, not `GET` requests.

14. A team builds a Docker image for their application using `FROM ubuntu:latest` in their `Dockerfile`. Two months later, a CI build fails even though no application code changed. The most likely cause is that `latest` resolved to a different Ubuntu version with a breaking OS-level change. What is the best practice to prevent this?

    A. Pin the base image to a specific version tag, such as `FROM ubuntu:22.04`.

    B. Build the image only once and store it permanently; never rebuild from the `Dockerfile`.

    C. Remove the `FROM` instruction and install the OS manually as a `RUN` step.

    D. Add a `RUN apt-get update` step to ensure the latest packages are always installed.

15. A deployment script needs to call a cloud provider's API to resize a database. A developer suggests storing the provider's access key and secret in an ENV file in the project repository. Why is this approach problematic?

    A. ENV files use a format that is incompatible with most cloud provider SDKs.

    B. Credentials stored in version control are accessible to anyone with repository access and are at risk of exposure through repository history.

    C. Environment variable files are not read by container runtimes, so they would be ignored.

    D. The cloud provider requires credentials to be stored in a dedicated credential file format, not ENV files.

16. A team's monitoring system sends an alert when CPU usage on any server exceeds 90 percent for more than five minutes. A Lambda function is configured to automatically add capacity when this alert fires. Which automation pattern does this represent?

    A. Polling; the Lambda function checks CPU metrics on a fixed schedule.

    B. Event-driven; an infrastructure event (the alert) triggers the automated response.

    C. Scheduled; the capacity change happens at a predetermined time.

    D. Pull-based; the Lambda function requests metric data from the monitoring system.

17. An order processing system receives spikes of up to 10,000 orders per minute but can only process 500 per minute. The team needs to ensure no orders are lost during peak periods and that each order is processed exactly once. Which architectural component is most appropriate?

    A. A publish-subscribe topic, because it fans out messages to multiple subscribers simultaneously

    B. A message queue, because it provides durable storage and decouples ingestion rate from processing rate

    C. A webhook endpoint, because it allows the order source to push directly to the processor

    D. A polling script that checks for new orders every second

18. A team wants to run a small piece of code that resizes images whenever a new file is uploaded to cloud storage. The code runs for less than a second and is triggered hundreds of times a day. They want to pay only for actual execution time and have no interest in managing servers. Which compute model is most appropriate?

    A. A dedicated virtual machine running a background daemon that polls storage for new files

    B. A containerized application deployed to a Kubernetes cluster with autoscaling

    C. A function as a service (FaaS) triggered by the storage upload event

    D. A bare-metal server co-located with the storage system to minimize latency

19. A team's CI pipeline should run the full test suite automatically whenever any developer pushes code to any branch, but should only build and publish Docker images when code is merged to the `main` branch. Which pipeline configuration approach implements this correctly?

    A. Define two separate pipelines: one triggered on any push, one triggered only on merges to `main`.

    B. Run both the test suite and Docker build on every push, but tag images as `draft` on non-`main` branches.

    C. Use conditional logic within the pipeline so test stages run on all branches and build/publish stages run only when the branch is `main`.

    D. Run the full pipeline only on `main`; rely on developers to run tests locally before pushing.

20. A CI pipeline must authenticate to a container registry to push built images. A developer suggests hard-coding the registry password directly in the pipeline definition file. What is the correct approach?

    A. Hard-code the password since the pipeline file is only accessible to the CI system.

    B. Base64-encode the password in the pipeline file to obscure it from casual readers.

    C. Store the password as an encrypted CI secret/variable and reference it by name in the pipeline.

    D. Create a separate credentials file in the repository and reference it from the pipeline.

21. After a successful CI build, the pipeline produces a versioned JAR file. The team needs to share this artifact with downstream deployment pipelines and preserve previous versions for rollback. Where should the artifact be stored?

    A. Commit it back to the Git repository alongside the source code.

    B. Email it to the deployment team for manual distribution.

    C. Publish it to a dedicated artifact registry with version metadata.

    D. Store it on the CI build agent's `local` filesystem for downstream pipelines to retrieve.

22. A CI pipeline runs a security scanner that detects a hard-coded AWS access key in newly committed code. The scanner is configured as a required quality gate. What should happen next?
    - A. The pipeline logs the finding as a warning and continues to deploy the code.
    - B. The pipeline fails, preventing the code from progressing to deployment until the secret is removed and the credential is rotated.
    - C. The pipeline automatically removes the hard-coded credential and replaces it with a placeholder.
    - D. The pipeline sends a notification to the developer but allows the deployment to continue.

23. A team wants to prevent developers from accidentally pushing code with trailing whitespace and tabs mixed with spaces. This check should happen before any code reaches the remote repository. Which mechanism should they implement?
    - A. A post-commit hook that emails the developer if violations are found
    - B. A pre-push hook on the CI server that scans code before accepting the push
    - C. A pre-commit hook on each developer's workstation that checks formatting before allowing a commit
    - D. A code review requirement in the pull request template reminding developers to check formatting

24. A company is migrating workloads from one cloud provider to another and needs their infrastructure templates to describe resources in both clouds using the same tooling and workflow. Which characteristic of Terraform makes it appropriate for this requirement?
    - A. Terraform generates cost estimates for cloud resources across providers.
    - B. Terraform uses provider plug-ins to support multiple cloud platforms from a single declarative language and workflow.
    - C. Terraform automatically migrates resources between cloud providers without changing templates.
    - D. Terraform is the only IaC tool that supports declarative syntax.

25. An Ansible playbook installs nginx and then starts the service. A team member runs the playbook on a server where nginx is already installed and running. What will Ansible do on the second run?
    - A. Ansible will reinstall nginx from scratch, overwriting the existing installation.
    - B. Ansible will skip the install task (reporting OK, no change) and skip the start task because the service is already running.
    - C. Ansible will fail because the install task encounters a conflict with the existing package.
    - D. Ansible will uninstall and reinstall nginx to ensure the latest version is applied.

26. An engineer writes a `curl` command to create a resource via a REST API. The server responds with a 415 Unsupported Media Type error. What is the most likely fix?
   A. Add the `-X POST` flag to specify the HTTP method.
   B. Add the `-H 'Content-Type: application/json'` header to tell the server what format the request body uses.
   C. Add the `-H 'Accept: application/json'` header to request a JSON response.
   D. Change the HTTP method from `POST` to `PUT`.

27. A developer runs `pip install requests` on a shared Linux server. The next day, a colleague's automation script that depends on an older version of requests begins failing. What would have prevented this conflict?
   A. Using sudo `pip install` to install the package systemwide with elevated permissions
   B. Creating a Python virtual environment for each project so dependencies are isolated per project
   C. Installing requests with the `--user` flag to limit it to the current user's home directory
   D. Downgrading to an older version of Python that is compatible with both versions of requests

28. An automation script calls a REST API and receives a JSON response. The engineer wants to extract only the value of the `status` field from the response to use in a conditional check. Which command correctly extracts this value?
   A. `grep 'status' response.json`
   B. `awk -F: '/status/ {print $2}' response.json`
   C. `cat response.json | sed 's/status//'`
   D. `cat response.json | jq -r '.status'`

29. A Windows administrator writes a PowerShell script that needs to find all running services whose names begin with `Win` and restart them. Which PowerShell approach is most appropriate?
   A. `Get-Service | grep '^Win' | restart`
   B. `Get-Service -Name 'Win*' | Where-Object {$_.Status -eq 'Running'} | Restart-Service`
   C. `net start | findstr Win | restart-service`
   D. `Get-Process Win* | Stop-Process -Force`

30. A development team uses a self-hosted Git server and a separate CI system. The team wants the CI pipeline to start automatically within seconds of a push to any branch. Which configuration establishes this?
   A. Configure the CI system to poll the Git server every 30 seconds for new commits.
   B. Configure the Git server to send a webhook to the CI system's endpoint on each push event.
   C. Have developers manually trigger the CI pipeline after each push via the CI web interface.
   D. Set up a scheduled CI job that runs every five minutes and checks for recent commits.

31. A team is releasing a significant update to a checkout service. They want to expose the new version to a small subset of real users first, monitor error rates for 30 minutes, and proceed with the full rollout only if metrics look healthy. Which deployment strategy matches this approach?

A. In-place deployment; replaces all instances simultaneously with minimal complexity

B. Blue-green deployment; switches all traffic at once after validating the new environment

C. Canary deployment; routes a small traffic percentage to the new version, expanding gradually after validation

D. Rolling deployment; replaces instances in batches until all run the new version

32. Immediately after deploying a new version of a web application, an automated pipeline step hits the application's `/health` endpoint and checks that it returns HTTP 200. If the check fails, the pipeline triggers an automatic rollback. What type of test is this?

A. Load test; measuring system performance under simulated traffic

B. Regression test; verifying that previously working functionality still works

C. Smoke test; a quick check that the deployment is alive and responding before declaring success

D. Integration test; verifying that the application correctly communicates with its dependencies

33. A deployment to production introduces a bug. The team initiates a rollback to the previous version. The rollback completes successfully, but users still report errors. Investigation reveals the deployment added a new column to the database that the old code does not know how to handle. What describes this situation?

A. The rollback failed because the CI pipeline was not configured to validate database changes.

B. The old code version is incompatible with the database schema left behind by the new version, making a code rollback alone insufficient.

C. The rollback introduced a new bug unrelated to the deployment.

D. The load balancer is still routing some traffic to the new version despite the rollback.

34. An engineering team sets an internal availability target of 99.95 percent per month for their API service, while the contractual commitment to customers is 99.9 percent. Why might a team deliberately set the internal target higher than the customer commitment?

A. To create a buffer so the team has time to detect and fix issues before the customer-facing SLA is breached

B. Because 99.95 percent is easier to calculate than 99.9 percent for monthly reporting

C. Because the customer SLA only covers business hours, whereas the internal SLO covers 24/7

D. Because internal SLOs are required to be higher than SLAs by industry regulation

35. An operations team is reviewing reliability metrics for two services. Service Alpha fails approximately once per week but is restored within five minutes each time. Service Beta fails approximately once per month but takes four hours to recover each time. Which service has higher availability?

A. Service Alpha, because it fails more frequently and the team is more practiced at recovery.

B. Service Beta, because failures are rare even though recovery is slow.

C. Service Alpha, because its short recovery time (low MTTR) outweighs its high failure frequency.

D. Both have identical availability because the total downtime per month is the same.

36. Two engineers simultaneously run `terraform apply` against the same infrastructure state. One is adding a new subnet and the other is resizing a compute instance. What risk does this create?

A. Both operations complete successfully because Terraform queues concurrent operations.

B. The state file becomes corrupted or produces conflicting changes because both runs read and modify the same state simultaneously.

C. The second apply automatically cancels and waits for the first to complete.

D. Terraform uses transactions to ensure concurrent applies are safe.

37. A team uses a golden image pipeline to build AMIs with all required software preinstalled. New instances are launched from these images. Six months later, some instances are missing a security patch released two months ago. What is the most likely explanation?

A. The golden image pipeline failed to install the patch during the original build.

B. Instances launched from the golden image have not been replaced or had configuration management applied since the image was built.

C. The patch is incompatible with the version of the OS baked into the golden image.

D. The cloud provider automatically reverts instances to their original image state.

38. An automation script sends a `GET` request to a `REST` endpoint and receives an HTTP 301 response with a Location header pointing to a new URL. The script does not follow the redirect and considers the request complete. What problem will this cause?

A. The script will read the 3XX response body, which contains the same data as a 200 response.

B. The script will miss the actual resource, which has permanently moved to the URL in the Location header.

C. A 301 response means the resource was deleted and is no longer available.

D. A 301 response is a success code; the script has completed correctly.

39. A security team asks the application team to provide a complete list of every software component included in a deployed application, including indirect dependencies pulled in by libraries the team explicitly chose. What document captures this information?

  A. `requirements.txt`, which lists all explicitly declared Python dependencies
  B. A software bill of materials (SBOM): a comprehensive inventory of all components, versions, and their licenses in the final artifact
  C. The `Dockerfile`, which describes how the image was built but not every transitive dependency installed
  D. The CI pipeline log, which records every command executed during the build

40. A CI pipeline runs three independent steps: a unit test suite, a security scan, and a code quality check. Currently they run sequentially, taking 15 minutes total. The team wants to reduce pipeline duration. Which change achieves the best result?

  A. Run only the fastest check and skip the other two to reduce duration.
  B. Run all three steps in parallel since they have no dependencies on each other.
  C. Run the security scan first since it is the most important check.
  D. Combine all three checks into a single script to eliminate orchestration overhead.

41. A small startup is evaluating deployment strategies for their web application. Their primary concern is minimizing infrastructure cost. They are comfortable with a few minutes of potential downtime during releases. Which deployment strategy is most appropriate for their constraints?

  A. Blue-green deployment, which provides instant rollback by maintaining two full production environments
  B. Canary deployment, which requires infrastructure to serve two versions simultaneously
  C. In-place deployment, which updates the existing infrastructure without maintaining a parallel environment
  D. Rolling deployment, which requires enough capacity to run old and new versions concurrently during the rollout

42. A team has good MTBF (failures are rare) but poor MTTR (when failures occur, they take hours to resolve). Which investment would most directly improve MTTR?

  A. Adding more unit tests to the CI pipeline to catch bugs before they reach production
  B. Implementing centralized logging, alerting, and runbooks so failures are detected and resolved faster
  C. Switching from weekly releases to daily releases to reduce the size of each change
  D. Adding more redundancy to reduce the impact of individual component failures

43. An engineer runs `git checkout` followed by a specific commit hash in order to examine old code. After making some experimental changes, they run `git status` and notice the message "HEAD detached at abc1234." What does this mean?

 A. The repository has been corrupted and needs to be re-cloned.

 B. HEAD is pointing directly to a commit rather than to a branch, so any new commits will not belong to any branch and may be lost.

 C. The current changes cannot be committed because the repository is in read-only mode.

 D. The engineer is on a protected branch that prevents direct commits.

44. A new engineer joins a team and is asked to understand how the CI/CD pipeline works. Rather than navigating a web interface with dozens of configuration screens, they find a `github-actions.yml` file in the root of the repository that defines every pipeline stage. What advantage does this approach offer?

 A. Pipeline definitions stored in files are executed faster than configurations stored in a web interface.

 B. Storing pipeline configuration as code means changes are version-controlled and reviewable, and the pipeline definition is visible alongside the application code it builds.

 C. YAML files are the only format supported by CI systems for pipeline configuration.

 D. Pipeline-as-code requires no knowledge of the CI platform, making it universally portable.

45. A team's 99.9 percent monthly availability SLO gives them approximately 43.8 minutes of error budget. On the 25th of the month, they have already consumed 40 minutes due to two incidents. A developer proposes deploying a complex, high-risk feature before month-end. What is the recommended response based on error budget principles?

 A. Proceed with the deployment; the team should not let operational concerns slow down feature delivery.

 B. Defer the high-risk deployment until the new SLO period begins, since only 3.8 minutes of budget remains.

 C. Reduce the SLO target to 99.5 percent for the remainder of the month to create more budget.

 D. Deploy to production without testing to minimize the deployment window and reduce risk.

Answers to Assessment Test

1. B. The `tee` command reads from standard input and writes simultaneously to both standard output and a file, allowing the engineer to see the output on screen while saving it. Option A redirects output to the file only; nothing appears on screen. Option C appends to the file but also does not display on screen. Option D redirects only standard error, not standard output. For more information, see Chapter 1.

2. A. Piping `grep` output to tail filters for the pattern first, then displays the last 20 matching lines. Option B tails the last 20 lines of the whole file first, then filters; if the last 20 lines have no `WARN` entries, the output is empty. Option C uses `sed` correctly but `head -20` takes the first 20 matches, not the last. Option D writes to a file rather than displaying on screen and retrieves all matches, not just the last 20. For more information, see Chapter 1.

3. A. The `$?` variable holds the exit code of the most recently executed command. A zero exit code indicates success; non-zero indicates failure. Checking `$?` allows the script to branch: run cleanup only when the backup exits cleanly. Option B uses `trap` for signal handling, which is not the same as checking exit codes. Option C with semicolons runs both commands unconditionally regardless of success or failure. Option D with `set -e` would exit the script on failure, preventing cleanup from running at all. For more information, see Chapter 2.

4. B. Variables declared with the `local keyword` in Bash are scoped to the function in which they are defined. Once the function returns, the `local` variable is no longer accessible. Option A is incorrect; Bash functions can absolutely define variables. Option C is incorrect; variables defined without `local` persist in the calling scope. Option D describes `export`, which makes variables available to child processes, not to the parent script. For more information, see Chapter 2.

5. A. A `try/except` block catches exceptions at runtime and allows the script to respond gracefully, logging the error and continuing rather than crashing. Option B checks status codes after a successful response, but a timeout raises an exception before any response is received. Option C silently ignoring all exceptions hides bugs and makes the script harder to debug. Option D, using `assert`, terminates the script on failure rather than recovering. For more information, see Chapter 2.

6. C. Feature branching creates short-lived branches for individual pieces of work, keeps `main` stable, and enforces review through pull requests before merging. It does not require maintaining long-lived release branches. Option A (Gitflow) maintains multiple long-lived branches, including release branches. Option B (trunk-based) allows direct commits to main without the isolation the team wants. Option D (release branching) explicitly introduces the long-lived release branches the team wants to avoid. For more information, see Chapter 3.

7. B. Semantic versioning (`MAJOR.MINOR.PATCH`) increments the minor version when new backward-compatible functionality is added. Adding an optional parameter extends the API without breaking existing callers. Option A (major bump) is reserved for breaking, backward-incompatible changes. Option C (patch bump) is for backward-compatible bug fixes only. Option D is incorrect; a version bump communicates to consumers that new functionality is available. For more information, see Chapter 3.

8. B. Declarative IaC expresses what the infrastructure should look like rather than how to build it step by step. The tool reconciles the current state with the desired state, handles resource dependencies, and can detect and correct configuration drift. Option A partially captures idempotency but overstates the speed benefit. Option C is incorrect; understanding the provider's resource model is still required. Option D is incorrect; declarative templates typically use domain-specific languages like HCL or YAML. For more information, see Chapter 4.

9. B. Immutable infrastructure means servers are never modified after deployment. When a change is needed, a new image is built and a new instance deployed, with the old one destroyed. This pattern makes ad hoc SSH modifications impossible by design because the instance is replaced rather than updated. Option A describes idempotency, which corrects drift but does not prevent the manual change from occurring. Option C addresses configuration values, not post-deployment mutations. Option D reduces impact scope but does not prevent the change. For more information, see Chapter 4.

10. B. Configuration drift occurs when a system's actual configuration deviates from its desired state as defined in the configuration management template. This typically happens through manual changes, failed updates, or OS-level variation over time. Option A (entropy) is not the standard term used in configuration management. Options C and D (state divergence, environment skew) are informal descriptions but not the standard term. For more information, see Chapter 5.

11. C. In a push model, the central configuration management system initiates the connection and pushes changes to all target hosts on demand. This allows immediate, operator-controlled delivery, ideal for time-sensitive situations like emergency patching. Option A is incorrect because pull agents check in on a schedule, introducing latency. Option B incorrectly claims pull is more secure as a general rule. Option D confuses push with agentless tools; push-based systems typically do require an agent, but agentless tools like Ansible use SSH instead. For more information, see Chapter 5.

12. C. `POST` is the correct method for creating a new resource when the server assigns the identifier. The client sends the resource data and the server creates it at a new URL (e.g., `/api/users/456`). Option A (`GET`) retrieves data; it does not create resources. Option B (`PUT`) creates or replaces a resource at a client-specified URL, which is not what the API describes here. Option D (`PATCH`) performs a partial update to an existing resource. For more information, see Chapter 6.

13. B. REST's statelessness constraint means the server holds no client session state between requests. Every request must include all information needed for the server to process it, including authentication credentials. There is no "session" that persists between calls. Option A is incorrect; headers are not automatically cached or re-sent by the HTTP client. Option C is incorrect; most APIs will return 401 Unauthorized, not merely log a warning. Option D is incorrect; authentication is required for any protected resource regardless of HTTP method. For more information, see Chapter 6.

14. A. Pinning the base image to a specific, immutable version tag ensures reproducible builds. The `latest` tag is a moving pointer and will pull a different image each time it is updated by the upstream maintainer, introducing unexpected changes. Option B creates a maintenance problem by never updating the image, accumulating security vulnerabilities. Option C is not possible; a Docker image must have a base image. Option D adds package updates but does not address the base image version instability. For more information, see Chapter 7.

15. B. Storing credentials in a file committed to version control exposes them to everyone with repository access, and the credentials remain in the commit history even after deletion. This is one of the most common causes of credential leaks. The correct approach is to use a secrets manager, environment variables injected at runtime, or cloud-native IAM roles. Option A is incorrect; ENV files can be read by many SDKs and tools. Option C is incorrect; containers can read ENV files when configured to do so. Option D is not a general rule about cloud providers. For more information, see Chapter 7.

16. B. An event-driven pattern is one in which a state change or condition—here, the CPU alert—automatically triggers an action without human intervention or polling. The monitoring system pushes the alert, and the function reacts immediately. Option A describes polling, where the function would repeatedly ask "is CPU high?" rather than being notified. Option C describes a time-based trigger, not a condition-based one. Option D describes a pull model where the function initiates data retrieval, which is the opposite of what happens here. For more information, see Chapter 8.

17. B. A message queue decouples producers from consumers. During spikes, orders accumulate in the queue and are processed at the rate the consumer can handle, with no orders lost. The durable storage ensures each message is held until successfully processed and acknowledged. Option A (pub-sub) broadcasts messages to all subscribers immediately and typically does not provide durable buffering between production and consumption rates. Option C (webhook) sends directly to the processor, which would be overwhelmed at 10,000 per minute. Option D (polling) introduces latency and does not solve the rate mismatch. For more information, see Chapter 8.

18. C. FaaS (such as AWS Lambda or Azure Functions) is designed exactly for this use case: short-lived, event-triggered code that runs on demand with no server management. Billing is per invocation and execution duration. Option A (a polling VM) wastes compute during idle periods and requires server management. Option B (Kubernetes) adds significant orchestration complexity for a simple, short-lived function. Option D (bare-metal) has the highest operational overhead and cost. For more information, see Chapter 8.

19. C. Conditional stage execution within a single pipeline is the standard solution. Using branch-based conditions (e.g., `only: main` or `if: branch == main`), test stages fire on all pushes for early feedback, while the build and publish stages are gated to `main` only. Option A works but adds maintenance overhead for two separate pipeline definitions. Option B publishes potentially broken images from feature branches, polluting the registry. Option D removes automated testing feedback from feature branches, one of CI's core benefits. For more information, see Chapter 9.

20. C. CI systems provide encrypted secret storage (e.g., GitHub Actions secrets, GitLab CI variables) that inject values into pipeline runs as environment variables without exposing them in logs or source code. Option A is incorrect; pipeline files are stored in version control, making hard-coded credentials visible to all repository users. Option B (Base64) is encoding, not encryption, and is trivially reversible. Option D stores credentials in the repository, which is the same problem as Option A. For more information, see Chapter 9.

21. C. Artifact registries (such as Nexus, Artifactory, or cloud provider equivalents) are designed to store, version, and distribute build outputs. They support access controls, retention policies, and integration with deployment pipelines. Option A bloats the repository with binary files and slows clone operations. Option B is manual, error-prone, and does not support rollback. Option D stores the artifact in an ephemeral location; CI build agents are typically cleaned or destroyed after each run. For more information, see Chapter 9.

22. B. A required quality gate that detects a hard-coded secret should fail the pipeline entirely. This prevents the compromised code from reaching deployment and forces the developer to both remove the secret from the codebase and rotate the exposed credential (since it may have already been seen in `git` history). Options A and D, allowing the pipeline to continue, defeats the purpose of the quality gate. Option C is not a standard behavior of security scanners in CI pipelines; scanners detect and report—they do not automatically remediate. For more information, see Chapter 9.

23. C. Pre-commit hooks run on the developer's local machine before a commit is recorded, making them the earliest possible intervention point. They prevent problematic code from even entering the local commit history. Option A (post-commit) runs after the commit is already made and cannot prevent the bad commit. Option B (pre-push on the CI server) is further down the chain; the commit is already local and the developer must make a corrective commit before pushing. Option D (code review reminder) is a manual process that depends on reviewers catching the issue. For more information, see Chapter 3.

24. B. Terraform's provider plug-in architecture allows teams to manage resources across AWS, Azure, Google Cloud, and others using the same HCL language and CLI workflow. Each provider exposes its resources through a plug-in, and a single template can reference resources from multiple providers. Option A describes a separate tool (Infracost). Option C is incorrect; Terraform does not migrate existing resources—it provisions and manages them. Option D is incorrect; AWS CloudFormation, Azure Bicep, and others also use declarative syntax. For more information, see Chapter 4.

25. B. Ansible tasks are idempotent by design. The package install task checks whether nginx is already at the desired state (installed) and reports OK with no changes. The service start task similarly checks whether the service is already running and takes no action if it is. This safe re-runnability is a core principle of configuration management. Option A describes imperative behavior, not declarative idempotent behavior. Option C is incorrect; Ansible's package modules handle already-installed packages gracefully. Option D describes an upgrade behavior, which requires an explicit state of latest rather than present. For more information, see Chapter 5.

26. B. HTTP 415 Unsupported Media Type means the server does not recognize or accept the format of the request body. Adding the `Content-Type: application/json` header tells the server the body is JSON. Option A (`-X POST`) sets the method, which is likely already set correctly. Option C (Accept header) tells the server which response format the client wants, not what format the request body is in. Option D, changing the HTTP method, does not address the content type mismatch. For more information, see Chapter 6.

27. B. Python virtual environments create isolated dependency sets per project. Installing requests into one project's virtual environment does not affect another project's environment. Option A (`sudo install`) installs globally and makes the conflict worse, not better. Option C
(--`user` flag) isolates by user, not by project, so all of that user's projects still share one package version. Option D (downgrading Python) is unnecessary and counterproductive; the issue is package version isolation, not Python version compatibility. For more information, see Chapter 7.

28. D. `jq` is a purpose-built tool for parsing and querying JSON data. The `.status filter` extracts the value of the top-level `status` field, and `-r` outputs raw text without JSON string quotes. Option A (`grep`) returns the entire matching line, not just the field value, and is fragile with nested JSON. Option B (`awk`) would parse incorrectly on nested JSON and would return the raw JSON value, including surrounding characters. Option C (`sed`) removes the word `status` rather than extracting its value. For more information, see Chapter 1.

29. B. PowerShell's object pipeline allows filtering and acting on service objects directly. `Get-Service -Name 'Win*'` uses wildcard filtering to find matching services, `Where-Object` filters to only running ones, and `Restart-Service` acts on each. Option A mixes PowerShell cmdlets with Bash-style `grep` and an invalid `restart` command. Option C uses `net start` (a legacy command) and `findstr`, producing text output that cannot be piped to `Restart-Service` as objects. Option D uses `Get-Process` and `Stop-Process`, which target processes rather than services and do not restart them. For more information, see Chapter 2.

30. B. A webhook from the Git server to the CI system enables event-driven pipeline triggering. When a push occurs, the Git server immediately sends an HTTP `POST` notification to the CI endpoint, which starts the pipeline within seconds. Option A (polling every 30 seconds) introduces lag and generates unnecessary API traffic. Option C (manual trigger) removes the automation entirely. Option D (scheduled job every five minutes) still introduces up to five minutes of lag and is wasteful during periods with no commits. For more information, see Chapter 9.

31. C. Canary deployment deliberately routes a small, controlled slice of traffic to a new version while the rest continues to the current version. Metrics from the canary cohort inform the decision to expand or abort. This is exactly the use case described. Option A (in-place) replaces everything at once with no gradual validation. Option B (blue-green) also switches all traffic at once, though it maintains a full parallel environment for rollback. Option D (rolling) replaces instances in batches but does not use weighted traffic routing for controlled exposure. For more information, see Chapter 10.

32. C. A smoke test is a minimal, fast verification that the newly deployed system is up and responding. It answers "Did the deployment succeed at a basic level?" before investing in more thorough validation. Option A (load test) measures throughput and latency under volume. Option B (regression test) reruns the full test suite to check for regressions in existing functionality. Option D (integration test) verifies interactions between components. Smoke tests precede all of these post-deployment validation types. For more information, see Chapter 10.

33. B. Code rollbacks do not automatically undo database schema changes. If the new version altered the schema in a way the old code cannot handle (e.g., adding a required column or renaming a field), rolling back the code leaves the schema in a state the old code cannot process. Resolving this requires either rolling back the schema change or applying a forward-fix. This is why backward-compatible schema migrations are a key practice in continuous delivery. Options A, C, and D describe different failure modes unrelated to schema compatibility. For more information, see Chapter 10.

34. A. Setting an internal SLO tighter than the customer-facing SLA creates an operational buffer. When the internal target is breached, the team knows to act before the contractual commitment is at risk. This gives time to investigate and remediate while still delivering on customer expectations. Option B is not the reason; both calculations are straightforward. Option C conflates SLO scope with time-of-day coverage, which is not the standard distinction. Option D is incorrect; there is no industry regulation requiring this relationship. For more information, see Chapter 11.

35. C. Availability = MTBF / (MTBF + MTTR). Service Alpha: MTBF ~ 168 hrs, MTTR ~ 0.083 hrs, giving availability of about 99.95 percent. Service Beta: MTBF ~ 720 hrs, MTTR 4 hrs, giving availability of about 99.45 percent. Despite failing more often, Alpha's extremely fast recovery results in far less total downtime. Option A is partly right (Alpha is higher) but for the wrong reason. Option B is incorrect; rare but long outages accumulate more downtime. Option D is incorrect; Alpha accumulates roughly 20 minutes of downtime monthly vs. Beta's 4 hours. For more information, see Chapter 11.

36. B. Terraform uses a state file to track the current infrastructure. Without state locking, two simultaneous applies can both read the current state, make decisions based on it, and write conflicting changes, corrupting the state file or producing unintended infrastructure changes. Most remote backends (like S3 with DynamoDB locking or Terraform Cloud) support state locking to prevent this. Options A and C incorrectly imply Terraform has built-in concurrency management, which it does not by default. Option D is incorrect; Terraform does not use database-style transactions for state. For more information, see Chapter 4.

37. B. Golden images capture a point-in-time state. Instances launched from them do not automatically receive subsequent patches. If instances are not replaced with updated images or managed by ongoing configuration management, they accumulate security debt. This is a fundamental limitation of a pure golden-image approach without complementary runtime management. Option A is possible but not the "most likely" explanation given the scenario's timeline. Option C is possible but speculative without evidence. Option D is incorrect; cloud providers do not revert running instances to image state. For more information, see Chapter 5.

38. B. HTTP 301 Moved Permanently indicates the resource has moved to a new permanent URL specified in the Location header. An automation script that does not follow the redirect will not retrieve the actual resource. Most HTTP clients handle redirects automatically, but scripts that construct raw requests must be configured to follow them. Option A is incorrect; a 3XX response body is typically empty or contains a brief HTML message, not the resource data. Option C is incorrect; 301 is a redirect, not a deletion (410 Gone indicates deletion). Option D is incorrect; 3XX is a redirection class, not a success class (2XX). For more information, see Chapter 6.

39. B. A software bill of materials (SBOM) is a formal, structured list of every software component in an artifact, including direct and transitive dependencies, their versions, and often their licenses. SBOMs are increasingly required in security-conscious environments to support vulnerability tracking and supply chain auditing. Option A (`requirements.txt`) lists only explicit dependencies, not transitive ones. Option C (`Dockerfile`) describes build steps but does not enumerate all installed packages. Option D (CI log) is unstructured and difficult to audit systematically. For more information, see Chapter 7.

40. B. Steps without dependencies on each other can run in parallel, reducing the total pipeline time to approximately the duration of the longest single step rather than the sum of all steps. If each step takes 5 minutes, parallel execution reduces the total from 15 to 5 minutes. Option A removes quality gates and defeats the purpose of CI. Option C reorders but does not parallelize; the total time remains 15 minutes. Option D combines steps into a script that still runs them sequentially and adds complexity. For more information, see Chapter 8.

41. C. In-place deployment updates the application on existing instances without spinning up parallel infrastructure. This minimizes cost at the expense of rollback speed and the possibility of brief downtime during the update. For a cost-sensitive startup comfortable with short maintenance windows, this is a reasonable trade-off. Option A (blue-green) doubles infrastructure costs by maintaining two full environments. Option B (canary) also requires running two versions simultaneously. Option D (rolling) requires excess capacity during the rollout to maintain availability. For more information, see Chapter 10.

42. B. MTTR (mean time to repair) is the average time to restore service after a failure. Reducing MTTR requires faster detection (alerting), faster diagnosis (centralized logging, tracing), and faster execution of fixes (runbooks, documented procedures). Options A and C address defect rates and change risk, which affect MTBF (failure frequency) rather than repair time. Option D (redundancy) reduces the user impact of failures but does not speed up repair; it addresses MTBF and availability differently. For more information, see Chapter 11.

43. B. A detached HEAD state means HEAD points directly to a commit object rather than to a named branch. Any commits made in this state are not tracked by any branch and may be garbage-collected after switching away. To preserve work done in a detached HEAD state, the engineer should create a new branch to capture the commits before checking out another branch. Option A is incorrect; detached HEAD is a normal Git state, not a corruption. Option C is incorrect; commits can be made in detached HEAD—they just risk being lost. Option D describes protected branch rules, which is a different concept. For more information, see Chapter 3.

44. B. Pipeline-as-code stores the pipeline definition in a file in the source repository. This means pipeline changes go through code review, are tracked in `git` history, can be rolled back, and are visible to anyone reading the repository. New team members can understand the pipeline without navigating an external UI. Option A is incorrect; execution speed is unrelated to where configuration is stored. Option C is incorrect; some CI systems support JSON, Groovy (`Jenkinsfile`), and other formats. Option D is incorrect; pipeline files use platform-specific syntax and are not universally portable across CI systems. For more information, see Chapter 9.

45. B. Error budget is a quantitative tool for making deployment decisions. With only 3.8 minutes remaining and five days left in the month, a high-risk deployment could easily exhaust the budget and breach the SLA. The prudent decision is to defer until the new period, preserving the remaining budget for unavoidable incidents. Option A ignores the risk management purpose of error budgets. Option C, retroactively changing the SLO, defeats its purpose and may breach contractual SLAs. Option D, reducing testing, increases the probability of an incident at the worst possible time. For more information, see Chapter 11.

Coding Your Job Away

PART I

Chapter 1

Working on the Command Line

THE AUTOOPS+ EXAM TOPICS COVERED IN THIS CHAPTER MAY INCLUDE, BUT ARE NOT LIMITED TO, THE FOLLOWING:

✓ **1.0: Automation Coding Concepts**

- 1.1. Given a scenario, use code to support automation.
- 1.4. Given a scenario, troubleshoot common issues with the code life cycle.

✓ **2.0: System Configuration**

- 2.2. Compare and contrast basic approaches to automation.

How do you start to automate your world? Just open the command line. Whether you're on a Windows machine, macOS, Linux, or some variant, you can leave behind the mouse clicks and drag-and-drop of the user interface and take up your keyboard instead. Working from the *command line*, or *terminal*, you're able to perform most, if not all, of the tasks you'd do with the UI through text-based input—input that can be saved, corrected, rewritten, shared, and even version controlled. Working effectively on the terminal and learning its unique ecosystem of commands is the first and most important step to automating systems management and operations.

Navigating Command-Line Variants

In this book, we'll primarily focus on automating deployment, provisioning, and configuration in Unix-like environments or on Windows. This section uses examples and describes tools that will work in any POSIX-compliant operating systems. *POSIX* stands for Portable Operating System Interface (plus an X to make it feel extra Unix-y) and is a standard that defines how Unix and its many variants work under the covers. Ubuntu, CentOS, Amazon Linux, and even your macOS command line are examples of current-day POSIX-compliant systems. Still, even with POSIX compliance making these environments work very similarly, they each developed over many years along different branches of the POSIX family tree, so keep in mind that there are some variations in seemingly identical commands across them. When in doubt, append `-h` or `--help` to learn more about the supported functions of the command you're using in your particular environment.

Even if you're on Windows, it's possible to get a Unix-style terminal experience; however, Windows' journey to Unix compatibility takes some explaining.

A Brief History of the Windows Command Line

At one time, the command line on Windows was something of an afterthought. Once the visual experience of Windows came along in the '90s to provide a user interface over Disk Operating System (DOS), Microsoft placed their emphasis there, focusing on improving that interface and relegating the terminal to a second-class citizen with limited support for keyboard shortcuts and command-line tooling. This created a challenge for those who wanted to be able to easily script and automate tasks in Windows.

The good news is that the Windows terminal experience is no longer stuck in the era of dial-up and Encarta. Microsoft has made substantial investments to bring the Windows command-line interface into the modern age, providing powerful options for both native scripting and cross-platform automation.

Improvements came in a few different ways. The year 2006 saw the first release of *PowerShell*. PowerShell is both a scripting language and a *shell* (aka command-line terminal) unto itself, providing robust commands for automating common Windows tasks. It is the definitive tool for automating Windows administration and orchestrating configuration within the Microsoft ecosystem, and we'll get into it more in the next chapter. It was the beginning of a transformed Windows command-line experience, but it didn't provide the Linux-style environment that some administrators sought. Microsoft wouldn't deliver a native Linux experience in Windows until a decade later.

Soon, other options came along, like Cygwin, which offers a POSIX-compatible terminal support as a thin layer over the traditional Windows OS, and Git Bash, first bundled with Git for Windows in 2010. This shell gave Windows developers a lightweight Bash emulation layer that included many of the most-used Unix tools, and we were happy, for a time.

The real breakthrough, though, was the introduction of the *Windows Subsystem for Linux (WSL)* in 2016. WSL allows users to run a genuine Linux environment natively on Windows, without the overhead of a virtual machine. The first version, WSL 1, provided a compatibility layer that translated Linux system calls into Windows calls, making it possible to run Linux binaries without modification. In 2019, WSL version 2 went even further, using a lightweight virtual machine with a full Linux kernel for near-native performance and compatibility.

WSL made it possible to install and run popular Linux distributions (like Ubuntu, Debian, Fedora, and more) directly from the Microsoft Store. Suddenly, Windows users could run `apt-get`, `systemd`, `bash`, and `cron` natively, without emulation or the need to dual-boot.

All of this means that Windows users now have real options. You can write PowerShell scripts to manage your system the Windows way, or you can spin up WSL and manage everything like you're on native Linux.

Mac Unix Compatibility

The story is a bit more straightforward on Macintosh operating systems. Today's macOS has its roots in BSD Unix and is fully POSIX-compliant. Most Unix or Linux tools and commands work natively on a Mac with no modification necessary. This compatibility was complicated somewhat by Apple's shift to their own ARM64-based microprocessor architecture, called Apple Silicon, but the change was largely invisible to users, as the terminal now either runs binaries compiled natively for ARM64 or runs them through a compatibility layer called Rosetta. In either case, we can pretty universally run Linux commands on a Mac terminal in its `zsh` shell.

So now that we know how to get that Linux feeling on all the major operating systems, let's get to automating. We'll start with some important basics.

Environment Variables

Variables are the key to making any automation reusable. It's a classic programming truism that you should never hard-code any values that may change over time or from environment to environment. To see why, imagine a step in a Linux shell script that invokes an API over HTTP using `curl`:

```
curl -H "Authorization: Bearer my_api_key_123"
https://api.example.com/api/some_endpoint
```

Two elements make this script hard to reuse: the hard-coded API key and the API URL. What if you have a development or testing environment for the app? Both the API key and URL are likely to be different. Let's parameterize this script so it can work in multiple contexts. In Linux, you'd define the variables, then refer to them by name in the command:

```
export API_KEY=my_api_key_123
export API_BASE_URL=https://api.example.com/api
curl -H "Authorization: Bearer $API_KEY" $API_BASE_URL/some_endpoint
```

With this modification, those two variables can be defined outside the script, which now becomes generic and reusable. Note that *export* is needed to ensure that these variables are accessible in child shells. Without it, invoking something like `bash -c 'echo $API_BASE_URL'` wouldn't work because the value would not be in scope for the child session spawned by `bash -c`. In PowerShell, this command would look like this:

```
$env:API_KEY = "my_api_key_123"
$env:API_BASE_URL = "https://api.example.com/api"

curl -Headers @{ Authorization = "Bearer $env:API_KEY"
} "$env:API_BASE_URL/some_endpoint"
```

TIP Fun fact: In PowerShell, `curl` is an alias for the `Invoke-WebRequest` cmdlet and not the Linux executable of the same name. They behave similarly, but this explains why the parameters are passed slightly differently from the Linux version.

Externalize Configuration

In all your automations, you should strive to externalize as much configuration as possible. This separation of configuration from code has several key benefits:

- It makes scripts easier to share with others.
- It allows you to more easily update configuration without needing to update your code.
- It often allows configuration updates without any redeployment necessary.
- It creates good habits that help avoid security concerns, like pushing code with secrets into version control.

There are many good ways of managing external configuration (in other words, of securely maintaining and setting environment variables), which we explore more in later chapters. For now, just remember the importance of using variables for any values that may change.

Slice and Dice Text Like a Pro

One of the most common and essential command-line skills for a system administrator, DevOps professional, or app developer is the ability to quickly and efficiently manipulate text. After all, everything on the command line is text, whether it's a log file, a list of processes, or an error message.

You'll want to process large volumes of log files, hunting for specific error codes, warnings, application output, or stack traces. You'll want to search through source code to find relevant lines to troubleshoot a deployment problem or debug a configuration file. You'll write scripts where you need to extract just the domain name from a URL or count how many times a specific user tried to log in (and failed).

In short, if you plan to script or automate anything, you need to master the art of slicing and dicing text.

Unix-compatible environments treat text as the lingua franca of the command line. When commands are chained together with *pipes* (|), it's text that flows through the pipeline. Knowing how to speak, read, and dissect that text is what turns a shell user into a shell wizard.

Regular Expressions

Regular expressions (commonly abbreviated *regex*) are a special syntax for describing patterns in text. Regex lets you describe patterns that would be tedious or impossible to match manually. Want to find every log line that contains a date? Or extract all email addresses from a file? Or match every line that starts with `ERROR` but not `OK`? It's time to break out a regex.

However, regular expression syntax can be cryptic. They're famously terse, occasionally unreadable, and fairly challenging to master. Every developer or admin knows the pain of carefully crafting a long or detailed regex with nested quotation marks or extensive character escaping. Still, learning a handful of common patterns gives you 90 percent of what you need to use tools like `grep`, `sed`, and `awk` with confidence, and to carry those skills into scripts written in any other language that supports regex.

We'll start with the basics, talking first about pattern matching in a general sense; later, you'll see how to use tools like `grep` to apply these patterns in practice. Regular expressions are often bracketed by forward slashes, so we'll use that syntax going forward.

Literal Characters

Most characters match themselves. The regex pattern `/dog/` matches the string `"dog"` and only that.

Pattern Matches

In regular expressions, certain special characters let you match longer strings, wildcards, or express where a searched-for string should appear when matching. Here are a few examples, followed by what they match or indicate:

. Any single character

* Zero or more of the previous character

+ One or more of the previous character

? Zero or one of the previous character

[] Any one character inside the brackets

^ Start of the line

$ End of the line

When used in a regular expression, these elements are called *metacharacters*, and they allow us to do more than match single words:

`/^ERROR/` matches any line that starts with `ERROR`.

`/404$/` matches any line that ends in `404`.

`/[Uu]ser/` matches `User` or `user`.

`/n*/` matches the letter `n` when it occurs zero or more times. It would match `lunch`, with one `n`, `dinner` with two consecutive, and even `breakfast` with zero.

`/n+/` matches `n` when it appears one or more times, so `lunch` and `dinner`, but not `breakfast`.

We can be specific with character counts by using curly braces:

`/n{1}/` matches `lunch` only, while `/n{2}/` would match `dinner` only.

Escaping Characters

To match one of these metacharacters literally, you escape it with a backslash (`\`). When would you use this? Say you're hunting for the domain name `example.com`. Here's how it can go wrong: The expression `/example.com/` matches `example.com`, but also `examplexcom`, `example9com`, and more, because the unescaped period matches any single character. To make it match the actual period character, change your regex to `/example\.com/`.

To match `[hello]` literally, you'd escape both brackets: `/\[hello\]/`. As you can see, escaping special characters can quickly increase the complexity of regular expressions. It's important to build them carefully so your automation scripts don't end up missing important matches or over-matching strings that shouldn't be flagged.

Character Classes

Character classes let you match any one character from a set. You'll put them in square brackets:

- `[aeiou]` matches any lowercase vowel. You can put any list of characters you like to create a set.
- `[0123456789]` matches any single numeric character, but ranges, shown below, are easier.
    - `[0-9]` matches any digit.
    - `[A-Za-z]` matches any letter.
    - `[^a-z]` negates the set (matches anything but a lowercase letter).

> **TIP** When used inside square brackets, the ^ (caret) character has a different meaning. Alone, it indicates the beginning of a line; in conjunction with a character class, it represents negation.

There are a few shortcuts to these character classes supported by different systems. These, beginning with backslashes, are called "Perl-compatible" expressions, since they originated in that programming language.

`\d` is equivalent to `[0-9]`. Its inverse, `\D`, matches any non-digit.

`\w` matches any "word character" and is equivalent to `[a-zA-Z0-9_]`. Its inverse is `\W`.

`\s` matches whitespace characters such as tabs, spaces, and newlines. You can do the opposite with `\S`.

In addition to Perl, some tools support these out of box.

There are also POSIX character classes, which achieve many of the same shortcuts in a more verbose, but often more readable format:

`[[:digit:]]`	Digits (0–9)
`[[:alpha:]]`	Alphabetic characters
`[[:alnum:]]`	Alphanumeric (letters or digits)
`[[:space:]]`	Any whitespace (like spaces, tabs, newlines)
`[[:punct:]]`	Punctuation characters
`[[:upper:]]`	Uppercase letters
`[[:lower:]]`	Lowercase letters
`[[:xdigit:]]`	Hex digits (0–9, a–f, A–F)

Want to find email addresses in a log file? You could search with a regex pattern like this:

```
/[a-zA-Z0-9._%+-]+@[a-zA-Z0-9.-]+\.[a-z]{2,}/
```

Let's break that down. `[a-zA-Z0-9._%+-]+` matches everything in an email that comes before the @ sign. Notice that it defines one character class (between square brackets), allowing any lowercase letter, uppercase letter, or digit, period, underscore, percent sign, plus sign, or minus sign.

The Text Manipulation Toolbox

Now that you understand regular expressions (at least enough to be dangerous!), let's look at the power trio of text manipulation: `grep`, `sed`, and `awk`.

grep

The *grep* command is ubiquitous for command-line pros: as common as a flathead screwdriver and just as useful. It's so often used that, until this moment, I didn't know how it got its name. I just thought of it as "grep," that useful command. It turns out it stands for "global regular expression print," which is itself a reference to a commonly used command in the old editor tool `ed: g/re/p --` literally, globally apply this regular expression, then print the result. Unix lore is just full of delightful historical details like this.

In any case, `grep` is one of your best friends on the command line. Let's see how it works. Here's the basic format of a `grep` command:

```
grep [options] 'pattern' filename
```

Let's look at some examples. First, to find all lines containing the word `ERROR` in a log file, you'd use:

```
grep "ERROR" app.log
```

Or to use the `-r` flag to search a directory of source code for the string `"TODO"`, enter:

```
grep -r "TODO" src/
```

You can use the `-c` flag to count matches:

```
grep -c "failed" auth.log
```

You can also use the aforementioned pipes to send text input into `grep`. The `cat` command (a binary with its own lore; it stands for "concatenate") prints out files. So let's pipe an Apache web server log into `grep` and search for "401 unauthorized" errors:

```
cat apache.log | grep '401'
```

I use `grep` all the time when checking for running processes on a Linux machine. For instance, to see if Apache (the `httpd` process) is running, use:

```
ps -ef | grep httpd
```

The first command lists all processes, with the `-ef` flag telling it to list all processes in a fully formatted list. `grep` then prints out the lines that match `httpd`. Either I get a result and know Apache is online, or I get nothing, and realize it's gone down—again. Note that the quotes are not strictly necessary to `grep`, but you'll want them whenever quotes appear in your search string and you need to remove ambiguity.

TIP Add `-i` for case-insensitive searches and `-v` to invert the match (i.e., show lines not matching your pattern).

Using *grep* with Regex

Now, let's use `grep` to try out some regular expressions and see how `grep` supports the various styles you learned earlier. I'm using the `echo` command to output the word `dinner` (maybe I'm hungry!) and piping it as input to `grep`. Let's see what works and what doesn't.

```
> echo "dinner" | grep n{2}
# no result means no match

> echo "dinner" | grep -e 'n\{2\}'
dinner

# let's try extended mode to avoid escaping curly braces
> echo "dinner" | grep -E 'n{2}'
dinner
```

What do you learn from this? You see that `grep` needs a flag, `-e`, to use regular expressions, and that by default, every special character needs escaping. The `-E` is `grep`'s "extended" regular expression support mode, allowing you to get by without those extra backslashes.

However, I'm running this on a Mac. If you try these exercises on a native Linux machine or Windows running WSL, the supported parameters may vary. Much like our favorite comic book heroes, `grep` and its counterparts have variants.

Into the *grep*-verse

Not all `grep` commands are the same. While the name stays consistent, the behavior can shift slightly depending on your environment:

- macOS ships with BSD `grep`, which lacks support for `-P` (Perl-compatible regex) and behaves a bit differently around extended regex.
- Most Linux distros use GNU `grep`, which supports `-E`, `-P`, and other niceties. Most online examples will be in a GNU-compatible syntax.
- WSL (Windows Subsystem for Linux) runs genuine Linux binaries, so you'll get GNU `grep` by default.
- Cygwin tries to mimic GNU behavior, but compatibility isn't always perfect.
- Git Bash for Windows includes a pared-down `grep`—usually GNU-based, but sometimes with missing or different features or command parameters.

Basically, if you try a command you found online and it doesn't work on your machine, check which version of `grep` you're using with `grep --version` and check its help pages for specific parameter support.

sed

The *sed* command stands for "stream editor," which is refreshingly straightforward after `grep`. It's designed for editing text on the fly, substituting, deleting, inserting, or transforming lines as they flow from one place to another. In practicality, `sed` and `grep` can often be used to achieve similar results, but `sed` excels in a few areas that differ from `grep`.

While `grep` is a searchlight looking for patterns in text, `sed` is designed to change that text as it goes by. You feed `sed` input, describe a text transformation, and it spits out the modified version. That's especially handy when you want to do simple replacements without firing up a text editor. Basically, `sed` is what the name implies: a stream editor that reads input line-by-line, applies a set of editing rules (which you provide), and sends the result to standard output.

The most common use case is substitution—the `s/` command—and it's one you'll see in a million shell scripts:

```
sed 's/foo/bar/' filename
```

That tells `sed` to look for the first instance of `foo` on each line and replace it with `bar`. If you want to replace all instances of `foo` on each line, add the `g` (for "global") at the end:

```
sed 's/foo/bar/g' filename
```

Substitution with `sed` comes in handy when you're trying to clean up log files, config files, or even the output of other commands. Suppose a config file uses `http://` but you're migrating everything to `https://`. Ignoring the fact that you should not still be operating unencrypted HTTP servers in this day and age (at least you're fixing it, right?), here's a `sed` one-liner to the rescue:

```
sed 's|http://|https://|g' config.yaml
```

Note the use of | as a delimiter—you're not stuck with slashes. This helps avoid escaping those slashes when your patterns include them, keeping your `sed` commands much more readable. Essentially, whatever character you use after the "s" will become the delimiter between sections, so choose wisely.

Also (and I digress) it's not always a crime to run plain text HTTP. Maybe your web server is safely behind a load balancer that only accepts HTTPS connections and terminates TLS before passing unencrypted traffic to a server protected inside your data center. That's fine. Just be careful out there!

The previous examples spit the modified text to *standard output* (`STDOUT`; basically, the command-line output). If you want to modify the file in place, use `-i`:

```
sed -i 's/debug=true/debug=false/' .env
```

Here's a good one for git pre-commit hooks (a topic for later in this book): Strip out trailing whitespace.

```
sed 's/[[:space:]]*$//' file.txt
```

More *sed* Examples

Here are a few quick one-liners you'll find yourself reaching for again and again.

Tabs to Spaces

```
sed 's/\t/    /g' file.txt
```

Use this code to change all tabs in `file.txt` to a series of four spaces. Just make sure you have the reverse command ready to go when your developers revolt (as if they could ever come to a consensus on this topic).

Get Rid of Blank Lines

```
sed '/^$/d' file.txt
```

This one deletes blank lines in file.txt. Note that `^$`, with nothing in between, designates the beginning of a line (`^`) followed immediately by the end of a line (`$`). The `/d` at the end tells sed to delete the matching character strings from the input stream.

Piping

```
cat app.log | sed 's/error/ERROR/g'
```

As with `grep`, you can use `cat` to output a file, then pipe it into `sed` with a vertical pipe character. This one outputs everything in `app.log`, but with every instance of `error` replaced with `ERROR`. Now, your logs can really shout at your developers when a bug needs fixing.

Don't Get Sedentary

Now that you're comfortable using sed to do simple substitutions, let's kick things up a notch.

Target Specific Lines

```
sed '1s/DEBUG/INFO/' app.log
```

In this example, you prefix the substitution command `s` with the number `1`, narrowing `sed`'s scope to just the first line. The command itself replaces any instance of `DEBUG` with `INFO` on line 1.

Target a Range of Lines

```
sed '3,6s/error/ERROR/' errors.log
```

Here, you specify only to make changes on lines 3–6, inclusive, casting `error` to uppercase.

Referencing the End of the Doc/Line

```
sed '$s/$/ Ka-chow!/' file.txt
```

This one uses the dollar sign in two distinct ways. First, when it precedes the `s` substitution command, it indicates that `sed` should target the last line of the stream. Then, when the last line is encountered, the dollar sign works like the one in `grep`, indicating the end of the line. As a result, this `sed` command makes sure that the last word in the transformed stream is an enthusiastic `Ka-chow`!

Run Multiple Commands

```
sed '
  s/DEBUG/INFO/
  s/http:/https:/
  s/localhost/127\.0\.0\.1/
' config.yaml
```

If you use single quotes, you can give multiple commands to `sed` when you delimit them with newlines. This lets you run multiple commands (like substitutions or line deletions) at once without sacrificing legibility. This snippet runs three different substitutions, which will be executed in sequence against the incoming stream.

Inserting Lines and a More Complicated Example

You can do more than just search and replace. As with the `/d` command, you can use `/i` and `/a` to insert and append new text, respectively. Let's assume you have a web server configuration file `nginx.conf` that contains the following:

```
http {
    include       mime.types;
    default_type  application/octet-stream;
    ...(more)...
}
```

Here, we are writing a script where we want to insert a new config line into our nginx configurations (potentially something we'll copy out to many servers). We want to add a line like this:

```
log_format  main  '$remote_addr - $remote_user [$time_local] "$request"';
```

Let's use `sed` to perform this change. We'll use the `-i` that overwrites the original file, rather than just outputting modified text.

```
sed -i '/^http {/i\
log_format  main  '"'"'$remote_addr - $remote_user
[$time_local] "$request"'"'"';
' nginx.conf
```

Okay, that's a bit complicated. Let's break it down.

- `^http {` means we're finding the line that *begins* with `http {`.
- `/i` means we'll insert whatever comes next *before* the matched line.

This means this command results in the following:

```
log_format  main  '$remote_addr - $remote_user
[$time_local] "$request"';
http {
    include       mime.types;
    default_type  application/octet-stream;
    ...(more)...
}
```

How about appending something at the end? Let's create a new `location` block after the `http` block:

```
sed -i '/^}/a\
location /status {\n\
    return 200 '\''ok'\'';\n\
}
' nginx.conf
```

In nginx-speak, this creates a static URL `/status` that always returns a `200 OK` HTTP response, but all you need to understand is how the location block is appended. Again, breaking it down:

- `-i` replaces the file with the new content.
- matching on `^}` means we're looking for a closing curly brace to appear right at the start of the line (indicated by `^`).
- `/a` means we're going to append.

sed vs. *grep*

So when do you reach for `sed` instead of `grep`? Here's some general guidance:

- Use `grep` when you're filtering lines (i.e., showing only the ones that match a pattern).
- Use `sed` when you're transforming lines (i.e., changing the content but keeping all lines).

And if you need to both find and transform, you can start piping commands together into clever one-liners.

Clarity Over Cleverness

Yes, you could craft some impressively clever, lengthy command chains that accomplish wonders with nary a line break to be found. Text manipulation commands like `sed` are good at that, and there's a kind of cachet among Linux enthusiasts for those that can craft the most powerful and esoteric one-line command. But please, resist. Because while programmers love to be clever, there's one thing far more valuable than cleverness, and that's readability. Programming is not just about accomplishing a task; it's about communication.

When you write code, you're communicating to future maintainers, and often, your future self. Fancy one-liners are like run-on sentences. They exhaust the reader and fail to communicate effectively. You or your colleagues won't want to carefully parse your past intentions from a 500-character line of `sed` script. You're not getting paid to conserve newlines, and "Faulknerian" is not an adjective to which coders should aspire.

When the task gets complicated, it's time to start writing scripts: scripts that strive for clarity, that decompose complex commands into legible, distinct functions. But we'll get to that. For now, let's look at the last of the three best-known command-line text manipulators: `awk`.

awk

With `grep`, you've got a tool for rapid pattern-matching; `sed` goes a step further and gives you powerful tools to match, replace, and edit text. Rounding out the classic trio of Unix text editing tools is *awk*, a command designed not just for pattern scanning and text processing. `awk` is often used to perform small data analysis jobs, particularly when text is laid out in rows and columns, like CSVs, TSVs, or your average log file.

Unlike `grep` or `sed`, which are shorthand for specific functions, `awk` gets its name from its creators: Alfred Aho, Peter Weinberger, and Brian Kernighan. Kernighan is also known for co-authoring the C Programming Language—no small addition to one's résumé!

Because it's technically an acronym, `awk` is sometimes rendered `AWK`, but not consistently. When you use the command on a terminal, it'll be lowercase, so we'll stick with that.

Power and Terseness

`awk` was created as a kind of successor to `sed`. Its purpose is to match patterns and then take an action on the matched text. In fact, `awk` bills itself as "the AWK Programming Language," which implies the depth contained within. It essentially has a run loop like a programming language, and it's stocked with functions that will remind you of C.

Wikipedia notes that the "power and terseness of early AWK programs . . . were important inspirations for the Perl language." Perl was one of my first coding experiences, and I've often noted that idiomatic Perl looks like the result of someone banging their head against the keyboard a few times. So as advised above, do your best to use `awk` in a way that folks can follow, or at least comment your scripts thoroughly!

I don't use `awk` as much as `sed` or `grep`, but it's powerful and useful in the right situations, so let's equip ourselves with some knowledge.

When to Use *awk*

awk reads input line-by-line, splits each line into fields (by default, on whitespace), and lets you write mini-programs to decide what to do with each line. It shines when you're working with structured data like:

- Tabular reports
- Space- or comma-delimited logs
- Config or log files with predictable structure
- Output of other commands like ps, df, ls, etc.

You'll use awk to filter, calculate, and summarize. It's like Excel, if Excel only had one cell and ran entirely in your terminal.

awk Basics

The canonical awk command looks like this:

```
awk 'pattern { action }' filename
```

Often, you're parsing the output of some other command with a pipe:

```
command | awk 'pattern { action }'
```

By default, awk splits each line into fields using whitespace, and you can reference them as $1, $2, $3, etc. $0 is the entire line.

Back to our nginx example, let's say you had an nginx log file like this:

```
127.0.0.1 - - [10/Aug/2025:13:00:00 +0000] "GET /index.html HTTP/1.1" 200 612
```

To print just the HTTP method (which is the sixth field, counting from 1), use:

```
awk '{ print $6 }' nginx.log
```

The result:

```
"GET
```

You'll get a bunch of "GET or "POST" strings, with those quotes included, since they're in the raw log. Remember, awk is separating tokens by whitespace, so it's looking at the single spaces around that string.

To clean it up:

```
awk '{ gsub(/"/, "", $6); print $6 }' nginx.log
```

What's going on here? Note the semicolon in the middle. This indicates that, in between the brackets, we are executing two distinct commands. First, we do a `gsub`, or "global substitution" on the item at `$6`. The first parameter you'll recognize as a regex bracketed by forward slashes, matching a double-quote character. The second parameter is delimited by double quotes and is an empty string. So this `gsub` command says, "find any double-quotes in the pattern at `$6` and replace them with nothing." Then, we print `$6`.

This demonstrates an important point about `awk`, which is that these pattern-match variables have a state within your `awk` command, and those states can be mutated. `$6` starts off as one thing and ends up as another before being printed. The result:

```
GET
```

We can even use those variables in conditional statements, like in a traditional programming language. Let's look for any failed HTTP requests by checking for lines where the response code is not 200:

```
awk '$9 != 200 { print $0 }' nginx.log
```

Note that I use `$9` (the status code) to check the condition, but `print $0` for the whole matching row.

Let's mix up the delimiter `awk` uses. The `/etc/passwd` file uses colons as delimiters, not whitespace, so tell `awk` about that with the `-F` command:

```
awk -F: '{ print $1 }' /etc/passwd
```

This will take an `/etc/passwd` file like this:

```
root:x:0:0:root:/root:/bin/bash
daemon:x:1:1:daemon:/usr/sbin:/usr/sbin/nologin
bin:x:2:2:bin:/bin:/usr/sbin/nologin
sys:x:3:3:sys:/dev:/usr/sbin/nologin
alice:x:1000:1000:Alice Smith:/home/alice:/bin/bash
bob:x:1001:1001:Bob Jones:/home/bob:/bin/zsh
```

and print this:

```
root
daemon
bin
sys
alice
bob
```

This prints the username. Note that because `$0` represents the entire line, awk pattern variables are essentially "base 1 indexed." The first match is `$1`.

While the exam only requires that you know a bit about awk and when to use it, there's much more to this diverse and powerful tool. Look for any of the numerous online tutorials or e-books available, such as the one at `https://opensource.com/article/20/9/awk-ebook`, to learn more.

Structured Text: JSON, YAML, INI

While the tools we've been learning are great at helping us wrangle unstructured text, it's structured documents that make the world go 'round. Formats like JSON, YAML, and INI are the critical foundation for many systems, defining standardized ways to clearly express environment variables, configuration values, infrastructure requirements, and more. Let's start with the one that's practically everywhere: JSON.

JSON

JSON, or JavaScript Object Notation, was designed to make data interchange easy and predictable. The specification was created, at least in part, as a response to the growing complexity of XML (itself inspired by HTML), with its complex combination of opening and closing tags, angle brackets, and object attributes that so often produces a wall-of-text effect.

As an example, imagine a response from a weather API returning something like this in XML:

```
<weatherResponse>
  <location>
    <city>South Bend</city>
    <state>IN</state>
    <country>USA</country>
  </location>
  <current>
    <temperature unit="F">73</temperature>
    <condition>Partly Cloudy</condition>
    <humidity>64</humidity>
    <wind>
      <speed unit="mph">9</speed>
      <direction>SW</direction>
    </wind>
  </current>
  <forecast>
    <day name="Friday">
      <high>78</high>
```

```
      <low>62</low>
      <condition>Scattered Showers</condition>
    </day>
    <day name="Saturday">
      <high>80</high>
      <low>65</low>
      <condition>Sunny</condition>
    </day>
  </forecast>
</weatherResponse>
```

The same, in JSON, is less verbose, requiring fewer characters and providing enhanced readability:

```
{
  "location": {
    "city": "South Bend",
    "state": "IN",
    "country": "USA"
  },
  "current": {
    "temperature": {
      "value": 73,
      "unit": "F"
    },
    "condition": "Partly Cloudy",
    "humidity": 64,
    "wind": {
      "speed": 9,
      "unit": "mph",
      "direction": "SW"
    }
  },
  "forecast": [
    {
      "day": "Friday",
      "high": 78,
      "low": 62,
      "condition": "Scattered Showers"
    },
    {
      "day": "Saturday",
      "high": 80,
      "low": 65,
      "condition": "Sunny"
    }
  ]
}
```

Much nicer. JSON is also fairly permissive with its structure. For instance, this snippet:

```
"wind": {
    "speed": 9,
    "unit": "mph",
    "direction": "SW"
}
```

can just as easily be rendered on a single line, like this:

```
    "wind": {"speed": 9, "unit": "mph","direction": "SW" }
```

Both are valid, machine-parseable, equivalent JSON, but while the latter may conserve a little space, it sacrifices readability. REST responses are often "minified" in this way to reduce the number of bytes transmitted over the web. As a result, developers commonly use browser plug-ins or editor extensions that will "prettify" JSON into the nicely tabbed, clearer format shown previously.

In JSON, anything between two brackets is an object, and an object has fields or attributes. Objects can be nested within other objects. If you need to define a list of values (or a list of objects), that list must be enclosed in square brackets, delimited by commas, like so:

```
{
  "user": {
    "id": 42,
    "first_name": "Alice",
    "roles": ["admin", "editor", "viewer"],
    "profile": {
      "email": "alice@example.com",
      "preferences": {
        "theme": "dark",
        "notifications": true
      }
    }
  }
}
```

This example shows all of those conditions. The `user` object has both simple values, like `first_name`, as well as arrays, like `roles`, which has three string values separated by commas. The `profile` object has some scalar values like `email`, but also has a nested object, `preferences`. For an example of an array of objects, see the `forecast` object in the weather example earlier.

One advantage of JSON's ubiquity is that, like XML before it, it has been blessed with developer support and tooling to help make it easier to work with. An example is the command `jq`, which helps parse JSON.

Navigating JSON with *jq*

jq is a command-line JSON processor. It reads JSON input, applies a filter or transformation, and prints the result. You can think of it as `awk` or `sed`, but for structured JSON data.

Let's assume the previous JSON snippet is in the file `alice.json`. With `jq`, you can reference nested values like this (first the command, then the output):

```
jq '.user.first_name' alice.json
"Alice"
jq '.user.profile.email' alice.json
"alice@example.com"
```

To lose the quotes, include -r:

```
jq '.user.profile.email' alice.json
alice@example.com
```

You can fetch Alice's first-listed role by using square brackets:

```
jq -r '.user.roles[0]' user.json
admin
```

You can also create new JSON by filtering the original:

```
jq '{name: .user.first_name, email: .user.profile.email}' alice.json > new_
output.json
```

Here, I use the > character to pipe the usual console output into a file. This command renders the file `new_output.json` as this:

```
{
  "name": "Alice",
  "email": "alice@example.com"
}
```

As a command-line tool, `jq` is great for parsing the JSON-based output of other commands. Here, we ask the Amazon Web Services command-line interface for information on a cloud server. The output of AWS EC2 `describe-instances` returns information about the virtual machines running in your AWS account. The output is much too verbose to show in its entirety, but it starts like this:

```
{
    "Reservations": [
        {
            "ReservationId": "r-07b991feb612345",
            "OwnerId": "03187812345",
            "Groups": [],
            "Instances": [
                {
                    "Architecture": "x86_64",
                    …many other fields…
                    "InstanceId": " i-0123456789abcdef0"
```

You need to understand the structure of your JSON before you can parse it with `jq`. We're after the instance IDs of our virtual machines. From reading the unfiltered output, we know that it returns a `Reservations` array, that each `Reservation` object has an `Instances` array, and that each `Instance` object has an `InstanceId` attribute. We can then pipe that output into `jq` and have it grab the one value we want: the instance ID.

```
aws ec2 describe-instances | jq -r
'.Reservations[].Instances[].InstanceId'
```

Using the square brackets but omitting an index, causes `jq` to fetch all array elements. The output looks a bit like this:

```
i-0123456789abcdef0
i-0fedcba9876543210
i-0fedcba9876543999
```

`jq` is extremely helpful, as are similar packages in node, Python, and other languages. The existence of such tools is a big part of JSON's appeal. Now that you know how to navigate JSON with ease, let's look at JSON's little cousin, YAML.

YAML

YAML's whole deal is that it's a data interchange format that's even more human-friendly than JSON. One of my favorite fun facts is that it stands for Yet Another Markup Language, a nod to the fact that markup languages were a dime-a-dozen back in 2001, when it was first created. Since then, the lore has been revised to say that the acronym stands for YAML Ain't Markup Language, acknowledging YAML's growing diversity of use. For what it's worth, that's what's called a recursive acronym. As with PHP, which stands for PHP: Hypertext Preprocessor, the acronym incorporates itself into its definition. Try not to think about it too long.

I love YAML. JSON is great and incredibly widely used, but JSON can be tedious and more than a bit touchy, treating you to a constant need to match curly braces, quote strings, escape special characters, and use extra tools to force it into a human-readable format—not to mention the endless comma management.

YAML, on the other hand, eschews all that. As in Python, indentation in YAML documents is syntactically significant. This means you're required to format documents well, which makes them instantly more readable. Even better, it's rarely required in YAML to enclose strings in quotation marks, so you're less often required to escape characters and are free to type in a more natural way.

Let's take our weather example and express it in YAML:

```
location:
  city: South Bend
  state: IN
  country: USA

current:
  temperature:
    value: 73
    unit: F
  condition: Partly Cloudy
  humidity: 64
  wind:
    speed: 9
    unit: mph
    direction: SW

forecast:
  - day: Friday
    high: 78
    low: 62
    condition: Scattered Showers

  - day: Saturday
    high: 80
    low: 65
    condition: Sunny
```

You can see how YAML can be a better experience. If you're getting one thing from this chapter, it's that I'm a big fan of readability. Code and configuration files are ultimately processed by computers, but they are written, read, and maintained by humans. The easier they are for people to parse, the better.

In YAML, most things are key-value pairs. Nesting, indicated in JSON by nested braces, is depicted with indentation:

```
location:
  city: South Bend
  state: IN
  country: USA
```

Indentation is commonly kept to two spaces only. Four is fine as well, but you must be consistent. Oh, and don't even think about using tabs! YAML will not allow it.

In this case, `location` comprises three fields: `city`, `state`, and `country`.

Multivalue arrays are designated with hyphens, a style YAML shares with another document markup format popular with developers, Markdown:

```
ports:
  - 80
  - 443
```

In this web server–based example, the value of `ports` is an array of two values, 80 and 443.

You Can Comment YAML

Another great feature YAML has over JSON is that it supports Python-style comments. Use a hash symbol, like this:

```
# expose ports for HTTP and HTTPS. Any HTTP traffic will be redirected to
HTTPS by
# the load balancer
ports:
  - 80
  - 443
```

You Still Need Quotes, Sometimes

In YAML, you often don't need quotation marks around values, but there are a few exceptions. Primarily, anything that uses special characters needs quotation marks. For example, in this case the use of the colon in the movie title requires the title to be enclosed in quotes:

```
film:
  title: "Mission: Impossible"
  release_year: 1996
```

The same goes for any string with brackets, asterisks, question marks, and more.

If you want values to be parsed literally, use single quotes. If you want escape characters interpolated, use double. For example:

```
# this is a newline
my_value: "\n"

# this is a backslash followed by the letter n
another_value: '\n'
```

Multi-line Strings

You can also define multi-line strings using a pipe, giving you even more flexibility in defining long values:

```
description: |
  This is a multi-line
  string in YAML.

  It preserves all line breaks,
  including blank lines.
```

You'll find YAML in all kinds of places, from Ansible playbooks to infrastructure-as-code templates. For instance, AWS's CloudFormation, which lets you define cloud architectures via text files, initially required JSON but now fully supports YAML. Guess which one I use?

INI Files

JSON and YAML are both commonly used formats for defining configuration files. However, Windows has one style of config file that goes back decades and persists to this day: the *INI file*. That's INI as in "initialization": these files were first used to tell Windows how to configure things as it started up.

INI files are wonderfully simple, defining key-value pairs using equals signs and designating sections via square brackets. INI is not really a properly defined specification in the same way as JSON or YAML, so your mileage may vary, but they look a lot like this:

```
[database]
host=localhost
port=5432
user=postgres
password=secret

# this is a comment
; this is also a comment
[server]
port=8080
debug=true
```

These files are less common today, but they still show up in some Windows contexts. For instance, a file called `desktop.ini` maintains user preferences for the display of things like hidden folders or displaying file extensions on users' desktops.

The simplicity of INI files is very similar to that found in `.env` (dotenv) files, which are often used in modern application stacks to define environment variables. Python's `dotenv` package expects a file called `.env` that might contain the following:

```
AWS_ACCESS_KEY_ID=ASIAABC123XYZPXG
AWS_SECRET_ACCESS_KEY=RA123fdakl35+fda928123
```

This format, similar to INI syntax, loads in key-value pairs and sets them in the environment.

Externalizing Secrets

One big use case for these kinds of files is externalizing configuration or secrets. You never want to embed (or hard-code) passwords, API keys, or other sensitive information in application code (or any code that goes into version control).

Not only is it a security risk, but these values can change. If a password is compromised, you want the ability to update it without the overhead of redeploying code. When your secrets or other configuration files are separated from your code, you can often update the configuration only, then reboot the software to have the new values be picked up.

Working with Application and System Logs

We've discussed how to navigate the terminal and work with common commands, we've seen how to wield powerful tools to manipulate and process text, and we've learned about the text formats that drive so much of our infrastructure's critical configuration. With this knowledge, we turn our attention to one of the most important text-based sources of system information you'll encounter: logging.

Types of Logs and Where to Find Them

System logs, server logs, application logs, and more: Your computing resources are constantly generating a chatty stream of helpful (if at times overly verbose) information. Logs are the first place you'll go to troubleshoot issues, perform security audits, and analyze performance. As a systems administrator, operations engineer, or DevOps professional, you need to know how to work with logs to successfully manage your environments.

System Logs

On Linux, you'll find systemwide activity in `/var/log/`. Windows keeps its records in the *Event Viewer* (see Figure 1.1), neatly split into categories like System, Security, and

FIGURE 1.1 The windows event viewer.

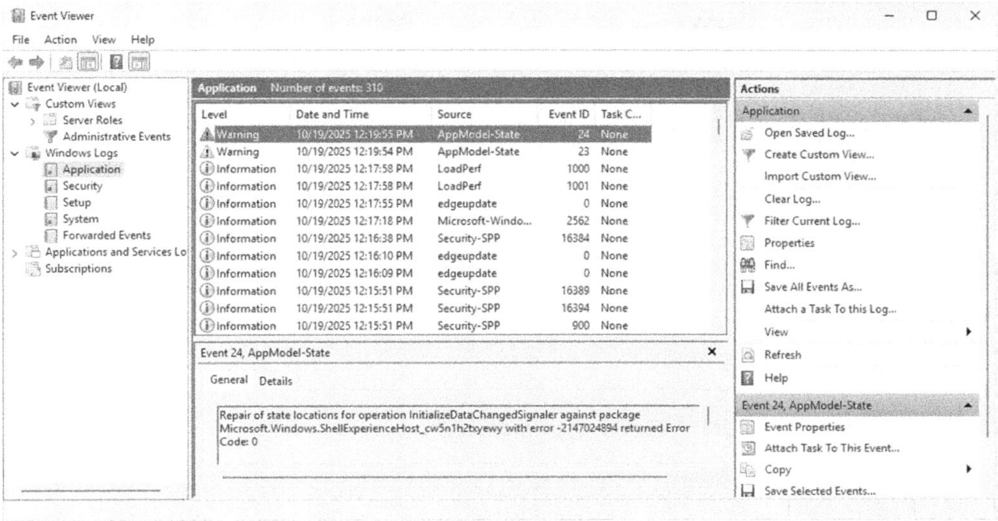

Application. These logs are your first stop when the machine itself is acting up—things like failed logins, hardware errors, or a service that mysteriously stopped at 2:00 in the morning.

Application Logs

Individual apps often keep their own journals of behavior. Frameworks like Python's `logging` module or Java's `log4j` allow developers to emit structured messages about what's happening inside their code. These are crucial for debugging; if your company's e-commerce site crashes whenever someone tries to make a purchase, detailed application logs should give you plenty of clues as to why (or at least leave you a cryptic stack trace to puzzle over). While developers decide what to log and how, using these frameworks can make it easier to parse large log dumps for relevant information.

Server Logs

Web and database servers can be especially chatty. Apache and nginx write access and error logs that show every request. Database engines like MySQL and PostgreSQL do the same for queries and performance issues. Server logs are often the first stop for performance tuning and intrusion detection.

Log Locations

Where you'll find logs depends on the environment and ecosystem in which you're working. Here are a few of the most common places to look:

- **Linux/Unix:** Almost everything funnels into `/var/log/`.
- **Windows:** Event Viewer (`eventvwr.msc`) is the control center for watching your system's logs.
- **Containers:** Logs usually print to `stdout` or `stderr`. You can monitor Docker logs at runtime with the command `docker logs`, or configure your Docker runtime to route output to another location.
- **Cloud:** Centralized services like CloudWatch (Amazon Web Services), Cloud Logging (Google Cloud Platform), and Log Analytics (Microsoft Azure) aggregate most logs in their respective cloud infrastructure systems.

In short, system logs explain the machine, application logs explain the code, server logs explain the services, and the location depends on your operating system and environment. Table 1.1 shows a few of the more common log locations for Linux variants.

Applying the Text Parsing Toolkit

Once you know where logs live, what do you do with them? Not only can application and system logs be quite verbose, but they can also grow very quickly. It can be a challenge to find what you're looking for in a sea of fast-moving logs. That's where our text parsing

TABLE 1.1 Common log locations

File	What it Tracks
`syslog` or `messages`	General system activity, kernel messages, daemons, and services
`auth.log/ secure`	Authentication attempts, sudo use, SSH logins, failures
`dmesg`	Kernel ring buffer; hardware and driver initialization
`kern.log`	Kernel-specific events (warnings, errors, panics)
`cron`	Scheduled jobs run by `cron`, including errors
`boot.log`	Boot process details, useful if startup goes sideways
`apt/`	Subdirectory of logs related to package management (Debian/Ubuntu)
`yum.log`	Package installation/removal on Red Hat/CentOS systems
`httpd/` or `nginx/`	Web server access/error logs, if those services are installed

toolkit of `grep`, `sed`, `awk`, and `jq` comes in. These tools turn a wall of log noise into something you can reason about. Let's look at a few real-world examples.

Catch Logs by the Tail

We haven't covered it yet, but the `tail` command in Unix-compatible systems shows you the last few lines of a file. Add `-f` to follow the file as it grows in real time:

```
tail -f /var/log/syslog
```

It's the system administrator's equivalent of watching a security camera feed. If you know a problem is taking place *right now*, or you have a collaborator who can trigger an error, tailing a log can be a great way to see what's going on.

Combine `tail` with `grep` for quick filtering. Maybe you're looking for web requests coming into `nginx` from a known malicious IP address (using a fake address here):

```
tail -f /var/log/nginx/access.log | grep "130.8.23.XY"
```

Now, the only thing streaming across your screen will be access log lines that contain this IP. Combining `tail` with `grep` can be a great way to get a handle on the real-time state of your system while you troubleshoot.

More Log Parsing

Let's look at some of our other commands. Our old pal `sed` is perfect for fixing text in bulk. Although best practice says that developers should avoid logging out sensitive values, you may still encounter logs that contain API keys, passwords, or other text that should not be shared. With `sed`, we can do some filtering to clean things up before passing the logs downstream for analysis. Let's redact any API keys, which in this example, we know begin with `sk-` and are always followed by a space in this log. Assuming the target lines look like this:

```
access granted with key sk-1289bDFx12 at 12:35
```

then the following command will clean them up:

```
sed 's/sk-[0-9a-zA-Z]* /\[REDACTED\] /' app.log > sanitized.log
```

Note how we're bringing in our knowledge of regular expressions to match keys that can contain numbers, lowercase letters, and uppercase letters, as well as how we must escape the square brackets so they are treated as literals. This turns each matching line into something safe, like this:

```
access granted with key [REDACTED]at 12:35
```

We can use awk to split Apache web server log lines into columns and process them. For a file that looks like this:

```
10.10.10.5 - - [05/Oct/2025:08:24:16 -0400] "GET /dashboard HTTP/1.1" 200 18321
"https://example.com/login" "Mozilla/5.0 (iPhone; CPU iPhone OS 17_0 like Mac
OS X)"
203.0.113.55 - - [05/Oct/2025:08:24:28 -0400] "GET /favicon.ico HTTP/1.1" 404
162 "https://example.com/" "Mozilla/5.0 (X11; Ubuntu; Linux x86_64)"
198.51.100.99 - - [05/Oct/2025:08:24:33 -0400] "PUT /api/items/129 HTTP/1.1"
201 67 "-" "PostmanRuntime/7.39.0"
```

We can get a summary of the URLs access like this:

```
awk '{print $7}' httpd.log
```

This pulls the seventh column (the URL) and prints it.

Admins use these tools daily to triage problems, generate reports, or monitor systems. A well-crafted command can save hours of log-diving, and once you've written it, you can add it to a script it for next time.

Best Practices for Log Management

Before we move on from logging, consider these additional points.

First, logs are both a powerful asset and a potential threat to your runtime system. Why? Because they can grow so quickly that they can fill up your system's drives if you're not careful. Use tools like Linux's `logrotate` to regularly archive or delete old log files to keep logs manageable.

Second, although it is somewhat beyond the scope of this book, many organizations centralize their logs into systems that aggregate information from many different sources. Sometimes this may be a locally run system, like an Elasticsearch/Logstash/Kibana (ELK) stack, a well-liked open source trio for centralizing log analytics; other times it may be a cloud service like Splunk that does the work. Often, these services provide not only log storage and access, but powerful analytics tools to help you gain more insights from your logs than you might be able to do on your own.

Summary

In this chapter, we explored the command line and dove into tools that help manipulate and extract meaning from plain text. We used regular expressions and command-line tools like `grep`, `sed`, and `awk`. You practiced parsing structured data with `jq` and learned how JSON, YAML, and INI formats are used to store configuration cleanly and predictably.

Finally, you turned these same skills toward application and system logs, the running commentary of your systems' behavior. You learned how to locate logs, tail them for real-time updates, and filter them for patterns or errors of interest.

Exam Essentials

Understand the role of text-processing tools. Remember what each tool does best: `grep` filters text, `sed` transforms it, and `awk` analyzes structured text. Be able to recognize how these tools can be combined in pipelines to clean or extract data from logs or other text sources.

Know the basics of regular expressions. Regex defines search patterns used by many automation tools. Recognize how metacharacters such as `^`, `$`, `*`, and `[]` affect pattern matching and how escaping special characters changes behavior.

Recognize structured data formats and tools. Be able to identify and read JSON, YAML, and INI syntax. Know that `jq` allows you to query and transform JSON output, such as filtering API responses or command-line tool output for specific fields.

Understand application and system log analysis. Know what logs are used for, where they're commonly located (e.g., `/var/log` on Linux and the console on macOS), and how to inspect them with commands like `tail` for streaming output. Understand how `grep`, `awk`, or `jq` can extract useful insights such as error codes or timestamps.

Know why separating configuration and secrets matters. Recognize the security and maintainability benefits of keeping credentials and environment-specific values outside of code. This prepares you for later topics in configuration management and secrets handling.

Review Questions

1. On a Windows system, you want to run Bash scripts that use common Linux commands like `grep` and `sed`. Which tool provides the most native Linux experience without needing a full virtual machine?

   A. Git Bash

   B. Cygwin

   C. Windows Subsystem for Linux (WSL)

   D. PowerShell

2. You've written a shell script that calls an API using `curl`, but you've hard-coded the API key and base URL. What is the best way to make this script reusable across multiple environments?

   A. Leave the values in the script but comment them out for reference.

   B. Use environment variables to externalize the API key and base URL.

   C. Create separate copies of the script for each environment.

   D. Store the API key in the script but obfuscate it with base64 encoding.

3. While working with logs, you want to find all lines ending in the string `404`. Which regular expression would you use with `grep`?

   A. `grep '^404'`

   B. `grep '/404/'`

   C. `grep '404$'`

   D. `grep '.*404.*'`

4. You need to replace every instance of `http://` with `https://` in a configuration file using `sed`. Which of the following commands is both correct and avoids unnecessary escaping?

   A. `sed 's/http:\/\/https:\/\//g' config.yaml`

   B. `sed 's|http://|https://|g' config.yaml`

   C. `sed 'replace http:// with https://' config.yaml`

   D. `sed 's/http:/https:/g' config.yaml`

5. You have a structured JSON file with user information. Which tool allows you to extract the user's email address directly from the command line in a clean, predictable way?

   A. `awk`

   B. `grep`

   C. `jq`

   D. `sed`

6. You're documenting config formats for your team. Which format is indentation-sensitive, supports inline comments with #, and represents lists with leading hyphens?
   A. JSON
   B. YAML
   C. INI
   D. XML

7. On macOS (BSD grep), you want to match the string `"dinner"` specifically by detecting two consecutive n characters without backslash-escaping the curly braces. Which command works?
   A. `echo "dinner" | grep -e 'n{2}'`
   B. `echo "dinner" | grep -E 'n{2}'`
   C. `echo "dinner" | grep -P 'n{2}'`
   D. `echo "dinner" | grep 'n{2}'`

8. You have a text file where each line contains several words separated by spaces. You want to print only the *sixth word* from every line. Which command is the best choice?
   A. `grep "word6" file.txt`
   B. `sed 's/ .*//' file.txt`
   C. `awk '{ print $6 }' file.txt`
   D. `jq '.fields[5]' file.txt`

9. A Bash script defines `API_BASE_URL="https://api.example.com"` and then calls `bash -c 'echo $API_BASE_URL'`, but nothing prints. What single change ensures child processes see the value?
   A. Prepend the script with `set -a` (export all variables).
   B. Use `export API_BASE_URL="https://api.example.com"` before invoking the child.
   C. Quote the assignment: `API_BASE_URL='"https://api.example.com"'`.
   D. Use `declare -g API_BASE_URL="https://api.example.com"` to force global scope.

10. When you type `ps -ef | grep httpd`, what role does the pipe (`|`) play in this command?
    A. It comments out the first command.
    B. It redirects standard output from the first command into the second.
    C. It joins two files together for `grep` to read.
    D. It prevents both commands from running simultaneously.

Answers to Review Questions

1. C. The correct answer is C. Windows Subsystem for Linux (WSL) runs genuine Linux distributions directly on Windows, offering near-native performance and compatibility. Options A and B (Git Bash and Cygwin) provide partial emulations, but not full Linux binaries. Option D, PowerShell, is powerful for Windows automation but is not Linux-compatible.

2. B. Option B is correct. Externalizing values into environment variables makes scripts reusable, portable, and more secure. Option A is incorrect because commenting values out still risks exposure. With option C, multiple copies of the script lead to poor maintainability, and option D uses base64 encoding, which does not secure secrets.

3. C. The correct answer is C. The dollar sign (`$`) in regex means end of line, so `grep '404$'` matches lines ending in `404`. Option A (`^404`) would only match lines starting with `404`. Option B is syntactically incorrect for `grep` unless using `-E` with slashes removed. Option D (`.*404.*`) matches lines containing `404` anywhere, not just at the end.

4. B. The correct answer is B. Using | as the delimiter keeps the command readable without escaping slashes. Option A works but is messy. Option C is not valid `sed` syntax. Option D would only replace the string `http:` and leave the rest unchanged.

5. C. The correct answer is C. `jq` is designed for parsing and filtering JSON and can directly access nested fields like `.user.profile.email`. While `awk`, `grep`, and `sed` can be made to work, they are text-based tools and not as suitable for structured JSON parsing.

6. B. The correct answer is B (YAML). YAML is indentation-significant, allows # comments, and uses leading hyphens for lists. Option A, JSON, does not support comments and isn't indentation-sensitive. Option C, INI files, support comments (# or ;) but not indentation-based structure or hyphenated lists. Option D, XML, uses tags, not indentation or hyphens, and comments use `<!-- ... -->`.

7. B. The correct answer is B. BSD `grep` supports extended regex via `-E`, which lets you use `{}` without escaping. Option A (`-e`) needs the braces escaped on many platforms. Option C uses `-P` (PCRE), which BSD grep doesn't support. Option D (no flags) treats { literally and won't match as intended.

8. C. The correct answer is C. `awk` automatically splits each line into fields (separated by whitespace) and lets you print any field by its position number. `$6` means "the sixth word." Option A uses grep to for text patterns, but `word6` is only going to match that literal value. In Option B, `sed` will edit the text rather than extracts columns, and `jq` (Option D) only works with structured JSON data.

9. B. The correct answer is B. Environment variables must be exported to be visible to child processes like a `bash -c` subshell. Option A uses `set -a`, which could work, but changes behavior for all subsequent assignments (not the simplest, single fix). In Option C, quoting doesn't export. Option D uses `declare -g`, which affects shell scope, not environment inheritance to child processes.

10. B. The correct answer is B. The pipe sends the standard output of `ps -ef` into `grep httpd` as input, letting `grep` filter only the matching lines. Option A confuses it with a comment symbol; C and D are incorrect interpretations of the pipe's function.

Chapter 2

Scripting Basics

THE AUTOOPS+ EXAM TOPICS COVERED IN THIS CHAPTER MAY INCLUDE, BUT ARE NOT LIMITED TO, THE FOLLOWING:

✔ **1.0: Automation Coding Concepts**

- 1.1. Given a scenario, use code to support automation.
- 1.4. Given a scenario, troubleshoot common issues with the code life cycle.

✔ **2.0: System Configuration**

- 2.2. Compare and contrast basic approaches to automation.
- 2.3. Given a scenario, interact with representational state transfer–compliant (RESTful) systems to perform create, read, update, and delete (CRUD) operations.

Now that you've got a few commands under your belt, it's time to start structuring those commands into repeatable, reusable documents. The idea of "scripting" can be as simple as that, but experienced system administrators and DevOps professionals go further, creating shell scripts in Bash, automating with PowerShell, or programming in Python to get things done in languages that support variables, conditions, loops, and more. Let's see some examples.

Coming Out of Your Shell

We've talked a lot about the command line as a concept; sometimes we refer to it as the terminal. Another word for this text-based interface is a *shell*, a word that is commonly used in Unix-based systems. One of the most common shells in Unix-land is *Bash*, which stands for the Bourne Again Shell. It's a successor to the original Bourne shell that formed the basis for so much of today's concept of a command line environment.

As mentioned in Chapter 1, "Working on the Command Line," even among POSIX-compliant shells, not every command is 100 percent the same. While they often have much in common, they have developed along sometimes parallel, sometimes divergent lines. Just remember to double-check the particulars of this book's examples with your specific operating system's help pages.

With that, let's take a look at some shell scripting basics. Shell scripting lets you blend typical command-line commands—everything from tool calls like `grep` and `sed` to basic commands like changing directories, `cd`—with higher-order programming constructs like variable declaration, conditional logic, looping, and functions. For instance, if you wanted to write a script that archives log files and gives them a name based on the hostname and current time but makes sure to skip already processed files, you can do that by combining basic terminal commands with shell scripting.

Shell scripts are the next step up from doing everything manually on the command line; indeed, it's the first step many system administrators take to automating their work.

Let's look at some basics. You probably know what these concepts are in a general sense, and this section isn't intended to teach programming. What you do need to know is shell scripting's unique syntax and quirks. There are more than a few!

Running Shell Scripts

Every example in this chapter can be run by saving the code into a file, then running it in one of two ways. First, by invoking the `bash` command followed by the script name:

```
>  bash my_script.sh
```

Second, you can invoke the `bash` executable at the start of a script, and then run the script directly. Doing this requires you to know the path to your local machine's `bash` script, and to set permissions to make your script executable. I'll track down my computer's `bash` with the `which` command:

```
> which bash
/bin/bash
```

Then, I'll use the `#!` (sometimes called the "shebang" operator) in my file:

```
#! /bin/bash
echo "hello!"
```

Finally, I'll use `chmod` to make the script executable, then run it directly:

```
> chmod +x my_script.sh
> ./my_script.sh
hello!
```

You can follow these steps to try any of the scripting examples in this chapter.

Comments and Variables

Comments are important in any programming context; in shell script, they're behind hash symbols. Variables are named and assigned with = but referenced with `$`.

```
# comments are behind hash symbols
# variables are assigned with equal signs -- no spaces!
message="hello world!"

# Variables are referenced with a dollar sign.
# Always reference variables within quotes.
# This preserves any spaces or special characters.
echo "$message"

# For example:
my_filename="some file.txt"
cat $my_filename # fails due to space
cat "$my_filename" # succeeds
```

You can weave in command-line commands, as well:

```
API_URL="https://api.example.com"
curl "$API_URL/pets"
```

This example will print the output of the `curl` command to the console.

Conditionals

You have conditionals:

```
if [ "$message" = "hello world" ]; then
    echo "Hello to you, too!"
else
    echo "Where is my greeting?"
fi
```

Note a few things here. First, `if` statements are denoted by `if`, a condition in square brackets, a semicolon, and the word `then`. You can have an optional `else`, and then the conditional block continues until the keyword `fi`.

Also note that in order to compare strings, I put the variable in double quotes and used the `$` to interpolate the variable into its value. As a result, this code prints "Hello to you, too!"

Comparing numbers is a little different. Shell scripts don't use the traditional > or < kind of signs.

```
# this checks if $COUNT is greater than 10
if [ $COUNT -gt 10 ]; then
  echo "Too many."
fi
```

Table 2.1 shows the comparison operators available in a Bash script.

There is an alternate syntax that lets you use more traditional operators. Use double parentheses, as shown, instead of square brackets, to get the option to use things like > and >=.

```
if (( $COUNT > 10 )); then
    echo "greater than 10 in double parentheses"
fi
```

Just make sure to keep track of which style you're using, and as always, stay consistent.

TABLE 2.1 Shell scripting comparison operators

Operator	Meaning
`-eq`	Equal to (integers)
`-ne`	Not equal to (integers)
`-lt`	Less than (integers)
`-le`	Less than or equal to (integers)
`-gt`	Greater than (integers)
`-ge`	Greater than or equal to (integers)
`=`	Equal to (strings)
`!=`	Not equal to (strings)
`<`	Less than (strings must be quoted)
`>`	Greater than (strings must be quoted)
`-z`	String is empty
`-n`	String is not empty

Looping

Shell scripting also offers loops. One style is denoted by `for`, followed by a condition, then a semicolon. Use `do` and `done` to enclose what happens in the loop:

```
for file in *.log; do
    echo "Processing $file"
done
```

This `for...in` example loops over the contents of the current folder, as long as they end in `.log`. This is similar to running an `ls` statement on the command line.

You can also write `while` loops:

```
COUNT=0
while [ $COUNT -lt 5 ]; do
  echo "Count is $COUNT"
  COUNT=$((COUNT + 1))
done
```

Note that in order to assign COUNT the value of COUNT+1, it's necessary to enclose the *arithmetic expression* in double parentheses.

Command Substitution

You can also assign variables to the output of shell commands:

```
current_date=$(date)
my_files=$(ls -l)
```

This puts the text result of the ls command into a variable, which you can then manipulate with other bash commands.

Functions

When code gets sufficiently complicated or you find yourself performing the same kind of action more than once, it's time to write some functions.

```
say_hello() {
  echo "Hi there, $1"
}
say_hello "friend"
```

In this case, we take the echo command and place it into a function, which can then be called with many different parameters. Inside the function, $1 refers to the first passed-in parameter—in this case, the word friend.

Functional decomposition is the act of creating reusable functions from code that you might reuse regularly or copy for different purposes. For instance, let's say you have a series of steps you perform to prepare log files before they are sent to a centralized log aggregator. This activity might be performed on many different input files, but the steps are the same. Rather than replicating code for different circumstances, turn that code into a function that allows you to pass in different filenames:

```
prepare_log() {
    local input_file="$1"

    # Check if file exists
    if [[ ! -f "$input_file" ]]; then
        echo "Error: File '$input_file' not found."
        return 1
    fi

    echo "Preparing log file: $input_file"
```

```
    # Remove blank lines
    sed -i '/^$/d' "$input_file"

    # redact sensitive values
    sed -i 's/sk-[0-9a-zA-Z]* /\[REDACTED\] /' "$input_file"

    # Compress the cleaned log
    gzip -f "$input_file"

    echo "Finished: ${input_file}.gz created."
}

# Example usage:
prepare_log "/var/log/syslog.log"
prepare_log "/tmp/custom_app.log"
```

This script accepts a filename as input, which becomes $1 inside the function. The syntax [[-f <filename>]] checks to make sure a file exists and returns a Boolean suitable for an if statement. The exclamation mark negates it, so we're checking if the file does *not* exist and outputting an error if that's the case. From there, we do some sed transformations, zip the file, and output a status update.

This function can then be used on many different input files without repeating code and becomes a useful tool in the rest of a larger script. You'll want to use functional decomposition often in Bash, Python, and any script you write.

TIP Just like functions, your shell scripts can accept parameters. When you invoke a shell script from the command line, any input given after the script's name will become parameters accessible by variable names $1, $2, etc.

Checking Exit Codes

Because shell scripts often incorporate command-line commands, it's important to know how to use them. You've seen how the standard output of a command can be captured into a variable. You can also see the command's *exit code* with the built-in variable $?. The value of a script's exit code indicates the outcome of the command. Zero tends to mean success; anything else is usually some sort of failure.

```
curl http://non-existent-url.com
if [ $? -ne 0 ]; then
  echo "Web request failed"
fi
```

Shell scripting in Bash and similar shells is incredibly powerful, but if you're on Windows, you have another fantastically useful tool at your disposal: PowerShell.

PowerShell: Cmdlet Clarity

PowerShell arose out of a need to make Windows scripting and administration more comprehensible, and it has, in fact, become an invaluable tool for Windows system administrators, programmers, and operators.

To understand PowerShell, you should understand how its design is, in some ways, a response to the heterogeneous sprawl of Unix. Given its history, it's amazing that the Unix command-line experience coheres as well as it does. Unix and its many tools were built by many different teams and individual contributors over time, with few formal standards to align their behavior (though de facto standards often emerged). Unix tools tend to adhere to the tenet of "do one thing well," a philosophy that has led to many Unix commands being fairly specialized. Even more ad hoc is how they exchange data: through text. In POSIX-compliant operating systems, we are most often using pipes to flow plain text between commands. This is, of course, a big part of the reason we rely on tools like `grep`, `sed`, and `awk` so much.

PowerShell is different. It was designed from the ground up as a unified command-line experience. The developers of PowerShell learned the lessons of Unix well and conceived of an ecosystem with a set of tools that work similarly and exchange data in a predictable, structured way. Although often more verbose than shell scripting, PowerShell programs offer more clarity to the reader.

Inputs and outputs in PowerShell are not just text; they are objects with documented structures, fields, and data types. As a result, learning PowerShell may be said to have a shorter learning curve than Bash scripting, and the resulting scripts may be less prone to errors.

Cmdlets: Consistent by Design

PowerShell commands are called *cmdlets* (pronounced "command-lets"). They follow a strict Verb-Noun naming convention. For example:

- `Get-Process`
- `Stop-Service`
- `New-Item`

Unlike the esoteric mix of Unix commands like `ps`, `kill`, `ls`, or `cat`, each cmdlet follows this specific formula. PowerShell also makes discovery easy. `Get-Command` lists all available cmdlets, and `Get-Help` gives you usage examples. If you forget the syntax for stopping a service, no worries: you can just ask PowerShell directly. Here, we fetch the first five cmdlets:

```
C:\Windows\system32> Get-Command -CommandType Cmdlet -TotalCount 5

CommandType     Name
-----------     ----
Cmdlet          Add-History
Cmdlet          Clear-History
Cmdlet          Connect-PSSession
Cmdlet          Debug-Job
Cmdlet          Disable-PSSessionConfiguration
```

You can see the Verb-Noun format there, along with two parameters prefixed with hyphens. PowerShell convention is to always use InterCaps format for commands and parameters. This can make typing PowerShell commands a little slower than one might like, but it's worth it to become adept at a fantastic tool.

If you're curious whether a certain command exists, you can always try constructing one from known verbs and nouns. In fact, the set of all available verbs is something you can browse with PowerShell. Here's a small sample of the verbs listed by the cmdlet `Get-Verb`:

```
> Get-Verb
Verb        Group
----        -----
Add         Common
Clear       Common
Close       Common
Copy        Common
Enter       Common
Exit        Common
Find        Common
```

Then, you can view everything you can do with a certain verb. Let's find all the cmdlets that begin with `Start` using a filtered `Get-Command` cmdlet. The pipe into `Select` limits the columns returned so the output is easier to read. Here are the first few responses:

```
> Get-Command Start-* -CommandType Cmdlet | Select CommandType, Name

CommandType Name
----------- ----
     Cmdlet Start-A2IRHumanLoop
     Cmdlet Start-AABIngestionJob
     Cmdlet Start-AARDeployment
     Cmdlet Start-ACCTPrimaryEmailUpdate
     Cmdlet Start-ACDConfigurationSession
```

To learn more, use `Get-Help` and supply a cmdlet name as the first parameter. In this way, PowerShell gives you plenty of ways to learn how to use it.

Objects, Not Strings

One of PowerShell's most useful innovations is that every command returns a well-documented, structured object with named fields and subfields. For example, when you run `Get-Process`, you're not getting a chunk of text. You're getting an array of .NET objects with properties like `Id`, `CPU`, and `ProcessName`. That means you can filter, sort, and manipulate data without writing a single regular expression. In this example, multiple cmdlets are chained together with the familiar "pipe" operator we know from Unix:

```
Get-Process | Sort-Object CPU -Descending | Select-Object -First 5
```

That gives you the five most CPU-hungry processes on the machine. No parsing through bespoke text-based output that varies with each command (or varies further depending on the parameters you supply). No iterating on highly specific and brittle `grep`, `sed`, and `awk` commands to parse. You just ask for the property you want, and PowerShell gives it to you.

You can even drill directly into objects:

```
(Get-Process -Name explorer).Id
```

That line returns the process ID for Windows Explorer.

PowerShell objects can contain nested properties and lists, much like a JSON object. Let's take a more complex example to demonstrate. Remember that PowerShell is a scripting language in addition to being a shell, so we can assign variables like this:

```
$proc = Get-Process -Name powershell
```

This snippet selects the Windows process associated with PowerShell. What properties does it have?

```
$proc | Format-List

Id      : 6668
Handles : 910
CPU     : 70.890625
SI      : 2
Name    : powershell
```

`Format-List` returns the first few properties; `Format-List *` returns a much longer, complete list. We can use *dot notation* to address these properties directly. Right now, I can check out much RAM PowerShell is using by checking this property:

```
C:\Windows\system32> $proc.WorkingSet64
164880384
```

Doing a little more scripting, if we wanted to write a warning when the process's RAM usage exceeds a certain threshold, we could do this:

```
if ($proc.WorkingSet64 -gt 200MB) {
    Write-Output "The $($proc.Name) service is using more than 200 MB of RAM."
}
```

Note that comparison operators in PowerShell resemble those in Bash scripts with operators like `-gt` for "greater than." The literal value `200MB` is a bit of convenient syntactical shorthand provided by PowerShell to help you write legible RAM values. It evaluates to `209715200` (200 MB in bytes).

Object Nesting

Also, note properties whose values are contained within curly braces, such as the `Modules` property of the process. This indicates a nested object. From the output of `$proc | Format-List *`, we see the following:

```
Modules                            :
{System.Diagnostics.ProcessModule (powershell.exe),
System.Diagnostics.ProcessModule (ntdll.dll),

System.Diagnostics.ProcessModule (KERNEL32.DLL),
System.Diagnostics.ProcessModule
                             (KERNELBASE.dll)...}
```

Let's drill into `Modules` to investigate. This output is long, so I'll pipe it into `Select-Object` to limit the results to three rows.

```
C:\Windows\system32> $proc.Modules | Select-Object -First 3

   Size(K) ModuleName        FileName
   ------- ----------        --------
       444 powershell.exe    C:\Windows\System32\WindowsPowerShell\v1.0\
powershell.exe
      2460 ntdll.dll         C:\Windows\SYSTEM32\ntdll.dll
       804 KERNEL32.DLL      C:\Windows\System32\KERNEL32.DLL
```

With these examples, you can clearly see a few foundational concepts in PowerShell: cmdlets, objects as both input and output, and how to understand and address the values in a PowerShell object. By the way, if you'd ever like to see the full, nested hierarchy of a PowerShell object, you can see a JSON representation with the following command: `$proc | ConvertTo-Json`.

Scripting PowerShell

As the examples have hinted, PowerShell is a full scripting language, not just a shell. You get variables, prefixed with `$`, as shown earlier. Conditionals work like this, with Unix-style comparison operators:

```
$Name = "Alice"
if ($Name -eq "Alice") {
    Write-Output "Hello, Alice."
} else {
    Write-Output "Who are you?"
}
```

Loops can be traditional `for` loop style:

```
for ($i = 1; $i -le 5; $i++) {
    Write-Host "Current iteration: $i"
}
```

Working with objects means that you can do some aggregate functions without the need for loops. In this example, we get all the `ChildItem` objects from a directory (i.e., the files in a folder), pipe that output into a filter using `Where-Object`, and then finally pipe the results into `Remove-Item`:

```
Get-ChildItem "C:\Logs\*.log" |
    Where-Object { $_.LastWriteTime -lt
(Get-Date).AddDays(-7) } |
    Remove-Item
```

The `Where-Object` line makes use of a special variable: `$_`. This variable refers to each given `ChildItem` returned by the first cmdlet. Even though we're not iterating through a loop, you can think of it somewhat like the loop variable from a `foreach`.

Remote Management

Remote management with PowerShell lets you administer systems without being physically logged into them. Without PowerShell, a Windows administrator might use Remote Desktop Protocol (RDP) to remotely log into a server and configure it as needed. With PowerShell, instead of using RDP to connect to a dozen servers to run the same patching command or configuration tweak, you can execute a PowerShell command or script from your own machine and have it fan out to remote systems automatically.

PowerShell remoting is built on *Windows Remote Management* (WinRM), Microsoft's implementation of the WS-Management protocol. Once WinRM is enabled and configured on a system, you can connect to it using `Enter-PSSession` for an interactive shell, or `Invoke-Command` to run scripts and commands remotely. For example:

```
Enter-PSSession -ComputerName Server01
Invoke-Command -ComputerName Server01,Server02 -ScriptBlock { Get-Service
wuauserv }
```

The first command logs into a server called `Server01` interactively. The second example queries the Windows Update service on multiple systems simultaneously, showing a small taste of PowerShell's parallel-processing power. Remote sessions can also be *persistent*, meaning you can reuse an authenticated connection for multiple commands, or *disconnected*, letting long-running jobs continue after you log off.

To access remote systems, you'll need credentials, and PowerShell supports multiple authentication mechanisms, including Kerberos for domain environments, NTLM for IP-based connections, and certificate-based authentication for workgroup setups. For more on security options for WinRM connections, see `https://learn.microsoft.com/en-us/powershell/scripting/security/remoting/winrm-security?view=powershell-7.5`.

Finally, PowerShell remoting isn't confined to Windows. Modern versions of PowerShell can use SSH (Secure Shell) connections, allowing cross-platform management of Linux and macOS systems with the same familiar syntax. These connections, very familiar to Linux and Unix system administrators, let you run a PowerShell command on a Linux box without ever leaving your Windows desktop. If PowerShell is your most comfortable language of choice, give it a try; otherwise, I'd recommend sticking to a more POSIX-native scripting solution like Bash, or moving to something even more common in multiplatform environments: Python.

Python: Your Go-To Cross-Platform Scripting Language

Python is currently the world's most popular programming language, and not by a small margin. As of this writing, according to the index maintained by software quality company TIOBE at tiobe.com, Python has outstripped all competitors, owning more than a quarter of web conversation about programming languages as of 2025 (Figure 2.1).

Long valued by coders for its clear, concise syntax and extensibility, Python began to gain serious ground in the mid-2010s, moving beyond its traditional niche as a tool for system scripting and web application development to become the language of choice for data science, cloud functions, infrastructure-as-a-service scripting, and most recently, AI programming.

FIGURE 2.1 Programming language popularity over time.

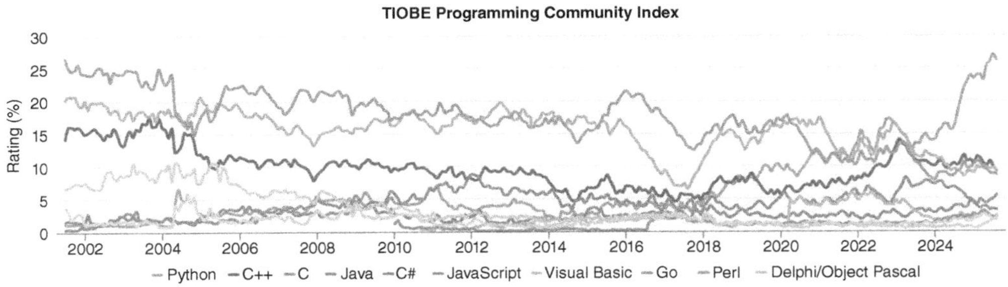

Source: www.tiobe.com.

Why Python for Automation?

When DevOps professionals and system administrators want a scripting language to automate their environments, Python is one of the first tools for which they'll reach, due to its clarity, versatility, and enormous ecosystem of libraries. It's both a fantastic general-purpose language and a wonderful special-purpose tool for everything from web development to data analysis. Its syntax and formatting requirements make it easy to read, and its support for higher-level data structures and objects make it a tool that is as complex as you need it to be. Let's take a closer look at some of the qualities that make Python such a valuable tool.

Community Support

One of the big reasons for Python's consistent adoption is its community support. There is a massive pool of libraries, documentation, tutorials, and Q&A posts waiting to help out new and existing Python coders. If you hit a snag trying to automate a task in Python, chances are someone else has already written a solution and posted it to GitHub, PyPI, or Stack Overflow. In fact, the prevalence of Python code and instruction on the Internet means that large language models are particularly adept at coding in it, making AI coding assistants particularly effective. All of this contributes to momentum that continues to carry Python to new heights of usage and support.

Cross-Platform Capabilities

Python runs on almost every operating system one might care about, from Windows, macOS, and Linux to embedded devices and cloud runtimes. Its standard library (browsable in full at `https://docs.python.org/3/library/index.html`) is famously described as coming with "batteries included." Out of the box, you can read and write files, parse JSON, work with dates, spin up a simple web server, or make HTTP requests—all without installing a single external dependency. For automation, this means less time fiddling with setup and more time solving problems.

Readability as a Design Principle

Python was designed to be read, not just executed. Not only does Python strive for readable syntax and function names, but in Python, proper indentation is required for code to run. This code will not run:

```
if domain == "www.example.com":
    found = True # indentation not consistent
  print("Example domain detected")
else:
  found = False
```

You'll get an error like this: `IndentationError: unexpected indent`. Rather, you must ensure consistent formatting, like so:

```
if domain == "www.example.com":
  found = True
  print("Example domain detected")
else:
  found = False
```

And don't even try to mix up tabs and spaces! You can use either one, but Python will ensure you stay consistent.

Getting Started

You can find instructions for installing Python at python.org. This will install the latest version of Python 3. You can run Python code in one of two ways. First, by giving a script to the `python3` executable:

```
python3 hello.py
```

or by working interactively with the "Read–Eval–Print Loop" tool, `REPL`, which is invoked by just typing **`python3`**.

```
$ python3
Python 3.12.3 (main, Apr  5 2025, 10:10:42)
>>> print("Hello, automation!")
Hello, automation!
```

This mode lets you quickly try out commands. To leave `REPL`, type **`exit()`** or press Ctrl/Cmd+D (Linux/macOS) or Ctrl+Z followed by Enter on Windows.

Dependency Management with *pip*

Sooner or later, you'll need more than the standard library. That's where Python's *package manager*, `pip`, comes in. Package managers help you download, update, and manage external libraries that you use with programming languages like Python (or in fact, with operating systems like Windows or Linux). With `pip`, you can install libraries from the Python Package Index (PyPI) with a single command:

```
pip install requests
```

That one line installs a popular HTTP library called `requests` that is ready to automate web calls. Include it in your next script with `import requests`.

Often, your Python scripts will have many dependencies on external libraries like this one. `pip` allows you to bundle these together into a file called *requirements.txt* so they can be tracked through version control and installed in one step. Here's an example requirements file:

```
requests==2.31.0
PyYAML>=6.0
```

This snippet says we need an exact version of the requests library (2.31.0) and will take any version of PyYAML higher than or equal to 6.0. When you run **`pip install -r requirements.txt`**, the `pip` command will consult with PyPI and fetch the libraries that meet your requirements. This approach is a great way to make sure you or your collaborators don't miss something essential to running your code.

Once you've installed dependencies, you `import` them into Python scripts, usually at the top. This can take a few forms, so familiarize yourself with these examples:

```
import os                  # import a whole module
import math as m           # import with an alias
from datetime import date  # import specific names
```

The last example imports just the `date` object from `datetime`. This can be a way to save memory when you only need a subset of the functionality of a larger library. You'll see each import method used in Python you encounter in the world.

The Python ecosystem offers many helpful tools to supplement the standard library. Among the most popular are `requests`, which simplifies HTTP requests; `PyYAML`, which reads and writes YAML; and `psutil`, which handles process and system monitoring. Explore more at `https://pypi.org`.

Virtual Environments

While `requirements.txt` helps keep track of your dependencies, you're still installing those packages globally. Whether this is on your own laptop (where you may be coding on multiple, distinct projects) or on a server (where you may be hosting multiple, distinct projects), installing packages globally can get messy fast. If different projects need different versions of the same library, you'll run into conflicts. The solution is to use *virtual environments*. A virtual environment is like a sandboxed Python installation that keeps dependencies neatly separated.

To create one:

```
python3 -m venv <name_your_venv>
```

This creates some files that allow Python to treat the current folder like its own private world (for purposes of installing libraries). Often, developers just name their virtual environment "venv," in which case the command is `python3 -m venv venv`. The resulting virtual environment must be "activated" before it can be used.

Assuming the name "venv," on Linux/macOS this command is:

```
source venv/bin/activate

And on Windows:
.\venv\Scripts\Activate
```

When the virtual environment is active, any `pip install` packages go into that virtual environment instead of your system's global Python. You'll know it's active when your shell prompt shows `(venv)` in front of it. When you're done, enter **`deactivate`** to go back to normal "everything installed globally" mode. Keeping environments like this distinct is essential, especially as we advance in automating deployments.

Python Basics

Let's take a quick tour of basic Python syntax and concepts.

Variables and Data Types

Python is loosely typed, so to create variables, just start assigning values:

```
name = "Alice"      # string
count = 42          # integer
speed = 5.195       # float
is_ready = True     # boolean
```

Conditionals and Loops

You've seen an `if` statement already, but here's a complete example:

```
if count > 10:
    print("Plenty")
elif count > 0:
    print("Some")
else:
    print("None")
```

Note the use of colons after the keywords. This is common in Python syntax, as you'll see.

Looping can be done as `for` or `while`:

```
for item in ["a", "b", "c"]:
    print(item)

while count > 0:
    count -= 1
```

Functions and Parameters

Functions rely on the keyword `def`:

```
def greet(name="stranger"):
    print(f"Hello, {name}!")

greet()        # Hello, stranger!
greet("Bob")   # Hello, Bob!
```

Note that the parameter `name` is given a default value. This is a common and helpful trait of Python functions, letting the function work whether or not the value is supplied by the caller.

F-strings

You may have noticed some unique syntax in the previous example: the character "f" preceding a double-quoted string. These so-called *f-strings*, introduced in Python 3.6, provide a concise way to embed expressions directly inside string literals. You create one by prefixing the string with an `f` or `F`, then placing variables or expressions inside curly braces. For example, `name = "Alice"; print(f"Hello, {name}!")` prints "Hello, Alice!" Inside those braces, you can even run small expressions, such as `f"{2 + 2}"` producing `"4"`. F-strings are preferred over methods like string concatenation or `.format()` because they're faster, more readable, and easier to maintain.

Handling Exceptions (*try/except*)

Errors can occur in any code. Like many programming languages, Python lets you handle exceptions with `try`, followed by `except` blocks that can catch both specific and generic exception types. In this example, you can stack up `except` blocks for as many named exception types as you like before catching the default case with `except Exception`:

```
try:
    value = int("not-a-number")
except ValueError as e:
    print(f"ValueError occurred: {e}")
except Exception as e:
    print("Generic error occurred")
```

Working with Files and Directories

The `open` command lets you interact with files. Use modes `r`, `w`, and `a` for read, write, and append, respectively.

```
# Write (overwrites)
with open("notes.txt", "w" ) as f:
    f.write("Hello, filesystem!\n")
```

```
# Append
with open("notes.txt", "a" ) as f:
    f.write("Another line.\n")

# Read whole file (good for small files)
with open("notes.txt", "r" ) as f:
    content = f.read()

# Stream lines (better for large files)
with open("logs/app.log", "r" ) as f:
    for line in f:
        if "ERROR" in line:
            print(line)
```

The standard library module `os` lets you interact with the operating system for tasks like iterating through files in a directory:

```
import os

log_dir = "/var/log/myapp"

for filename in os.listdir(log_dir):
    if filename.endswith(".log"):
        full_path = os.path.join(log_dir, filename)
        print(f"Found log file: {filename}")
```

This example (and the one before it) also demonstrates another form of iteration. `for filename in` iterates over the list of files returned by `os.listdir`.

Modules and Packages

For those interested in system automation, the Python Standard Library has plenty to offer. `os` and `sys` let us interact with the operating system, including retrieving environment variables:

```
import os, sys

print("Platform:", sys.platform)
print("User:", os.environ.get("USER"))
print("Args:", sys.argv)  # arguments passed to the script
```

For more sophisticated command-line argument wrangling, check out the standard library `argparse`.

Use `subprocess` to execute shell commands:

```
import subprocess

result = subprocess.run(["ls", "-l"], capture_output=True, text=True)
print(result.stdout)
```

This code runs a file listing with `ls`, then uses the `capture_output` parameter to pull that into the `result` variable. Python has many ways of interacting with other systems, such as standard library functions for iterating over files or SDKs for working with cloud providers, but in a pinch, you can always just run shell commands, as shown.

dotenv and Environment Variables

When your scripts need API keys or other secrets, don't hard-code them. As described in Chapter 1, a common pattern is to put them in an ENV file, often called a *dotenv file* due to its name `.env`, and load them with the `python-dotenv` package. This lets you keep secrets out of your code and version control. For example, your ENV file might have this:

```
API_KEY=supersecret123
```

Your Python code can then load that value like so:

```
from dotenv import load_dotenv
import os

load_dotenv() # fetches all values from the plaintext .env file and loads them
into the environment
print(os.getenv("API_KEY"))
```

Never place your ENV file in version control. That file is only to be shared or distributed securely. When we look at automating deployments, you'll see how we can use third-party secrets management tools like Hashicorp's Vault or AWS Secrets Manager to store and fetch such values in an even more robust way. With this approach, your secrets stay safe and are never part of your source code, helping you avoid leaking valuable passwords or keys to attackers.

Text Processing and Regex

We've seen how important string processing can be in the earlier conversations about `sed`, `grep`, `awk`, and regular expressions. Python comes with many string parsing tools out of the box:

```
line = "ERROR: Disk full"
if line.startswith("ERROR"):
    print("We have a problem.")
```

Other common helpers you can call on string objects are `.split()`, `.strip()`, `.replace()`, and `.find()`. To apply regular expressions, use the `re` library:

```
import re

pattern = re.compile(r"ERROR (\d{3})")
match = pattern.search("ERROR 404: Not found")
```

```
# matched patterns (possibly more than one) are pulled into the "match"
variable
if match:
    print("Error code:", match.group(1))

You can parse JSON with the package of the same name:
import json

data = json.loads('{"user": "alice", "active": true}')
print(data["user"])  # alice
```

Or handle YAML with the previously mentioned `PyYAML`, imported with just the `yaml` keyword. Let's say you have this `settings.yaml` file:

```
database:
  host: localhost
  port: 5432
```

You can get at those values with `PyYAML`:

```
import yaml

with open("config.yaml") as f:
    config = yaml.safe_load(f)

db_host = config["database"]["host"]
db_port = config["database"]["port"]
```

As you can see, Python's many libraries can save you a lot of heavy lifting for common tasks.

Working with APIs

Another very common task is working with APIs. The PyPI package `requests` is great for this. In this example, after `pip install requests`, we'll call a public weather API and use the `json` package to inspect the results:

```
import requests
import json

url = "https://api.weather.gov/alerts/active/area/CO"
resp = requests.get(url)

if resp.status_code == 200:
    data = json.loads(resp.text)
    print("Title:", data["title"])
    print("Number of alerts:", len(data["features"]))
```

A Practical Automation Script

Let's bring it all together into a practical example. We'll start with a `requirements.txt` file:

```
requests
python-dotenv
PyYAML
```

Imagine we have this configuration file, which describes a remote API and some details about how we should log output:

```
# Configuration the script can change without code edits
api:
  url: "https://api.weather.gov/alerts/active/area/CO"
logging:
  file: "alerts.log"
  level: "INFO"   # DEBUG, INFO, WARNING, ERROR
output:
  max_items: 5
```

You can imagine two versions of this file existing: one with values for a development environment, and another with values for production.

If this API required an API key, we might store that in an ENV text file:

```
API_KEY=abc123
```

This script combines multiple techniques to load the configuration and secrets, set up logging, query the API, and parse the results:

```
import os, json, logging, requests, yaml
from pathlib import Path
from dotenv import load_dotenv

load_dotenv()
cfg = yaml.safe_load(Path("config.yaml").read_text())

logging.basicConfig(
    filename=cfg["logging"]["file"],
    level=getattr(logging, cfg["logging"]["level"]),
    format="%(asctime)s %(levelname)s %(message)s"
)

headers = {}
if os.getenv("API_KEY"):
    headers["Authorization"] = f"Bearer {os.getenv('API_KEY')}"
```

```
resp = requests.get(cfg["api"]["url"], headers=headers)
data = json.loads(resp.text)

for f in data["features"][: cfg["output"]["max_items"]]:
    p = f["properties"]
    msg = f"{p.get('event')} — {p.get('severity')}: {p.get('headline')}"
    print(msg)
    logging.info(msg)
```

The output:

```
Flood Watch — Severe: Flood Watch issued September 13 at 3:25AM MDT until
September 14 at 12:00AM MDT by NWS Grand Junction CO
Frost Advisory — Minor: Frost Advisory issued September 13 at 1:29AM MDT until
September 14 at 9:00AM MDT by NWS Pueblo CO
```

This information is also logged to `alerts.log`, per the config file specification.

Why Python Matters for Automation

With its robust standard library, extensive ecosystem of third-party packages, readable syntax, and wide platform support, Python has become the go-to tool for DevOps professionals and system automation engineers. There is more to explore beyond this overview. Browse through PyPI or seek out advanced examples on the web to go deeper. Throughout this book, we'll rely frequently on Python as our language of choice for scripting.

Summary

In this chapter, we moved from one-off terminal commands to real automation. You learned how to write and run shell scripts, use variables, branch with conditionals, iterate with `for/while`, capture command output, and factor repeated logic into functions. You saw how scripts accept parameters (`$1, $2,` …) and how to check success with exit codes (`$?`).

On Windows, we explored PowerShell's Verb-Noun cmdlets, object pipelines, and predictable property access features. We then moved to Python: installing packages with `pip`, isolating them with virtual environments, keeping configs in `requirements.txt`, and writing clean, readable code for files, JSON/YAML parsing, and HTTP calls. Finally, we wrote a complete script that loads config and secrets, calls a REST API, prints results, and logs them, tying together core exam themes around scripting, troubleshooting, automation approaches, and interacting with RESTful systems.

Exam Essentials

Know how to run and structure shell scripts. Be able to add a shebang, set execute permissions, and run scripts directly or by using Bash. Use comments, variables, conditionals, loops, command substitution, and functions to make scripts readable and reusable.

Use parameters and exit codes correctly. Recognize how positional parameters (`$1, $2, ...`) pass input into scripts and how to test "`$?`" to branch on success/failure for reliable control flow and error handling.

Understand comparison operators in Bash. Identify when to use `[ ]` with `-eq`, `-gt`, string =/!=, and when `(( ))` enables familiar operators like > and >=. Stay consistent within a script to avoid subtle logic bugs.

Leverage PowerShell's object pipeline. Know that cmdlets return objects, not strings; you can sort, filter, and select properties without regex. Remember Verb-Noun naming, `Get-Command`, and `Get-Help` for discovery.

Apply Python for cross-platform automation. Use `pip` and `requirements.txt` for dependencies and virtual environments to avoid conflicts. Read/write files, parse JSON/YAML, handle exceptions, and call REST endpoints with requests to build small, testable automations.

Keep configuration and secrets out of code. Externalize environment-specific values to improve security and portability. This reduces code changes between environments and prevents accidental secret commits.

Compare basic automation approaches (local vs. remote; shell vs. PowerShell vs. Python). Recognize when a quick local shell one-liner is sufficient, when PowerShell's typed objects are safer on Windows, and when Python's libraries/portability are a better fit for more complex logic or REST integrations.

Interact with RESTful systems from scripts. Understand the basics: methods (`GET/POST/PUT/PATCH/DELETE`), headers, and status codes. Be able to recognize or compose simple curl calls in Bash and `requests.get()` patterns in Python.

Review Questions

1. You need a Bash command to replace every "myapp-test.example.com" with "myapp.example.com" in a file called `config.txt` *and* overwrite the file in place. Assume Linux. Which command does this correctly?

   A. `sed 's/myapp-test.example.com/myapp.example.com/g' config.txt`

   B. `sed 's/myapp-test.example.com/myapp.example.com/g' > config.txt`

   C. `sed -i 's/myapp-test.example.com/myapp.example.com/g' config.txt`

   D. `grep -r 'myapp-test' config.txt | replace 'myapp'`

2. You're writing a Bash script to read a file that may contain spaces in its name. Given the following snippet, which line correctly reads the file's contents?

   `my_filename="some file.txt"`

   A. `cat $my_filename`

   B. `cat "$my_filename"`

   C. `cat 'my_filename'`

   D. `cat ${my_filename without spaces}`

3. Your Windows ops box is accumulating logs in `C:\Logs`. You want a one-liner that removes .log files older than 7 days. Which PowerShell command best matches that goal?

   A. `dir C:\Logs\*.log | findstr /v 7d | del`

   B. `Get-ChildItem "C:\Logs\*.log" | Where-Object{ $_.LastWriteTime -lt (Get-Date).AddDays(-7) } | Remove-Item`

   C. `Get-Process | Sort-Object CPU -Descending | Select-Object -First 5 | Remove-Item`

   D. `Get-ChildItem "C:\Logs\*.log" | Select-Object -First 7 | Remove-Item`

4. You're troubleshooting a Windows Explorer issue and need its PID quickly using PowerShell's object model. Which single command returns the process ID?

   A. `tasklist | findstr explorer | awk "{print $2}"`

   B. `(Get-Process -Name explorer).Id`

   C. `Get-Command explorer | Select-Object -ExpandProperty Id`

   D. `Get-Help explorer -Id`

5. You're building a small Python automation that calls a REST API and prints a few items, but you must (1) keep secrets out of code and (2) allow environment-specific settings without code changes. Which is the best approach?

   A. Hard-code API keys and URLs in the script; commit to Git for convenience.

   B. Use an ENV file for secrets via `python-dotenv`; store non-secret settings (URL, logging, limits) in `config.yaml`; list third-party libs in `requirements.txt`.

   C. Keep everything in one JSON file—including secrets—and check it in; parse with `json` only.

   D. Install all packages globally; rely on OS environment variables set by hand each time.

6. You're writing a Bash `while` loop that counts from 0 to 4. Which snippet correctly increments the integer variable?

   A.
```
COUNT=0
while [ $COUNT -lt 5 ]; do
  echo "$COUNT"
  COUNT=$((COUNT + 1))
done
```

   B.
```
COUNT=0
while [ $COUNT -lt 5 ]; do
  echo "$COUNT"
  COUNT="$COUNT + 1"
done
```

   C.
```
COUNT=0
while ($COUNT < 5); do
  echo "$COUNT"
  let COUNT=COUNT+1
done
```

   D.
```
COUNT=0
while [ $COUNT -lt 5 ] {
  echo "$COUNT"
  COUNT=$COUNT++
}
```

7. Given this Bash function and call, what is the output?

```
say_hello() {
  echo "Hi there, $1"
}
say_hello "friend"
```

   A. Hi there, $1

   B. Hi there, friend

   C. Hi there, “friend”

   D. friend

8. Which PowerShell command lists the set of approved verbs and their groups to help you discover consistent cmdlet names?

   A. `Get-Command -Verb`

   B. `Get-Help Verb-Noun`

   C. `Get-Verb`

   D. `Show-Command -Verbs`

9. Your draft Python function is meant to greet a user with an f-string and a default parameter. Which corrected version actually runs in Python 3?

   A.
   ```
   def greet(name="stranger"):
       print f"Hello, {name}!"
   ```

   B.
   ```
   def greet(name="stranger"):
       print(f"Hello, {name}!")
   ```

   C.
   ```
   def greet(name="stranger"):
       print("Hello, " + {name} + "!")
   ```

   D.
   ```
   def greet(name="stranger"):
       print(f"Hello, {name}!")
   ```

10. You want to run `ls -l` from Python and capture the output text into a variable. Which snippet is the best approach?

    A.
    ```
    import subprocess
    out = subprocess.check_output("ls -l")
    print(out.stdout)
    ```

    B.
    ```
    import subprocess
    result = subprocess.
    run(["ls", "-l"], capture_output=True, text=True)
    listing = result.stdout
    ```

    C.
    ```
    import os
    listing = os.system("ls -l")
    ```

    D.
    ```
    import subprocess
    result = subprocess.
    run(["ls -l"], capture_output=True, text=True)
    listing = result.text
    ```

11. In a `bash` script, what symbol introduces a comment?

    A. //

    B. #

    C. --

    D. ;

12. Which `bash` line correctly captures today's date into a variable named `today`?
    A. `today="date"`
    B. `today=$(date)`
    C. `date=today`
    D. `today={date}`
13. PowerShell cmdlets always use what naming convention?
    A. CamelCase
    B. snake_case
    C. Verb-Noun
    D. Shorthand abbreviations
14. Which of the following is **not** a valid way to import a module or function in Python?
    A. `import os`
    B. `import math as m`
    C. `from datetime import date`
    D. `include "sys"`
15. You're managing five Windows servers and want to restart the Print Spooler service on each of them without logging in manually. Which PowerShell command accomplishes this most efficiently?
    A. `Restart-Service -Name Spooler`
    B. `Enter-PSSession -ComputerName Server01`
    C. `Invoke-Command -ComputerName Server01,Server02,Server03, Server04,Server05 -ScriptBlock { Restart-Service -Name Spooler }`
    D. `Start-Job -ScriptBlock { Restart-Service Spooler }`

Answers to Review Questions

1. C. The correct answer is C. The `-i` flag performs in-place editing, overwriting the original file with the modified contents. Option A just prints the result to STDOUT; option B is a malformed command that doesn't provide `sed` an input file, but nevertheless writes STDOUT to `config.txt`, leaving it empty. Option D uses some commands incorrectly; `grep` is used incorrectly and there is no `replace` command. As an aside, it may be more precise to replace `myapp-test` only, rather than try to match the entire domain, if it is not necessary, as the dots in the domain should be escaped to precisely match periods.
2. B. The correct answer is B. Quoting variable expansions in Bash preserves spaces and special characters so that `"$my_filename"` opens the intended file. Option A fails when

the variable contains spaces because the shell splits on whitespace. Option C treats `my_filename` literally (not the variable). Option D is not valid Bash syntax.

3. B. The correct answer is B. PowerShell pipelines pass objects, not plain text; `Where-Object` filters on the `LastWriteTime` property and `Remove-Item` deletes only those older than 7 days. Option A uses text tooling and ignores file metadata; C targets processes, not files; D deletes the first seven files regardless of age.

4. B. The correct answer is B. `Get-Process` returns .NET objects, and selecting `.Id` reads the property directly. Option A doesn't use PowerShell and instead depicts the use of baseline DOS commands with text parsing. Option C uses PowerShell, but queries commands, not running processes. Option D asks for help, not process metadata.

5. B. The correct answer is B. You've seen how externalizing secrets to an ENV file (loaded with `python-dotenv`), keeping configuration in YAML (PyYAML), and pinning dependencies in `requirements.txt` helps you maintain secrets and dependencies in clean, source-control compatible ways. This approach keeps secrets out of source control and lets you swap environment settings without editing code. Options A and C violate "never hard-code secrets" guidance. D is brittle; global installs and manual `env var` fiddling are error-prone and make it difficult to manage multiple projects on the same server.

6. A. The correct answer is A. Bash integer math is done with arithmetic expansion `$(())`, so `COUNT=$((COUNT + 1))` properly increments the value. Option B stores a literal string, not math. Option C mixes non-POSIX test syntax and uses `( )` improperly for `while`. Option D borrows C-style braces and post-increment that Bash doesn't support in that form.

7. B. The correct answer is B. `$1` expands to the first positional parameter passed to the function; here that's the word "friend," sans quotes. The output from option A would occur only if the `$` were escaped. Option C would require the quotes to be part of the argument, escaped with backslashes. Option D omits the literal text echoed inside the function.

8. C. The correct answer is C. `Get-Verb` returns the approved verbs (e.g., `Get`, `Set`, `Start`) and their groupings, which helps you "guess" valid cmdlet names. Option A isn't a valid parameter combo, while option B shows help and examples but doesn't list all verbs. Finally, option D is wrong because it opens a UI helper for commands, not a verb catalog.

9. D. The correct answer is D. Python 3 requires parentheses with print, and f-strings must be inside them: `print(f"...")`. Option A uses Python 2-style syntax and is invalid with f-strings. Option B has broken indentation. Option C attempts string concatenation with a dictionary-like `{name}` expression, which is invalid.

10. B. The correct answer is B. `subprocess.run([...], capture_output=True, text=True)` returns a `CompletedProcess` with `.stdout` as a decoded string. Option A mixes APIs (`check_output` returns bytes by itself and doesn't have `.stdout`). Option C returns an exit code only, not output. Option D passes a single string inside a list (not split args) and then accesses a nonexistent `.text` attribute.

11. B. The correct answer is B. In shell scripts, comments start with #. Option A is from C/Java, option C from SQL, and option D is just a command separator in languages like Bash scripts.

12. B. The correct answer is B. Command substitution with `$(...)` captures a command's output into a variable. Option A stores the literal string `"date"`. Option C assigns the variable `date` (but does not run the command). Option D is not valid syntax.

13. C. The correct answer is C. PowerShell cmdlets always follow the Verb-Noun format (`Get-Process`, `Start-Service`). Options A and B describe casing styles. Option D is more of a description of Unix commands (`ls`, `cat`).

14. D. The correct answer is D. Python uses the `import` keyword for all imports; `include` is not a valid Python statement. Options A through C are all correct and commonly used import styles.

15. C. The correct answer is C. `Invoke-Command` runs the specified script block on multiple remote computers simultaneously, making it ideal for managing a fleet of systems. Option A only affects the local system. Option B opens a single interactive session with one machine at a time. Option D starts a background job locally, not on remote systems.

Chapter 3

Source Control

THE AUTOOPS+ EXAM TOPICS COVERED IN THIS CHAPTER MAY INCLUDE, BUT ARE NOT LIMITED TO, THE FOLLOWING:

✔ **1.0: Automation Coding Concepts**

- 1.1. Given a scenario, use code to support automation.
- 1.2. Given a scenario, use source control techniques to version code.

Half the reason to turn infrastructure, automation, and configuration into code is so that we can version-control it. Honestly, there are very few problems in life that can't be improved with version control. Good version control practices are the foundation of backup, recovery, collaboration, code review, automated quality checks, and even deployment triggers for application and system automation code.

Why Version Control?

The idea of version control comes from a simple, yet powerful concept: What if you could create checkpoints as you work on changes to your code? Then, if you ever make a mistake, change your mind, or just need to revert back to an old version, you can easily return to one of those checkpoints and restore the state of your files from that point.

Many developers reading this book will already be familiar with version control in Git. If that's you, feel free to skim the next few sections as we lay out the basics, then tune back in when we start talking about more sophisticated techniques for team collaboration, branching strategies, and more.

Source Control Everything

Source control systems, also called version control systems, have existed almost as long as computers. Even back in the punch card days, computer programmers sought ways to track changes to their programs over time. The first true source control system was invented by Bell Labs in 1972. Source Code Control System (SCCS) allowed developers to track and revert changes to files over time, but it was limited to a single user at a time.

In the 1980s, Revision Control System (RCS) and Concurrent Version System (CVS) advanced the ideas of SCCS with more efficient methods of storing updates and introducing the idea of branching code paths.

Version control really took off in a huge way with the creation of Subversion by CollabNet in 2000. SVN, as it's often called, is a centralized system wherein multiple users maintain change history on a common copy of code files stored in some central SVN server. I used it myself for years, and while it is powerful in its own right, one does eventually see the limitations of SVN's centralized nature and its ad hoc approach to multiuser collaboration. A few years later, a new system would come along to focus on enhancing the experience of team-oriented version control.

The modern era of version control kicked off in 2005, when Linus Torvalds, already famous for creating Linux, released the first version of *Git*. Unlike SVN, Git is a *distributed version control system*, designed explicitly to let multiple users maintain complete, local copies of code repositories while interacting together with remote instances of the same. With Git, developers can work locally with a fully realized set of tools for tracking changes, reverting to past code, experimenting on branches, and more, before connecting to remote Git servers that allow them to work with others on the same codebase.

Git has become the de facto industry standard for how developers, system administrators, and DevOps professionals manage, store, and share code. It is supported by a robust ecosystem of tools, platforms, and integrations, built into IDEs like VS Code and JetBrains, and used as the trigger point for almost all continuous integration and delivery pipelines. Along with scripting fundamentals, knowledge of Git is one of the foundational pillars of this book, so it's a good time to dive into how it works.

Git Concepts

Git has a sprawling set of commands that can feel quite intimidating to the uninitiated. In fact, it has so many esoteric, situation-specific keywords that it spawned a parody site at `https://git-man-page-generator.lokaltog.net`, where the "git man (manual) page generator" will make up entirely new, entirely fake `git` commands with every refresh. However, you needn't fear. All you need to know to take your first steps with Git are a few simple verbs.

Managing Git State with Add, Commit, and Reset

In a Git *repository*, files can exist in a few states. You move files between these states with the verbs add, commit, and reset (see Figure 3.1).

- *Untracked* files have not yet been put under version control. Any brand-new file you create in a Git repo starts as untracked. Certain files may always remain untracked, such as temporary files you intend to delete, build artifacts that only appear after compilation steps, or files containing secret or configuration values. For files like the latter that you wish to remain persistent without introducing them to version control, the `.gitignore` file lets you specify paths and file patterns Git should never track. Files in `.gitignore` never show up anywhere to get; it's like they don't exist. To start tracking a new file, we *add* the file.

FIGURE 3.1 States of files in a Git repository.

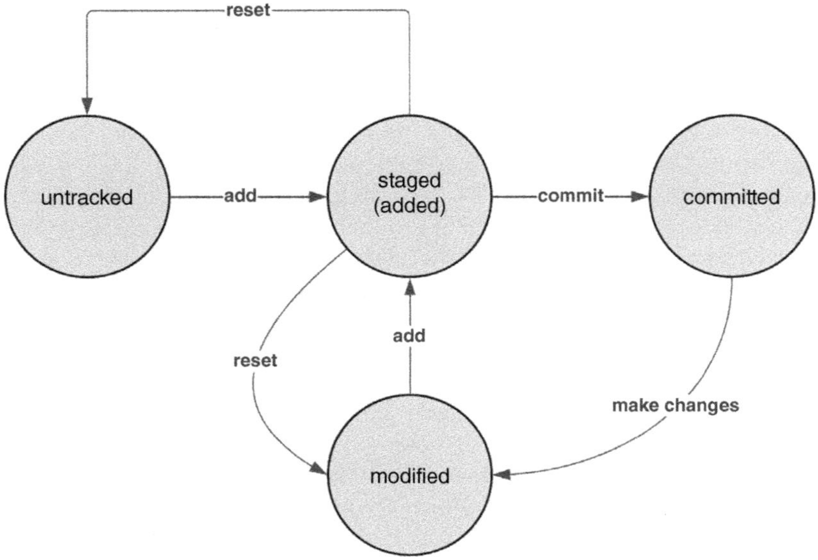

- *Staged* files are files that have been *added*. Added files become tracked. You can stage as many new or modified files as you want before committing them. A *commit* is a collection of changes with a description of the change contents (the "commit message"). Each commit is a point in time to which you can return. The idea is to stage related changes, then commit them with a common commit message. For instance, if it takes updates to three files to add a Redis cache to your application's configuration code, you can make changes to all three files, test your updates, then *add* and *commit* all three changes at once with the message like "added Redis caching to the index page to reduce loading times"—whatever is most relevant. If you wish to unstage a file, the command is *reset*.
- *Committed* files are those that have been updated, staged, and committed, but have not yet been modified further.
- *Modified* files are tracked files that have been edited in some way and are ready to be staged again.

That's the clinical view. I like to imagine that staging and committing files is like loading containers onto a ship (not to be confused with shipping Docker containers!). When you add a collection of changed files, it's like loading them onto a platform on the dock. Committing files is like a crane lifting that platform and loading the containers onto the ship (see Figure 3.2). Pushing your changes to a Git remote is like the ship leaving the harbor for its destination, but I'm getting slightly ahead of myself.

FIGURE 3.2 Imaging the Git file life cycle as shipping containers.

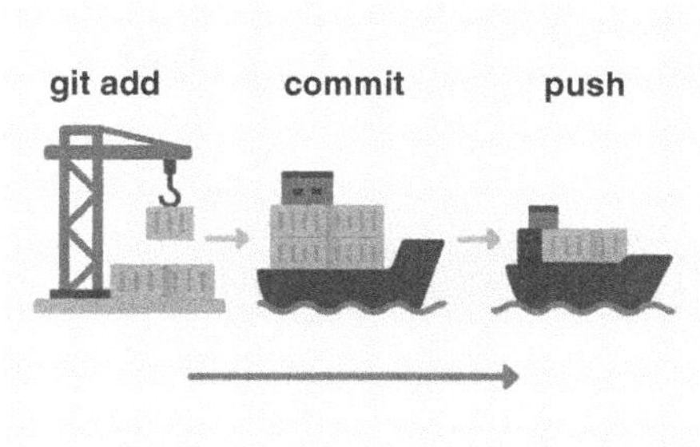

Equipped with this understanding, let's see how adds and commits work on the command line.

Local and Remote

When you're first getting started with Git, the best thing to do is to experiment locally, without necessarily engaging with a Git remote like GitHub. When working with Git on your own machine only, you can use all the core features of Git for version control. Just know that everything remains confined to your local machine for now, so using Git in this way doesn't save you from device failure.

Act Local

This section assumes you have Git installed and configured. If not, the Git web page can help: `https://git-scm.com/book/en/v2/Getting-Started-Installing-Git`. Now, let's assume you have a folder with one file of shell script in it:

```
> ls -lart
total 4
drwxr-xr-x 11 root root 352 Aug 13 09:22 ..
-rw-r--r--  1 root root  19 Aug 13 09:23 script.sh
drwxr-xr-x  3 root root  96 Aug 13 09:23 .
```

This script is very simple. `script.sh` contains this:

```
echo "hello world"
```

To start working with Git in this folder, type **`git init`**. This starts a local Git repo in this folder and creates a (usually hidden) folder called `.git`. Careful with that folder—it's where all your version control data will be stored. If you want to fully delete all your version control information and start over, you can delete that folder.

Now, let's check `git status`, a frequently used command to observe the stages of your files.

```
> git status
On branch main

No commits yet

Untracked files:
  (use "git add <file>..." to include in what will be committed)
          script.sh

nothing added to commit but untracked files present (use "git add" to track)

Our script is untracked, so let's add it:
> git add script.sh
```

I won't show `git status` for every step, but running it now will show `script.sh` is staged. At this point, you can create new files to add; you can use `git reset <filename>` to unstage a file. You can even make additional changes to the script and optionally add it again. When you're satisfied with what is staged, we can commit.

```
> git commit -m"initial revision"
```

The `-m` flag lets us set the commit message inline. Executing this creates your first commit. You might be required to set your Git config first. If you get this warning, follow its instructions:

```
  git config --global user.email "you@example.com"
  git config --global user.name "Your Name"
```

Then, run the commit. You can view it with **`git log`** to understand what's happening.

```
> git log
commit 953204a8746ffd96bd166e374e664942f82cd07d (HEAD -> main)
Author: John Doe <john@example.com>
Date:   Sat Aug 16 13:05:29 2025 +0000

    initial revision
```

You can see the commit author, date, message, and up at the top, that long string? That's the *commit hash*, a value that uniquely identifies this commit. Let's modify the file, then add and commit a second and third time. After this, you see three commits in the Git log.

```
> git log
commit bafc27af6e6c726f6125baddb88ef0b3561f3344 (HEAD -> main)
Author: John Doe <john@example.com>
Date:   Sat Aug 16 13:35:18 2025 +0000

    added nginx config

commit 095859c1bdde5219e673dacc4aa973ab4fa34eb0
Author: John Doe <john@example.com>
Date:   Sat Aug 16 13:09:48 2025 +0000

    added another output statement

commit 953204a8746ffd96bd166e374e664942f82cd07d
Author: John Doe <john@example.com>
Date:   Sat Aug 16 13:05:29 2025 +0000

    initial revision
```

You can see the version history being built up right here, in a string of commits, with the newest on top. At any time, if you want to jump back to a previous commit, you can do so with **`git checkout`**. Let's go back to the first commit.

```
git checkout 953204a8746ffd96bd166e374e664942f82cd07d
```

TIP The first seven characters of a Git commit hash are the commit's "short form" hash and can be used interchangeably with the long form.

Using the short form commit hash, this command is equivalent to the above:

```
git checkout 953204a
```

This, indeed, restores your repo and all its code to the state it was at the original commit. However, you also get this warning:

```
You are in 'detached HEAD' state. You can look around, make experimental
changes and commit them, and you can discard any commits you make in this
state without impacting any branches by switching back to a branch.
```

If you want to create a new branch to retain commits you create, you may do so (now or later) by using `-c` with the `switch` command. Example:

```
git switch -c <new-branch-name>
```

FIGURE 3.3 Visualizing a series of Git commits.

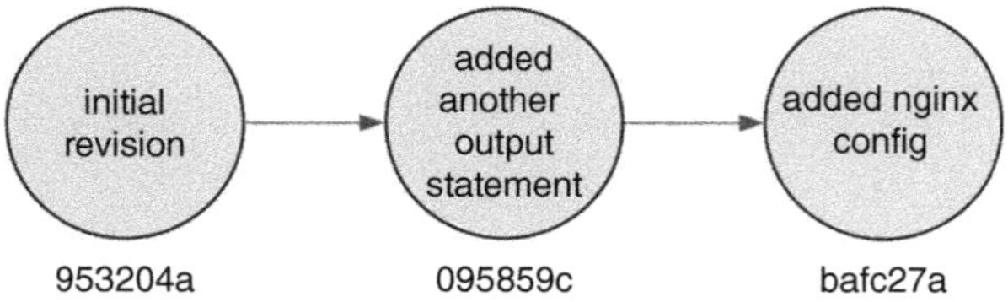

Or undo this operation with:

```
git switch -
```

To understand why, realize that your commits are in sequence, oftentimes likened to a string of Christmas lights (see Figure 3.3).

Your terminal is now pointed at the first node, but commits can only be added to the *end* of a sequence. In other words, the HEAD pointer that is your current point in the string is usually meant to be on the latest commit. You're not pointing there anymore, so you're in the humorously named "*detached HEAD*" state. So, Ichabod, what happens if you commit in this state? Your commit becomes free-floating, attached to nothing, and is potentially subject to being swept by Git's garbage collection. Git advises that you still have a chance to preserve it:

```
Warning: you are leaving 1 commit behind, not connected to
any of your branches:

  abf85ac added nginx config file
```

If you want to keep it by creating a new branch, this may be a good time to do so with this:

```
git branch <new-branch-name> abf85ac
```

In my personal experience, detached HEAD state is usually just for when you want to observe the previous state of a repo, or in some rare cases, when you want to revert a deployment back to a certain commit. It's not typically used in developers' workflows. That's because, more often than not, Git users aren't jumping to specific commits; they're switching between *branches*.

Understanding Branches

In Git, a *branch* is literally a label pointing to a particular commit in your project's history. In practicality, you can think of it like one branch in a timeline, a "what if" scenario of code changes you can choose to keep or not.

FIGURE 3.4 Creating a branch from `main`.

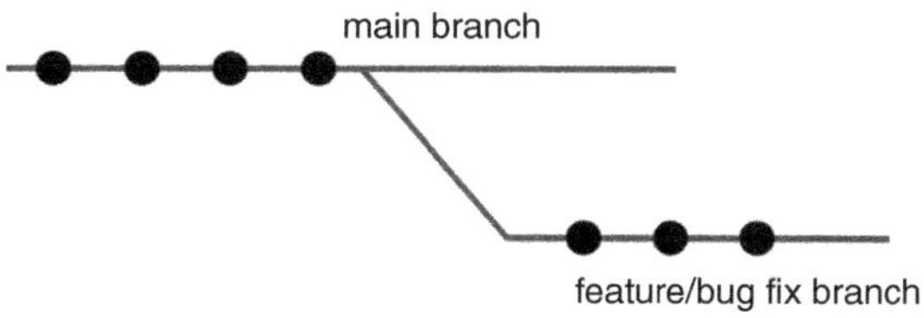

Developers create branches so they can experiment, work on features, fix bugs, or try out ideas in isolation. A new branch creates a, well, branching point from the commit at which you created it, letting you work without impacting others until you are ready to merge your changes back in with the main branch. It always makes me think of that scene in *Back to the Future Part II* when Doc Brown describes the way timelines diverge. Once you branch, you're off on your own timeline, but the good news is, it doesn't take a tricked-out DeLorean to get back home.

By default, Git creates a branch named `main` when you initialize a repository. So far, everything we've done has been on this main branch. All commits you make go on that branch until you create a new one. Figure 3.4 shows how this looks.

Key Commands for Branching

Let's say we've just cloned a repository and we're on the `main` branch. We'll create a feature branch called `new_dashboard`. There are a few ways to do this:

```
# create a branch and switch to it
git branch new_dashboard
git checkout new_dashboard

# create a branch and switch to it in one command
git checkout -b new_dashboard

# create a branch and switch using newer syntax
# introducded in git 2.2.3
git branch new_dashboard
git switch new_dashboard
```

The last example uses the `git switch` command, which is intended to make the action of switching branches more explicit. Because `git checkout` does a few different things, this can aid clarity in your scripts.

From here, you can work as before, editing files and creating commits. If your work runs into a wall, no problem; you can always `checkout` or `switch` to the branch where you started and branch again, abandoning the failed experiment. Instead, if you are happy with your changes and testing, you can *merge* the branch back into `main`.

It's important to keep in mind that merging on the command line is done from the destination branch. Commit all your branch changes, then do this:

```
git switch main
git merge new_dashboard
```

If none of your changes conflict with newer changes on `main`, you're in good shape, and your branch changes are now integrated into the main branch. If not, you'll have to resolve some conflicts.

Resolving Merge Conflicts

If someone made or merged a change on `main` that affects the same files you changed, you'll get a lovely message indicating a *merge conflict*:

```
> git switch main
> git merge new_dashboard
Auto-merging script.sh
CONFLICT (content): Merge conflict in script.sh
Automatic merge failed; fix conflicts and then commit the result.
```

Now, `git status` will help you understand the state of things:

```
git status
On branch main
You have unmerged paths.
  (fix conflicts and run "git commit")
  (use "git merge --abort" to abort the merge)

Unmerged paths:
  (use "git add <file>..." to mark resolution)
        both modified:   script.sh

no changes added to commit (use "git add" and/or "git commit -a")
```

As you can see, `script.sh` has been modified on both branches. If you open up the file now, you'll see that Git has added some text that flags the conflicting sections, like this:

```
> cat script.sh
echo "hello world"
echo "making changes"
<<<<<<< HEAD
echo "change made on main"
=======
echo "making a change on new_dashboard"
>>>>>>> new_dashboard
```

FIGURE 3.5 Managing Git conflicts in VS Code's native merge editor.

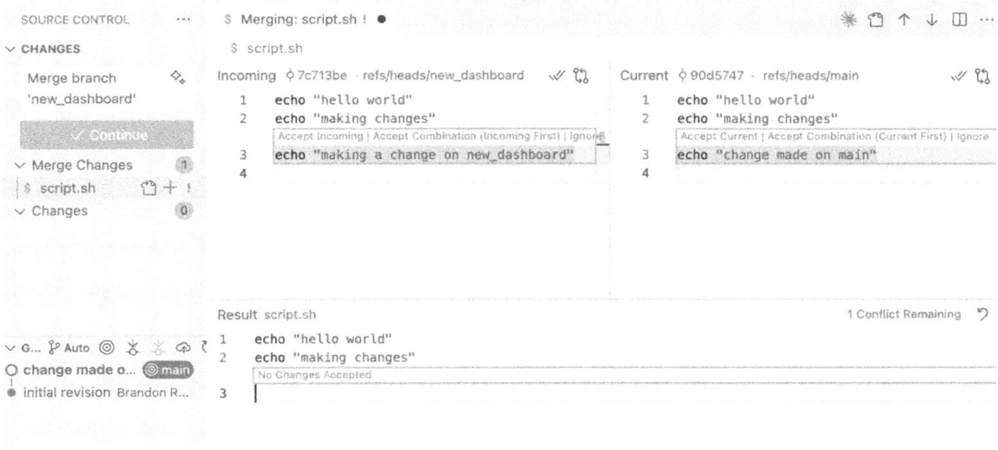

In this case, the conflict is simple: a line added from a commit on `main`, and another on `new_dashboard` (the changes are simple `echo` statements to keep this example clean). Under `HEAD` you see what's on the `main` branch, and then after the row of equals signs, the incoming changes. If you're using a graphical IDE, you probably have tools to resolve these changes in a more visually understandable way, as in the VS Code example in Figure 3.5.

It's up to you to edit the file into the state you desire. Then, save the file, `add` it, and `commit` with a new message indicating you merged the changes. This creates one new commit: the `merge commit` that is autogenerated with a message stating which branch was merged.

Remotely Interesting

Local Git usage has its advantages. It's easy to get started, and if you screw up a file and have a recent commit, no worries—you can always recover it. However, if you drop your laptop in a lake, you have no recourse. You might start to wish all that versioned code was not just on your laptop, but that it was securely stored somewhere else.

That's where *Git remotes* like GitHub or Bitbucket come into play. Whereas you've used a local repository thus far, GitHub allows you to create repositories in their cloud environment. When you configure a local repository to connect to a remote repository, you gain some new available actions, the most prominent of which are `git push` and `git pull`. Pushing a branch to a Git remote uploads everything on the current branch, along with its history of commits. Later, you or a colleague can pull that information down to your local machine (see Figure 3.6).

Creating the actual Git remote is outside the scope of this book, but if you head to github.com and create an account, you'll be able to create a repository there. You can then either

FIGURE 3.6 Collaborating with a Git remote.

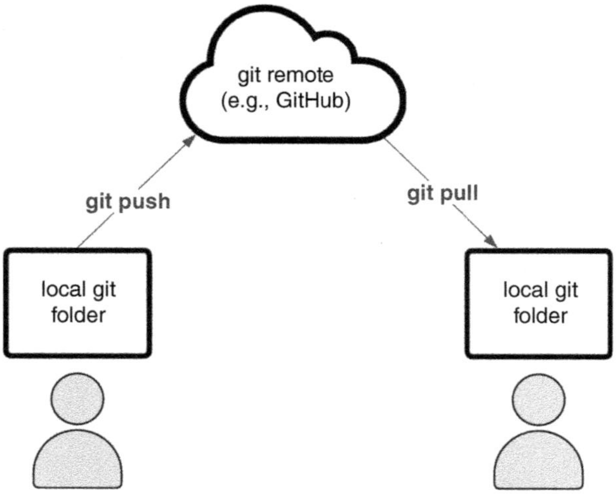

clone the repo locally, which automatically establishes a link between the local repository and the remote, or you can take an existing local repository and associate it with the URL of the remote.

Let's say you have an existing local repo you want to house on GitHub. Create a remote repo, copy the URL, then execute this command locally in your project's directory:

```
git remote add origin <https://github.com/yourname/project.git>
```

This command adds a remote called `origin`. That is the default name for the default remote, but not only can it be changed, you can also have multiple remotes! This is a great way to migrate code from one Git remote platform to another. If my default remote of `origin` was associated with GitHub, and I wanted to migrate to (or store a backup on) Bitbucket, I could create a repo at Bitbucket, then add it as a second Git remote with the name Bitbucket. Then, I could pull from one remote location and push to the other with ease.

How does that work? Well, with this connection established, you can push branches to the remote:

```
git push origin <name of branch>
```

If I had two remotes, as described above, I could migrate the main branch code this way:

```
git pull origin main
git push bitbucket main
```

In this case, your local machine is the go-between as you move code from one cloud provider to another.

There are many ways to interact with a Git remote on the command line. The `https://` URL will prompt you to log in with a username and password whenever you attempt to push code, but cloning a public repo is fine. You might also authenticate with an SSH key or a GitHub Personal Access Token. To learn more, visit `https://docs.github.com/en/authentication/keeping-your-account-and-data-secure/managing-your-personal-access-tokens`.

Git fetch

`git fetch` is a tool you'll use often. It updates your local repository with any new commits, branches, or tags from the remote, but it doesn't modify your working files or change your current branch. It simply refreshes your view of what's happening on the remote so that you can review changes before merging or rebasing. Here are some examples:

```
# Fetch updates from the default remote (usually "origin")
git fetch

# Fetch from a specific remote
git fetch origin

# Fetch updates for a specific branch only
git fetch origin main

# Fetch all remotes (useful if you have more than one)
git fetch --all

# Fetch all branches only. You can also specify "tags"
git fetch --branches
```

This command helps make sure you're never missing something that has been pushed to a remote by a colleague.

Merge Strategies with Remotes

When other developers get involved, there's always the possibility that someone makes an update to a branch after you've checked it out. Let's say you cloned a repository and checked out the `main` branch. Meanwhile, through the normal course of development, another developer's work is merged into `main` at the Git remote. This means there are changes out there for `main` that don't exist on your local machine, and you need to do something about it.

If you haven't touched `main` on your own computer (say, because you immediately created a branch to work on), then everything is easy. Run this:

```
git pull origin main
```

Git will automatically pull down and merge the remote changes into your `main` branch.

If you have made a change, there's a chance you'll have to handle merge conflicts. Don't worry! This works just the same way merge conflicts were described earlier. However, it's possible to run into a message like this and become alarmed:

```
hint: You have divergent branches and need to specify how to reconcile them.
hint: You can do so by running one of the following commands sometime before
hint: your next pull:
hint:
hint:   git config pull.rebase false  # merge
hint:   git config pull.rebase true   # rebase
hint:   git config pull.ff only       # fast-forward only
```

What is all that? Again, fear not. Git is saying that your local copy of `main` has changes that differ from what's coming down from the remote, and therefore it needs your input on how to handle things. You are advised to use the `git config` command to specify your default preference flags, but what are these options, and how do they work?

Merge is going to work the way we've seen before: by creating a dedicated merge commit. However, there is another option.

Git Rebase

When you merge a feature branch into another, you're bringing the full history of one branch to the target branch—every commit in chronological order. *Rebasing* is another approach for moving feature branch commits. Instead of merging, it takes your commits, replays them on top of another branch, and gives the appearance that your work was always based on that newer point in history.

To use it, start on your feature branch, then use `git rebase`. For example, if you've branched from `main`, created `my-feature-branch`, made a few commits, and now want to apply those commits to `main`, do this:

```
git checkout my-feature-branch
git rebase main
```

Figure 3.7 shows how this works.

As opposed to `git merge`, `rebase` rewrites the feature branch (i.e., `my-feature-branch`) by creating new commits (with their own new, unique commit IDs) that replay your work on top of the target branch's (i.e., `main`'s) latest commit. This makes it appear

FIGURE 3.7 Using `git rebase` on your feature branch updates its source to be the latest of `main`. Note that X, Y, and Z would get fresh commit hashes in the process.

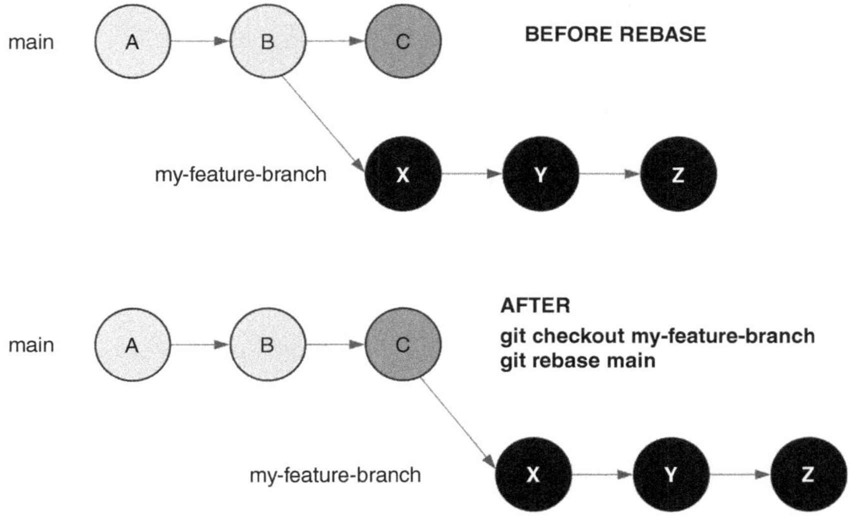

as though the work started from that newer point in history and, by itself, doesn't create a merge commit.

If your ultimate intention is to merge `my-feature-branch` into `main` at this point, it's very straightforward because your branch is now identical to `main`—plus your feature commits.

When working on a feature branch, use `git rebase` regularly to incorporate external changes happening on your source branch. For instance, if your colleague makes a change on `main`, follow these steps to stay in sync:

```
git checkout main
git pull origin main
git checkout my-feature-branch
git rebase main
```

Assuming no conflicts, you're back in business—with the latest updates from `main`!

Rewriting History

`git rebase` also has another power: Before you tack those feature branch commits onto another branch, you can edit your commit history. This is wonderfully handy when your commit history is full of micro-commits of the "fixed typo," "really fixed typo this time" sort. Use the following commands to enter interactive mode, which lets you clean and consolidate history.

```
git checkout my-feature-branch
git rebase -i main
```

In interactive mode, you're thrust into a text editor and given a special view of all the commits on your feature branch. If you made three changes, it might look something like this:

```
pick a1b2c3d added login form
pick e4f5g6h fixed typo in login form
pick i7j8k9l really fixed the typo this time
```

Think of this view as Git's sequential plan for how to add those three changes to the ones from `main`. The word `pick` is a command, and if you change that word before saving this file, you can influence how these commits will look when they're added to `main`. Here are a few of your choices:

`pick` just runs the commit as is. It's the default option.

`reword` lets you also change the commit message.

`edit` pauses the process at this point and lets you do anything, including adding and committing new files before proceeding.

`squash` keeps the commit's changes, but makes them part of the previous commit.

That last one is great for cleaning up the history. Let's edit the plan like this:

```
pick a1b2c3d added login form
squash e4f5g6h fixed typo in login form
squash i7j8k9l really fixed the typo this time
```

This version keeps all our changes but results in only one commit. That typo is fixed, but it's part of the commit whose message is "added login form." Note that Git actually pauses once more to confirm how the squashed commit message should look, then saves everything once you decide. So now, your Git log can have just one commit that looks like this:

```
commit a1f359d00ce127726d9933b141463aa583309202 (HEAD -> my-feature-branch)
Author: John Doe <john@example.com>
Date:   Sat Jan 25 21:00:54 2026 -0400

    added login form and fixed some typos you'll never know about!
```

Figure 3.8 shows how this works.

FIGURE 3.8 Interactive `git rebase` allows you to manipulate your branch's commit history before rebasing.

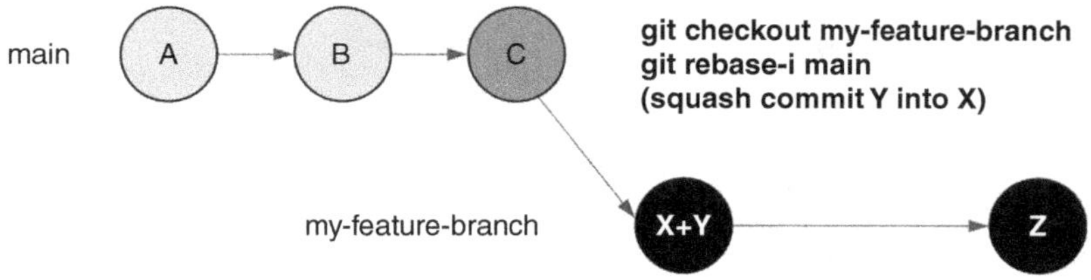

With this, you can keep your history clean.

> **TIP** Be warned! If you *delete* a line from the interactive `git rebase` plan, that commit will be lost forever. Type carefully.

Branching Strategies and Naming

We've talked a little about how branching works, but how is it actually used in practice?

Semantic Versioning and Tagging

Tags in Git are human-friendly names attached to specific commits. They're often used to mark release points, like when your project reaches its polished "1.0" version. When pushed to GitHub, tags show up prominently as "Releases" and are usually the way that mature, well-governed projects (e.g., many open source projects) publish milestones. As with all software, not every release is equally significant, and the way you name your tags is a great way to reflect this.

Most projects use *semantic versioning*, a convention that uses this format:

```
MAJOR.MINOR.PATCH
```

In this convention,

- `MAJOR` is for significant releases. They may contain large collections of enhancements or bug fixes, or just a few significant changes that impact the user experience or software functionality. Sometimes, developers use major versions to mark releases that contain some non-backward-compatible change, also known as a "breaking change" because it may disrupt other software that is dependent on the project being changed.
- `MINOR` is for smaller individual changes or collections of changes, and is almost always assumed to be backward-compatible with previous releases.

- PATCH is for even more tightly scoped releases; however, patches are often significant in their impact, because small changes rolled out quickly are often those done in response to deployment mistakes, significant but small-in-scope errors, or security vulnerabilities.

Here are two examples. Note that small variations, like preceding the version with a lowercase "v" or extending the version with details like -beta, are decisions made at the project or the repository level. Decide what works best for your team or project.

```
# third patch of the second minor release of version 1
v1.2.3

# a pre-release tag for version 2
v2.0.0-beta

To create a tag:
> git tag v1.0.0
> git push origin v1.0.0
```

Many projects accompany their tags with rich documentation of exactly what was changed in that release. Increasingly, these detailed messages can be generated by large language models (LLMs), where the AI can review the GitHub issues associated with the release, compare it to the code that has been changed, and write a nicely formatted set of release notes. Whether you do this yourself or have a robot step in, the way to provide this rich message is this:

```
git tag -a <your tag label here>
```

This command will open your default text editor to let you create a detailed message.

Tags are especially useful when you want to deploy or revert to a known good state. You can check one out like a branch:

```
git checkout v1.0.0
```

(Just watch out for that detached HEAD again.)

Tags vs. Branches

Branches and tags are two flavors of the same thing in Git. They are both labels that get applied to your current location along the Git timeline, but they differ in key ways. Table 3.1 outlines these differences.

Branching is one of the most powerful concepts in Git, giving you the power to experiment with code changes confidently. You should be comfortable with branching any time you take on a new feature request, bug fix task, or hotfix, and perhaps even branching again as you explore coding rabbit trails and discover what works. Branching not only makes changing code easier, but it makes it easier to collaborate on the same

TABLE 3.1 Git tags vs. branches

Feature	Git Branch	Git Tag
Purpose	Represents a movable pointer to a series of commits; used for ongoing development	Marks a specific point in history, typically for a release
Mutability	Moves with new commits	Fixed to a single commit (immutable)
Use case	Feature development, bug fixes, collaboration	Releases, versions, milestones
Naming	Typically descriptive (e.g., `feature/login`)	Often semantic versioned (e.g., `v1.2.3`)
Life cycle	Created, updated, merged, or deleted during development	Created once, rarely deleted or changed
Merging	Can be merged into other branches	Cannot be merged; just a reference
Checkout behavior	Moves `HEAD` to latest commit on that branch	Moves `HEAD` to specific commit in `detached HEAD` state
Shared via remote?	Yes, using `git push`	Yes, using `git push --tags` or `git push origin <tag>`

codebase with colleagues, letting you work independently until it's time to merge your efforts. Taking the time to learn to use and manage branches well will pay dividends for all your coding tasks.

Pull Requests and Team Collaboration

Another reason to adopt a Git remote is collaboration. Working on the same codebase at the same time as others can be challenging in the best of circumstances, but not only do Git's powerful branching and conflict management tools help you avoid problems, Git remote platforms like GitHub help even more by introducing the concept of *pull requests*.

Instead of manually and unilaterally merging code into a parent branch, pull requests (PRs) allow developers to push a branch to the remote repo, then initiate a workflow in which a colleague can review the proposed merge, inspect the specific code changes (often in a side-by-side view of differences), and initiate conversation about specific choices made by the developer before deciding to merge the altered code.

The developer's workflow typically proceeds like this:

1. Create a branch.
2. Edit files, make changes, and test locally.
3. Push the branch to the Git remote.
4. Open a pull request in the web interface (e.g., GitHub).
5. Have a teammate review or make comments on the changes.
6. Iterate on these comments, pushing additional commits to the branch until the reviewer approves.
7. The reviewer approves and merges the PR with the destination branch.

PR reviews are critical to today's team-based application development; the final merge of a PR is, in many cases, the trigger that kicks off automated testing or deployments. It's the human quality check that precedes many kinds of automation, so it's really important!

Branching Strategies and Naming

Once you've got the hang of using branches, your next step is to create some consistency in your naming. Clear, consistent branch naming strategies help teams collaborate without stepping on each other's toes, avoiding the headache of sorting through mysteriously named branches like `added_stuff` or `hotfix`.

A branching strategy defines how and when developers create branches, how they get merged, and what naming conventions to follow. This is especially important when you're working with remotes and pull requests as part of a team.

De facto standards have coalesced around a few different workflows. They differ in their complexity; choose the one that is most suited for the size and scope of the team or project with which you're working. Let's look at some examples.

GitHub Flow

This is the simplest model, often used for smaller teams or projects deploying continuously:

- `main` is always deployable, meaning it is fully tested and either represents what is currently in production or ready to be deployed to production.
- Every new feature or fix gets its own branch off `main`.
- When complete, open a pull request back to `main`.
- Once approved and merged, `main` gets deployed.

```
Example branches:
feature/login-form
bugfix/handle-timeout
hotfix/reset-password-bug
```

The key here is speed and simplicity. It assumes you're deploying often and that `main` is always stable.

Git Flow

Git Flow is a more structured branch management model for handling longer release cycles. It's popular in larger or more traditional teams. You'll notice it uses slashes in branch names, which is allowed by Git!

- `main` holds production-ready code.
- `dev` is a persistent, shared integration branch for new features. It often triggers a deployment to a nonproduction environment where internal users can test merged code before it goes live.
- `feature/*` branches are made off `dev`.
- `release/*` branches prepare code for release.
- `hotfix/*` branches are made off `main` for urgent fixes.

This approach creates more process and protection around what gets into production. It's useful when you need to support multiple versions or have strict QA requirements.

Here's an example:

```
feature/user-profile-page
release/1.3.0
Hotfix/1.2.1
```

If this feels like too much overhead for your use case, that's okay. Many teams opt for a simplified variant of GitHub Flow with just `main` and `feature` branches.

Naming Branches

As with commit messages, you want to establish good habits, even when you're working solo. A well-named branch tells you what the branch does and why it exists. Here are some suggestions:

- Use prefixes to indicate the branch type, such as `feature/`, `bugfix/`, `hotfix/`, `release/`, etc.
- Use hyphens to separate words, not underscores.
- Include ticket or issue numbers if you're using a tracker (e.g., `feature/1234-add-login`).
- Keep it lowercase and avoid punctuation.

Good examples:

```
feature/add-oauth-support
bugfix/fix-null-pointer-on-startup
Release/v2.1.0
```

Less good examples:

```
foo
temp-changes
johns-feature-branch
```

A branch name should tell a short, readable story about the work it contains.

No matter which branching strategy you adopt, the goal is the same: Help your team (and your tools) know what's happening, avoid unnecessary conflicts, and make it easy to manage the flow of code into production.

Protecting Branches

A *protected branch* is a branch you've locked down so important code can't be accidentally (or impulsively) changed. Platforms like GitHub or GitLab let you mark branches, such as `main` or `release`, as protected, blocking force pushes, deletions, and direct commits. Changes must come through pull requests, reviews, and passing tests.
In short, it's a safety net that protects your production code from "helpful" late-night edits. Protected branches are a common strategy when implementing multi-developer Git workflows.

Commit Life Cycle: Hooks, Linters, Secrets Detection

Every action you take with a Git repository, whether local or remote, is part of the overall code life cycle, consisting of events such as commits made, pushes initiated to remote branches, PRs created, PRs merged, tags pushed, and more. Each of these events is an opportunity to introduce some automation.

In a local repository, developers can set *pre-commit hooks* in Git to kick off basic quality checks that precede a commit being written. Common use cases include:

- **Linting:** Checking that code follows formatting rules
- **Secrets detection:** Preventing values such as database passwords or API keys from being committed
- **Test execution:** Blocking commits if tests fail

Developers can define a pre-commit hook by placing an executable script in `.git/hooks/pre-commit`.

Note that locally defined commit hooks are ignored when pushing code to the remote repository; they are local to the developer and must be shared out-of-band with the repo if you want your team to run them consistently.

Pre-commit hooks, as their name implies, run checks before a commit can even occur, and reject the commit if they fail. If this process is not quick enough, it can create delays that disrupt developers' flow and even discourage commits, which otherwise ought to be frequent and descriptive. Some tasks, like preventing secrets from ever leaving the local machine, can really only be done at this stage. However, quality-oriented tools, such as linters, can often be built right into the editor via extensions or plug-ins that alert developers to feedback as they type. You always want to create a balance between automation, developer feedback, and speed.

To create hooks that enforce team policies, you'll want to explore how to trigger activity on the server side via tools like GitHub Actions, Jenkins, or Google Cloud Build, all of which we'll discuss in later chapters.

Common Git Errors and How to Fix Them

We've discussed a few ways you might get into trouble with `git`. Here's a recap, plus a few more, with suggestions on how to set things right.

Unstage a File

You added a file by mistake. Unstage it with this:

```
git reset <filename>
```

Undo Commit

You committed a change that wasn't quite ready or (just as common) you made and committed a change on the wrong branch. Undo the latest commit with this:

```
git reset --soft HEAD~1
```

This command moves the `HEAD` pointer to the commit before the current one. It leaves your working directory and staging area untouched. The changes introduced in the now-undone commit will remain in your staging area, ready to be committed again. See `--mixed` and `--hard` in the documentation for variants.

Grab a File from Another Branch

You or a colleague changed a file on another branch, and you'd like that version of the file in your current branch. This command fetches just that one file and overwrites your current copy.

```
git checkout <branch_name> -- <filename>
```

This can be a good way to pull in a change from a colleague's branch without needing to go through the effort of a full branch merge.

Summary

When you version-control your code, you gain an incredible range of benefits. You get backups of your code, and you get the ability to revert back to known good states. Developers get a convenient way to try new ideas or implementation methods without risk of failure. Service owners can track changes to help determine the root cause of issues. Teams can more easily collaborate on the same codebase with greater confidence that their changes can be merged successfully. They can use pull requests to implement mature, quality-increasing review practices, and they can use Git remotes to communicate with users, share their work, and document releases over time. Code and version control are a match made in heaven. If only everything could be code!

Exam Essentials

Know the purpose and benefits of version control. Understand that version control systems like Git track changes to code and configuration files over time. Recognize how this enables rollback, collaboration, auditing, and automation triggers for builds or deployments.

Understand local vs. remote Git workflows. Be able to distinguish between local operations (`git add, git commit`) and remote operations (`git fetch, git pull, git push`). Know that local commits are stored on your machine until you push them to a shared repository.

Know key Git commands and their roles. Identify what each command does in context. For example, `git add` stages changes, `git commit` records them, and `git push` publishes them to a remote repository. Recognize common error conditions like merge conflicts or detached `HEAD` states.

Understand semantic versioning. Know the format of version numbers (`MAJOR.MINOR.PATCH`) and when to increment each.

Recognize common branching strategies. Be familiar with feature branching, release branching, and mainline protection. Understand why protected branches prevent accidental overwrites and how pull requests enable review before merging.

Identify best practices for collaboration and security. Know why secrets should never be committed to version control and how pre-commit hooks, linters, and scanners help detect them. Understand how commit hooks can enforce standards and trigger CI/CD pipelines.

Know how to resolve and prevent Git errors. Recognize the causes of merge conflicts, authentication errors, and detached `HEAD` states, and understand the general process to recover from them without data loss.

Review Questions

1. You just ran git checkout 953204a to inspect the very first commit in your repo. You make a quick hotfix and try to git commit, but you see a warning about being in a detached HEAD state. What is the safest next step if you want to keep this new commit and later merge it back into main?
   - A. Run **git push origin 953204a** to attach the commit to the remote history.
   - B. Run **git switch -c hotfix/initial-state** to create a branch at this point, then commit.
   - C. Run **git reset --hard main** to reattach HEAD, then commit again.
   - D. Run **git tag v1.0.1** to anchor the commit, then continue committing in detached HEAD.
2. On your feature branch you've finished changes to three files. You want all three to be part of one logical commit with the message "add Redis caching for index page." What is the correct sequence to achieve this cleanly?
   - A. Edit files → git commit --all "add Redis caching..."
   - B. Edit files → git add <all three files> → git commit -m "add Redis caching..."
   - C. Edit files → git commit (opens editor) → write message → git add
   - D. Edit files → git push → git commit -m "add Redis caching..."
3. You merged feature/cart_updates into main and got a conflict in shopping_cart.js showing the <<<<<<< HEAD and >>>>>>> feature/cart_updates markers. After editing the file to the desired final state, what must you do next to complete the merge?
   - A. Run **git commit -m "merged feature/cart_updates into main"**.
   - B. Run **git merge --continue** without staging the file.
   - C. Run **git reset --hard** to clear the markers and auto-resolve.
   - D. Run **git push** so GitHub can finish the merge automatically.
4. Your team wants to publish releases that clearly communicate significance and compatibility, and you also want an immutable reference to each release point. Which approach best fits?
   - A. Use branch names like release/important vs release/minor and retain them indefinitely.
   - B. Use tags named with semantic versions (e.g., v1.2.3, v2.0.0-beta) and push them.
   - C. Use commit messages starting with MAJOR, MINOR, or PATCH followed by details of the release.
   - D. Create a releases folder in the repo and commit versioned ZIPs to source control.

5. You maintain a shared repo and want to improve quality without slowing developers down. Which combination best balances local speed and team enforcement?
   - A. Heavy local pre-commit hooks that run full test suites; no server-side checks.
   - B. Light local hooks (secrets scan, quick lint) + editor integrations; deeper checks in server-side triggered by GitHub actions (or similar tool) on pull request creation.
   - C. No hooks; rely only on code owners to review manually before merging.
   - D. Put all checks in a shared `.git/hooks/` folder and expect them to run everywhere automatically.
6. You cloned a repository and created a new branch called `feature/api-refactor`. Before pushing, you realize the remote also has a branch with the same name that diverged days ago. What is the safest way to reconcile your local work with the remote one?
   - A. Force-push your branch to overwrite the remote copy.
   - B. Delete the remote branch so your push succeeds.
   - C. Fetch, then rebase your local branch onto the remote tracking branch before pushing.
   - D. Merge the remote main branch directly into your local branch.
7. You just committed a secret API key by accident. It's now in your most recent commit on a feature branch but has not been pushed. What's the proper fix?
   - A. Delete the file and commit a new change, overwriting the key.
   - B. Use **`git reset --soft HEAD~1`** to uncommit, remove the key, then recommit safely.
   - C. Run **`git stash`** to trash the file.
   - D. Push and then open a PR explaining the mistake.
8. You have multiple small commits like "fix typo" and "really fix typo this time." Before merging to `main`, your team prefers a single tidy commit. Which command helps you combine them interactively?
   - A. `git squash`
   - B. `git rebase -i HEAD~N`
   - C. `git commit --multiple 3`
   - D. `git commit --amend`
9. You want each commit message in your repo to include a ticket number from your issue tracking system. Which Git feature enforces this automatically before commits are accepted?
   - A. Pre-commit hook script
   - B. Server-side post-receive hook
   - C. Branch naming convention
   - D. Signed commits (`-S` flag)

10. You want to ensure that only reviewed code can reach main. Which GitHub feature helps enforce that policy?
    A. Protected branches requiring pull request reviews.
    B. Git hooks in each developer's local repo.
    C. Establish team norms that all pushes to main use a pull request.
    D. Tagging commits with "approved."

Answers to Review Questions

1. B. The correct answer is B. In `detached HEAD` you're not on a branch; new commits can become unreachable. Creating a new branch at the current commit (`git switch -c hotfix/initial-state`) preserves your work and lets you merge it later. Option A is incorrect because `git push origin 953204a` pushes a branch or a tag, not individual commits. Option C is incorrect because `git reset --hard main` moves your working tree back to `main` and discards the detached context; you'd lose the commit you were about to make. Option D is incorrect because it creates a tag, which marks a point in history but doesn't give you a branch for continued commits. Committing further in `detached HEAD` remains risky.

2. B. Option B is the correct answer. Stage the related changes together with `git add`, then create one commit with a descriptive message. This add → stage → commit life cycle is the central action loop of working in `git`. Option A is not quite correct. It uses the nonexistent `--all` flag to `git commit`. Option C is backward; you can't commit unstaged changes. Option D is also out of order; you can't push before you commit, and push sends existing commits to a remote.

3. A. The correct answer is A. After manually resolving, you stage the file (`git add shopping_cart.js`) and then commit the merge to finish it. (You can use `git commit` with or without `-m`.) Option B is incomplete in this context; `git merge --continue` still requires that you stage resolved files first. Option C discards your work and doesn't resolve anything. Option D won't complete a local merge; you must commit the resolution locally before pushing.

4. B. The correct answer is B. Tags mark specific commits immutably and, combined with semantic versioning (`MAJOR.MINOR.PATCH`, optional pre-release), communicate release intent and compatibility. Pushing tags publishes them to your remote and, at least in GitHub, makes them available on the Releases page. Option A uses branches, which are not immutable, and therefore unsuitable for permanent releases. Option C depends on commit message conventions without stable pointers for each release. Option D clutters the repo with binaries and still lacks immutable references tied to code history.

5. B. The correct answer is B. Keep in mind how to strike a balance between centrally-imposed quality checks and developer speed. Keep fast pre-commit hooks locally (linting/secret

detection) to prevent obvious or high-impact issues without blocking flow, and push heavier checks (full tests, security scans) to server-side CI tied to pull requests. Option A can slow commits and discourage frequent, descriptive commits, which we want. Option C is incorrect because it over-relies on humans and misses automation benefits. Option D misunderstands Git's behavior: local hooks don't propagate with pushes; they must be shared by other means or enforced server-side.

6. C. Option C is the correct answer. Running **`git fetch origin`**, followed by **`git rebase origin/feature/api-refactor`**, preserves both histories cleanly and reapplies your commits on top of the remote version. Option A is not a good idea, as it overwrites others' work; same with option B, which is likely to get you in even more trouble. Option D is viable, but doing so frequently creates many merge commits in your branch, and it's not as clean as using rebase. In cases like these, someone (you) must do the careful work of merging code. Make sure to communicate with the owner of that existing branch, as well, to make sure you're on the same page.

7. B. Assuming you have *not* pushed your code yet, option B is your best choice. `git reset --soft HEAD~1` rolls back the commit while preserving the working changes. You can remove the secret and commit again without ever exposing it remotely. Option A leaves the secret in history; option C only hides changes temporarily; and option D publishes the secret, which, of course, you should never do.

8. B. Option B is correct. Interactive rebase (`git rebase -i`) lets you squash (that is, combine) or reorder multiple commits before merging. Option A is not a real command; it is actually a command used only within an interactive rebase plan. Option C includes the non-existed `--multiple` flag. Option D changes only the message of the most recent commit.

9. A. Option A is correct. A local pre-commit hook can validate commit messages and block commits that lack the required format. Option B runs after pushing, so it can't stop a non-compliant commit locally. Option C is useful policy but unenforced. Option D signs commits cryptographically; it doesn't check format.

10. B. The correct answer is A. Branch protection rules can require PR reviews, confirm passage of automated checks, and prohibit direct pushes. Option B is local-only and unenforced remotely. Option C is great, but only Option A pairs it with protected branches, which can enforce the rule. Option D would be purely informational and would not enforce any action.

Chapter 4

Infrastructure-as-Code

THE AUTOOPS+ EXAM TOPICS COVERED IN THIS CHAPTER MAY INCLUDE, BUT ARE NOT LIMITED TO, THE FOLLOWING:

✔ **1.0: Automation Coding Concepts**

- 1.1. Given a scenario, use code to support automation.
- 1.3. Explain concepts related to infrastructure-as-code (IaC).
- 1.4. Given a scenario, troubleshoot common issues with the code life cycle.

✔ **2.0: System Configuration**

- 2.2. Compare and contrast basic approaches to automation.

Can everything be code? Today, the answer is a resounding "yes." Not only do cloud infrastructure providers like Amazon Web Services, Google Cloud, and Microsoft Azure expose all their services as APIs, making resources like virtual machines, load balancers, and network security rules scriptable out of the box, but they also go a step further by letting you define infrastructure as templated code.

Now, developers can bring all the benefits of code from the world of software to the realm of hardware. In this chapter, we'll explore how you can take the guesswork out of building cloud infrastructure, creating everything from simple cloud resources to complex, interconnected, and scalable architectures using the same technologies that we've already covered earlier in this book. So grab your JSON, brush up on YAML, and fire up the Python editors, because it's time to learn about infrastructure-as-code.

What Is Infrastructure-as-Code and Why Use It?

The umbrella term for defining things formerly consigned to physical hardware using code is *infrastructure-as-code (IaC)*.

Defining infrastructure-as-code is a bit like writing a recipe: It defines the ingredients and how they should be assembled. Deploying that code is like cooking the recipe; you're selecting ingredients (defining parameters) and preparing the meal (deploying the code). The completed dish is the set of resources created by your code. And as with a real recipe, infrastructure-as-code *templates* can be reused again and again, creating the same dish multiple times, or applying different ingredient choices to make variations on a common idea.

Infrastructure-as-code is a very powerful concept—one that drives a lot of automation in the cloud space—and it comes in two basic flavors: declarative or imperative.

Declarative vs. Imperative Approaches

There are two ways to think about defining infrastructure-as-code. The first is *imperative*. In an imperative approach, you issue commands in the same way—and in the same order—and you'd need to do them manually. Let's take a simple example architecture (Figure 4.1).

FIGURE 4.1 Infrastructure we want to create with code.

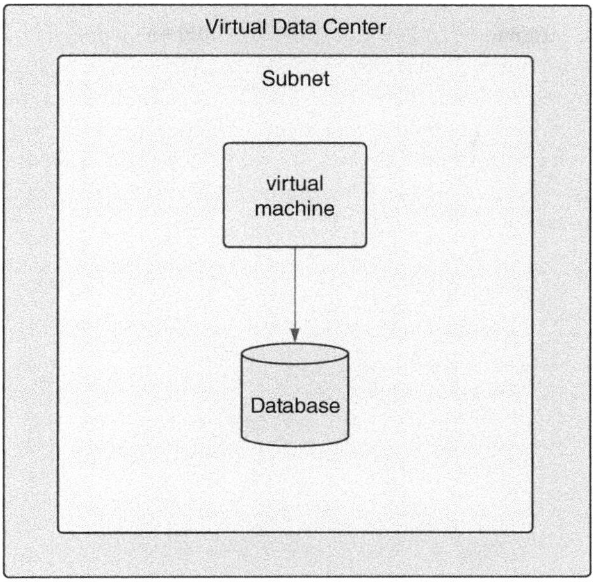

To be clear, a real web stack involves more elements than this. Most minimum-viable-product web stacks would at least include a load balancer so that the web application can run on multiple virtual machines and so that a web server itself is not exposed directly to the Internet. However, our goal is to demonstrate infrastructure-as-code, so we'll keep it simple.

Even with this design's simplicity, many elements of infrastructure are implied here. Before you can create any parts of the actual web stack, you must build your virtual data center and networking infrastructure. In Amazon Web Services (AWS), the virtual data center is a virtual private cloud (VPC). It's the network "container" within which all other resources reside. After establishing a VPC, you divide its address space into subnets, some of which you'd build to allow Internet traffic, and some of which you'd keep private. To achieve these variants, each subnet needs unique routing tables (not shown in the figure) between them. You'll also need a resource called an Internet gateway (again, not shown) to allow traffic to leave the subnet. That's the foundation of this design.

From there we create a virtual machine (called an EC2 instance in AWS) and place it in the subnet. We'll also have to create a database, and before anything can begin to work, we must create security rules that allow the traffic we want: public HTTPS traffic to the instance and private database traffic between the instance and the database. So, even a relatively straightforward deployment has many moving parts, especially when you factor in baseline networking infrastructure and intra-resource communication. Wouldn't it be great if we could lay all that down as code?

We'll start by demonstrating an imperative approach, using Python pseudocode that approximates how you'd build this in AWS. Amazon provides AWS software development kits (SDKs) for most languages. In Python, the AWS SDK has a special name: boto. We can build this stack in boto, but we'll have to assemble the pieces in order. In this example, EC2 refers to Elastic Computer Cloud, the part of AWS used to build virtual machines and other cloud resources needed for launching a web stack. For brevity's sake, we will assume the VPC and subnets already exist and focus on the web stack infrastructure comprised by the load balancer, instances, and database. This pseudocode creates the virtual machine and database infrastructure:

```
import boto3
region = "us-east-1"

# hard-coded infra you already have
VPC_ID = "vpc-0123456789abcdef0"
APP_SUBNET_ID = "subnet-aaa111"        # instance lives here (public subnet)
DB_SUBNET_A  = "subnet-bbb222"         # private subnets for DB
DB_SUBNET_B  = "subnet-ccc333"
AMI_ID = "ami-xxxxxxxx"                # pick a Linux AMI for your region

# Create a security rule to allow public HTTPS. This is
# a three-step process.
# First, we create the group.
web_sg = ec2.create_security_group(
    GroupName="web-sg",
    Description="HTTPS to web",
    VpcId=VPC_ID
)["GroupId"]

# Then, add a rule to it (TCP 443 from the world)
ec2.authorize_security_group_ingress(
    GroupId=web_sg,
    IpPermissions=[{
        "IpProtocol": "tcp",
        "FromPort": 443,
        "ToPort": 443,
        "IpRanges": [{"CidrIp": "0.0.0.0/0"}]
    }]
)

# Next, create a security group that will allow postgres
# database traffic on port 443.
db_sg = ec2.create_security_group(
    GroupName="db-sg",
    Description="DB from web-sg",
    VpcId=VPC_ID
)["GroupId"]
```

```
# Note that now, our source is not an IP address, but another security group.
# This is a great feature of AWS that lets you define rules
# where the source is any other resource posessing a certain security group.
ec2.authorize_security_group_ingress(
    GroupId=db_sg,
    IpPermissions=[{
        "IpProtocol": "tcp",
        "FromPort": 5432,
        "ToPort": 5432,  # postgres
        "UserIdGroupPairs": [{"GroupId": web_sg}]
    }]
)

# Create the instance in the app subnet and attach its SG
instance_id = ec2.run_instances(
    ImageId=AMI_ID,
    InstanceType="t3.micro",
    SubnetId=APP_SUBNET_ID,
    SecurityGroupIds=[web_sg]
)["Instances"][0]["InstanceId"]

# Create the database and attach its SG
rds.create_db_instance(
    Engine="postgres",
    DBInstanceClass="db.t4g.micro",
    DBSubnetGroupName=rds_subnet_group,
    VpcSecurityGroupIds=[db_sg]
)
```

The catch with this imperative approach is that you must create resources in the right order and remember IDs between steps. If you wanted to make a change to some configuration that occurs halfway through the sequence (say, updating the instance type of the database), you don't have many good options. Depending on the types of resources you create, rerunning a script like this one would lead to either a script error or duplicate resources, or both. Plus, if something does go wrong, it takes extra coding on your part to recover to a good state; you must carefully delete resources or reverse changes in a way that doesn't create compounding inconsistencies.

CloudFormation and other *declarative* IaC tools make things easier by letting you declare your desired end state. It determines order of execution, wires references for you, shows the anticipated change impact before you apply, and lets you reuse the same template for updates:

```
AWSTemplateFormatVersion: '2010-09-09'

Parameters:
  VpcId:
    Type: AWS::EC2::VPC::Id
  AppSubnetId:
    Type: AWS::EC2::Subnet::Id
```

```
  DbSubnetA:
    Type: AWS::EC2::Subnet::Id
  DbSubnetB:
    Type: AWS::EC2::Subnet::Id
  AmiId:
    Type: AWS::EC2::Image::Id

Resources:
  WebInstance:
    Type: AWS::EC2::Instance
    Properties:
      ImageId: !Ref AmiId
      InstanceType: t3.micro
      SubnetId: !Ref AppSubnetId
      SecurityGroupIds: [!Ref AppSg]

  AppSg:
    Type: AWS::EC2::SecurityGroup
    Properties:
      GroupDescription: Allow public HTTPS to instance
      VpcId: !Ref VpcId
      SecurityGroupIngress:
        - IpProtocol: tcp
          FromPort: 443
          ToPort: 443
          CidrIp: 0.0.0.0/0

  DbSg:
    Type: AWS::EC2::SecurityGroup
    Properties:
      GroupDescription: Allow DB from instance SG
      VpcId: !Ref VpcId
      SecurityGroupIngress:
        - IpProtocol: tcp
          FromPort: 5432
          ToPort: 5432
          SourceSecurityGroupId: !Ref AppSg

  DbInstance:
    Type: AWS::RDS::DBInstance
    Properties:
      DBInstanceIdentifier: demo-postgres
      Engine: postgres
      MasterUsername: !Ref DbUsername
      MasterUserPassword: !Ref DbPassword
      DBInstanceClass: db.t4g.micro
      AllocatedStorage: 20
      VPCSecurityGroups: [!Ref DbSg]
      DBSubnetGroupName: !Ref DbSubnetGroup
      PubliclyAccessible: false
```

```
DbSubnetGroup:
  Type: AWS::RDS::DBSubnetGroup
  Properties:
    DBSubnetGroupDescription: private subnets for RDS
    SubnetIds: [!Ref DbSubnetA, !Ref DbSubnetB]
```

At first glance, this snippet might not seem that different from the previous one. However, although this template achieves the same result as the imperative example given in Python, how it achieves these goals is much different.

Understanding the Dependency Graph

In the Python example, it was very important to get things in the right order. After all, you can't associate a security group with an instance if you have not yet created the security group. In contrast, take a close look at the CloudFormation example, and you'll notice that I deliberately placed some things out of order. This is because infrastructure-as-code engines don't care about the order of your declared resources. Instead, they analyze your template and determine the necessary order for you. This internal representation of relationships between resources is called a *dependency graph* (see Figure 4.2).

The purpose of an IaC engine like CloudFormation is to take away the effort of maintaining this ordering yourself. As shown in Figure 4.2, the tool's preprocessing service recognizes when one part of the template references a resource defined elsewhere, so that when it executes the underlying API calls required to actually build your resources, it can do so in the right order.

Note that for relationships that are not so easily inferred, IaC tools always give you ways to declare relationships explicitly. For CloudFormation, this is done through a property called `DependsOn`.

In addition, some dependencies are not based on resource creation but on external factors. For instance, you might want a web server to be created only after a database migration takes place. The IaC tool knows when the database is live, but not when the

FIGURE 4.2 Infrastructure-as-code engines maintain an internal dependency graph representing order-of-operations relationships between resources.

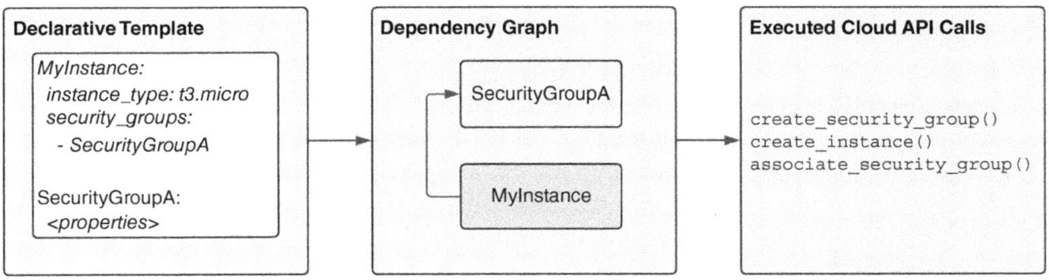

data has fully updated. IaC tools give you commands that let your template execution wait for certain events or "all clear" signals before proceeding. In CloudFormation, this is done through a `WaitCondition`.

Idempotency and Reusability

A few more key principles of infrastructure-as-code are exemplified in the CloudFormation example: idempotency and reusability.

Idempotency

A script or template can be called *idempotent* if you are able to run it multiple times and end up in the same state. In an IaC template, the first execution might create resources, but the second execution should do nothing.

Back when my job involved writing database migration scripts by hand to achieve idempotency, I'd have to carefully order statements and wrap many of them in exception handling code, because the database engine could not handle executing certain commands twice. For instance, a `CREATE TABLE` statement might throw an error if the table already exists. Writing a script such that a second or third execution was nondestructive was a challenge; with today's declarative IaC templates, idempotency is a built-in feature.

In CloudFormation, the same engine that intuits the dependency graph is the one that checks for template changes to determine if an action should take place. If you update one resource in your YAML but not another, the IaC engine is smart enough to only touch the latter. If you've made no changes, no updates will occur. This is idempotency, and it means you don't have to worry about destructive changes happening when you don't intend them to.

Reusability

Good infrastructure-as-code templates are modular and reusable. Notice the `Parameters` section at the beginning of the CloudFormation snippet earlier. CloudFormation templates are often executed by a human who enters the template into AWS's CloudFormation web interface. During this process, the user gets prompted for values for each parameter listed. In this way, the same template can serve to build multiple sets of similar infrastructure.

In CloudFormation, each set of resources created by one template is called a *stack*. In this example, we could use our example template to create a development stack by supplying a private subnet ID and a smaller instance size, and we could later create a production stack by placing the instance in a public subnet with a larger, more powerful instance size. This same reusability can be done even in fully automatic IaC deployments by supplying parameter values as input to the tool's deployment command. Reusing templates or template snippets means more consistency across your entire environment, as resources are stamped from the same pattern.

Managing Related Resources

One of the nicest aspects of infrastructure-as-code is that the resulting stacks share a life cycle and can be managed together. In short, this means that resources that are created from a single template are represented as a collection by the IaC tool and can be updated or torn down together, using a single command. This is especially useful when you're first working out how your infrastructure should be defined, because IaC makes it easy to iterate: build, evaluate, tear down, and build again.

Drift Detection and Change Tracking

Drift is what happens when a live environment no longer matches its template. Maybe someone fixed a production issue in the console, or a script tweaked a setting out of band. Declarative tools help you spot and correct that. CloudFormation can compare the stack's current state to the template and flag modified or missing resources. Before you touch anything, you can also generate a *change set*—a summary of the anticipated changes that will result from an update—to see what would be created, updated, replaced, or deleted. That preview is your safety net, letting you make the final decision about whether or not to execute an update.

Version Control for IaC

One of the best reasons to use IaC is to treat your infrastructure code like application code: Put your templates in Git and every benefit version control offers to software development becomes part of your operations. You get code review on infrastructure, a history of who changed what and why, and the ability to roll back to known good states. The same template can stand up development, test, and production environments with only parameters changing, so teams stop hand-crafting unique snowflakes. In addition, having your templates version-controlled helps pave the way for automated deployments, a concept covered later in this book.

Pitfalls: Bad Templates and Troubleshooting

Infrastructure-as-code can make things easier, but it doesn't eliminate every challenge. This section explores a few common issues you may meet along the way.

Circular Dependencies

Overly entangled resources can confuse dependency graphs. To avoid this, break components into smaller modules or use explicit depends-on hooks.

Zombie Stacks

Sometimes an IaC template can get into a state where it refuses to properly roll back or delete resources. This is one reason it's good to divide your IaC templates into smaller, more focused sections. For example, put foundational shared networking setup in one file, load balancing infrastructure in another, and virtual machines in their own. This helps you avoid ever getting too stuck if one template gets into a difficult state.

Configuration Drift

Someone (let's face it, probably you) changed a resource manually instead of updating the IaC template. This is known as *configuration drift* because your real-life infrastructure state has "drifted" away from what is declared in the template. IaC works best when your template is always the source of truth, so be consistent and always make updates through IaC. Some tools, such as CloudFormation, have ways of alerting you to drift over time.

Configuration drift is more than an annoyance; it can undermine your entire infrastructure-as-code approach by breaking your templates entirely. For instance, if you have a template that defines several virtual machines and security rules, then make a manual modification that causes one of those VMs to be re-created with a different identifier, your IaC template may no longer recognize its existence. Subsequent effects are difficult to predict, but here are a few likely ones:

- The template will no longer be able to make updates to the changed resource; it is now unmanaged by the template.
- Deploying the template again is likely to create a new, duplicate virtual machine to replace the one it can no longer find.
- The template may throw errors because of its newly inconsistent state and be unable to issue new updates to any resources in the stack.
- The template may be unable to perform a rollback of any kind, leaving untethered all the other resources you didn't manually alter.

As you can see, configuration drift can be a big deal. Once you commit to IaC, it's a good idea to make it your primary means of editing infrastructure, lest you get into an undesirable state.

Recovering from configuration drift is not impossible, but it can be a significant challenge. Your goal is to get reality to align with the template, so it's best if those changes are few and low impact. Revert any changes that can be reverted to match the template, and you'll have a good chance of keeping your IaC code working. To catch changes early, use platform-native drift detection and revert manual changes as soon as possible.

Because of the possibility of IaC code getting into an unrecoverable state, it's best to structure your templates with a "blast radius" in mind, thinking in layers or groups of related entities. For instance, build basic networking infrastructure like subnets and routing tables in one template, then create another to build the components of a single web app. It can also be fruitful to divide IaC templating responsibilities across organizational lines—perhaps having a database team manage templates for a data layer. Just keep in mind that while more templates can reduce the risk of configuration drift, they also increase the level of coordination that is required to make everything work together.

Unintended Deletes

Sometimes, you might expect that an IaC update will change a resource in place. However, updates can be destructive. Your chosen tool can often tell you before you proceed whether a change will be low-impact (like stopping and starting an AWS instance when resizing it) or destructive (like terminating an instance to change its operating system). Make sure to use the tools provided to you to preview changes.

Surveying Infrastructure-as-Code Tools

With today's cloud computing, you have many options for building and deploying your infrastructure-as-code. In this section, we'll take a look at some of the most prominent tools available for your service of choice.

AWS CloudFormation

As the first major cloud-native infrastructure-as-code templating language, Amazon Web Services' CloudFormation looms large over the space. CloudFormation runs natively in AWS, meaning that to get started, you don't need to install anything. You can just log into your AWS account, navigate to the CloudFormation section, and start by uploading a template.

Template Syntax

We've already shown examples of CloudFormation, so you have a good idea of how it looks. The CloudFormation template has just a few sections:

- **`AWSTemplateFormatVersion`**—Declares the version of the template format. This value has been set at `2010-09-09` for more than a decade, so just copy it as is!
- **`Description`**—A human-friendly string describing the template; a good place to remind your future self why you made certain decisions.
- **`Metadata`**—Stores arbitrary data about the template, often used by tools or the AWS console.
- **`Parameters`**—Lets you define user-supplied values when the stack is created or updated.
- **`Mappings`**—Can provide lookup table for static values (like AMI IDs by region).
- **`Conditions`**—Defines whether certain resources are created or properties are assigned based on logical condition statements.

- **`Transform`**—Used to alter basic syntax, reference macros, or frameworks like the AWS::Serverless transform (SAM). This one's for power users.
- **`Resources`**—Defines the actual AWS resources (EC2 instances, S3 buckets, IAM roles, etc.). Every template you write will have this section.
- **`Outputs`**—Declares values you want returned after stack creation, such as ARNs, URLs, or IDs. When working with multiple templates, this section is critical for passing information between stacks.

The only required sections of a CloudFormation template is the `Resources` section. All others are optional.

Resources

Understand the `Resources` section in CloudFormation, and you'll have a large part of what you need to understand both this tool and the others like it in this section. Recall that a "resource" is just about any service within AWS, be it an S3 bucket for storing objects, an EC2 virtual machine, a subnet definition, or a user policy document. For all these resources, Amazon provides a JSON or YAML representation and thorough documentation of its parameters. We'll create a brief and incomplete example to demonstrate:

```
AWSTemplateFormatVersion: 2010-09-09
Resources:
  MyEC2Instance:
    Type: AWS::EC2::Instance
    Properties:
      ImageId: ami-79fd7eee
       InstanceType: t2.micro
```

This example doesn't have every element it needs to be deployed correctly, but it does demonstrate a few things: first, that every resource has a user-defined name—in this case, `MyEC2Instance`. This name is used inside the template anytime you need to refer to this resource elsewhere (say, to associate the instance with a load balancer). Second, it has a type, which defines what kind of resource you're building. Finally, the `Properties` section lets you enumerate the parameters of the instance. These are the exact same options as those you'd define in the web console, were you to build your instance in a browser interface.

In this example, the instance's configuration is defined with hard-coded values, but much of the power of infrastructure-as-code templates occurs when we start to parameterize these property values.

Parameters

Let's add a new section to our IaC template. The `Parameters` section lets you make values user-definable.

```
AWSTemplateFormatVersion: 2010-09-09
Parameters:
```

```
  MyAMI:
    Type: String
    Default: ami-1234
  MyInstanceType:
    Type: String
    Default: t3.micro
Resources:
  MyEC2Instance:
    Type: AWS::EC2::Instance
    Properties:
      ImageId: !Ref MyAMI
      InstanceType: !Ref MyInstanceType
```

Now, both the `ImageId` and `InstanceType` of this template are no longer hard-coded, but will be provided from the value of a user-defined prompt. When you go to the AWS web console to deploy this template (or deploy it from a command line), you'll be required to give values for these parameters; see Figure 4.3. The default values ensure that there's always something defined, and provide a helpful hint to users as to the kind of values expected.

FIGURE 4.3 A user is prompted for CloudFormation property values in the AWS web console. Default values are pre-filled.

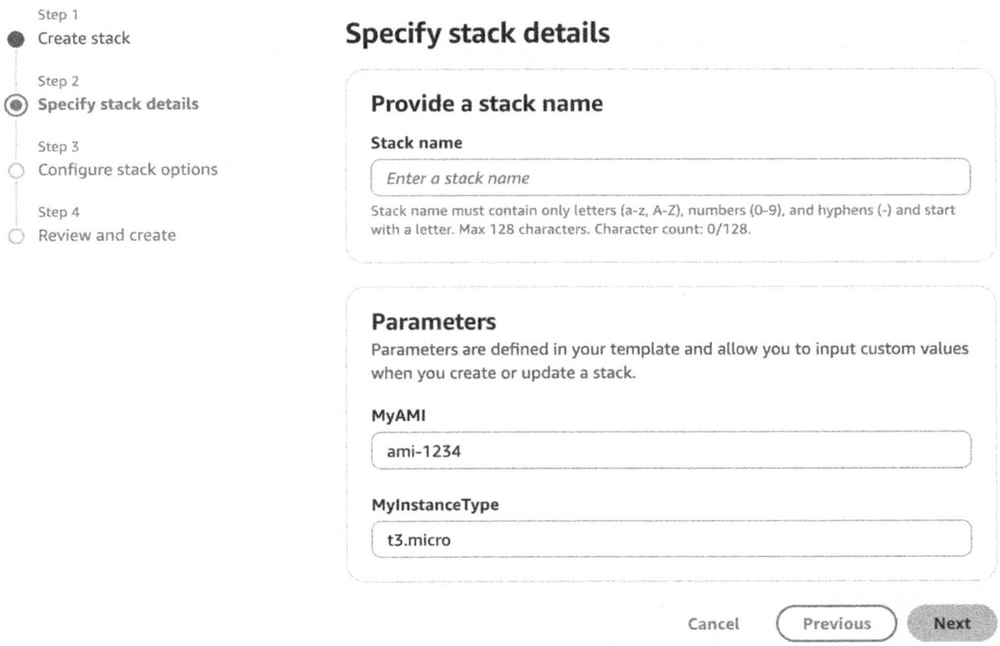

FIGURE 4.4 CloudFormation parameters with `AllowedValues`.

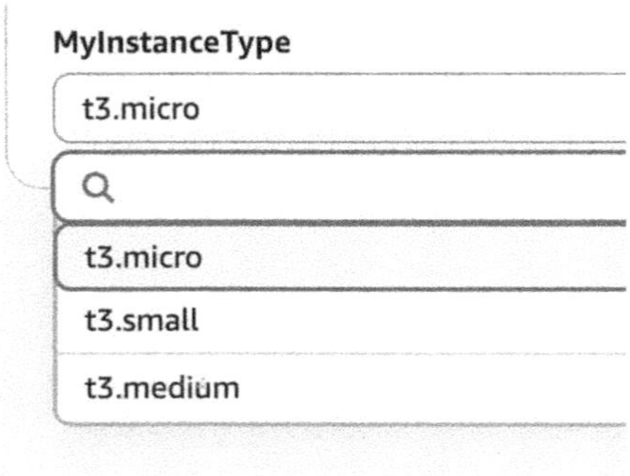

CloudFormation parameters can also be defined with `AllowedValues`, which creates a drop-down list for the user (see Figure 4.4):

```
AWSTemplateFormatVersion: 2010-09-09
Parameters:
  MyAMI:
    Type: String
    Default: ami-1234
  MyInstanceType:
    Type: String
    AllowedValues:
      - t3.micro
      - t3.small
      - t3.medium
    Default: t3.micro
Resources:
  MyEC2Instance:
    Type: AWS::EC2::Instance
    Properties:
      ImageId: !Ref MyAMI
      InstanceType: !Ref MyInstanceType
```

In this way, template writers can create infrastructure definitions that are flexible and that can be used with different parameter inputs to create multiple, similar stacks.

Inputs and Outputs

The `Outputs` section of a CloudFormation template serves two purposes. At its most basic, it allows you to print values to the CloudFormation console when the stack has finished being built. In this way, you can get easy access to values that are not known until after resources come into existence. Suppose you have an application load balancer (ALB) defined in your template by the name AppLB. You can make sure its DNS names appears in the web console with this code:

```
Outputs:
  AppLBDNS:
    Description: DNS name of the Application Load Balancer
    Value: !GetAtt AppLB.DNSName
```

In this example, we use the function !GetAtt to get the DNSName attribute from AppLB via dot notation. This attribute is defined by AWS and only has a value after the ALB is created. Including it here will make the value appear on the Output tab in CloudFormation. Now, if we want to make this value available to other CloudFormation stacks, we can include the Export option:

```
Outputs:
  AppLBDNS:
    Description: DNS name of the Application Load Balancer
    Value: !GetAtt AppLB.DNSName
    Export:
      Name: WebALBDomainName
```

Here, we specify that this output should be exported with the name WebALBDomainName. Other stacks can make reference to this value like so:

```
Resources:
  AppDNSRecord:
    Type: AWS::Route53::RecordSet
    Properties:
      HostedZoneName: example.com.
      Name: app.example.com.
      Type: CNAME
      TTL: 300
      ResourceRecords:
        - !ImportValue WebALBDomainName
```

Here, we use AWS's Route53 service to create a DNS alias for the load balancer's address. In the last line of the sample, we call !ImportValue with the name exported by the other stack. As long as the previous stack has already successfully run in the same account, this value will resolve to the one exported by the first stack.

Change Sets

It's not always possible to change resources in an IaC template nondestructively. For instance, AWS can always change an instance's sizing with a simple reboot, but it can't magically change a Linux instance to a Windows instance. If you wish to make that kind of change, only a full deletion and recreation of the instance will do.

To help you understand in advance how your updates will affect your resources, let's take a look at some other options in the cloud IaC ecosystem.

HashiCorp Terraform

Terraform is the open source heavyweight of multicloud IaC. It uses its own language (HCL—HashiCorp Configuration Language), derived from JSON. Due to its ability to work with multiple cloud providers, Terraform is widely adopted in industry, sometimes even chosen over CloudFormation for AWS. Being able to train your team in just one templating language and having those skills apply in AWS, Azure, or Google Cloud can be very valuable.

Multiple Providers, One Syntax

Terraform is the closest thing we have to a universal translator for infrastructure. While tools like AWS CloudFormation, Azure Resource Manager, and Google Deployment Manager each speak their provider's native language, Terraform speaks them all.

Terraform's defining feature is provider-based extensibility. Each supported platform (AWS, Azure, GCP, VMware, even GitHub) plugs in through a provider module, exposing its resources in HCL, making it cloud-agnostic.

However, just because Terraform can work with multiple cloud providers doesn't mean its code is 100 percent portable between those providers. Terraform provides a *lingua franca*, but each provider still has some unique configuration parameters or resource types that could see multicloud practitioners maintaining branching copies of IaC code even if they're using Terraform. The strength is in having a common syntax, even as underlying resources may vary.

Terraform also has a large library of third-party modules built by its users. These open source templates can help accelerate your work by encapsulating complex or unique infrastructure in short commands.

Let's take a look at the basic syntax of Terraform:

```
resource "aws_instance" "demo" {
  ami           = "ami-123456"
  instance_type = "t2.micro"

  tags = {
    Name = "demo-instance"
  }
}
```

In this example, we create a single AWS instance with a provided Amazon Machine Image identifier (AMI ID) and an instance type, then give it a few metadata tags. As you can see, HCL has similarities to JSON, making it easy to both read and write.

Client-Side Execution

Unlike CloudFormation, which runs entirely inside AWS, Terraform runs client-side, meaning it must be launched from a machine you own. This could be a laptop or a dedicated host within your cloud account. Terraform builds and maintains its own state file—a snapshot of what's been deployed and how it maps to your configuration. This gives Terraform enormous flexibility but also means state management becomes your responsibility. Lose that file, and you'll lose track of the state of your infrastructure. Version control is very important when working with Terraform!

Another unique strength of Terraform is its execution plans. When you run the command **`terraform plan`**, you'll be shown exactly what will change before you commit. That plan output becomes a kind of living "diff" between intent and reality, similar to CloudFormation's change sets.

Installing Terraform

As client-side software, Terraform must be installed before you can use it. HashiCorp provides packages for some of the major packages managers. On a Mac, users of the Homebrew package manager can run the following:

```
brew tap hashicorp/tap
brew install hashicorp/tap/terraform
```

Terraform can also be directly installed on Windows using the package manager Chocolately using **`choco install terraform`**. Linux users on Debian variants have an `apt-get` option. Otherwise, you have the option to choose manual installation or even compile the tool yourself at `https://developer.hashicorp.com`.

Primary Terraform Commands

Let's look at a few Terraform basics.

Initializing a Provider

To get started with Terraform, start a template (a file ending in `.tf`) in an empty directory. This file can be blank to begin, but let's initialize a provider by using this for the contents of `main.tf`:

```
provider "aws" {
  region = "us-east-1"
}
```

This tells Terraform that we're going to use Amazon Web Services and provides the AWS region as a parameter. After this, run **`terraform init`** to initialize the directory for use with Terraform, and it'll download everything it needs to work with AWS.

Defining a Resource

Let's add an S3 bucket to the template:

```
resource "aws_s3_bucket" "MyDemoBucket" {

  # AWS bucket names must be globally unique
  bucket = "demo-bucket-auto-ops-plus"

  tags = {
    Environment = "Development"
  }
}
```

This template defines a single bucket with minimal configuration. It has a *resource type* of `"aws_s3_bucket"` (the official type designation from HashiCorp for an AWS S3 bucket) and a user-provided name, in this case, `MyDemoBucket`. These two fields make up the *resource address* of the resource in the form `aws_s3_bucket.MyDemoBucket`.

There are many more parameters we could provide and resource we could create; see the directory at `https://registry.terraform.io` for full details of available resources from each provider.

Establishing Credentials

Before you can do anything with Terraform, you need to have established credentials to execute commands on your provider of choice. For AWS, this means having the AWS command-line interface installed and configured with credentials. It also means the credentials you use must have permission to create, update, and delete the resources you'll be managing with Terraform. In this example, we must have configured an AWS account that can create an S3 bucket.

Similarly, to use Azure, Google Cloud, or any of the other cloud providers, you must set up access to accounts on those services. Note that Terraform doesn't directly execute command-line commands but rather executes API calls using the provided credentials.

There are multiple ways to authenticate to each provider, including methods that use service accounts or OAuth flows. Exploring these methods is important once you're ready to deploy Terraform in production. You should not use an individual's credentials in a live setting, but instead establish service accounts with the least necessary privileges to execute your IaC templates, reducing the blast radius of any potential problems, misconfigurations, or exploits.

Planning Is Everything

Now it's time to run `terraform plan`. This step will give you a detailed breakdown of what's about to happen:

```
> terraform plan

Terraform used the selected providers to generate the following execution plan.
Resource
```

```
actions are indicated with the following symbols:
  + create

Terraform will perform the following actions:

  # aws_s3_bucket.MyDemoBucket will be created
  + resource "aws_s3_bucket" "MyDemoBucket" {
      + acceleration_status         = (known after apply)
      + acl                         = (known after apply)
      + arn                         = (known after apply)
      + bucket                      = "demo-bucket-auto-ops-plus"
      + bucket_domain_name          = (known after apply)
      + bucket_prefix               = (known after apply)
      + bucket_region               = (known after apply)
      + bucket_regional_domain_name = (known after apply)
      + force_destroy               = false
      + hosted_zone_id              = (known after apply)
      + id                          = (known after apply)
      + object_lock_enabled         = (known after apply)
      + policy                      = (known after apply)
      + region                      = "us-east-1"
      + request_payer               = (known after apply)
      + tags                        = {
          + "Environment" = "Development"
        }
      + tags_all                    = {
          + "Environment" = "Development"
        }
      + website_domain              = (known after apply)
      + website_endpoint            = (known after apply)

      + cors_rule (known after apply)

      + grant (known after apply)

      + lifecycle_rule (known after apply)

      + logging (known after apply)

      + object_lock_configuration (known after apply)

      + replication_configuration (known after apply)

      + server_side_encryption_configuration (known after apply)

      + versioning (known after apply)

      + website (known after apply)
    }

Plan: 1 to add, 0 to change, 0 to destroy.
```

This is the set of changes Terraform will execute when you `apply` this template. To make sure nothing changes the plan between execution, you can save the plan with the `-out` parameter and provide it in the next step. If you don't, Terraform will execute `terraform plan` on its own before applying changes. In either case, you'll see the plan, which should help avoid surprises!

Apply the Plan

Run `terraform apply` and confirm the change, and you'll get output like this:

```
aws_s3_bucket.MyDemoBucket: Creating...
aws_s3_bucket.MyDemoBucket: Creation complete after 1s
[id=demo-bucket-auto-ops-plus]

Apply complete! Resources: 1 added, 0 changed, 0 destroyed.
```

Now your bucket is created in AWS.

A Peek Behind the Curtain

Run **`terraform show`**, and you'll see a much more detailed version of the template you wrote. Remember that bucket names must be unique, so yours will be different from this:

```
# aws_s3_bucket.MyDemoBucket:
resource "aws_s3_bucket" "MyDemoBucket" {
    acceleration_status         = null
    arn                         = "arn:aws:s3:::demo-bucket-auto-ops-plus"
    bucket                      = "demo-bucket-auto-ops-plus"
    bucket_domain_name          = "demo-bucket-auto-ops-plus.s3.amazonaws.com"
    bucket_prefix               = null
    bucket_region               = "us-east-1"
    bucket_regional_domain_name = "demo-bucket-auto-ops-plus.s3.us-east-1.
amazonaws.com"
    force_destroy               = false
    hosted_zone_id              = "ABCDEFGHIJ123"
    id                          = "demo-bucket-auto-ops-plus"
    object_lock_enabled         = false
    policy                      = null
    region                      = "us-east-1"
    request_payer               = "BucketOwner"
    tags_all                    = {}

    grant {
        id          = "86c2da35ef60528dac4317220c5ecb473763375b2b99d78013e"
        permissions = [
            "FULL_CONTROL",
        ]
        type        = "CanonicalUser"
        uri         = null
    }
```

```
    server_side_encryption_configuration {
        rule {
            bucket_key_enabled = false

            apply_server_side_encryption_by_default {
                kms_master_key_id = null
                sse_algorithm     = "AES256"
            }
        }
    }

    versioning {
        enabled    = false
        mfa_delete = false
    }
}
```

This shows you everything that Terraform is tracking in its internal state management—quite a bit for one simple S3 bucket! But that's the point: your template can stay simple, while Terraform handles all the nitty-gritty details.

Updating Resources

Now we can see how `terraform plan` can help us as we update resources. Let's try changing the bucket name:

```
provider "aws" {
  region = "us-east-1"
}

resource "aws_s3_bucket" "MyDemoBucket" {

  # AWS bucket names must be globally unique
  bucket = "demo-bucket-auto-ops-plus-changeme"

}
```

S3 bucket names can't change in place; they can only be destroyed and re-created with the new name. Terraform warns us of this when we run `terraform plan`:

```
> terraform plan
aws_s3_bucket.MyDemoBucket: Refreshing state...
[id=demo-bucket-auto-ops-plus]

Terraform used the selected providers to generate the following execution plan.
Resource
actions are indicated with the following symbols:
-/+ destroy and then create replacement

Terraform will perform the following actions:
```

```
  # aws_s3_bucket.MyDemoBucket must be replaced
-/+ resource "aws_s3_bucket" "MyDemoBucket" {
      + acceleration_status         = (known after apply)
      + acl                         = (known after apply)
      ~ arn                         = "arn:aws:s3:::demo-bucket-auto-ops-plus"
-> (known after apply)
      ~ bucket                      = "demo-bucket-auto-ops-plus-1234" ->
"demo-bucket-auto-ops-plus-changeme" # forces replacement
```

If this is what you want, great! If not, Terraform's "think first" approach is a great help.

For an easier change, let's add versioning to this bucket without updating the name. For this, we add versioning not as a configuration to the bucket resource, but as a distinct resource that refers back to the bucket by its full name:

```
resource "aws_s3_bucket_versioning" "MyDemoBucketVersioning" {
  bucket = aws_s3_bucket.MyDemoBucket.id
  versioning_configuration {
    status = "Enabled"
  }
}
```

Note how we refer to the bucket by its fully qualified name, `aws_s3_bucket.MyDemoBucket`, and how we use dot notation to refer to its `id` property. As you now understand from IaC principles, this relationship is one Terraform will use to construct its internal dependency graph, ensuring that resources will be created in the right order. Now, `terraform plan` shows us exactly what will happen:

```
> terraform plan
aws_s3_bucket.MyDemoBucket: Refreshing state...
[id=demo-bucket-auto-ops-plus-1234]

Terraform used the selected providers to generate the following execution plan.
Resource actions are indicated with
the following symbols:
  + create

Terraform will perform the following actions:

  # aws_s3_bucket_versioning.MyDemoBucketVersioning will be
created
  + resource "aws_s3_bucket_versioning" "MyDemoBucketVersioning" {
      + bucket = "demo-bucket-auto-ops-plus-1234"
      + id     = (known after apply)
      + region = "us-east-1"

      + versioning_configuration {
          + mfa_delete = (known after apply)
          + status     = "Enabled"
        }
    }
```

When we run **terraform apply**, we see the change is made:

```
aws_s3_bucket_versioning.MyDemoBucketVersioning: Creating...
aws_s3_bucket_versioning.MyDemoBucketVersioning: Creation complete after 2s
[id=demo-bucket-auto-ops-plus]

Apply complete! Resources: 1 added, 0 changed, 0 destroyed.
```

Pretty simple.

Tear Down Resources

Finally, let's tear down the stack with terraform destroy.

```
aws_s3_bucket_versioning.MyDemoBucketVersioning: Destroying...
[id=demo-bucket-auto-ops-plus-1234]
aws_s3_bucket_versioning.MyDemoBucketVersioning: Destruction complete after 0s
aws_s3_bucket.MyDemoBucket: Destroying... [id=demo-bucket-auto-ops-plus-1234]
aws_s3_bucket.MyDemoBucket: Destruction complete after 0s

Destroy complete! Resources: 2 destroyed.
```

Terraform's Strengths

Terraform is a fantastic tool for anyone working in multiple clouds or who just wants a well-supported, well-thought-out tool for use building infrastructure in their native cloud provider. Its strength lies in its balance of flexibility and control. Execution plans make changes transparent before they happen, and its modular design encourages reuse and collaboration. It's a tool any DevOps professional or operations engineer should keep handy.

Azure Resource Manager (ARM)

Microsoft's answer to CloudFormation and Terraform is Azure Resource Manager (ARM). ARM uses JSON for its templating language:

```
{
  "$schema": "https://schema.management.azure.com/schemas/2019-04-01/
deploymentTemplate.json#",
  "resources": [
    {
      "type": "Microsoft.Compute/virtualMachines",
      "apiVersion": "2023-03-01",
      "name": "demoVM",
      "location": "eastus",
      "properties": {
        "hardwareProfile": {
          "vmSize": "Standard_B1s"
        },
```

```
        "storageProfile": {
          "imageReference": {
            "publisher": "Canonical",
            "offer": "UbuntuServer",
            "sku": "18.04-LTS",
            "version": "latest"
          }
        },
        "osProfile": {
          "computerName": "demoVM",
          "adminUsername": "azureuser",
          "adminPassword": "ReplaceMe123!"
        }
      }
    }
  ]
}
```

This example is fairly readable: You can clearly observe that one resource is specified as type Microsoft.Compute/virtualMachines. This VM will have certain configuration values set, such as the `imageReference` that specifies the latest Ubuntu Linux operating system and the `osProfile` section that defines the login information.

However, ARM syntax can get complicated, so in order to simplify the language, Microsoft flexed its ARM and came up with Bicep (get it?):

```
param adminUsername string = 'azureuser'
param adminPassword string

resource demoVM 'Microsoft.Compute/virtualMachines@2023-03-01' = {
  name: 'demoVM'
  location: 'eastus'
  properties: {
    hardwareProfile: {
      vmSize: 'Standard_B1s'
    }
    storageProfile: {
      imageReference: {
        publisher: 'Canonical'
        offer: 'UbuntuServer'
        sku: '18.04-LTS'
        version: 'latest'
      }
    }
    osProfile: {
      computerName: 'demoVM'
      adminUsername: adminUsername
      adminPassword: adminPassword
    }
  }
}
```

This example is similar in length, but notice that Bicep syntax largely does away with the need for quotation marks and reduces the number of required commas, bringing it a little closer to YAML-style syntax and making things easier to read.

IaC as You GUI

One of the nicest features of Azure as a cloud infrastructure provider is that it was built with infrastructure-as-code in mind as a first principle. In contrast to AWS, where you must make a choice as to whether to build with code, the Azure service is constantly creating ARM templates for you as you work. For example, when you log in to Azure through your browser and set through the wizard to create a virtual machine, you'll notice a button on the bottom of the screen that says "Download a template for automation." This link takes you to a screen where all of your choices are encoded as an ARM template, ready for you to download (see Figure 4.5).

This code uses ARM syntax, but Azure command-line tools (largely out of scope for this book) can convert them to Bicep code using `az bicep decompile`.

Similar to AWS, Azure allows you to download templates reflecting existing infrastructure as well. Not only does this give you a way to get started quickly with IaC, but this feature also helps alleviate one of the infrastructure-as-code's initial challenges, which is

FIGURE 4.5 Microsoft Azure creates infrastructure-as-code ARM templates as you work in the web portal.

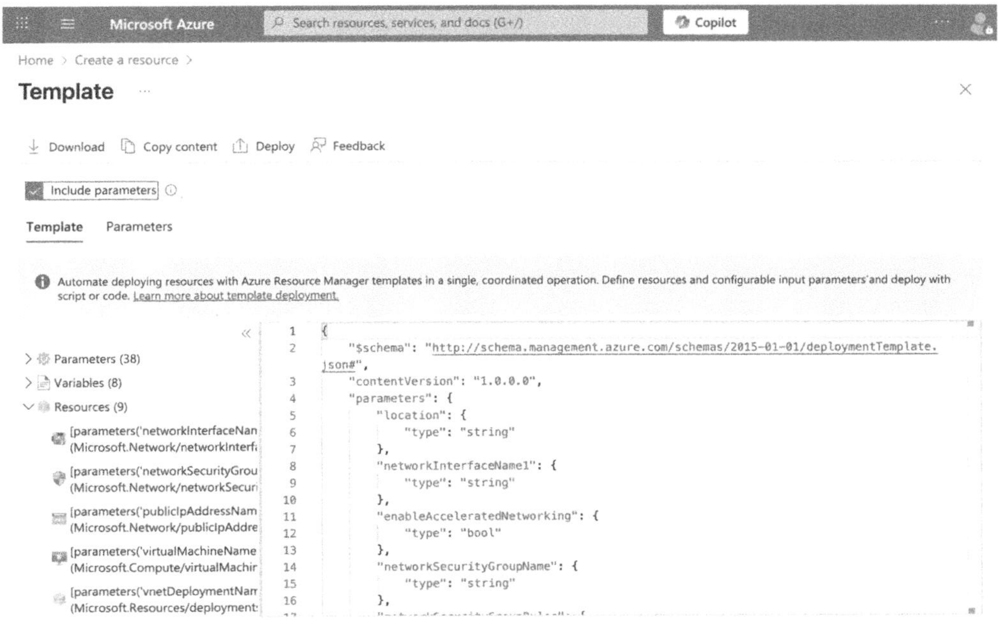

the trial-and-error process it sometimes takes to get a template working. Being able to immediately see working, Microsoft-authored syntax that expresses your choices is a great way to understand how ARM templates work without succumbing to frustration.

Google Cloud Deployment Manager

Google has their own take on IaC for use on the Google Cloud Platform (GCP). Called Google Cloud Deployment Manager, Google's service is YAML-based with all the readability that comes with that syntax. To create an instance:

```
resources:
- name: my-vm
  type: compute.v1.instance
  properties:
    zone: us-central1-a
    machineType: zones/us-central1-a/machineTypes/f1-micro
    disks:
    - deviceName: boot
      type: PERSISTENT
      boot: true
      autoDelete: true
      initializeParams:
        sourceImage: projects/debian-cloud/global/images/family/debian-11
    networkInterfaces:
    - network: global/networks/default
```

By now, you've seen enough IaC templates to recognize a virtual machine declaration with a device type (`f1-micro`), an operating system image (`debian-11`) and a default network interface.

However, Google Cloud Deployment Manager has not gotten the love that other tools enjoy, neither from the community nor from Google itself. It often lags behind in support for new and updated cloud services, leaving you without the ability to build the latest and greatest cloud infrastructure with code. You know the writing is on the wall when even Google's own GCP documents refer users to Terraform, which is often much quicker to implement support for new cloud features. So while Cloud Deployment Manager is an option, most GCP practitioners look to Terraform for their IaC needs.

AWS Cloud Development Kit

AWS Cloud Development Kit (CDK) both asks and answers the question: "What if infrastructure-as-code was more like code?" We discussed earlier how one of the core IaC principles (along with idempotency and reusability) is that it is declarative. Indeed, it is often seen as a strength of IaC that it does not get bogged down in complex logic and variables (use CloudFormation's `Condition` directive sparingly!).

CDK attempts to bring together the best of infrastructure-as-code and imperative languages. CDK lets you code infrastructure in many of your favorite languages, including Python, JavaScript, Java, C#, and Go, using a native SDK with a consistent set of functions implemented in each.

Three Levels of Constructs

CDK defines three "levels" of what it refers to as "constructs." These constitute three levels of abstraction: the higher the level, the more CDK is doing for you.

Level 1 puts all the control in your hands, with Level 1 constructs essentially being language-native wrappers around CloudFormation concepts. They expose all the same resource parameters as CloudFormation, making them just as verbose and just as reliant on you deciding everything.

Level 2 constructs, also known also as "curated" constructs, offer a higher-level abstraction by simplifying the parameters needed to create resources. With Level 2 constructs, CDK supplies default values to many attributes. This is the sweet spot of CDK. For example, in this JavaScript-based snippet, we create an EC2 instance, relating it to an already-created security group and VPC:

```
// EC2 instance
new ec2.Instance(this, 'DemoInstance', {
  vpc,
  instanceType: new ec2.InstanceType('t3.micro'),
  machineImage: ec2.MachineImage.latestAmazonLinux(),
  securityGroup: sg,
});
```

CDK retains a fairly imperative approach, but because you're working in a full-fledged programming language, you get all the power of that language, such as loops, conditionals, variables, functions, and classes. This lets you organize CDK code the way you would any automation script. For example, you might use a loop to create multiple instances, calling a user-defined function around the instance creation, as in this example:

```
// Variable
const instanceTypes = ['t3.micro', 't3.small', 't3.medium'];

// Function
function createInstance(name, type) {
  return new ec2.Instance(this, name, {
    vpc,
    instanceType: new ec2.InstanceType(type),
    machineImage: ec2.MachineImage.latestAmazonLinux(),
  });
}

// Loop
```

```
instanceTypes.forEach((type, i) => {
  const instance = createInstance.call(this, `DemoInstance${i}`, type);

  // Conditional
  if (type === 't3.micro') {
    instance.instance.addPropertyOverride('Tags', [
      { Key: 'Environment', Value: 'Dev' },
    ]);
  }
});
```

Finally, Level 3 constructs are available to let CDK take the wheel and define infrastructure in an opinionated manner. Referred to as "patterns," Level 3 constructs create many related resources at once, often reflecting popular architecture patterns. For instance, use the Level 3 construct `ApplicationLoadBalancedEc2Service` and CDK will create a complete, working web stack, automatically standing up virtual machines, attaching security groups, and wiring them to a load balancer without you needing to stitch those pieces together by hand.

Summary

Infrastructure-as-code tools are incredibly powerful, letting you manage cloud resources with the same tools you use to write automation scripts. In this chapter, we explored how declarative templates mean you have a clearly documented source of truth for your infrastructure—one that you can put into version control and share with collaborators. We saw how managing collections of related resources as a single unit also dramatically improves your ability to stay on top of the complexity of your cloud environments. It's a great choice for any cloud engineer, DevOps professional, or systems automation expert.

We explored key principles like *declarative* design (describing the end state, not the steps), *idempotency* (running the same template twice without side effects), and *immutability* (rebuilding rather than patching). We also saw how IaC tools like CloudFormation, Terraform, ARM templates, and CDK translate human-readable configuration into consistent, automated infrastructure deployment.

Finally, you learned how treating infrastructure like code brings all the benefits of version control—reviews, change tracking, and rollback—into the world of servers and services. In short: It's not just automation, it's automation with discipline.

Once the servers are up, though, you'll need a way to configure what runs on them, keep them patched, and ensure they stay in the right state. That's where the next chapter's topic, configuration management, comes in.

Exam Essentials

Understand what infrastructure-as-code (IaC) means. IaC expresses infrastructure configuration—such as servers, networking, and permissions—as code stored in version-controlled templates. Know that this replaces manual provisioning with consistent, repeatable deployment.

Know the difference between declarative and imperative approaches. Declarative IaC describes the desired end state ("what" the system should look like), while imperative scripting defines the steps to get there ("how" to build it). Recognize examples of each and know that declarative tools like Terraform or CloudFormation focus on state reconciliation rather than command sequences.

Understand idempotency and why it matters. Idempotency means running the same configuration multiple times without producing unintended changes. Recognize that this principle enables drift detection and safe reapplication of templates without breaking running systems.

Recognize the benefits of version-controlling infrastructure. Know how storing infrastructure templates in Git provides traceability, peer review, rollback, and integration with CI/CD pipelines. IaC makes your infrastructure testable, reviewable, and auditable—just like software.

Understand immutability and reusability in IaC. Immutability means replacing rather than modifying resources in place to avoid configuration drift. Reusability means defining modular templates or stacks that can be reused across environments for consistency.

Be familiar with common IaC tools and their characteristics. Understand that AWS CloudFormation, Terraform, Azure Resource Manager, and Google Deployment Manager are all examples of declarative IaC tools, while higher-level frameworks like AWS CDK generate declarative templates through code. You should recognize which are cloud-specific and which are multicloud.

Know the risks and limitations of IaC. Recognize that bad IaC templates can reproduce bad configurations at scale. Understand that IaC requires strong version control and testing practices to prevent errors from being codified and propagated.

Review Questions

1. You've inherited a Python script that provisions a small web stack in AWS using boto calls in a strict sequence. You need to change only the database instance class from `db.t4g.micro` to `db.t4g.small` without risking duplicate resources. What's the best approach?
   - **A.** Rerun the existing Python script; because it's "just code," it will update the database instance in place.
   - **B.** Update an AWS CloudFormation template and apply it using a change set so that only the database is modified.
   - **C.** SSH to the instance and change the class by editing a config file on the server.
   - **D.** Delete the stack manually in the console and rebuild everything with the new database class.
2. Your template should launch an app server only after a one-time database migration completes (the migration is run by a separate process and not represented as a CloudFormation resource). What CloudFormation feature is the most appropriate to model this?
   - **A.** Add `DependsOn` from the app server to the database instance.
   - **B.** Use a `WaitCondition` that signals completion before creating the app server.
   - **C.** Pass a parameter called `MigrationDone=true`.
   - **D.** Export the database endpoint as an output and import it into the app stack.
3. A teammate hot-fixed a security group directly in the console, and you suspect the live environment no longer matches its template. Before updating the stack, what's the most appropriate next step?
   - **A.** Delete and re-create the entire stack to purge the drift.
   - **B.** Run a drift detection, review differences, then generate a change set to preview the update.
   - **C.** Edit the security group again in the console to match "what you think" the template says.
   - **D.** Disable stack termination protection so updates won't fail.
4. You want one reusable template to stand up both dev and prod stacks that differ by subnet IDs and instance sizes. What's the best IaC technique?
   - **A.** Hard-code dev values; copy the file for production and hand-edit the differences.
   - **B.** Define parameters for IDs and sizes; pass environment-specific values at deploy time.
   - **C.** Use outputs so the template picks "dev" or "prod" automatically.
   - **D.** Create two templates and keep them in separate repos to avoid confusion.

5. Your team is building on Google Cloud and needs to provision a new service that isn't yet supported by Deployment Manager. You still want a single, portable IaC workflow across providers. What's the most pragmatic choice?
   A. Stick with Deployment Manager; it always ships first for new services.
   B. Use Azure Resource Manager/Bicep; it's Microsoft, but close enough.
   C. Use Terraform with the GCP provider and community modules for faster support cadence.
   D. Use AWS CloudFormation to generate GCP resources via cross-cloud exports.
6. Which Terraform command displays the changes about to be performed by deploying the current template?
   A. `terraform deploy`
   B. `terraform plan`
   C. `terraform detect-drift`
   D. `terraform init`
7. You've defined an AWS CloudFormation template that provisions an S3 bucket and an EC2 instance. A teammate manually deletes the bucket in the console, but the stack still shows `CREATE_COMPLETE`. What happens the next time you update the stack?
   A. CloudFormation silently re-creates the missing bucket.
   B. The update fails because a declared resource no longer exists.
   C. CloudFormation ignores the missing resource and updates only what changed.
   D. The template's outputs automatically remove any reference to the deleted bucket.
8. In Terraform, what's the purpose of the state file?
   A. It defines the desired configuration for your environment.
   B. It records the current mapping between deployed resources and your configuration.
   C. It stores provider credentials for faster authentication.
   D. It replaces the plan command by showing pending changes.
9. Which of the following best describes idempotency in an infrastructure-as-code tool?
   A. Reapplying the same configuration results in the same infrastructure state.
   B. Each resource is immutable and must be replaced for every change.
   C. The tool supports running multiple environments concurrently.
   D. Parameters are evaluated only once per deployment.

10. Your organization maintains several IaC templates that each define a subset of resources, including files containing resources for networking, application servers, and databases. What's the main benefit of this modular design?

A. Each stack can be deleted only by its original author.

B. It limits the blast radius of changes and simplifies troubleshooting.

C. It eliminates dependency graphs between stacks.

D. It guarantees faster deployment times.

11. A developer modifies a Terraform file to rename an existing AWS S3 bucket. The next `terraform plan` output shows "-/+ destroy and then create replacement." What is Terraform warning you about?

A. The bucket will be updated in place using a rolling restart.

B. The change will be applied without downtime.

C. Terraform must destroy and re-create the bucket, causing data loss unless handled manually.

D. The change won't take effect until you manually delete the bucket.

12. Your CloudFormation template defines two AWS security groups that reference each other: `AppSG` allows inbound from `DbSG`, and `DbSG` allows inbound from `AppSG`. The stack fails with a circular dependency error. What's the most appropriate fix consistent with the chapter's dependency-graph guidance?

A. Use `AWS::EC2::SecurityGroupIngress` as separate resources to define the cross-referencing rules outside the security group definitions.

B. Remove one ingress rule from the initial template, deploy the stack, then add it back via a stack update.

C. Replace one security group reference with a CIDR block matching your VPC range, then update to use the security group reference after deployment.

D. Add `DependsOn` attributes to establish explicit dependency order between the security groups.

13. You're using Azure Bicep to define virtual machines. Compared to raw ARM templates, what's the main advantage Bicep provides?

A. Bicep templates can be executed locally without Azure access.

B. Bicep introduces a simplified, less verbose syntax that compiles to ARM JSON.

C. Bicep supports cross-cloud deployments like Terraform.

D. Bicep is the only Azure tool that supports change sets.

14. You're explaining AWS CDK to a teammate who only knows declarative IaC tools. Which statement best captures how CDK differs conceptually?

A. CDK uses imperative programming languages to generate declarative templates.

B. CDK executes resource creation commands directly, skipping CloudFormation.

C. CDK templates can only be written in Python or JavaScript.

D. CDK is less reusable than CloudFormation because it lacks parameter support.

Answers to Review Questions

1. B. Option B is correct. Use CloudFormation's declarative model and idempotent updates to safely change only what differs; a change set previews impact before execution, reducing risk. Option A is risky because imperative scripts often create or error when rerun out of order. Option C doesn't change the managed service class. Option D is unnecessary and disruptive.

2. B. `DependsOn` (option A) guarantees resource creation order, not external events. Because the migration is outside the resource graph, a `WaitCondition` gate with a completion signal is the right tool. Parameters (option C) don't enforce sequencing, and outputs/imports (option D) wire values, not event readiness.

3. B. Option B is correct. First, confirm and visualize configuration drift, then use a change set to preview exactly what CloudFormation will create, update, or replace. That preserves safety and traceability. Option A is heavy-handed. Option C repeats the antipattern. Option D is unrelated to detecting or reconciling drift.

4. B. Option B is correct. Reusability is a core IaC concept. Parameters let one template be applied across environments by supplying values at deployment. Options A and D fragment source of truth. Outputs (option C) publish values but don't parameterize inputs.

5. C. Option C is correct. Terraform is widely adopted for multicloud and often supports new resources faster via providers and modules, enabling a consistent IaC workflow across clouds. Deployment Manager support lags, ARM/Bicep targets Azure, and CloudFormation (AWS) can't provision GCP resources.

6. B. Option B is correct. The `terraform plan` command displays the delta between the current state of the infrastructure and what will be deployed. Option A is technically incorrect; however, any execution of `terraform deploy` begins with a fresh `terraform plan` being executed. Option C is not a valid Terraform command. Option D is not correct because it is the command used to start a new Terraform project.

7. B. Option B is correct. CloudFormation tracks resources via internal metadata. If a declared resource is deleted manually, drift is detected and updates typically fail until reconciled. IaC tools can't "guess" at lost resources, so the stack must be corrected before continuing. Option A is incorrect because CloudFormation will attempt the creation but fail. It will not silently succeed. Option C is incorrect because the missing resource will cause an error. Option D is incorrect for the same reason.

8. B. Option B is correct. The state file is Terraform's record of what exists in real infrastructure and how it maps to configuration code. Lose it, and Terraform can no longer safely apply or destroy resources. It's distinct from the template itself and should be version-controlled carefully (or stored remotely). Option A is incorrect; this definition fits your template, not the state file. Option C is incorrect because credentials are not stored in the state file. Finally, Option D is incorrect; this is the function of `terraform plan`.

9. A. Option A is correct. Idempotency ensures that applying the same template more than once yields the same end result. Declarative tools like CloudFormation and Terraform rely on this behavior for predictable automation. Option B is incorrect; ideally, your templates will not need to replace every resource when updating a template. Whether they do depends on the nature of the change requested. Option C describes a real capability (nothing stops you creating more than one template simultaneously), but this is nothing to do with idempotency. Option D is a true but irrelevant statement.

10. B. Option B is correct. Breaking templates into focused stacks reduces the risk that a bad update will cascade through unrelated components, making recovery and troubleshooting easier. It also keeps drift or rollback issues more contained. Options A, C, and D are all false statements.

11. C. Option C is correct. Some resource attributes (like virtual machine operating systems) can't be modified in place. Terraform highlights this with a destroy-and-re-create indicator. Always review plans carefully to avoid unintentional destructive operations. Option A is not a real behavior of Terraform, nor is option B. Option D is incorrect because Terraform can, in fact, handle the deletion, as it manages all resources created by the stack.

12. A. Option A is correct. Although we did not cover `AWS::EC2::SecurityGroupIngress` exactly, the point is to find a way to break the self-referencing cycle. These resources define inbound rules separately from the security groups themselves, allowing you to retain the group definitions without error. Extract the mutually referencing ingress rules into separate `AWS::EC2::SecurityGroupIngress` resources outside the security group definitions. Now, both security groups can create first (with no or minimal ingress rules in their properties), then the standalone ingress resources reference them afterward, creating a valid acyclic dependency graph, all in one template. Option B works but requires two deployments and leaves infrastructure incomplete initially. It's a workaround, not the proper solution. Option C creates a security gap with overly permissive inbound rules and requires manual post-deploy cleanup. Option D is impossible—`DependsOn` can't resolve circular dependencies because it only enforces order when a valid creation sequence exists; if A needs B and B needs A, no ordering solves it.

13. B. Option B is correct. Bicep is a domain-specific language that simplifies the syntax of Azure Resource Manager (ARM) templates but compiles down to standard ARM JSON. Option A is wrong because Bicep still needs Azure permissions and deployment context. Option C is wrong because Bicep is Azure-only, not multicloud. Option D is incorrect because Azure doesn't use the change set concept; that's CloudFormation terminology.

14. A. Option A is correct. CDK lets you define resources using full programming languages (Python, JS, C#, etc.), but the result is still a generated CloudFormation template, which means it's declarative at deployment time while being imperative in written style.

    Option B is false; CDK still compiles to CloudFormation under the hood. Option C is incorrect because multiple languages are supported, including Java, Go, and C#. Finally, Option D is wrong, because CDK supports parameters, constructs, and reuse more effectively via code.

PART II

Managing Systems at Scale

Chapter 5

Configuration Management

THE AUTOOPS+ EXAM TOPICS COVERED IN THIS CHAPTER MAY INCLUDE, BUT ARE NOT LIMITED TO, THE FOLLOWING:

✔ **1.0: Automation Coding Concepts**

- 1.1. Given a scenario, use code to support automation.
- 1.3. Explain concepts related to infrastructure-as-code (IaC).
- 1.4. Given a scenario, troubleshoot common issues with the code life cycle.

✔ **2.0: System Configuration**

- 2.2. Compare and contrast basic approaches to automation.

In the previous chapter, we used infrastructure-as-code (IaC) to stand up cloud resources in a predictable, repeatable way. Now we get to turn our freshly minted servers into something useful. How do we go from an out-of-the-box, bare-bones operating system to a system that is patched, hardened, and loaded with the necessary software packages to run your workload? More importantly, how do we perform that task at scale, managing not just one, but many different hosts in our environment? In this chapter, we'll explore configuration management, a concept—supported by tools like Ansible and Puppet—that allows us to provision and maintain servers at any scale, from a few dozen instances to a fleet of thousands.

What Is Configuration Management?

Once upon a time (and maybe still today!) organizations had only a few servers, and those servers were built and maintained by hand. They were given affectionate, nerdy names by their creators and users; indeed, every server-equipped organization, without fail, had a machine called "gandalf." These lovingly configured servers were maintained by another sort of wizard: the system administrator. Things were good, but this is a pattern that doesn't scale well.

As organizations mature, they often run more and more servers, and this bespoke, artisanal approach to server maintenance starts to introduce complexity. It takes a lot of documentation, ad hoc scripting, and individual human memory to maintain increasingly large fleets in this way. Configuration management changes this paradigm. Somewhere around 2012, Microsoft engineer Bill Baker is said to have originated an analogy about server maintenance that persists to this day. Bill urged listeners to treat servers as "cattle, not pets."

The idea of "cattle, not pets" is that you should consider your server fleet like a herd of cattle, managed all at once, instead of like family pets, who receive individual, special treatment. It may sound a bit crass, but the point is that your servers ought to be interchangeable and easily replaceable, not beloved and unique creations. This management of servers at scale is what drives the ideas in this chapter.

Configuration management is the discipline that ensures your servers, virtual machines, containers, and server instances remain consistently configured across their lifetime. Instead of thinking of individual machines, you group machines according to their purpose and role in your infrastructure, and configure them accordingly. As with IaC, configuration management is built around the concept of declarative templates, which describe your desired state, and idempotent execution, which ensures you can run a template multiple times as you update, troubleshoot, or extend it.

Let's take a look at where configuration management fits in the big picture of systems automation.

The "Last Mile" of Provisioning

When you provision infrastructure via CloudFormation, Terraform, or your cloud provider's web console, you get building blocks, such as compute instances, network architecture, security rules, subnets, and load balancers. It's like you've built a building, including electrical wiring, plumbing, and climate control, but you haven't yet filled that building with anything to give it a purpose. The contents of that building are going to look very different depending on whether your goal is to create an office building, a yogurt shop, or a dentist's office.

This is what configuration management does for computing infrastructure. By installing packages, configuring services, writing application settings, applying file permissions, and enforcing security policies, configuration management turns generic compute instances into machines with specific roles to play.

In the world before configuration management, this kind of work was performed either manually or by custom-built shell scripts maintained by system administrators. The latter approach can work very well for provisioning brand-new systems; a remote script can configure users, user groups, packages, and more, but the same scripts are often not as effective at maintaining state over time.

Just as with infrastructure-as-code, configuration management tools let you declare a desired state, then run that template to align the target compute instance with your wishes. It doesn't matter if you run the script more than once; it will bring the target into compliance. Also like infrastructure-as-code, the concept of idempotence makes our lives easier. Of course, achieving idempotence with ad-hoc scripting can be quite challenging. It requires the script writer to think ahead to all the ways that a state might change, and to catch, anticipate, and react to those differences in a way that produces the right outcome. It needs to account for partial failures, missing files, extra files, incorrect permissions, inconsistent package versions, and unexpected service states. Configuration management tools take on that burden for you, letting you focus on defining the desired state while the system handles the details of implementing it safely and repeatably.

Configuration Management in the DevOps Life Cycle

Where does configuration management fall within the larger flow of building, deploying, and running software? Consider the following stages of operations: provisioning, configuration, deployment orchestration, and monitoring. Figure 5.1 depicts this life cycle.

FIGURE 5.1 DevOps life cycle.

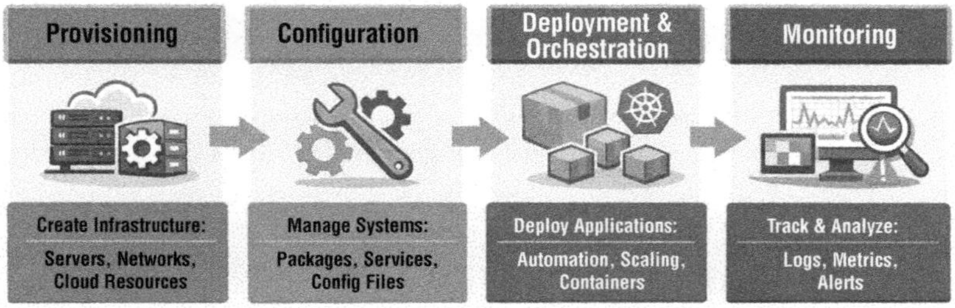

Provisioning

In the Provisioning step, you're using tools like Terraform, CloudFormation, ARM, or CDK create the infrastructure that will run your applications and services. This includes servers, networks, policies, load balancers, and managed services. The provisioning can take place on local infrastructure (either physical or virtual), but often takes place in a cloud provider like Amazon Web Services (AWS) or Google Cloud Platform.

Configuration

In the Configuration stage, we'll use configuration management tools manage packages, services, system files, permissions, app configuration, and OS-level security.

Deployment Orchestration

In the Deployment phase, you'll get applications and services running on the now-configured infrastructure. The concept of *orchestration* is how you do this deployment, as well as manage scaling, failover, and resource utilization on that infrastructure. Deployment may be done with automated scripts or through continuous integration and delivery tools like AWS CodePipeline or Jenkins. For container-based deployments, higher-level orchestration tools like Kubernetes and Amazon's Elastic Container Service decide what runs where within a container infrastructure and scale workloads up or down based on your parameters.

Monitoring

In the Monitoring phase, tools like Datadog and AWS CloudWatch, along with log aggregation and analytics services like Splunk or your own ELK (Elasticsearch, Logstash, Kibana) stack, ensure that everything is behaving correctly, and tell you when it isn't.

It's worth noting that these phases are descriptive, not prescriptive, and that some tools and practices can span multiple steps. For instance, in addition to configuring servers, Ansible can provision cloud infrastructure, and you can use IaC or configuration management tools to deploy code, rather than making deployment a distinct phase with its own toolchain. The right mix of technologies is the one that works best for your workload.

Configuration Management vs. Golden Images

Before configuration management tools were mainstream, teams relied on a few other approaches to achieve consistent system states. One popular method that still has its uses today is to produce golden images.

Golden images are snapshots one can take of a system after it has been fully configured. Whether provisioning was done by an automation or by hand; it's that finished state that a golden image lets you replicate. In theory, golden images ensure identical server builds, because once you create one, you can stamp that image onto a generic machine to produce a clone with minimal effort. In practice, however, they grow stale almost immediately. Plus, reimaging a fleet of machines (or even a single machine) can be fairly disruptive; depending on how the machine is configured or the situation into which it is deployed, you could easily lose user data that has been stored on the soon-to-be-reimaged drive. As a result, systems engineers that rely exclusively on golden images for configuration management may be unwilling to push changes as often as is needed or desired, which can result in unhappy users or insecure systems.

Still, golden images can be an effective, and at times necessary, tool in your toolbox. For instance, some configuration management tools use agents that run on a compute instance to regularly request configuration updates from a central server. Having this agent preinstalled on a machine makes it much easier to bring it into configuration management just as it is built. We'll talk about this "pull model" more in this chapter.

Similarly, golden images can be useful in auto-scaling situations. When you need an instance to come online as quickly as possible, you may not have time for a configuration management script to do its job. Standing up a pre-imaged machine can let you scale much, much faster. In fact, rapid deployment of prebuilt, validated images is one of the hallmarks of container-based workflows, which we'll explore in Chapter 8, "Patterns of Automation Architecture."

Configuration Management vs. Containers

It's tempting to think that container orchestration and serverless functions mean you don't need configuration management. After all, if you deploy immutable Docker images or Lambda functions, how much do you need to manage system state?

In reality, most organizations aren't 100 percent containerized or serverless. Most enterprise ecosystems continue to operate persistent systems, whether on Linux, Windows, or another operating system. These systems are running legacy workloads, hosting databases, acting as bastion hosts, or running builds and tests for deployments. They're your company intranet or your static file servers. Not only that, but even teams using container orchestration are not always running in managed cloud services; rather, they run their own hardware locally or manage their own server fleet in AWS or Azure. Those servers need managing, too.

All these systems need consistent configuration to stay up to date, secure, and running as expected. Plus, if your environment is subject to any kind of audit process, configuration management is your best tool to be ready, helping you demonstrate compliance around file permissions, patch cycles, certificate rotation, access control lists, and more.

Declarative Templates, Desired State

As with infrastructure-as-code, configuration management tools use declarative templates, defining for a server which packages must be present, which services should be running, which files should exist, what their contents should be, and what permissions they should carry. Instead of imperatively telling the tool how to achieve this, you're defining the result and letting the engine take responsibility for reconciling reality with the specification.

Expressing Desired State at the System Level

Declarative templates define the target characteristics of a system. This includes:

- Required software packages and versions
- Configuration files and their contents
- Service state (running, stopped, enabled at boot)
- User accounts and permissions
- Filesystem ownership and mode
- Security baselines and system policies

Rather than writing logic to check and implement these things, you state them. For example, instead of scripting:

```
if ! dpkg -s nginx; then
    apt install nginx
fi
systemctl enable nginx
systemctl start nginx
```

you declare in Ansible:

```
- name: Ensure nginx is installed and running
  apt:
    name: nginx
    state: present

- service:
    name: nginx
    state: started
    enabled: yes
```

This example may prompt a common objection from those unfamiliar with configuration management: Isn't the declarative syntax more verbose? Sometimes, the answer is yes; however, this is not always the case. Configuration management engines like Ansible pack a lot of logic behind the scenes to execute your wishes and preserve idempotency. If you were covering all the same bases in a traditional script, your code might not be as concise. In addition, consider the benefits you gain in readability from a declarative configuration management template: because you are constrained to a certain syntax, your templates are much more consistent (and therefore maintainable) than imperative scripts are likely to be.

Testing and Validating Declarative Configurations

Even though declarative templates handle state logic for you, the templates themselves deserve scrutiny. Syntax errors, inconsistent indentation, or incorrect module parameters can cause embarrassing failures during rollout. Tools provide several safety nets:

Syntax and Lint Checks YAML and JSON are strict, and linters catch subtle issues like extra spaces or misaligned keys.

Dry-run or "Check Mode" For Ansible, this is `--check`. It previews all proposed changes, showing exactly what would be altered without touching the system. Running your updates in a dry run mode before committing to changes is essential for:

- Risky file updates
- Configuration affecting shared services
- Certificate rotations
- Major version upgrades

An example of this output is shown in Figure 5.2.

FIGURE 5.2 Ansible check mode output.

```
> ansible-playbook -i inventory.ini nodeapp.yml --check

PLAY [Configure Node.js hello world host] *****************************************************

TASK [Gathering Facts] ************************************************************************
ok: [localhost]

TASK [Ensure apt cache is up to date (Debian / Ubuntu)] ***************************************
changed: [localhost]

TASK [Install Node.js, npm, and git] **********************************************************
ok: [localhost]

TASK [Ensure nodeapp group exists] ************************************************************
ok: [localhost]

TASK [Ensure nodeapp user exists] *************************************************************
ok: [localhost]

TASK [Ensure base application directory exists] ***********************************************
ok: [localhost]

TASK [Ensure current application directory exists] ********************************************
ok: [localhost]

TASK [Copy hello.js application code] *********************************************************
ok: [localhost]

TASK [Install express dependency locally for the app] *****************************************
ok: [localhost]

TASK [Create systemd service for Node.js app] *************************************************
ok: [localhost]

TASK [Ensure nodeapp service is enabled and started] ******************************************
ok: [localhost]

PLAY RECAP ************************************************************************************
localhost                  : ok=11   changed=1    unreachable=0    failed=0    skipped=0    rescued=0    ignored=0
```

With these tools, configuration becomes safer, more predictable, and easier for new teammates to understand and maintain.

Push vs. Pull Approaches

Configuration management tools vary in style and design philosophy, but most of them fall into one of two operational models: *push* or *pull*. Understanding the distinction is essential, because the model you choose affects scalability, access control, and how you apply configuration updates across your fleet.

At a high level, *push models* send configuration to nodes from a central control point via remote protocols like SSH, whereas pull models have the nodes initiate contact and fetch configuration on their own schedule.

This section breaks down how each model works, explores their strengths and weaknesses, and walks you through real-world scenarios where one model clearly outperforms the other.

Push Models

A *push model* is straightforward: You operate a central machine that initiates configuration runs and sends instructions to all target systems. When you run a playbook or configuration routine, the controller reaches out to your fleet using protocols like SSH and WinRM. The nodes don't need agents running on them; they just listen and respond. Ansible is the most visible example of the push model.

Push models give you immediate control and feedback. When you trigger a run, you see the results right away. Push models are often selected for environments that meet some combination of these conditions:

- Systems are short-lived or ephemeral.
- Updates need to be applied immediately.
- The environment is relatively small.
- Secure, consistent inbound connectivity to each host is available.
- Agents are not allowed for policy reasons.

Push is often the simplest place to start, especially for small teams or mixed environments where you want to avoid installing yet another service or runtime on each node. Figure 5.3 depicts how updates flow in a push model, originating from a central control node that reaches out to target hosts over SSH or WinRM.

As you can see, in a push approach it's important that the centralized server have direct network access to each remote host.

FIGURE 5.3 Push model configuration management.

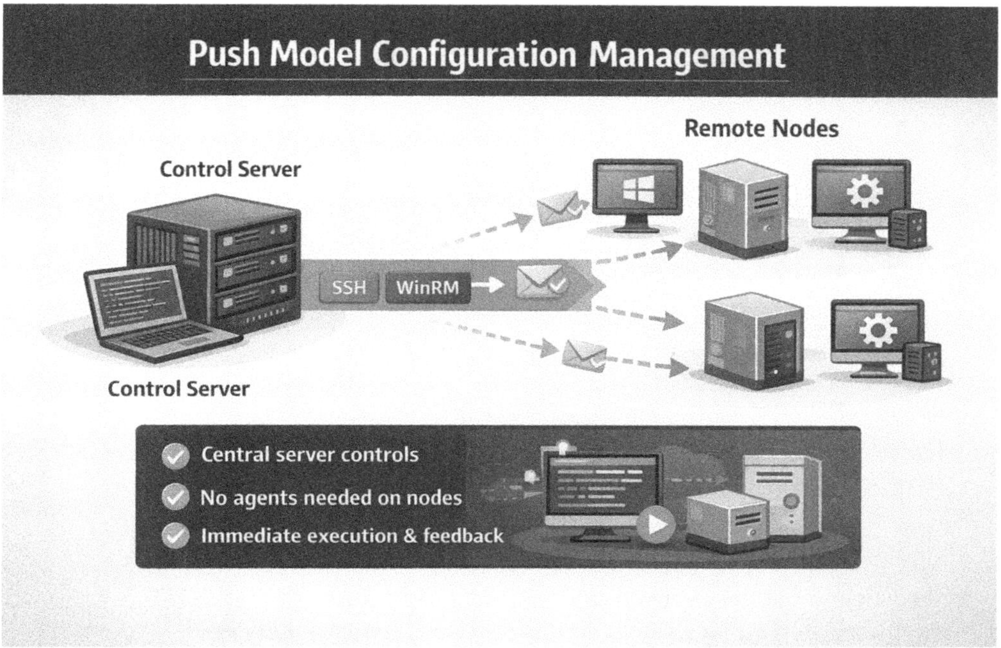

Pull Models

A *pull model* inverts the push approach. Instead of the controller reaching out to nodes, each node reaches out to a central server or orchestrator. The node fetches configuration instructions, applies them locally, and reports back. The biggest advantage of this mode is that unresponsive target machines don't just miss updates; they initiate a pull whenever they come online. While this does offer a lot more flexibility, it comes at the cost of requiring an *agent* to run on the target machine—a software package that must be installed and configured ahead of time (perhaps in a golden image) that checks with a control node and asks for updates.

Pull models decentralize the enforcement of configuration. Nodes decide when to check in, which means they operate more independently. This works particularly well for large or globally distributed fleets where connectivity to every node from a central controller might not be reliable.

Puppet and Chef are pull models by default. A Puppet agent, for example, wakes up on a recurring schedule and checks for updates. If the configuration has changed or if the node has drifted, it applies the necessary actions and records the results in a central reporting system.

FIGURE 5.4 Pull model configuration management.

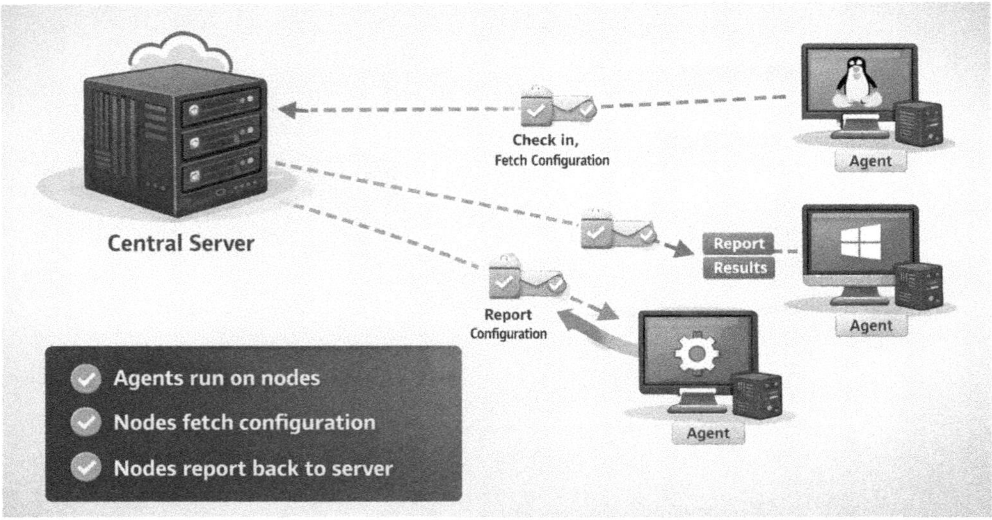

Pull configurations are ideal when:

- You have very large fleets.
- Nodes may come online or go offline at any time.
- You need continuous enforcement without manual intervention.
- The network prevents controllers from initiating inbound connections.
- Long-term scalability is more important than immediate updates.

Pull models encourage a consistent, predictable rhythm of configuration across the environment. If the node misses one check-in cycle, it tries again next time. Figure 5.4 shows how, in a pull model managed hosts request data from the central control node, rather than waiting for updates to be pushed their way.

In a pull model, your environment can change more easily, without the need to update a centralized inventory.

Pull models have unique failure modes, often involving stale or missing agents, misconfigured check-in schedules, or certificate issues. The distributed nature of pull systems means you may need to manually inspect target systems to troubleshoot.

Choosing Your Model

These days, many systems operators choose tools with push models for managing their fleets. The reason is that push not only allows for more immediate feedback, but it also allows tools like Ansible to play more of a role in orchestration, coordinating multiple related or sequential steps to bring up web applications or services that span multiple parts of your infrastructure. Some also find the additional burden of ensuring agents are running on remote hosts makes pull-based tools undesirable. Ansible will continue working on other hosts even when one host fails to respond, and several configuration options let you control its behavior when hosts are unreachable, such as `ignore_unreachable: yes` and the `retries` parameter, which controls how many attempts the system will make.

While pull-based tools are quite viable and still used in many large-fleet contexts, push models are adaptable enough that their benefits may outweigh those of pull-based tools. When starting from a green field, consider the range of work you want your configuration management tool to perform, and choose appropriately.

Drift Detection and Remediation

Configuration drift is the enemy of consistent systems. It creeps in when a server's actual configuration diverges from the configuration you intended. The causes vary: A teammate makes a manual fix during an outage; a package update pulls in a conflicting dependency; an unexpected edge case arises on certain operating systems. Whatever the cause, drift erodes predictability and makes troubleshooting far more difficult.

Drift detection and mitigation helps bring systems back to the declared state, and with our templates, we have a clear definition of what "correct" looks like.

How Tools Detect Drift

Configuration management tools use their declarative specifications as a reference point. They examine the current state of the system, compare it to the declared configuration, and identify the differences.

Typical drift checks include:

- Verifying package versions
- Checking service state
- Validating file contents and permissions
- Confirming user and group definitions
- Detecting unmanaged changes to configuration directories
- Reviewing ACLs or certificate validity

Some tools provide dedicated drift reports or dashboards. Others expose check-only or diff modes that show exactly what would change during enforcement. For example, Ansible's check mode (`--check`) displays proposed modifications without applying them. Puppet publishes compliance reports that highlight discrepancies for each node.

In well-managed environments, you'll run drift detection tools on a regular schedule or ad hoc as needed, taking steps to bring systems back into compliance.

Making Targeted Changes

Server fleets are heterogenous, ever-evolving things. Configuration management helps keep servers looking the same, but sometimes, it's necessary to make some ad hoc changes. That's okay! Having some one-off configurations in your fleet is not a crime, nor is it the same as drift. It could be that your team needs to apply a temporary patch to resolve an outage, or a developer requests some environment-specific logging configuration to troubleshoot a problem. Perhaps a host firewall might require an emergency rule to restore connectivity.

In such cases, you'll want to use the tools of configuration management to make these changes. If you need to tweak a single machine, it's often still better to define host-specific rules in your configuration management tool than to make a change manually.

Resist the temptation to SSH into a machine for a quick fix. If you do, you may find yourself fighting against your well-crafted configuration management system, which might try to "correct" your fix on the next push or pull.

If circumstances don't allow you to do things the right way, follow this pattern:

1. Make the emergency fix.
2. Record what changed.
3. Update the configuration template.
4. Reapply for consistency.

Not following this pattern creates long-term inconsistencies and increases operational risk.

The Goal: Continuous, Predictable Configuration

Configuration management is most effective when drift detection and mitigation happen routinely. Instead of discovering inconsistencies during outages, teams surface them early and correct them automatically. The result is a fleet that converges toward a known-good state, even in the presence of manual changes, environmental differences, or unpredictable workloads.

With drift detection and mitigation in place, configuration management becomes more than a deployment tool. It becomes a safety mechanism that keeps your systems consistent, compliant, and reliable over their entire lifetime.

Survey of Configuration Management Tools

Configuration management has a long history, and while the individual tools differ in design patterns, syntax, and architecture, they all aim for the same outcome: consistent, predictable systems.

The major tools you are most likely to encounter today are Ansible, Puppet, Chef, Salt, and CFEngine. Each brings a particular worldview to how configuration should be expressed and enforced.

Ansible

Ansible is the most approachable of the major configuration management systems. It favors readability and accessibility. Playbooks are written in YAML, it runs over SSH or WinRM, and it does not require an agent on each host. This makes it ideal for small to medium environments and hybrid fleets where agent installation might be difficult.

Strengths include low operational overhead, fast onboarding, and strong community support. It fits teams that want a push-based model with clear, explicit execution. Ansible is an oft-chosen first step into configuration management for many teams.

Puppet

Puppet is built around a robust pull-based model. Each node runs an agent that checks in at scheduled intervals, retrieves a configuration catalog, and applies changes locally. This makes Puppet resilient and predictable at scale. Nodes that miss a check can catch up later, which is ideal for global infrastructure or frequently disconnected systems.

Puppet uses its own declarative language, which has a bit of a learning curve, but one that comes with copious online support. Puppet also has an extensive ecosystem of modules that can support a wide variety of configuration tasks that might not come out of the box.

Chef

Chef takes a hybrid approach. It uses a Ruby-based DSL and has configuration syntax that feels more like programming. This brings significant flexibility for complex or conditional configurations that go beyond simple resource declaration, not entirely unlike how Cloud Development Kit brings a programming paradigm to infrastructure-as-code in AWS.

At one time, Chef and Puppet were the two most prominent configuration management options; however, these days, Chef's adoption rate seems to be declining. Still, Chef has the flexibility to operate in both push and pull modes, and it remains a viable choice, especially for those already comfortable in Ruby.

Salt (SaltStack)

Salt positions itself as both a configuration management tool and a remote execution engine. It supports event-driven workflows, parallel operations, and both push and pull models. By default, Salt's architecture uses "masters" and "minions," the latter of which are agents running on the remote hosts. A persistent connection using queuing system ZeroMQ allows Salt to communicate quickly to many hosts in parallel, making it potentially faster than SSH-based push models.

Its strengths include high-speed orchestration, real-time triggers, and the ability to react automatically to events like package updates or state changes. Salt excels in environments that need rapid response or complex automation across thousands of nodes.

CFEngine

CFEngine is the oldest tool on this list and arguably the most efficient. It uses lightweight agents and a highly optimized engine that can enforce configuration on extremely large fleets with minimal resource usage. Many security-focused or regulated industries appreciate CFEngine for its stability and audit reliability.

Its configuration language is more abstract than others, and the tool is less widely adopted in new deployments, but it remains a solid choice for organizations that prioritize minimal footprint and predictable performance above all else.

Table 5.1 shows a brief comparison to help clarify where each tool fits.

TABLE 5.1 Comparing configuration management tools

Tool	Model	Agent	Language	Best for
Ansible	Push	No	YAML	Small to mid-sized fleets, hybrid environments
Puppet	Pull	Yes	Puppet DSL	Large fleets, compliance-heavy environments
Chef	Pull or Push	Yes	Ruby DSL	Complex logic, enterprise DevOps pipelines
Salt	Hybrid	Yes	YAML-like SLS	Event-driven automation, massive scale
CFEngine	Pull	Yes	CFEngine DSL	High-scale, resource-constrained environments

Choosing the Right Tool

There is no single "correct" configuration management tool. Teams choose based on culture, scale, network layout, compliance needs, and operational norms. A team that loves YAML and quick iteration will gravitate toward Ansible. A team that values continuous enforcement across thousands of nodes may choose Puppet or Salt. A team with deeply customized workflows might prefer Chef.

The important part is understanding the architectural patterns each tool favors and how that approach aligns with your environment.

Common Configuration Tasks with Ansible

To better understand configuration management tools, we will dive into the syntax and commands for one of the space's most widely adopted platforms. Ansible is often the first configuration management tool professionals choose because it is both powerful and approachable. It does not require agents, it uses plain SSH or WinRM to reach systems, and its configuration files are written in readable YAML. Most importantly, you can get useful work done very quickly. This section demonstrates Ansible basics and shows how common tasks map to real, everyday work in operations.

Ansible's workflow has three main parts: an *inventory* that identifies what systems you want to manage, a *playbook* that describes the desired state, and *modules* that apply those changes. You run the playbook from a control machine, and Ansible orchestrates the rest.

Understanding the Inventory

Ansible's inventory is a list of hosts you want to manage. It can be a simple static file with hostnames or IP addresses, a directory of group-specific files, or a dynamic inventory script that pulls from AWS, Azure, GCP, VMware, or other sources.

A minimal static inventory might look like this:

```
[webservers]
web-01.example.com
web-02.example.com

[databases]
db-prod-01.example.com
db-prod-02.example.com
```

Groups (defined in square brackets) let you organize systems by purpose. For example, you might have a `windows` group for patching via WinRM, or an `internal-services` group for identity or monitoring servers.

Inventories can store per-host variables such as SSH usernames, private key paths, or custom ports. They can also be hierarchical, splitting development, staging, and production into separate groups. In more advanced pipelines, inventories are generated dynamically from cloud APIs so Ansible always has an up-to-date list of running systems.

Authenticating to Remote Hosts

The second piece is authentication and transport. For Linux and other Unix-like hosts, Ansible uses SSH. For Windows hosts, it uses WinRM. Most teams adopt key-based SSH authentication, which avoids interactive passwords and is easy to automate. A typical host entry might specify the user and SSH key to use:

```
web01.example.com ansible_user=ubuntu ansible_ssh_private_key_file=~/.ssh/
id_rsa
```

You can also define these defaults at the group level or in `ansible.cfg`, keeping your inventory clean and readable. Ansible will automatically use your SSH agent if one is running, which simplifies rotation and short-lived credentials. For Windows environments, you can configure WinRM with Kerberos or certificate-based authentication so that Ansible has the same single sign-on experience administrators normally rely on.

Inventories and connection settings are what allow Ansible to treat a fleet as a single logical surface. Whether you define two hosts or two thousand, the playbook looks the same. You target a group and let Ansible handle the logistics of fan-out, authentication, and connection management.

Running Your First Ad Hoc Command

Before writing playbooks, many users start with ad-hoc commands to test connectivity or apply quick fixes. For instance, to check available disk space on all hosts in a group called `workstations`:

```
ansible workstations -m shell -a "df -h"
```

Or to ensure a Windows Time service is running across several Windows hosts (assuming an inventory group named `windows`):

```
ansible windows -m win_service -a "name=W32Time state=started"
```

Ad hoc commands are useful for immediate tasks, but playbooks are where you get into actual management of servers.

Anatomy of a Simple Playbook

A playbook applies configuration using tasks, each powered by an Ansible module. A basic playbook might look like this:

```
- hosts: workstations
  become: yes
  tasks:
    - name: Ensure basic troubleshooting tools are installed
      package:
        name:
          - curl
          - git
        state: present
```

This is one of the simplest playbooks you can write, and it demonstrates the power of declarative configuration management template by making sure two critical packages, `curl` and `git`, are always present. The `become:yes` line allows the playbook to use `sudo` at runtime to install packages as root. Run this template a second time, and it'll take no action, unless someone has come along and deleted one of the packages. In that case, Ansible makes sure they both are installed!

Organization with Roles

While a full explanation is beyond the scope of this book (and the exam!), it's worth understanding that Ansible and similar tools allow you to break up and organize templates in ways that help avoid repetition and keep shared configuration in one place, even as you expand to other contexts. In Ansible, the primary means of this organization is the *role*.

Ansible roles are a way to package configuration into self-contained, reusable units that represent a specific responsibility or function, such as "web server," "database," or "monitoring agent." This is distinct from the way that nodes (servers) can be divided up into groups in an inventory. A role follows a standard directory structure that separates tasks, variables, files, templates, and handlers, making complex playbooks easier to read and maintain. Instead of writing one large playbook with everything in it, you compose playbooks from roles, applying the same role to many hosts or environments with different variable values. This encourages consistency and reuse, and it makes it easier for teams to share and review configuration without wading through unrelated logic.

Check the official Ansible docs at `https://docs.ansible.com` for more on how to structure a role folder to separate components in an easy-to-follow way.

Understanding Modules

Ansible's modules are the building blocks that do the actual work in an Ansible playbook. Each module performs a specific type of action on a target system, such as installing a package, creating a file, managing a service, or querying system information. For example, the `package` module lets you install packages:

```
- name: Install Git
  package:
    name: git
    state: present
```

while the `service` module lets you manage the existence and run state of OS-level services:

```
- name: Start and enable the SSH service
  service:
    name: ssh
    state: started
    enabled: yes
```

Modules are defined around domains you'd expect, such as `user` (define and configure users), `group` (define and populate groups), and `file` (upload, modify, or delete files), as well as some that may not be as obvious, like the `git` module, which lets you do things like clone a Git repo. The latter is one of the many indicators that Ansible's authors want you thinking beyond configuration management and more about how Ansible can help manage deployments.

Two notable modules are `shell` and `command`, each of which let you run arbitrary command-line commands. Be careful with these, because they will always run any time the module is encountered in a template; they are not idempotent by default. If you want this behavior, you have to code it into your shell command yourself.

Installing and Managing Software Packages

Installing software is one of the most common tasks in configuration management. As we've just seen, Ansible's `package` modules abstract away distribution differences.

For example, you can make sure `git` is installed everywhere:

```
- name: Ensure git is installed
  package:
    name: git
    state: present
```

This works across multiple Linux distributions as long as the package name is consistent. You can also define environment-specific variables if different platforms use different names.

A real-world scenario: installing cloud provider CLIs for developer environments:

```
- hosts: workstations
  become: yes
  tasks:
    - name: Install AWS CLI
      package:
        name: awscli
        state: present
```

Managing Configuration Files

One of Ansible's strengths is handling file content. Whether it is an application config, a system file, or a script, Ansible can ensure it stays correct and consistent.

Here's an example—deploying a companywide SSH config that strengthens security defaults:

```
- name: Enforce SSH security settings
  template:
    src: sshd_config
    dest: /etc/ssh/sshd_config
    owner: root
    group: root
    mode: 0644
  notify: Restart SSH
```

Using the `template` module lets you parameterize values such as allowed ciphers or idle timeouts.

What's this `notify` directive at the end? This leads us to handlers.

Using Handlers for Safe Service Restarts

Handlers run only when triggered; they are a bit like function definitions. Following the SSH example:

```
handlers:
  - name: Restart SSH
    service:
      name: sshd
      state: restarted
```

Here, we define a handler called `Restart SSH`. Unlike traditional code, it's fine to have a space in this function-like construct's name. As in the previous section's example, other parts of the template can reference this name using a `notify` tag to trigger the handler as needed. Use names that clearly describe the action being triggered.

If the configuration file does not change (i.e., results in a `changed` status), the handler won't run. That's Ansible's idempotency in action.

Managing Users and Permissions

System engineers often need to manage local accounts or groups. Ansible supports this with the `user` and `group` modules.

Here's an example—ensuring the operations team has correct access on internal servers:

```
- name: Ensure operations user exists
  user:
    name: opsadmin
    state: present
    groups: wheel
    shell: /bin/bash
```

This task handles account creation, group membership, and shell settings declaratively.

Starting and Enabling Services

Controlling services is routine for system administrators. For example, use this to ensure a monitoring agent stays active:

```
- name: Ensure monitoring agent is running
  service:
    name: telegraf
    state: started
    enabled: yes
```

This is especially useful when onboarding new servers or enforcing compliance rules.

Understanding Variables and Scope

Variables in Ansible let you write flexible playbooks that work across different hosts, environments, and use cases without duplicating logic. Instead of hard-coding values like package names, ports, or file paths, you define variables once and reference them wherever needed. This keeps playbooks readable and makes it far easier to adapt the same automation to development, staging, and production systems.

Ansible variables can be defined in many places, but scope matters. A variable defined inside a playbook applies only to that playbook. A variable defined for a host or group applies only to those targets. When multiple variables with the same name exist, Ansible follows a particular precedence order to decide which value wins. In general, more specific definitions override more general ones.

Here's a basic example of playbook-level variables:

```
- hosts: webservers
  vars:
    app_port: 3000
  tasks:
    - name: Show application port
      debug:
        msg: "Application runs on port {{ app_port }}"
```

This value applies to all hosts in the webservers group for this playbook only.

Now contrast that with inventory-based scoping. You can place variable definitions in your inventory like this:

```
[webservers]
web01.example.com
web02.example.com

[webservers:vars]
app_port=3000

[webservers_prod:vars]
app_port=8080
```

If a host belongs to both groups, the more specific group variable takes precedence. This allows you to keep a single playbook while tailoring behavior per environment.

Variables are most powerful when combined with templates. For example, a systemd service file might reference variables like this:

```
ExecStart=/usr/bin/node app.js --port {{ app_port }}
```

Changing the port no longer requires editing the service file itself. You update the variable, rerun the playbook, and Ansible handles the rest.

In addition to playbook and inventory variables, Ansible supports role variables, which help keep larger playbooks organized and reusable. Each role can define default values in roles/<role_name>/defaults/main.yml and higher-precedence values in roles/<role_name>/vars/main.yml. Defaults provide sensible baseline values that can be overridden elsewhere, while role vars are intended for values that should rarely change. At the inventory level, group_vars/all.yml acts as a global variable file that applies to every host unless overridden by something more specific. This makes all.yml a convenient place for organizationwide settings such as standard paths, logging conventions, or default users.

One common pitfall is redefining the same variable in multiple places without realizing it. A variable set in `group_vars`, overridden in a role, and redefined in a playbook can lead to confusing behavior if you are not careful. When troubleshooting unexpected values, tools like `ansible-playbook --check` and `debug:` statements (shown above) help reveal which value Ansible is actually using.

Understanding variable scope is essential for writing maintainable Ansible code. When used thoughtfully, variables allow a single playbook to manage many systems cleanly. The key is to define variables at the most appropriate scope and keep overrides intentional and well documented.

A Look at Windows Support

Ansible supports Windows using WinRM rather than SSH. Modules are prefixed with `win_` and handle Windows-specific features.

Here's an example—enforcing password complexity settings across domain-joined Windows servers:

```
- name: Ensure password complexity is enabled
  win_security_policy:
    section: System Access
    key: PasswordComplexity
    value: 1
```

For organizations with mixed fleets, this cross-platform capability makes Ansible appealing.

A Complete Example

Let's pull everything into a single playbook that prepares a server to host a NodeJS web application. This is one continuous playbook example interspersed with commentary. This template assumes that wherever the template is run from, a simple single-file web application exists called `files/hello.js`. Remember, Ansible uses a push model, so this could be run from a local machine connected to a target on a remote host over SSH. The NodeJS app uses the `express` framework, which Ansible will have to install.

```
---
- name: NodeJS Web App Playbook
  hosts: node_web
  become: yes
```

The beginning of the playbook gives a name, and the `hosts` attribute describes the inventory group to which this will be applied: all hosts under the label `node_web`. The attribute `become: yes` means that this playbook is allowed to use privilege escalation—namely, sudo for Linux systems—while it runs. Because this template needs to create users and set privileges, this is appropriate, but make sure to use this only when needed.

```
vars:
  nodeapp_user: nodeapp
  nodeapp_group: nodeapp
  nodeapp_base_dir: /opt/nodeapp
  nodeapp_current_dir: /opt/nodeapp/current
  nodeapp_service_name: nodeapp
  nodeapp_exec: /usr/bin/node
  nodeapp_entrypoint: server.js
  nodeapp_port: 3000
```

This section defines variables for use in this template only. If, for example, you had multiple groups that run NodeJS applications for different purposes, you might move some of these variables out of this template and into shared variables at the role level.

```
pre_tasks:
  - name: Ensure apt cache is up to date (Debian / Ubuntu)
    apt:
      update_cache: yes
      cache_valid_time: 3600
    when: ansible_os_family == "Debian"
```

The pre-tasks section contains directives that are guaranteed to run before anything else. In this case, we're setting some caching parameters that will determine how the apt package module will behave. Note the when attribute that defines a condition: only run this section when the operating system is Debian-based.

```
tasks:
  - name: Install Node.js, npm, and git
    package:
      name:
        - nodejs
        - npm
        - git
      state: present
```

Here, we use the package command, which leverages apt when the host is Linux, applying the pre-task configuration earlier.

```
  - name: Ensure nodeapp group exists
    group:
      name: "{{ nodeapp_group }}"
      state: present
```

```
    - name: Ensure nodeapp user exists
      user:
        name: "{{ nodeapp_user }}"
        group: "{{ nodeapp_group }}"
        shell: /bin/bash
        create_home: yes
        state: present
```

These two sections make sure that necessary users and groups exist.

```
    - name: Ensure base application directory exists
      file:
        path: "{{ nodeapp_base_dir }}"
        state: directory
        owner: "{{ nodeapp_user }}"
        group: "{{ nodeapp_group }}"
        mode: "0755"

    - name: Ensure current application directory exists
      file:
        path: "{{ nodeapp_current_dir }}"
        state: directory
        owner: "{{ nodeapp_user }}"
        group: "{{ nodeapp_group }}"
        mode: "0755"
```

Here, Ansible ensures that certain directories exist, defined by the variables from the `vars` section. Note how task names double as comments describing the functionality.

```
    - name: Copy hello.js application code
      copy:
        src: files/hello.js        # relative to the playbook directory on the
control host
        dest: "{{ nodeapp_current_dir }}/hello.js"
        owner: "{{ nodeapp_user }}"
        group: "{{ nodeapp_group }}"
        mode: "0644"
      notify:
        - Restart nodeapp service
```

Here, you can see how the `file` module copies the application file to the remote host. We could easily turn the `hello.js` filename into another variable to avoid hard-coding.

```
    - name: Install express dependency locally for the app
      command: npm install express
```

```
    args:
      chdir: "{{ nodeapp_current_dir }}"
      creates: "{{ nodeapp_current_dir }}/node_modules/express"
    notify:
      - Restart nodeapp service
```

This is the command module in action, running a shell command to install express. It accepts arguments to set the working directory with chdir. It also uses a notification to restart the NodeJS app. What do you think would happen if the service didn't exist yet? It's not defined until later in this template. Ansible's internal dependency map tries to catch scenarios like this and update its internal order of operations. If it's unable, you might have to run this template again, but Ansible's idempotent defaults would make sure it doesn't run any other commands twice. This particular command, as a shell command, would run no matter what.

```
  - name: Create systemd service for Node.js app
    copy:
      dest: "/etc/systemd/system/{{ nodeapp_service_name }}.service"
      owner: root
      group: root
      mode: "0644"
      content: |
        [Unit]
        Description=Node.js application service
        After=network.target

        [Service]
        Type=simple
        User={{ nodeapp_user }}
        Group={{ nodeapp_group }}
        WorkingDirectory={{ nodeapp_current_dir }}
        ExecStart={{ nodeapp_exec }} {{ nodeapp_entrypoint }}
        Restart=on-failure
        Environment=NODE_ENV=production
        # App is assumed to listen on {{ nodeapp_port }}

        [Install]
        WantedBy=multi-user.target
    notify:
      - Reload systemd
      - Restart nodeapp service

  - name: Ensure nodeapp service is enabled
    systemd:
      name: "{{ nodeapp_service_name }}"
      enabled: yes
```

This relatively complex section defines a systemd service to keep the NodeJS application running. The majority of the text is the content section, which defines a service configuration inline. This is not Ansible syntax, but the file format expected by systemd to define this service. When it's done, it notifies two handlers, defined here:

```
handlers:
  - name: Reload systemd
    systemd:
      daemon_reload: yes

  - name: Restart nodeapp service
    systemd:
      name: "{{ nodeapp_service_name }}"
      state: restarted
```

Now, at the end of the template, we have two handlers that reload systemd and specifically restart the newly created NodeJS service. To run this template, let's create a file called inventory.ini. We'll put a local connection in the node_web group to test.

```
[example_host_group]
web01.example.com
web02.example.com

[node_web]
localhost ansible_connection=local
```

Then, we can save the template as node_app.yml and run this playbook with

```
ansible-playbook -i inventory.ini node_app.yml --check
```

Omit --check to run it with real changes. Once this entire template completes without error, the server will be up and running on port 3000, ready for users to interact with it.

A Closer Look at Puppet

Puppet is one of the most well-known configuration management platforms, and it is widely deployed in large enterprises and compliance-driven environments. Puppet exemplifies the pull model of configuration management, relying on managed nodes to request configuration on a schedule and converge toward a desired state. In this section, we'll take a closer look at Puppet and in the process, gain some familiarity with pull models.

Puppet's Architecture: Agent and Server

With Puppet, each managed machine runs a Puppet agent that regularly contacts a Puppet server. The agent asks, in effect, "What should I look like right now?" The server then dynamically creates a *catalog*, a document describing the node's desired state, which is based on your Puppet manifests, modules, and classification rules.

The workflow is straightforward:

1. The Puppet agent wakes up (on a schedule you define).
2. It sends node metadata (facts) to the Puppet server.
3. The server compiles a catalog tailored to that node.
4. The agent applies the catalog locally.
5. The agent reports back with what changed or stayed the same.

The catalog protects you from surprises. Even if a node gets rebooted, patched, or manually adjusted by an overenthusiastic coworker, the next Puppet run will correct anything that deviates from the declared configuration.

This is a key distinction from Ansible. With Ansible, you run a playbook whenever you want a change to occur. With Puppet, changes occur on a schedule whether you trigger them or not. That difference leads to a different operational mindset, with Puppet environments feeling more "self-healing," because drift is detected and remediated automatically.

Resources: Puppet's Basic Building Blocks

Puppet describes system state using *resources*, which are declarations like "this package should be installed" or "this file should have these contents." Resources are written in Puppet's own declarative DSL, which resembles a blend of JSON and Ruby-like syntax.

Here's a simple resource:

```
package { 'git':
  ensure => installed,
}
```

This tells Puppet: "On this node, the `git` package should be installed." Puppet determines how to make that true, whether by using `apt`, `yum`, `dnf`, or another provider.

Here's another example:

```
service { 'sshd':
  ensure => running,
  enable => true,
}
```

This declares that the SSH daemon should be running and enabled at boot.

Like Ansible tasks, Puppet resources are idempotent. If the service is already running, Puppet does nothing. If it is not, Puppet starts it.

Manifests, Classes, and Modules

Individual resources are useful, but real Puppet configurations organize them into manifests, classes, and modules. A *manifest* is simply a file (usually with a `.pp` extension) that contains one or more resource declarations. As configurations grow, Puppet encourages grouping related resources into *classes* so they can be reused and applied consistently.

Here's a simple class that establishes a basic system baseline:

```
class common_baseline {
  package { ['curl', 'vim']:
    ensure => installed,
  }

  service { 'rsyslog':
    ensure => running,
    enable => true,
  }
}
```

This class can then be applied to a node by including it in that node's configuration:

```
include common_baseline
```

Modules provide the directory structure that holds related classes, templates, and files. A typical module includes manifests, static files, templates, and metadata describing dependencies. Puppet modules serve a similar purpose to Ansible roles, but Puppet enforces a stricter structure and naming convention. This rigidity can feel limiting at first, but it pays dividends in large environments where consistency and predictability matter more than flexibility.

Facts and Conditional Configuration

One of Puppet's strengths is its built-in system for collecting *facts* about each node. Facts include information such as the operating system, kernel version, IP addresses, virtualization platform, and custom metadata you define. These facts are sent to the Puppet server during each agent run and can influence which resources or classes apply to a node.

For example, you might install different packages depending on the operating system family:

```
if $facts['os']['family'] == 'Debian' {
  package { 'apache2':
```

```
    ensure => installed,
  }
} else {
  package { 'httpd':
    ensure => installed,
  }
}
```

This approach allows Puppet to manage heterogeneous environments without maintaining separate configuration trees. Ansible supports similar behavior through facts and conditionals, but Puppet's catalog compilation process makes this per-node customization central to how the system works.

Ordering and Dependencies

Unlike imperative tools, Puppet does not assume resources execute in the order they appear in a file. Instead, it builds a dependency graph and applies resources in an order that satisfies those dependencies. When ordering matters, you must be explicit.

For example, if a configuration file change should trigger a service restart, you declare the relationship directly:

```
file { '/etc/myapp/config.yaml':
  ensure => file,
  source => 'puppet:///modules/myapp/config.yaml',
  notify => Service['myapp'],
}

service { 'myapp':
  ensure => running,
}
```

This relationship-driven model is a defining characteristic of Puppet. It forces you to think in terms of system state and relationships rather than execution steps. In contrast, Ansible executes tasks top to bottom, which can feel more intuitive but places more responsibility on the playbook author to manage ordering correctly.

Running Puppet

Most Puppet interactions revolve around the agent. On a managed node, an administrator can trigger an immediate run with:

```
sudo puppet agent -t
```

The output reports which resources were changed, which were already compliant, and whether any failures occurred. At steady state, most check-ins are going to report "no changes," which is exactly what you want. They will only trigger activity when administrators make changes or to correct drift.

Explore More Puppet

If you want to go deeper with Puppet, the next things to learn are how nodes are classified into environments and roles, how modules are structured and shared, and how reporting tools like PuppetDB surface drift and compliance information across a fleet. Those pieces show how Puppet scales beyond individual manifests to orchestration at scale.

Troubleshooting and Common Pitfalls

Most configuration failures fall into a few known patterns. Once you recognize them, you can fix issues more quickly and design future playbooks or manifests to avoid the same traps.

Inconsistent or Undocumented Starting States

One common source of trouble is making incorrect assumptions about the starting state of your fleet. In this case, you might experience packages missing that a script expects to exist, services running from a previous deployment, or unmanaged directories or files influencing system behavior.

The best way to mitigate this risk is to always start with configuration management; however, it's just as likely that you'll want to apply configuration management to existing, unmanaged compute nodes. If, say, a service is running when your manifest says it should be stopped, the tool will correct that. But when the divergence is too large (e.g., missing dependencies, partially installed packages, corrupted directories), the tool may error out in unexpected ways.

It's best to bring unmanaged systems under control gradually. Start with a baseline that ensures core dependencies and critical directories exist, then layer on more specific configuration once the ground rules are stable.

Order-of-Operations Conflicts

Declarative systems abstract away the need for you to understand precise execution order, but they still have dependency chains. Changing a configuration file before its directory exists, restarting a service before a needed package is installed, or modifying permissions before a user is created can all cause failures. Some tools automatically detect and order these dependencies. Others need explicit hints, especially for dependencies that can't easily be inferred.

Your first run of a new playbook or module will no doubt surface these kinds of issues quickly, but to reduce that first-run error deluge, group related tasks logically and make sure to flag notable order requirements. As you develop your templates, you may want to use an environment that lets you start fresh quickly without much difficulty. Lightweight local virtualization options like HashiCorp's Vagrant can be great for this.

Authentication and Connectivity Problems

These issues are some of the most irritating because they are showstoppers. SSH keys expire; WinRM certificates fall out of sync. Firewalls block access to certain nodes or DNS records drift, and suddenly you can't reach your host at all, in or out of the configuration management tool.

Test connectivity independently of the tool. If SSH does not work by hand, Ansible will not fix it. Automate key distribution and certificate rotation so that authentication is never a manual chore, and of course, use good change control practices so no one is making network changes without a documented reason.

Partial Failures That Leave Systems in Undefined States

Idempotence is a design principle for these tools, but it's not an iron-clad guarantee. If a run fails midway through an operation, you can end up with a half-updated system. This is especially dangerous for stateful services like databases or load balancers.

To help, use small, atomic configuration steps. Avoid large, monolithic tasks that apply multiple changes in one sweep. Roll back partial changes or rerun the configuration until convergence is achieved.

Overuse of Procedural Logic

A common mistake among new users of configuration management tools is writing their templates as if they were imperative scripts. Abusing conditionals, loops, and inline shell commands increases complexity and reduces the predictability that configuration management is meant to provide. This leads to brittle automation that breaks with minor changes in environment or timing.

Make sure to use tool-native modules and declarative resources whenever possible. Commands and scripts should be a last resort.

Summary

In this chapter, you learned how configuration management brings consistency and predictability to systems after they are provisioned. We defined configuration management as the layer that enforces system state over time and contrasted it with infrastructure-as-code, which defines the infrastructure itself. Declarative configuration and idempotency emerged as core ideas: You specify the desired end state, and tools reconcile reality to match it safely and repeatedly.

We compared push and pull approaches and saw how each model affects scalability, reliability, and operational workflows. Push models are simple and immediate; pull models excel at continuous enforcement and resilience across large or dynamic fleets. We also examined drift detection and remediation, exploring why drift occurs and how configuration tools correct inconsistencies to maintain compliance and security.

The chapter surveyed the major configuration management tools used in production (Ansible, Puppet, Chef, Salt, and CFEngine) and highlighted the environments in which they thrive. We then stepped through a complete Ansible example that configured a Node.js application, illustrating inventories, privilege escalation, handlers, and `systemd` integration.

Finally, we covered common pitfalls and troubleshooting techniques, including inconsistent starting states, conflicting automation systems, variable scoping issues, and connectivity failures. Together, these concepts give you a practical foundation for managing configuration at scale and understanding how the exam objectives map to real-world operations.

Exam Essentials

Understand configuration management and its role in automation workflows. Know how configuration management fits after provisioning in the DevOps life cycle and how it differs from infrastructure-as-code. IaC defines resources, whereas configuration management defines the state of the systems themselves.

Know the advantages of declarative configuration and idempotency. Declarative templates describe the end state, not the steps. Idempotency ensures that applying the same configuration multiple times never produces unintended changes. This underpins predictable, repeatable automation.

Compare push and pull models of configuration enforcement. Push systems are centrally managed and immediate. Pull systems rely on agents, scale well, tolerate offline nodes, and support continuous compliance. Understand when each model is appropriate.

Recognize causes of configuration drift and how to remediate them. Drift comes from manual edits, failed runs, or environmental differences. Tools detect drift by comparing actual and declared state, then correct it through idempotent actions or scheduled enforcement.

Identify major configuration management tools and their strengths. Ansible (agentless, push-based), Puppet (agent-based pull model), Chef (Ruby-based), Salt (hybrid and event-driven), and CFEngine (lightweight and scalable) each approach configuration with different philosophies. Know where these tools commonly appear in production environments.

Use Ansible fundamentals for basic system configuration. Be familiar with inventories, tasks, playbooks, handlers, modules, privilege escalation, and how to push files or configure services. Understand how Ansible connects to Linux (SSH) and Windows (WinRM).

Troubleshoot common configuration failures. Be prepared to diagnose issues caused by incorrect variable scope, missing dependencies, connectivity problems, partial configuration runs, unmanaged manual changes, or competing automation systems. Know how to use check mode, logs, and isolated testing to narrow root causes.

Review Questions

1. You've just added a new task to your Ansible playbook that installs an updated version of NGINX. When you run the playbook twice in a row, the second run shows no changes. What key configuration management concept does this behavior demonstrate?
   A. Immutability
   B. Convergence
   C. Declarative drift
   D. Idempotency
2. Your organization runs 1,000 Linux VMs. Each periodically checks in with a central configuration server to retrieve the latest approved policies. No manual trigger is required. Which approach is being used here, and what's one main advantage of it?
   A. Push model, which allows on-demand updates with minimal setup
   B. Pull model, which scales well for large, dynamic environments
   C. Push model, which simplifies auditing and drift detection
   D. Pull model, which avoids the need for agents on each host
3. You need to ensure that the SSH service is running on a group of servers and that it starts automatically on reboot. Which Ansible module is best suited for this task?
   A. `package`
   B. `service`
   C. `copy`
   D. `shell`
4. After a round of emergency maintenance, you discover several servers are running outdated configuration files that differ from your last approved playbook version. What's the best next step to bring them back into compliance?
   A. Rerun the playbook in check mode to detect drift, then reapply it in normal mode to reconcile.
   B. Delete and rebuild the servers from scratch.
   C. Manually edit the configuration files to match production.
   D. Disable the configuration management tool until the changes stabilize.
5. A team insists on manually patching "critical" servers by hand because they fear breaking configurations. As the automation engineer, how should you respond?
   A. Encourage manual patching for all production systems to minimize automation risk.
   B. Explain that manual changes create configuration drift and undermine reliability.
   C. Approve their request since configuration management can't handle updates safely.
   D. Suggest disabling configuration management on those servers to simplify troubleshooting.

6. You're tasked with deploying a configuration change across several web servers. The servers are occasionally offline, and you don't want the configuration to fail if they're temporarily unavailable. Which configuration management approach best fits this scenario?
   A. Push model using Ansible ad hoc commands
   B. Manual updates via SSH scripts
   C. Pull model using an agent-based system like Puppet
   D. Event-based triggers using Git webhooks
7. A configuration management tool runs in "check" mode and reports that two files differ from the desired state. What happens when you rerun it in normal mode?
   A. It replaces the files with the declared versions.
   B. It aborts since the files already exist.
   C. It updates only timestamps but not contents.
   D. It ignores files that have drifted.
8. Which situation best illustrates the "cattle, not pets" philosophy?
   A. You keep a list of each server's hostname and apply patches manually.
   B. You rebuild failed servers automatically from configuration templates.
   C. You SSH into production to tweak configuration files by hand.
   D. You name servers after movie characters for easier identification.
9. You have defined a variable named `app_port` in three different locations: the `role/defaults/main.yml` file, the `group_vars/all.yml` file, and directly within the `vars:` block of your playbook. When the playbook runs, which value will Ansible apply to the managed nodes?
   A. The value in `role/defaults/main.yml` because role defaults have the highest priority.
   B. The value in `group_vars/all.yml` because it is a global configuration.
   C. The value in the playbook's `vars:` block because it is more specific than group variables or role defaults.
   D. Ansible will fail with a "duplicate variable" error.
10. A junior engineer writes a task using the `command` module to generate an SSL certificate. Every time the playbook is executed, the task reports a status of "changed," even if the certificate already exists. What is the best way to make this task idempotent?
    A. Switch from the `command` module to the `shell` module.
    B. Add a `creates:` argument to the task specifying the path of the expected certificate.
    C. Use `ignore_errors: yes` to ensure the playbook continues if the file exists.
    D. Use a `handler` to run the command only when notified by another task.

11. Your company's compliance policy requires weekly remediation of configuration drift across a fleet of 10,000 mixed Linux and Windows hosts. Some hosts are intermittently offline, and others belong to development teams with custom configurations. You need a solution that ensures coverage, minimizes false positives, and avoids disrupting legitimate deviations. What's the most appropriate approach?
    - **A.** Schedule a weekly push-based enforcement job against all hosts simultaneously.
    - **B.** Configure agent-based pull checks with scoped configuration baselines per environment.
    - **C.** Run nightly SSH scripts to reimage any noncompliant servers.
    - **D.** Disable configuration management on development hosts to prevent conflicts.
12. You are using a `template` task to update a configuration file, which includes a `notify` trigger to restart a service. During a run, the template task completes with a status of OK (no changes), but a later task in the same play fails, causing the playbook to stop. After fixing the error and rerunning the playbook, the service never restarts. Why?
    - **A.** Handlers only run if the task notifying them returns a "changed" status during that specific execution.
    - **B.** The `template` module does not support the `notify` keyword.
    - **C.** Handlers are only executed at the very beginning of a playbook.
    - **D.** The failed task automatically flushed all pending handlers.
13. Your operations team manages hundreds of EC2 instances via Ansible. During a large-scale patch rollout, tasks intermittently fail with "Permission denied (publickey)" errors. Investigation shows some instances were recently replaced by autoscaling. What should you do to stabilize automation?
    - **A.** Reuse old SSH keys to maintain backward compatibility.
    - **B.** Implement dynamic inventory tied to AWS APIs to always discover current hosts.
    - **C.** Disable host key checking globally in the Ansible configuration file.
    - **D.** Switch to manual patching for autoscaled instances.
14. Your company's CI/CD system triggers configuration updates using Ansible playbooks. After a recent reorganization, several playbooks began failing mid-run with "resource temporarily unavailable" and "file descriptor limit reached" errors. You discover dozens of parallel runs executing simultaneously against overlapping host groups. What's the most effective corrective action?
    - **A.** Increase system file descriptor limits on the control node.
    - **B.** Serialize playbook execution by host group or implement a job queue mechanism.
    - **C.** Reduce the number of SSH connections per playbook by editing the `forks` parameter.
    - **D.** Run each playbook from a separate control node to distribute load.
15. A financial services company runs regular configuration audits using its Ansible-based compliance framework. Recently, audit runs have begun reporting inconsistent results. Certain servers show compliant one week and noncompliant the next, despite no manual

changes. After troubleshooting and introducing some additional logging, it becomes clear that certain OS package versions differ slightly between availability zones. What's the most probable root cause, and how should it be addressed?

A. Repository mirrors in different regions are serving different package versions; standardize repository endpoints.

B. The compliance tool's drift detection algorithm is incorrectly parsing YAML output.

C. Ansible's idempotency mechanism is overwriting correct versions with cached data.

D. The servers' clocks are desynchronized, causing time-based tasks to trigger inconsistently.

Answers to Review Questions

1. D. The correct answer is D. Idempotency ensures that reapplying the same configuration doesn't alter a system already in the desired state. Option A describes resources that cannot be changed at all. Option B (convergence) is related (systems converge toward the desired state), but idempotency is the specific behavior illustrated here. Option C is not a real concept.

2. B. Option B is correct. This is a pull model, where agents periodically fetch configuration. It scales efficiently across many nodes. Options A and C describe push-based models like Ansible. Option D is incorrect because pull-based systems depend on agents to perform check-ins.

3. B. Option B is correct. The `service` module manages system services, ensuring they're started, stopped, or enabled as needed. Option A installs packages but doesn't manage running state. Option C copies files, and option D executes arbitrary commands, which is less reliable and not idempotent.

4. A. Option A is correct. Running Ansible in check mode (`--check`), or performing the equivalent in other tools, identifies drift safely, then rerunning in normal mode restores desired state. Option B is overkill, option C introduces human error, and option D halts automation, allowing further drift.

5. B. Option B is correct. Manual patching leads to configuration drift and inconsistent system state. Automated, tested updates are safer and repeatable. Options A, C, and D all contradict configuration management principles and weaken reliability.

6. C. The correct answer is C. The pull model lets each node check in and update when available, handling transient connectivity gracefully. Option A's push model fails if a node is unreachable. Option B is manual and unscalable. Option D is unrelated to configuration enforcement.

7. A. Option A is correct. Running in normal (enforcement) mode reconciles system state with declared configuration. Option B misunderstands idempotency, option C confuses metadata

updates with state enforcement, and option D contradicts the purpose of configuration management.

8. B. Option B is correct. Automated rebuilds treat servers as disposable, interchangeable instances. Options A and C reflect "pet" thinking—manual, stateful, and error-prone. Option D is humorous but entirely beside the point.

9. C. Option C is correct. In Ansible's variable precedence hierarchy, playbook vars: override both `group_vars` and role defaults. Role defaults (`defaults/main.yml`) actually have the lowest precedence of all available locations, making them easy to override. Option A is incorrect because defaults are the weakest. Option B is incorrect as group variables are overridden by play-level variables. Option D is incorrect because Ansible is designed to resolve overlaps using a specific order of operations rather than failing.

10. B. Option B is correct. The `command` and `shell` modules are not inherently idempotent; they run every time unless instructed otherwise. When you use the `creates` parameter, Ansible will check for the existence of that file first; if it exists, the task is skipped. Option A is incorrect because `shell` behaves the same as `command` regarding change status. Option C does not fix the idempotency issue; it only ignores failures. Option D is incorrect because a handler would only run if another task changed, which doesn't address the primary need to check for the certificate's existence.

11. B. Option B is correct because agent-based pull checks allow each host to reconcile configuration when online, while scoped baselines accommodate intentional variation across environments. This design scales gracefully and reduces false positives. Option A is brittle and may fail on offline hosts. Option C introduces downtime and risk by reimaging entire systems unnecessarily. Option D undermines compliance and removes the very visibility drift detection provides.

12. A. Option A is correct. Ansible handlers are only triggered if the task containing the `notify` statement results in a "changed" status. Since the template was already up-to-date on the second run, the status was OK, and the notification was never sent. Note that there is a `force_handlers` option you can use to make handlers run no matter what. Option B is incorrect as `template` is a primary user of handlers. Option C is incorrect; handlers run at the end of the play. Option D is incorrect; a failure usually prevents handlers from running at all, rather than "flushing" them.

13. B. Option B is correct. Dynamic inventories query AWS for active instances at runtime, keeping automation synchronized with ephemeral infrastructure. This avoids stale host entries and authentication mismatches. Option A is insecure—reusing SSH keys across hosts violates best practice. Option C bypasses a useful security safeguard and risks adversary-in-the-middle exposure. Option D negates automation's entire benefit and introduces inconsistency across environments.

14. B. Option B is correct because it addresses the concurrency issue directly, preventing multiple instances of the playbook from running at once and overwhelming systems. Option A only postpones failure under load; while raising `ulimits` may temporarily mask symptoms, it doesn't prevent resource contention when dozens of playbooks compete for file handles

simultaneously. Option C can reduce parallelism within a single playbook, but doesn't solve race conditions between concurrent, separate playbooks. Option D complicates your setup tremendously, without resolving the issue, and creates more opportunities for drift and version conflicts.

15. A. Option A is correct. When using regional mirrors or content delivery networks, minor version mismatches can occur if repositories are not pinned to specific versions or URLs, leading to false drift detection. Standardizing repository configuration or enforcing version pinning resolves the inconsistency. Option B would cause parsing errors, not divergent state. Option C is incorrect because Ansible doesn't cache package versions between runs; rather, it queries the current state each time and enforces the desired state defined in playbooks, making this scenario impossible. Option D is incorrect, because while clock drift affects task scheduling and timestamp logging, package managers pull versions based on repository state at query time, not server clock values. Therefore, this cannot cause version inconsistencies across zones.

Chapter 6

Working with APIs

THE AUTOOPS+ EXAM TOPICS COVERED IN THIS CHAPTER MAY INCLUDE, BUT ARE NOT LIMITED TO, THE FOLLOWING:

✔ **1.0: Automation Coding Concepts**

- 1.1. Given a scenario, use code to support automation.

✔ **2.0: System Configuration**

- 2.2. Compare and contrast basic approaches to automation.
- 2.3. Given a scenario, interact with Representational State Transfer–compliant (RESTful) systems to perform create, read, update, and delete (CRUD) operations.
- 2.4. Given a scenario, troubleshoot common issues with system configuration.

✔ **3.0: Continuous Integration**

- 3.3. Given a scenario, analyze configurations to manage basic automation pipelines.

✔ **4.0: Continuous Delivery**

- 4.2. Explain concepts related to application service levels.

In this chapter, we'll unpack a concept that makes the computing world go 'round: the *application programming interface (API)*. When systems need to talk to each other, APIs are the common language between them. When programmers want to interact with an application or cloud service, the API of that service is how they do it. As you're building system automations, stitching disparate systems together to create pipelines and workflows, you'll work with APIs or their higher-level abstractions constantly. In this chapter, we'll start with the broad concept of APIs before focusing on the most common form seen today: the REST API. Let's get started.

What Is an API?

The concept of an API is an old one; it essentially defines any interface to a computing system. But while you may hear people talk about a system or service's API in a generic sense, these days when someone talks about an API, it's safe to assume that they're referring to a web API. Web APIs, sometimes also called *web services*, are interfaces that operate over HTTP and allow you to interact with a remote system, whether to retrieve information, update records, create a new record, or trigger an action. For instance, an API for a weather service might give you ways to fetch the forecast for Lincoln, Nebraska, while an API for a payment service might give you a way to make a credit card charge for a customer's purchase. The nature of the service shapes the API.

SOAP and the Road to REST

In the early days of the web, the dominant API format was Simple Object Access Protocol (SOAP). SOAP APIs typically expose operations as remote procedures, defined using copious amounts of XML text. SOAP is verbose, but those XML payloads adhere to strict schemas, and it was that type-driven design structure that made SOAP a widely adopted integration technology for so long. With SOAP, a request for records on all the dogs in a pet store (the canonical API example!) might look like this:

```
<?xml version="1.0" encoding="UTF-8"?>
<soapenv:Envelope
    xmlns:soapenv="http://schemas.xmlsoap.org/soap/envelope/"
    xmlns:pet="http://example.com/petstore">
    <soapenv:Header/>
    <soapenv:Body>
        <pet:GetPetsRequest>
            <pet:Category>dogs</pet:Category>
        </pet:GetPetsRequest>
    </soapenv:Body>
</soapenv:Envelope>
```

That's the HTTP payload of a SOAP request to the URL `http://example.com/petstore`. The corresponding response might look something like this:

```
<?xml version="1.0" encoding="UTF-8"?>
<soapenv:Envelope
    xmlns:soapenv="http://schemas.xmlsoap.org/soap/envelope/"
    xmlns:pet="http://example.com/petstore">

    <soapenv:Body>
        <pet:GetPetsResponse>
            <pet:Pets>
                <pet:Pet>
                    <pet:Id>123</pet:Id>
                    <pet:Name>Buddy</pet:Name>
                    <pet:Type>Dog</pet:Type>
                    <pet:Price currency="USD">499.99</pet:Price>
                </pet:Pet>
                <pet:Pet>
                    <pet:Id>124</pet:Id>
                    <pet:Name>Luna</pet:Name>
                    <pet:Type>Dog</pet:Type>
                    <pet:Price currency="USD">599.99</pet:Price>
                </pet:Pet>
            </pet:Pets>
        </pet:GetPetsResponse>
    </soapenv:Body>
</soapenv:Envelope>
```

Wordy, right? XML is very HTML-like, in that every element is wrapped by both opening and closing tags, and in XML, intra-tag attributes are used extensively. Still, this very rigid, machine-readable format led to many protocols and standards popping up around SOAP, dictating protocols for everything from response structures to authentication and authorization to security.

This structure and consistency meant an extensive ecosystem of tooling could develop around SOAP, but in the end, SOAP became too heavyweight and cumbersome for its own good, and developers sought a lighter, more agile way of defining server-to-server communications.

Then came REST, taking that lighter approach. With REST, that first call might look more like this:

```
GET http://example.com/petstore/pets/dogs
```

And the response:

```
{
  "pets": [
    {
      "id": 123,
      "name": "Buddy",
      "type": "Dog",
      "price": {
        "amount": 499.99,
        "currency": "USD"
      }
    },
    {
      "id": 124,
      "name": "Luna",
      "type": "Dog",
      "price": {
        "amount": 599.99,
        "currency": "USD"
      }
    }
  ]
}
```

Quite the improvement! REST's more laissez-faire approach to design, along with its reliance on familiar HTTP patterns, made it easy for developers to embrace. Throw in the fact that you can test a `GET` request right in a web browser or with a simple `curl` command, and you have a recipe for wide adoption.

What Is REST?

To understand REST, it helps to understand the concepts behind Hypertext Transfer Protocol (HTTP)—the technology that underpins the entirety of the web. When your web browser loads a website, it's acting as an HTTP client making an HTTP request. That request is composed of a few core elements: an HTTP *verb* describing the client's intent, a target *resource* (usually expressed as a Universal Resource Locator [URL]), and a set of *headers* carrying metadata about the request.

Most developers are familiar with the two most common HTTP verbs: `GET` and `POST`. When you type a URL into your browser and press the Enter key, you're issuing a `GET` request on a resource. When you submit a form, you're usually triggering a `POST` that sends information to the remote server. The verbs describe the action being taken.

Short for *Representational State Transfer*, REST takes these familiar HTTP concepts and applies them to programmatic communication between systems. Rather than inventing new protocols or command sets, REST leans into what HTTP already does well, and in fact, takes advantage of lesser-known HTTP verbs like `PUT`, `PATCH`, and `DELETE` to define a wide array of actions that API users can take on data.

Unlike HTTP, which returns HTML, CSS, JavaScript, and images for web page, REST responses come in the form of structured text—often JSON. In the last section's example, we receive a JSON array of multiple `pet` objects. Other verbs acting on the same or similar resources might retrieve a single pet record, delete a pet that has been sold, or update the details of a specific pet. We'll explore those patterns later in the chapter.

REST was formalized in the early 2000s by Roy Fielding as an architectural style, not a specification or standard. This is both the beauty and frustration of REST: It's deliberately not prescriptive. REST doesn't tell you exactly *how* to build an API, but it does describe a set of guiding principles that tend to produce systems that are scalable, predictable, and easy to reason about. It's flexible and easy to get started—qualities that allowed it to gain rapid ubiquity on the web while also inspiring two decades of arguments about exactly what constitutes "RESTful design." After this chapter, you'll be well equipped to join the debate yourself!

REST's Role in Automation

In continuous delivery pipelines, infrastructure provisioning, monitoring systems, and cloud platforms, REST APIs are the connective tissue. When you trigger a deployment, rotate a secret, create a virtual machine, or query system health, you're almost certainly talking to a RESTful API behind the scenes.

In fact, to understand how foundational web APIs are, it's worth connecting the idea of web services to the name Amazon Web Services (AWS). The genesis of AWS, Amazon's multi-billion-dollar cloud platform that underpins a large chunk of the world's computing infrastructure, can be traced to founder Jeff Bezos's mandate circa 2002 that all computing services being developed in-house to support their retail website must be built in an API-first manner. Bezos dictated that if a team created a service (such as early AWS components Simple Queuing Service and Simple Storage Service), it must have a web service interface that allowed other teams and systems to invoke its functionality remotely. It is this simple, yet powerful, idea that led to one of the world's most essential computing services.

Once you're comfortable with REST's core ideas, you can interact with nearly any modern platform using the same mental model and the same small set of tools. That consistency is what makes REST a foundational part of automation work. Let's dig into what makes an API a REST API.

Understanding REST Design

REST is designed to standardize how systems communicate and exchange data over a network. By adhering to a set of core philosophies, RESTful APIs provide a scalable and flexible foundation for modern web applications and automation tools.

Clients and Servers

REST assumes a clear separation between clients and servers. A client makes requests; a server responds to them. That's it. The client doesn't care how the server stores data, and the server doesn't care how the client presents it.

This separation is what allows automation tools to thrive. Your shell script or configuration management tool is just another client. Whether it's talking to AWS, GitHub, a monitoring system, or an internal service, the relationship stays the same: send a request, get a response.

Clients come in many forms; we'll talk about the most common ones later in this chapter, which include command-line tools and purpose-built client software.

APIs' Relationship to SDKs

There are also many abstractions that make working with APIs easier. For instance, when you use a language-specific SDK for a cloud service, like the Python library `boto` for Amazon Web Services, you are working with a Python-native wrapper around the underlying REST API. Additionally, when defining user or role permissions in AWS, you create Identity and Access Management policies that refer directly to API actions. This applies in similar ways to Azure, Google Cloud Platform (GCP), and other cloud providers. The REST foundations of today's cloud computing infrastructure are never far from the surface.

Actions Are Verbs

Generally, well-constructed RESTful APIs adhere to the following usage patterns with HTTP *verbs*, also called *methods*:

- `GET` retrieves a resource.
- `POST` creates a new resource.
- `PUT` replaces a resource.
- `PATCH` modifies part of a resource.
- `DELETE` removes a resource.

This isn't to say that RESTful API design decisions are always easy. What if you want to retrieve a report that takes five minutes to compile (longer than the typical web request timeout)? Do you `GET` that report or `POST` a request for a report? What if you don't wish to permanently delete database records, but instead soft-delete them by setting a `deleted` or `inactive` attribute on the record? Is that best expressed with a `DELETE` verb or a `PATCH`? REST is full of these kinds of trade-offs.

API designers can spend a lot of time striving for REST perfection, but as long as you are consistent in your approach across all your *endpoints* (verb + URL combinations) and document thoroughly, you'll be in great shape. As a consumer, make sure to read carefully to understand the behavior of an API before using it, lest you run into unexpected side effects.

Resources Are Nouns

A common mistake when designing REST APIs is thinking in terms of actions instead of resources. REST flips that mental model around. In REST, URLs identify nouns, not verbs. The verb comes from HTTP itself.

Avoid this:

```
POST /createUser
POST /deleteUser
```

and instead, let the verbs act on resources defined as nouns:

```
POST /users
DELETE /users/42
```

The second example is compatible with the REST philosophy. The URL describes the resource (`/users`), while the HTTP verb describes what you want to do with it. This separation of concerns leads to APIs that are more consistent and easier to explore.

This isn't to say that you won't see functionally RESTful APIs break this rule (at which point I'd argue that they are HTTP APIs and not really REST), but the most professional and well-structured APIs will adhere to this design principle.

Another point of RESTful pedantry is whether resource nouns should be singular or plural. Personally, I find plural to make the most sense (`GET /orders` sounds like a more complete sentence than `GET /order`), but it's down to your preference. Just make sure you stay consistent so that your users will always know what to expect.

Hierarchical Resources

One of the nice benefits of using the tried-and-true URL to name resources in a REST API is the ability to speak in terms of hierarchy. Imagine an API that returns information about college courses. The API might define the following:

- `GET /courses`, which returns all courses
- `GET /courses/{courseID}`, which returns the details of a specific course

If we were to call `GET /courses/ACCT101`, we might get a payload like this:

```
{
  "course_id": "ACCT101",
  "title": "Introduction to Accounting",
  "term": "Fall 2027",
  "credits": 3,
  "instructor": {
    "id": "u123",
    "name": "Dr. Elaine Porter"
  },
  "students": [
    {
      "student_id": "s456",
      "name": "Alex Martinez",
      "status": "enrolled"
    },
    {
      "student_id": "s789",
      "name": "Jordan Kim",
      "status": "enrolled"
    }
  ]
}
```

Just as user interface designers need to think about user interactions, API designers need to think about user experience. In this case, you can easily imagine wanting to "drill in" to fetch just the students in a class. The API design can leverage the ability to define resources hierarchically and allow a different endpoint:

```
GET /courses/{courseId}/students
```

This endpoint would return just this part:

```
[
    {
      "student_id": "s456",
      "name": "Alex Martinez",
      "status": "enrolled"
    },
    {
      "student_id": "s789",
      "name": "Jordan Kim",
      "status": "enrolled"
    }
  ]
```

At the same time, this API probably also should have a `GET /students/{studentId}` endpoint, which will return a much more detailed representation of a particular student. As you can see, there are many design decisions implicit in an API's interface.

Stateless Interactions

One of REST's most important constraints is statelessness. Each request from a client to a server must contain all the information the server needs to understand and fulfill it. The server doesn't rely on stored session state from previous requests.

Stateless APIs are easier to scale, easier to retry safely, and easier to troubleshoot. If a request fails, you don't need to reconstruct some invisible conversational context—you just look at the request and the response.

This property also fits neatly with automation patterns like retries, parallel execution, and idempotent operations, all of which show up frequently in automation and continuous integration/deployment systems.

Parameters

As you've probably noticed in the examples so far, APIs can be designed with parameters whose values are filled in by the client. There are two major ways that APIs accept parameters: the URL and the query string.

URL Parameters

A REST API endpoint is a unique combination of HTTP verb and resource URL. For instance, `GET /pets/123` and `DELETE /pets/123` are two endpoints with distinct identities: the former fetches information about the pet with ID 123, while the latter deletes the record. What about these two endpoints?

- `GET /pets/123`
- `GET /pets/456`

These two requests refer to the same endpoint; however, part of the resource URL is a *parameter*. Parameters in APIs are much like those in shell script arguments: they are variables whose values can be set to change the output or behavior of the service or script being called. In this case, the ID of the pet is a parameter. The documentation of the API might look like this:

```
GET /pets/{petID}
```

Those curly braces let you know that `petID` is a value for the client to fill in. Because they are part of the URL, these kinds of parameters are known as *URL parameters* or *path parameters*. However, you may encounter a different kind of parameter.

Query Parameters

Query parameters are those defined in key-value pairs after a URL. If you've ever used Google (say, to search "bananas"), you have seen query parameters in action:

```
https://www.google.com/search?q=bananas
```

Your search term comes after the URL, then a question mark. The key is `q` (in this case, for "query") and the value is `bananas`. Multiple query parameters may be separated by an ampersand (`&`).

The specific design of a REST API is always left to the implementation team, but often, URL parameters are used for those things that are part of the resource definition (i.e., when you want to "drill down" into a resource collection), whereas query parameters are for filtering. This is definitely not a hard-and-fast rule. Here's an example:

```
GET /courses/2027/fall?subject=ACCT&credit_hours=3
```

In this endpoint, `/2027/fall` are two URL parameters indicating the year and term, respectively. Calling `GET /courses/2027` would return all courses for 2027 and `GET /courses/2027/fall` returns all the courses for fall 2027. The API implementation also allows us to filter, so we provide two query parameters to filter the response to only those Fall 2027 classes that have the subject code `ACCT` for Accounting and that confer 3 credit hours.

Headers, Payloads, and Data Formats

Stored as HTTP *headers*, REST headers are key-value pairs that describe the request or response without being part of the resource itself.

Request headers are metadata that tell the server things like:

- How the client is authenticated
- What data formats it understands
- What kind of content it's sending

Response headers tell the client things like:

- The format of the returned data
- Caching behavior
- Rate limit information

Headers are especially important in automation because they often control authentication, versioning, and behavior that isn't obvious from the URL alone.

Authorization

The `Authorization` request header carries API keys, tokens, or credentials. A common form of authentication for APIs involves using this header to pass a *bearer token*. This is called *token-based authentication* and it shows up everywhere from cloud provider APIs to

CI/CD platforms. The value of the token may be a long-lived API key, but more often it's a short-lived token obtained through an authentication flow such as OAuth. An example of this header might look like this:

```
Authorization: Bearer ABCDEF123456
```

Note that the word `Bearer`, followed by a space, is just part of the value of the Authorization key-value pair. This is the de facto standard for bearer tokens.

Content-Type

`Content-Type` describes the format of the request body being sent to the server. This would be used with `POST`, `PATCH`, or `PUT` requests, since they may all contain an HTTP payload (i.e., the contents of a new or updated record). When you send JSON, this header is typically set to `application/json`. Without this value, the server may not know how to parse the payload at all, even if the body itself looks valid. Many REST errors trace back to a missing or incorrect `Content-Type` header.

Accept

`Accept` tells the server which response formats the client can handle. While most modern APIs default to JSON, some support multiple formats (e.g., XML). By explicitly setting `Accept`, the client can be explicit about which return format it is requesting and expecting.

User-Agent

`User-Agent` identifies the client making the request. Browsers set this automatically, but command-line tools and scripts often set a generic value, if it is set at all. Some APIs use `User-Agent` values for logging, debugging, or rate limiting, and others require one to be present. This value can be useful for API (or website) administrators looking to understand the makeup of their traffic or isolate issues to particular clients.

Misconfigured headers are one of the most common causes of API failures. When in doubt, inspect the headers.

Payloads and Message Bodies

The payload (or message body) contains the actual data being sent to the server. `GET` requests usually don't have one, but `POST`, `PUT`, and `PATCH` almost always do. For instance, using `curl`, we might define a new pet for a pet store API like so:

```
curl -X POST https://api.example.com/pets \
     -H "Content-Type: application/json" \
     -d '{
            "name": "Dodger",
            "species": "dog",
            "age": 2
        }'
```

We'll get more into `curl` shortly, but for now, notice that we explicitly name the `POST` verb, give the resource URL, and then set a `Content-Type` header to `application/json`. Finally, the `-d` flag lets us pass in a JSON-formatted pet definition. This definition format will vary; it is up to the API implementors to define and document what the API expects.

JSON and YAML Usage

As you've seen, JSON is the dominant format for REST APIs. It's compact, language-agnostic, and well supported by tooling (like `jq`) across every ecosystem you're likely to use.

YAML shows up less often in REST APIs themselves, but it's extremely common in configuration files, request templates, and infrastructure definitions, and is sometimes an option offered by an API in its `Accept` header. For automation work, it's important to be fluent in both.

Understanding REST Responses

Sending a REST request is only half the story. Every request receives a response of some kind that either returns data, conveys the results of a request, or informs you of an error.

A REST response is made up of three main pieces: a status code, headers, and (often) a response body.

Response Bodies

The response body contains the representation of the resource you asked for, or sometimes, a description of what went wrong. In most modern APIs, this body is JSON.

For example, a successful `GET /user/123` request might return something like this:

```
{
  "id": 42,
  "username": "alice",
  "role": "admin",
  "active": true
}
```

A failed request may still return a body, but instead of data, it contains error details:

```
{
  "error": "Unauthorized",
  "message": "Missing or invalid API token"
}
```

Note that whether an API returns such information is down to the implementor's choice: REST is not prescriptive, for better or for worse! What is more consistently implemented is the HTTP status code.

Understanding Status Codes

Every HTTP request returns a status code. You're probably familiar with the most widely used codes: `200 OK` for a successful request or `404 Not Found` for a missing resource. You can encounter the latter simply by mistyping a URL while browsing the web.

There are many more status codes defined by the HTTP specification, and a well-designed RESTful API will take full advantage of them to communicate clearly to clients what is happening inside the API.

Good automation logic will always check the status code of an API request first. If the code signals failure, there's no point trying to parse response body fields that may not exist.

Here's a simple example using `curl` and a shell script:

```
response=$(curl -s -o response.json -w "%{http_code}" https://api.example.com/
users/42)

if [ "$response" -eq 200 ]; then
  echo "User retrieved successfully"
else
  echo "Request failed with status $response"
fi
```

At a minimum, you always want to check for either a `200` or `not 200` response, but your automation scripts will be much more robust if you understand and handle a wider range of possible response codes. Let's take a look at what those are.

Status Code Categories

HTTP status codes are grouped into broad categories. You don't need to memorize every individual code, but you do need to understand what each category signals.

Always remember that, as with the design principles of REST, the use of HTTP status codes can vary. You can and will encounter APIs that return a `200 OK` no matter what, whether for success, missing resources, server errors. You'll see APIs use `GET` for delete operations or that expect tokens passed as URL parameters instead of `Authorization` headers. If you're lucky, this behavior is at least documented! Always be on the lookout for variances in API behavior, even across endpoints within a single API. Still, the status codes do have meanings prescribed by the HTTP spec, even if they leave some room for interpretation.

200: Success

Codes in the 200–299 range mean the request succeeded.

`200 OK` means the request completed successfully—the most common and satisfying of response codes!

`201 Created` indicates that a new resource was created. It's often used as a thumbs-up when you `POST` a new record.

`204 No Content` means success, but with no response body. It may be used interchangeably with `201 Created`, or possibly as confirmation of an action like `PUT` or `DELETE`.

300: Redirection

Codes between 300 and 399 indicate redirection. Redirects are more common on the web, but they may still occur in API contexts.

`301 Moved Permanently` means the requested resource has a new permanent URL, and clients should update any stored links or bookmarks to use the new location going forward.

`302 Found` is another type of redirect that may indicate a temporary relocation of a resource.

`304 Not Modified` is used for `GET` requests; it's a signal that the remote resource has not changed since a previous request and that the client should use its local cached copy.

Most REST clients and libraries follow redirects automatically. When writing low-level scripts, though, unexpected redirects can indicate misconfigured endpoints or deprecated URLs.

400: Client Errors

Codes in the 400–499 range mean the request was invalid in some way. These are client-side errors, meaning they happened on your side and you need to fix them.

`400 Bad Request` is a very common API error. It indicates malformed or invalid input, usually in the construction of a payload body. Double-check the API documentation to see what the API expects.

`401 Unauthorized` is another very common error indicating missing or invalid authentication. Either you forgot to add your `Authorization` header or the API key, your key is invalid, or you just don't have access to this particular resource.

`403 Forbidden` means you authenticated but the specific request is not allowed. For instance, you might be able to do `GET /pets/123` to see a pet record, but you're not allowed to `POST /pets/123/price` to change the price.

`404 Not Found` is the classic "resource doesn't exist" message.

In general, a 400-range error means you need to update your request and try again.

500: Server Errors

Codes from 500 to 599 indicate a failure on the server side. A response in this range doesn't mean you're out of options, but more often than not, it's someone else's fault. Here are two of the most common 500-style errors:

`500 Internal Server Error` is the generic "something went wrong" message. Servers will often use this as a default response when an exception occurs. Better-designed APIs will get more specific or provide details in the response body.

`502 Bad Gateway` relates to networking or request handling issues on the server side, usually to do with some proxy failing to get a response from an upstream server. This one is common in reverse-proxy setups (i.e., using nginx or Apache in front of an API) when the proxy is offline or unable to pass the request on to the backend.

Server-side errors are often transient. Automation systems frequently implement retries or backoff strategies when they encounter 500 responses.

Rate Limiting and Throttling

Many APIs enforce rate limits, whether it's on requests per minute, hour, or day. When a client hits those limits, they'll most often see `429 Too Many Requests`, or possibly `403 Forbidden` with a rate-limit message in the body or headers.

Good automation code respects limits. Your scripts should watch for these rate limit signals and implement retries with exponential backoff, an algorithm that steadily increases the time between retries to avoid triggering further blocks or penalties.

Authentication and Authorization

Every API needs a robust security layer around it. The kinds of APIs we encounter in systems automations can create resources, wipe databases, or spin up expensive infrastructure in seconds. These are powerful interfaces, often exposed directly to the public Internet, so they require strong guardrails.

Before our automation scripts can do anything useful with an API, they have to answer two questions for the server:

1. Who are you? (Authentication)
2. What are you allowed to do? (Authorization)

Clients make assertions about their identity through an authentication scheme, while authorization occurs when the service determines whether your requested action is allowed.

Who Are You?

APIs must be able to distinguish a legitimate request from a malicious actor, especially since they are so often accessible over the public Internet, where any person or system might attempt a request. Authentication allows the server to associate a request with a specific *principal*, or user identity. That could be an individual, a service account, or a containerized application. Mechanisms for this vary, but two common methods are *API key authentication* and *token-based authentication.*

Both types of values are usually passed in the request header, keeping the credentials out of the URL (where they could be logged by proxies) and the payload.

An *API key* is essentially a long-lived password for a service:

```
curl -H "Authorization: ApiKey abc123xyz" \
     https://api.example.com/pets
```

Although using a header is best practice (and the approach you should take, should you ever build your own API), it is not uncommon, especially in older systems, to see the API key required to be a query parameter.

Handling Short-Lived Tokens

Tokens (specifically bearer tokens or JWTs) are more sophisticated than API keys. They often include metadata like expiration dates or specific "scopes" (permissions) and are passed in the `Authorization` header with the word `Bearer` preceding the token.

```
curl -H "Authorization: Bearer eyJhbGciOi..." \
     https://api.example.com/pets
```

These tokens are usually obtained from an identity provider from an OAuth flow, the mechanics of which are outside the scope of this book.

Know that in many OAuth schemes, tokens are temporary, and must periodically be re-fetched from the identity provider. This behavior is more secure than having a long-lived API key, which, if compromised, stays useful to the attacker until you discover the breach. Short-lived (or *ephemeral*) keys are only useful for a short time, which helps keep your data safe. However, it does mean that your automation scripts need to take this into account.

FIGURE 6.1 Handling ephemeral key expirations.

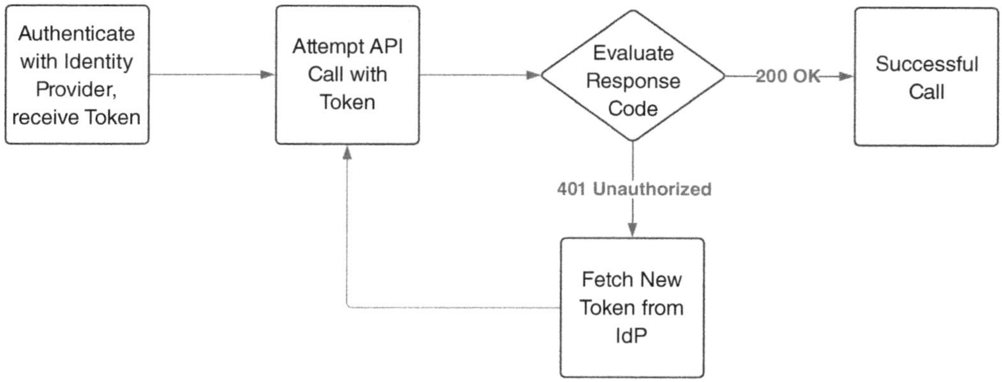

A common approach would be to wrap your API calls in a function that attempts the API call, but also watches for a status code that indicates an expired key. If this occurs, your code can fetch a fresh key and try again. Figure 6.1 depicts this logic flow.

Whether they are keys, tokens, or some other credential, these values are secrets that should never be hard-coded into your scripts. In a production pipeline, inject these via environment variables or fetch them from a dedicated secret manager, which we'll discuss in the next chapter.

Understanding Failure States

When authentication or authorization fails, the API's HTTP status codes should tell you what happened:

`401 Unauthorized` means the server doesn't know who you are. This usually means your token is missing or expired, or that you've got a typo in your header.

`403 Forbidden` typically means the server knows who you are, but you don't have permission to perform that specific action.

If you get a `401`, check your credentials. If you get a `403`, your credentials are fine, but you need to update your IAM policy or user permissions.

Interacting with REST from the Command Line

Now that you've seen a bit about how REST APIs work, how do we interact with them? As mentioned previously, `GET` requests are the standard mode of web browsers, so any `GET` endpoint can be tested in Chrome, Firefox, or Safari. For automation and scripting purposes, developers and systems administrators will reach for some more programmer-friendly tools.

curl

`curl` is the developer's go-to tool for testing web addresses, retrieving web-based install scripts, and talking to APIs. It's installed almost everywhere, supports every HTTP method you care about, and exposes nearly every part of the request and response.

A simple `GET` request looks like this:

```
curl https://api.example.com/users/42
```

Add headers for authentication, in this case, incorporating environment variables from the shell:

```
curl -H "Authorization: Bearer $API_TOKEN" \
     https://api.example.com/users/42
```

Send a `POST` request with a JSON payload (as in the example given earlier):

```
curl -X POST https://api.example.com/users \
     -H "Content-Type: application/json" \
     -d '{
"username":"alice",
"role":"admin"
}'
```

This syntax gets very cumbersome when your `POST` body is sufficiently large (which can happen quickly). `curl` allows you to point to a file instead of defining the body JSON in quotes on the command line. If you save your JSON as a file (e.g., `user.json`), you can run the previous command like this:

```
curl -X POST https://api.example.com/users \
     -H "Content-Type: application/json" \
        -d @user.json
```

The `-X` flag lets you define the HTTP verb, which a REST client will need to do frequently. `GET` is the default, but it's not a bad practice to always explicitly call out your intended verb.

Also by default, `curl` prints the response body to standard output, but using the `-o` flag lets you direct the output to a file. In this case, we route the output to a file called `user.json`:

```
curl -o user.json https://api.example.com/users/42
```

The verbose flag `-v` shows the full request and response exchange, including headers sent by both sides:

```
curl -v https://api.example.com/users/42
```

Of course, when interacting with REST URLs that return JSON, `curl` pairs naturally with tools like `jq`:

```
curl -s https://api.example.com/users/42 | jq -r '.username'
```

That one line fetches a resource, parses the JSON, and extracts the username value.

wget

`wget` is often thought of as a file-downloading tool, and that's largely how it's used. It's best used for retrieving files, not for crafting complex API requests.

That said, `wget` can interact with REST endpoints, especially for simple `GET` requests:

```
wget https://api.example.com/users/42
```

It also supports headers and authentication, but for REST, its requests are clunkier than just using `curl`.

Interacting with REST from Scripts

In practice, many of your interactions with REST APIs will be from automation scripts that you write.

Via Bash

When writing shell scripts in Bash, you'll be invoking `curl` to interact with any REST endpoint. You can capture both the response body and the HTTP status code and act on them explicitly.

However, recall that `curl` typically sends the response body to standard output (the console). Because we want *both* the body and response code, we need to be a little clever with how we invoke `curl`.

We can get the output to be just the response code by passing the argument `-w "%{http_code}"`. This syntax (standing for "write out") lets you extract metadata about the request. There are many options like `remote_ip` or `header{Accept}`. You can get all available output fields with `-w "%{json}"`. However, this output (for some reason!) does not include the actual HTTP response inside the JSON structure, so we'll take a slightly more circuitous approach.

To isolate just the HTTP code and to make sure we can get the output, we'll use `-o` to route the output to a file called `response.json`. Finally, we'll use the `-s` ("silent") flag to make sure `curl` doesn't output its default timing information (i.e., how long the request took) to standard output. We'll assign the command to a variable, and with that, we'll have the status code in the variable for inspection, along with the response body in the file `response.json`.

```
#!/usr/bin/env bash

API_URL="https://api.example.com/users"
API_TOKEN="abc123"
PAYLOAD='{"username":"alice","role":"admin"}'

response_code=$(curl -s -o response.json \
  -w "%{http_code}" \
  -X POST "$API_URL" \
  -H "Authorization: Bearer $API_TOKEN" \
  -H "Content-Type: application/json" \
  -d "$PAYLOAD")

if [ "$response_code" -eq 201 ]; then
  echo "User created successfully"
else
  echo "Request failed with status $response_code"
  cat response.json
  exit 1
fi
```

Now, you can invoke an API and check its response in a shell script, but if you're thinking "This would be easier in Python," you'd be right.

Via Python

To achieve the same functionality in Python, first install the `requests` library:

```
pip install requests
```

Then you can use the library like so:

```
import requests

url = "https://api.example.com/users"
headers = {
    "Authorization": "Bearer abc123",
    "Content-Type": "application/json"
}
payload = {
    "username": "alice",
    "role": "admin"
}
```

```
response = requests.post(url, json=payload, headers=headers)

if response.status_code == 201:
    print("User created successfully")
else:
    print(f"Request failed with status {response.status_code}")
    print(response.text)
    raise SystemExit(1)
```

You can see how much nicer it is to receive the full output details as a structured object—no manipulating of parameter flags necessary. It's also much easier to define both headers and the payload due to Python's native ability to work with dictionary values.

Postman

When you're scripting or want to do a quick test, `curl` is your friend, and Python will be your first choice for scripting automations. But when you are exploring an API and want a complete experience with a graphical interface, saved requests, and robust tools for testing APIs, you'll want to give Postman a try. It's excellent for learning an API, experimenting with payloads, and collaborating with teammates.

Collections and Requests

Postman is a tool with enough functionality to fill its own book, so we'll stick to the basics. One of the core ideas is that of the *collection*, a document that groups related API requests together. A collection is like a workspace for a single API comprising known endpoints, requests, documentation, variables, tests, and examples, all organized in one place.

A Postman collection usually represents a single API. Inside a collection, you define individual requests, each with its own URL, headers, authentication settings, and payload.

Each request is saved, named, and reusable. You don't need to retype URLs or headers every time you want to test something, which makes experimentation much faster than using the command line alone. Figure 6.2 shows an example of Postman loaded with a collection depicting the Okta (an identity provider service) API.

Collections can be shared with teammates, versioned, and even published as documentation. You can create them yourself based on an API you're working with, but often, API providers will create a Postman request for users to download, letting you quickly get started interacting with an API. This makes Postman useful as a common reference point between developers, providers, and testers.

Building and Sending Requests

Under the covers, Postman is still just sending HTTP requests. You choose the HTTP method, enter the URL, add headers, and optionally define a request body. When you click Send, Postman issues the request and displays the response in a structured, readable format.

This is particularly helpful when working with JSON payloads. Instead of subjecting you to raw text, Postman formats responses automatically, highlights syntax, and lets you

FIGURE 6.2 Postman collection.

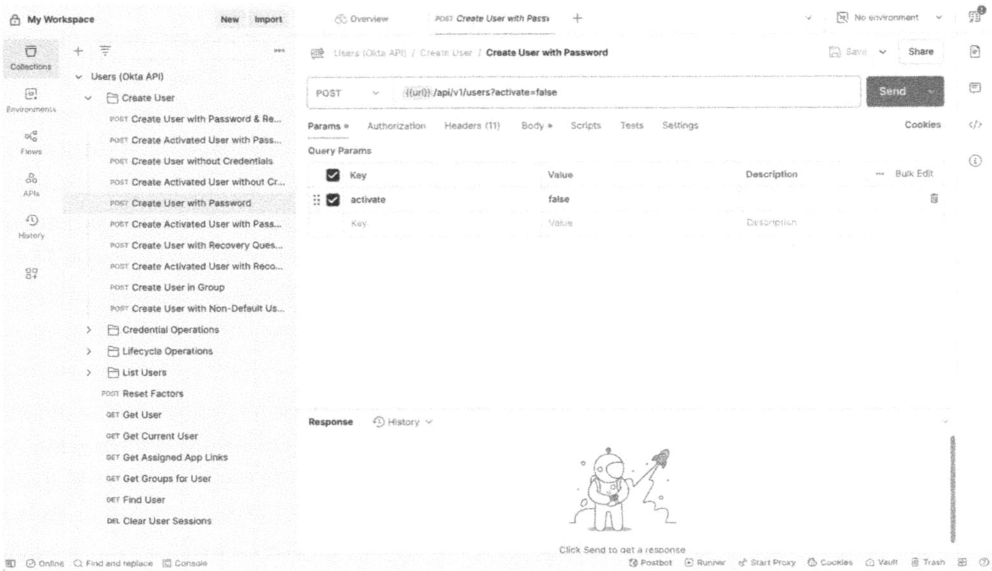

collapse or expand nested objects. When you're learning an API for the first time, this can help you understand its behavior much more quickly.

Postman also makes it easy to switch between variations of a request. To try a different payload or set of parameters, you can duplicate the request and try again.

Environments and Variables

One of Postman's most practical features is environments. Environments let you define variables such as base URLs, API tokens, or account IDs that change depending on context. The best use case for this feature is when an API is deployed to both a dev or test environment and a production environment. At minimum, the base URL is likely to be different.

For example, you might define:

`{{base_url}} = https://api.dev.example.com` in a development environment

`{{base_url}} = https://api.prod.example.com` in a production environment

As you can see, variables defined in a Postman environment can be referenced with double curly braces. Your requests can reference `{{base_url}}` instead of hard-coding

URLs, making it easy to use the same collection for both the development and the production instance of an API.

This separation of configuration from code is the same good design we've seen when scripting and that we'll continue to see with deployment automation.

Authentication in Postman

Postman supports all the authentication methods we've discussed, including API keys, bearer tokens, OAuth flows, and more. Instead of manually constructing headers, you select an authentication type and let Postman handle the mechanics.

When you're ready to use what you've learned in a script, inspect the generated Authorization header or export the request as a `curl` command to see the raw equivalent.

From Postman to Automation

For automations, Postman makes a great part of your workflow:

1. Explore the API in Postman.
2. Confirm behavior of endpoints, payloads, and authentication.
3. Export working requests as `curl` commands.
4. Integrate those requests into scripts or pipelines.

Postman provides built-in export options not just for `curl`, but for many other languages, from Python to JavaScript to Java and even PHP. Not only is Postman a great place to learn and experiment with an API, but these export abilities make it great launching point for scripting automations based on what you've learned.

REST in Real Automation Workflows

REST and other web APIs underpin many of the automation systems you'll work with in automations. When you provision infrastructure, trigger builds, deploy applications, rotate secrets, or query system health, you're almost always interacting with REST APIs under the hood.

The tools discussed in this book, like Terraform, Ansible, GitHub Actions, Jenkins, and cloud CLIs, are largely wrappers around API calls. Understanding REST lets you reason about what those tools are doing when something breaks, and helps you understand the identity and access control model around modern systems.

Automating with Webhooks

In this chapter, we've focused mainly on what happens when you are the client (aka consumer) of an API. However, many critical systems integrations rely on reversing those roles. Many services allow you to register *webhooks*—API endpoints that you host yourself in order to be notified of events on that system.

Webhooks are a powerful way to build *event-driven integrations* that take action based on some event. One way to understand webhooks is in the context of GitHub, which allows you to register webhooks for common events like pull request activity or pushing a branch. Figure 6.3 shows the user interface for adding webhooks.

While GitHub's REST API will let you query for this sort of activity, webhooks have some key advantages over using the REST:

No Risk of Rate-Limiting Without webhooks, if you want to know when a push event occurs on a repository, you must query (or *poll*) the REST API regularly to check for records of a push. With webhooks, you are notified exactly once: when the event occurs.

Closer to Real-Time Updates Depending on your request frequency, polling may introduce latency, whereas webhooks will notify you of an event right away.

FIGURE 6.3 Adding webhooks in GitHub.

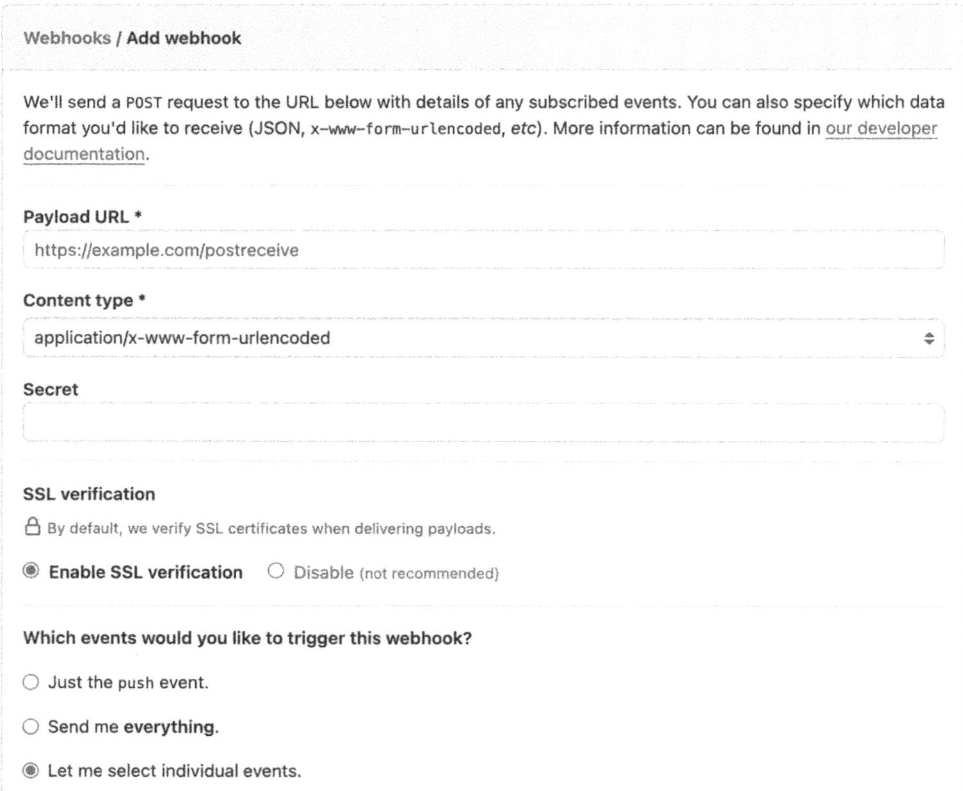

When you register to receive an event via webhook, you must host your own API with a URL as prescribed by the service. In GitHub's case, any URL you host will do. GitHub will issue an HTTP `POST` to your endpoint for whatever event or events you registered; the `POST` body will contain a JSON representation of the event that occurred. The GitHub developer documentation contains details on exactly what to expect with each of these. For instance, the default webhook sends information on each Git push. A significantly truncated example of the payload looks like this:

```
{
  "ref": "refs/heads/main",
  "before": "a1b2c3d4e5f678901234567890abcdef12345678",
  "after": "f6e5d4c3b2a1987654321098765432 1fedcba987",
  "repository": {
    "id": 987654321,
    "name": "example-repo",
    "full_name": "octocat/example-repo",
    "private": false,
    "owner": {
      "login": "octocat",
      "id": 583231,
},
    "url": "https://api.github.com/repos/octocat/example-repo",
    "created_at": 1612123456,
    "updated_at": "2025-12-01T12:34:56Z",
    "pushed_at": 1700000000,
    "default_branch": "main"
  },
  "pusher": {
    "name": "octocat",
    "email": "octocat@example.com"
  },
  "commits": [
    {
      "id": "abc1234abcdef5678abcdef901234567890abcd",
      "message": "Add new feature and update docs",
      "timestamp": "2025-12-26T15:00:00-05:00",
      "url": "https://github.com/octocat/example-repo/commit/
abc1234abcdef5678abcdef901234567890abcd",
      "author": {
        "name": "John Doe",
        "email": "john@example.com",
        "username": "john-doe"
      },
      "added": ["src/new-feature.js"],
      "removed": [],
      "modified": ["README.md"]
    }
  ],
}
```

As you can see, even in this shortened example, the payload contains many useful fields for understanding the full details of a push. With this much JSON to parse, you'll want to reach for what you learned about `jq`!

Handling Authentication

The service you work with will determine the necessary URL structure and authentication scheme. In GitHub's case, you can define a shared secret, which acts like an API key and will appear in the `X-Hub-Signature-256` HTTP header of any incoming request. Validate this secret before handling a webhook call, and you can be sure that the traffic originates from your own integration with GitHub.

Webhooks in the Context of Automation

What are webhooks for? There are many examples, but in this case, you can imagine hosting a webhook that listens for push events on a GitHub repository. If your API code detects that the target branch is named `test`, you can trigger a test build on the newly pushed code, then make the results available to your team via email or Slack message (posted with what else? The Slack API!). This flow is depicted in Figure 6.4.

This flow shows a realistic scenario of do-it-yourself build automation. First, you register a webhook with GitHub to be notified whenever a push event occurs, configured with a secret that you'll later validate. On your own infrastructure, you host the webhook. When it receives a request, you must first validate the secret, then check the `POST` body for details on what was pushed. In this case, we're looking for a particular branch (i.e., the `test` branch) to kick off a build.

FIGURE 6.4 Using webhooks to trigger builds.

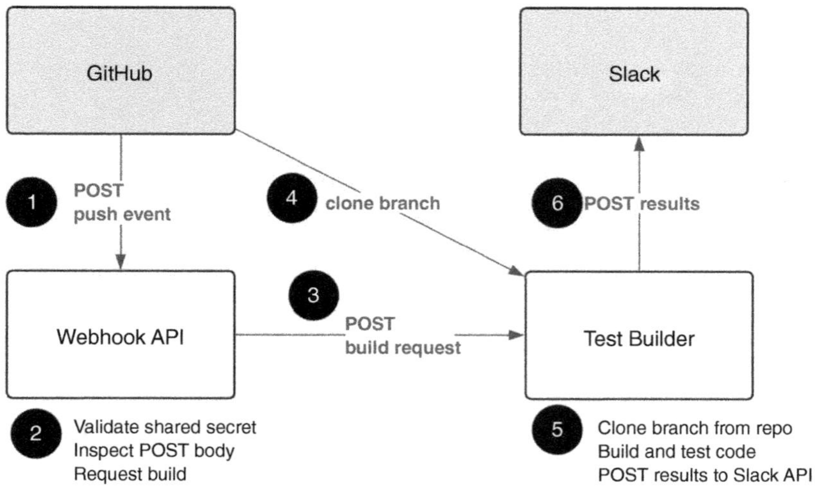

From here, we'll trigger a build. This could happen on the same server as the webhook, but in this diagram, it's a call to a different service. That service may have its own REST API to trigger builds; in this case, we `POST` to a `/build` endpoint (with the name of the branch as a parameter) and request a build.

On that build server, we receive the details of the branch the client wants to build, then use the GitHub API (or command-line interface) to clone the target branch. We'll run the build locally, collect the results, and `POST` them to one last API—the Slack API, where we'll notify teammates of the results. Automation in action!

Full details of hosting your own API are beyond the scope of this book, but if you are a web developer or work with a web development team, you likely have ways to deploy public-facing APIs. AWS's API Gateway service allows you to easily deploy a Lambda function with a world-accessible endpoint, as do Cloud Functions on Google Cloud Platform or Google's Firebase product. These services can become key integration points for event-driven integrations via webhook.

Documenting REST APIs with OpenAPI/Swagger

In this chapter, you may have noticed qualifiers like "often" and "typically" frequently used with respect to RESTful API behavior, because there's no one way to implement REST. The only guaranteed way of understanding an API's behavior and scope of capabilities is with good documentation from the creators.

OpenAPI is a standardized, machine-readable specification for documenting REST endpoints. *Swagger* is the original tooling ecosystem built around this idea, and today the terms are often used interchangeably. An OpenAPI document defines the available endpoints, supported HTTP methods, expected parameters, authentication requirements, request and response schemas, and example payloads. In other words, it's the contract that explains how to talk to an API without guessing.

Expressed in JSON or YAML formats, Swagger docs are not just a clear standard for documenting APIs; they are a way to create web-ready, user-friendly interfaces that let consumers explore and even test an API right from a browser. Swagger UI and other libraries can take source OpenAPI docs and render them in a nice, readable fashion, as shown in Figure 6.5.

Figure 6.6 shows how Swagger UI allows you to expand endpoints to reveal details like parameters and response structures, as well as ways to trigger an invocation of the endpoint from the web interface.

You won't need to know how to write OpenAPI docs for the exam, but if you're working with APIs, chances are you will encounter these kinds of docs in the wild. Along with provider-created Postman collections, OpenAPI docs are a welcome sight for developers looking to get up to speed on an API quickly.

FIGURE 6.5 OpenAPI documentation.

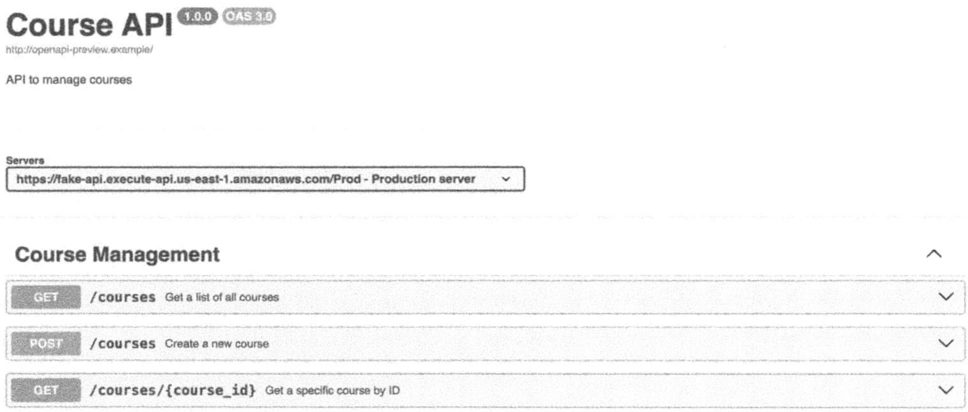

FIGURE 6.6 OpenAPI documentation expanded.

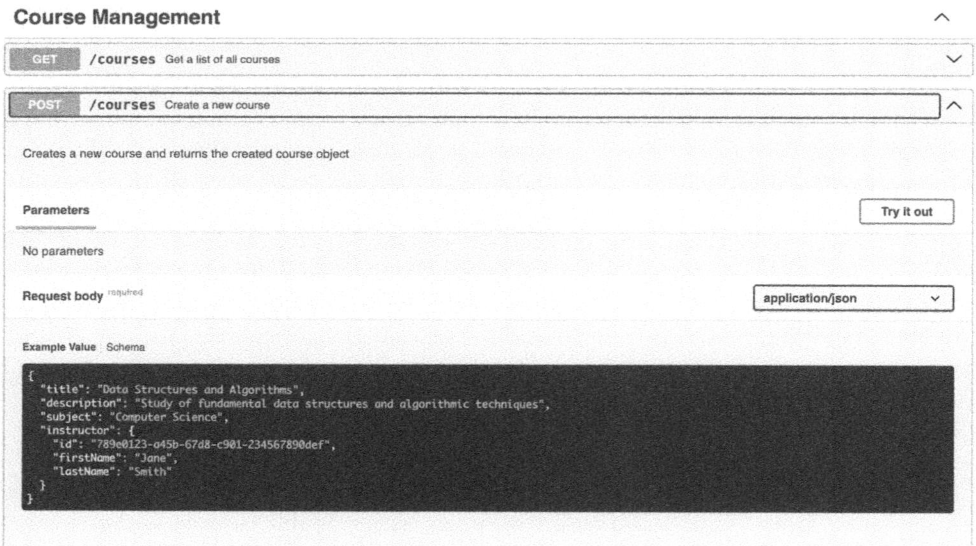

Summary

In this chapter, you learned how REST fits into the day-to-day reality of modern automation and operations work. We grounded REST in its HTTP roots, emphasizing stateless interactions, resource-oriented design, and the importance of expressing intent through standard HTTP verbs and response codes.

We walked through the practical mechanics of working with REST APIs: choosing the correct HTTP methods, interpreting responses, handling authentication and authorization, and interacting with APIs directly from the command line using tools like `curl` and Postman.

We also covered common failure modes like authentication errors, rate limits, and server-side issues, and you learned how to troubleshoot REST interactions using the signals APIs are designed to provide.

Another major piece of the automation puzzle is now in place. The next step is making sure the environment you're running in is ready to work safely and consistently. In the next chapter, we'll shift our focus to preparing the environment itself, covering network access, credentials, secrets, and dependencies, so that we can bring everything together as we pursue systems and deployment automation.

Exam Essentials

Understand REST as an architectural style built on HTTP. Know that REST is not a protocol or product, but an architectural style that uses standard HTTP concepts—methods, status codes, headers, and stateless requests—to interact with resources identified by URLs.

Know the core REST concepts that enable automation. Be able to explain clients and servers, resources and URLs, and idempotency. Understand why statelessness and idempotent operations matter for scalable, retry-safe automation workflows.

Understand how HTTP methods (verbs) are used in REST. Understand the purpose of `GET`, `POST`, `PUT`, `PATCH`, and `DELETE`, and how each expresses a different interaction with a resource.

Interpret REST responses correctly. Be able to use HTTP status codes as signals. Know the meaning of the 2XX, 3XX, 4XX, and 5XX categories and how automation should respond differently to client errors, server errors, and successful responses.

Understand headers, payloads, and data formats. Understand REST request headers and be familiar with common headers used in automation, including Authorization, Content-Type, and Accept. Understand how payloads are used in `POST`, `PUT`, and `PATCH` requests and why JSON is the dominant data format for REST APIs.

Interact with REST APIs from the command line. Be able to issue REST requests using command-line tools like `curl`. Understand why command-line interaction is critical for automation, scripting, and troubleshooting, even when GUIs or SDKs are available.

Understand authentication vs. authorization in REST APIs. Know the difference between authentication (who you are) and authorization (what you're allowed to do). Be familiar with API keys and tokens and how authentication failures (401) differ from authorization failures (403).

Recognize common REST failures and troubleshooting approaches. Be able to identify common REST issues, including authentication errors, malformed payloads, incorrect methods, missing resources, rate limiting, and server-side failures. Know how to diagnose problems using status codes, headers, and response bodies.

Understand REST's role in real automation workflows. Know how REST underpins infrastructure provisioning, pipelines, and event-driven automation through webhooks. Recognize REST as the connective layer between modern automation tools and platforms.

Review Questions

1. An automation pipeline successfully authenticates to a REST API, but receives a `403 Forbidden` response when attempting to delete a resource. What is the most likely cause?
   - **A.** The API endpoint does not exist.
   - **B.** The request payload is malformed.
   - **C.** The authenticated identity lacks permission for the operation.
   - **D.** The authentication token is missing or expired.
2. You are troubleshooting a REST API call in a deployment script. The request returns a `500 Internal Server Error`. What is the best automation-friendly response?
   - **A.** Retry the request with exponential backoff.
   - **B.** Immediately fail the pipeline and stop execution.
   - **C.** Regenerate authentication credentials.
   - **D.** Modify the request payload and retry immediately.
3. An architect is designing an API and insists that the server should not store any client context between requests. Each request from the client must contain all the information necessary to understand and complete the request. Which REST constraint is being applied here?
   - **A.** Layered system
   - **B.** Statelessness
   - **C.** Cacheability
   - **D.** Uniform interface
4. While running a script to sync data from a cloud provider, your application suddenly begins receiving HTTP `429 Too Many Requests` responses. To ensure your script completes successfully without being permanently blocked, what is the best immediate programmatic action to take?
   - **A.** Immediately retry the request until a `200 OK` is received.
   - **B.** Check the Retry-After header and implement an exponential backoff strategy.
   - **C.** Switch the HTTP method from `GET` to `POST` to bypass the limit.
   - **D.** Change the API key to a different user account to reset the quota.
5. You are consuming an API that supports multiple data formats, including JSON and XML. As the client, you want to explicitly request that the server sends the response data back in JSON format. Which HTTP header should you include in your request?
   - **A.** `Content-Type: application/json`
   - **B.** `Host: api.example.com`
   - **C.** `Accept: application/json`
   - **D.** `User-Agent: MyClient/1.0`

6. Which HTTP header is most commonly used to pass authentication credentials to a REST API?
   A. `Content-Type`
   B. `Accept`
   C. `Authorization`
   D. `User-Agent`
7. You are troubleshooting a REST API call made from a deployment script. The request fails with a `400 Bad Request` response. Which action is most likely to resolve the issue?
   A. Retry the request multiple times.
   B. Inspect the request payload and headers.
   C. Regenerate API credentials.
   D. Switch from HTTPS to HTTP.
8. You are testing a REST API from the command line and want to send a `POST` request with a JSON payload stored in a file named `user.json`. Which `curl` command is the best approach?
   A. `curl -X POST https://api.example.com/users user.json`
   B. `curl -X POST -d user.json https://api.example.com/users`
   C.
   ```
   curl -X POST -H "Content-Type: application/json" \
        -d @user.json https://api.example.com/users
   ```
   D.
   ```
   curl -H "Accept: application/json" \
        https://api.example.com/users < user.json
   ```
9. You have successfully tested a REST API using Postman and now need to integrate the request into a CI/CD pipeline. What is the best next step?
   A. Export the Postman collection and commit it directly to the pipeline.
   B. Translate the working request into a `curl` command or script.
   C. Continue using Postman manually for production deployments.
   D. Replace the API call with a scheduled polling job.
10. An automation workflow deletes a resource using a REST API and receives a `204 No Content` response. What should the automation infer from this response?
    A. The deletion failed but returned no error details.
    B. The resource was deleted successfully with no response body.
    C. The resource still exists but is marked inactive.
    D. The API endpoint does not support `DELETE`.

11. A REST API occasionally returns `502 Bad Gateway` responses during peak usage. Your automation currently fails immediately on any non-2XX status code. What is the *best* improvement to make?

    A. Convert all requests to `POST` to avoid gateway caching.

    B. Treat 5XX responses as retryable with limits and backoff.

    C. Disable TLS verification to reduce request latency.

    D. Ignore the response body and continue execution.

12. A developer is reviewing a pull request for a new API design. Which of the following endpoint definitions violates standard RESTful design principles?

    A. `POST /users/create`

    B. `DELETE /users/42`

    C. `GET /users/42/orders`

    D. `PATCH /users/42`

13. You are writing an automation script to update the `maintenance_mode` flag of a server resource from false to true. You do not wish to overwrite or resend the server's entire configuration object. Which HTTP verb is most appropriate for this specific action?

    A. `POST`

    B. `GET`

    C. `PUT`

    D. `PATCH`

14. You are using `curl` to send a JSON payload to create a new record. The server returns a `400 Bad Request` error indicating it cannot parse the body, even though the JSON syntax is correct. Which flag and value are likely missing from your command?

    A. `-X POST`

    B. `-H "Content-Type: application/json"`

    C. `-H "Accept: application/xml"`

    D. `-d @payload.json`

Answers to Review Questions

1. C. The correct answer is C. A 403 response indicates that authentication succeeded, but the identity is not authorized to perform the requested action. Option D would result in a `401 Unauthorized` response instead. Option A would typically produce a `404 Not Found`, while option B would more likely result in a `400 Bad Request`.

2. A. The correct answer is A. A 500-level status code indicates a server-side failure, which is often transient. Retrying with backoff is a common and appropriate automation strategy. Option B may be appropriate after repeated failures, but failing immediately reduces resilience. Option C addresses authentication issues, which would result in 401 or 403 responses. Option D assumes a client-side error, which is inconsistent with a 5XX response.

3. B. Option B is correct. The Statelessness constraint requires that the communication between the client and server contains all necessary information in every request; the server does not rely on "session" data stored on the server side. Option A refers to the ability to use intermediaries like proxy servers. Option C refers to the requirement that responses define themselves as cacheable or not. Option D refers to the consistent way resources are identified and manipulated.

4. B. Option B is correct. An HTTP 429 status code indicates that the client has sent too many requests in a given amount of time (rate limiting). Option A is incorrect because hammering the server with retries will likely lead to a longer or permanent ban. Option C is incorrect because rate limits usually apply to the client or IP regardless of the method used. Option D may work, but you're likely to find yourself running afoul of the API's Terms of Service. Plus, it doesn't solve the underlying architectural issue.

5. C. Option C is correct. The `Accept` header is used by the client to tell the server which content types the client is able to understand or prefers for the response. Option A is a common point of confusion; `Content-Type` is used to describe the media type of the data being sent in the body of the current request (e.g., in a `POST` or `PUT`), not the desired response format. Option B identifies the domain of the server. Option D identifies the client software making the request.

6. C. The correct answer is C. The `Authorization` header is used to pass API keys, bearer tokens, or other credentials. Option A describes the payload format. Option B specifies acceptable response formats. Option D identifies the client making the request.

7. B. The correct answer is B. A 400 response indicates the server could not process the request due to invalid input, such as malformed JSON or missing required fields. Option A is ineffective for client-side errors. Option C addresses authentication issues, which typically produce 401 or 403 responses. Option D introduces security risks and does not address input validation.

8. C. The correct answer is C. The `-d @user.json` syntax tells `curl` to read the request body from a file, and the Content-Type header correctly identifies the payload format. Option A does not send the file as a payload. Option B sends the literal string `user.json` rather than the file contents. Option D redirects input but performs a `GET` request and does not set the method or content type correctly.

9. B. The correct answer is B. Translating the request into a `curl` command or script makes it automatable, version-controllable, and runnable in headless environments like CI systems. Option A may be useful for documentation, but Postman collections are not ideal pipeline primitives. Option C does not scale and defeats automation. Option D changes the interaction model and does not address the need to automate the existing API call.

10. B. The correct answer is B. A 204 response indicates that the request succeeded and that there is no response body. This is common for `DELETE` operations. Option A incorrectly treats 204 as an error. Option C invents semantics not implied by the status code. Option D would typically result in a `405 Method Not Allowed`.

11. B. The correct answer is B. 5XX responses indicate server-side failures that are often transient. Retrying with backoff improves resilience without overwhelming the service. Option A does not address gateway errors. Option C introduces serious security risks. Option D hides failures and leads to inconsistent system state.

12. A. The correct answer is A. In REST, URLs should identify resources (nouns), and the action should be defined by the HTTP verb. `POST /users/create` includes the verb in the URL, which is not RESTful. The correct approach would be `POST /users`. Options B, C, and D are all reasonable RESTful endpoints.

13. D. Option D is correct. The `PATCH` verb is used to modify part of a resource. Option C, `PUT`, is incorrect, as it is typically used to replace the entire resource. Since you are only updating one flag without sending the whole object, `PATCH` is the correct choice. Option A would be for creating a resource, and option B for fetching; both are incorrect.

14. B. Option B is correct. When sending a payload, the server must know how to parse it. If the `Content-Type` header is not explicitly set to `application/json`, the server may attempt to parse it as plain text or form data, causing an error. Option A is incorrect, since the HTTP verb doesn't affect how the body is parsed. Option C is also incorrect; `Accept` relates to the response format the client expects. Option D is incorrect, but also plausible. This syntax specifies the payload as a file, so if the wrong file is specified or there is a syntax error in it, it could result in the 400 error.

Chapter 7

Preparing the Environment

THE AUTOOPS+ EXAM TOPICS COVERED IN THIS CHAPTER MAY INCLUDE, BUT ARE NOT LIMITED TO, THE FOLLOWING:

✔ **1.0: Automation Coding Concepts**

- 1.1. Given a scenario, use code to support automation.

✔ **2.0: System Configuration**

- 2.1. Given a scenario, use configuration management techniques to deploy a solution.

✔ **3.0: Continuous Integration**

- 3.1. Explain environmental factors related to continuous integration (CI) management.

✔ **4.0: Continuous Delivery**

- 4.3. Compare and contrast different methods to secure a connection to providers.

Working on the operations side of DevOps means having a broad understanding of many different topics. You need to understand scripting, automation, and integrations; you need to know a bit about infrastructure, networking, and systems administration. You don't have to be a full-stack developer, but you have to understand the full stack and what's going on at every stage of the development process. It can feel overwhelming, but it's also very empowering. The operations automation professional is someone who understands the entire system—a very valuable member of any team.

To this end, this chapter continues our system automation journey by rounding out some topics that will prepare you to head into end-to-end deployment operations further in this book. We'll get into the essential topics that take an environment from merely "online" to "production ready." This starts with *dependency management*, the practice of maintaining the libraries and packages necessary to make applications run. From there, we'll dive into secrets management and the ways in which we supply applications with sensitive values without compromising security. Finally, we'll put our infrastructure-as-code skills to work establishing the networking architecture necessary to run secure applications at scale.

Managing Dependencies

Modern applications are built on many layers of *dependencies*. A dependency is any software on which your runtime environment depends, from programming language libraries and frameworks to operating system patches and packages. In this section, we'll discuss how to manage dependencies to create well-defined, repeatable environments to ensure your applications run consistently whether they are on a developer's laptop, in a test container, or on a production server. Good dependency management turns the execution environment from an accident into a specification.

Understanding Packages and Libraries

To manage dependencies well, you need to understand what they are. The term "package" gets used casually, but it means slightly different things depending on context. Those differences matter when diagnosing problems or designing automation.

Language-Level vs. OS-Level Packages

At a high level, a package is a distributable unit of software that might live at different layers of the stack.

OS-level packages are installed by tools like `yum`, `apt`, `dnf`, Homebrew, or `winget`. They include system libraries, command-line tools, and language runtimes.

Language-level packages are installed by tools like `pip` (for Python), `npm` (for JavaScript), Maven (for Java), or NuGet (for C#). These are libraries designed to be consumed by applications written in a specific language.

Both types are dependencies, but they behave differently. OS packages are usually shared across the system. Language-level packages are often scoped to a project.

Direct vs. Transitive Dependencies

Most projects depend on more software than they explicitly list.

Direct dependencies are the packages you intentionally install using commands like `npm install`, `pip install`, or `yum install`.

Transitive dependencies are the packages *those* packages depend on. They are the iceberg of dependencies under the surface of your `package.json` or similar dependency file. Where you might manually install 10 packages for use in a web application, when all sub-dependencies are installed, the result might number in the multiples of dozens.

Even though you don't explicitly install transitive dependencies, they are still your responsibility to maintain. Why? For one, vulnerabilities can appear in transitive dependencies just as easily as direct ones, and version conflicts can arise several layers deep. Just ask anyone who has attempted a significant framework update on a web application, and they'll tell you that the upgrade path ripples out to transitive dependencies pretty quickly.

Luckily, modern tooling not only helps you track down and install transitive dependencies, but it also helps you understand the sprawling and interconnected web they weave.

GitHub Dependency Graph/Dependabot

One such tool is an open-source program that is also built directly into GitHub. It's called Dependabot, and it examines the source code you upload to surface key information about your dependencies. In fact, you can view this information for many popular open-source projects. Figure 7.1 shows one such view (no pun intended!) of the JavaScript web framework VueJS.

As you can see, GitHub allows you to filter the dependencies based on whether they are direct or transitive.

Visibility is great, but what most code maintainers are concerned with is whether any vulnerabilities have surfaced in their dependencies. Although you likely do not control the code of either your direct or transitive dependencies, you need to know when there's a potential security issue. These issues take the form of Common Vulnerabilities and Exposures (CVE) reports. Often, the solution to resolving a CVE is simply to upgrade that particular dependency to its latest patch level.

FIGURE 7.1 GitHub dependency graph.

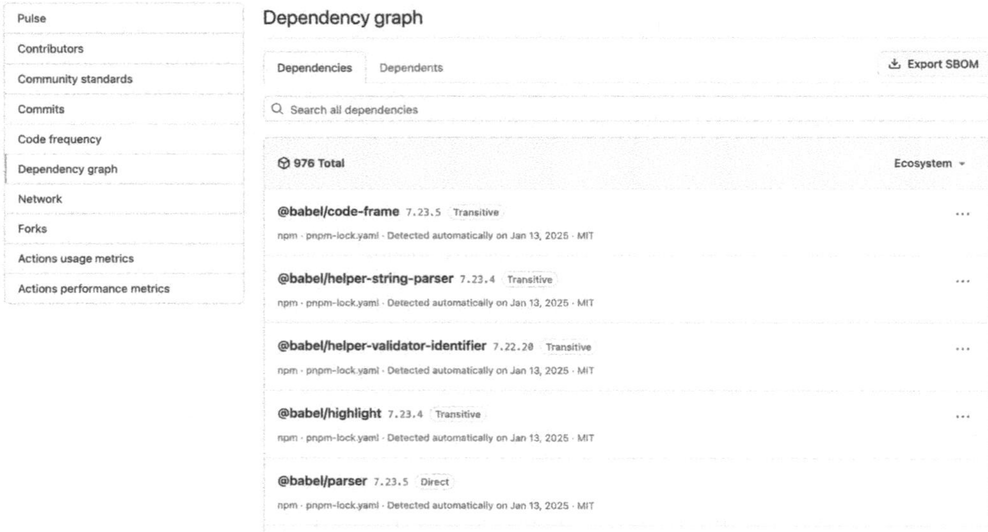

FIGURE 7.2 Dependabot vulnerability report.

Dependabot can scan your GitHub repository and send you regular emails on the status of vulnerabilities found in your dependencies. To demonstrate, Figure 7.2 shows an email from Dependabot, which has scanned a repo containing an abandoned Python Django web application.

The Django framework library in this repo is very out of date—no wonder there are critical vulnerabilities in the code! Dependabot suggests the lowest safe version to which the repo owner should upgrade, though Django has moved well past version 2.x by now! To keep your organization and your users safe, it's essential to use tools like this to stay on top of your dependencies.

Runtime vs. Build Time

Not all dependencies are needed at the same time:

- *Build-time dependencies* are required to construct the software (compilers, build tools, test frameworks).
- *Runtime dependencies* are loaded when the software is actually running (libraries, interpreters, shared objects).

A good example would be the JavaScript library `tsc`. It's required at build time to convert TypeScript code to vanilla JavaScript, but it's not needed by the application that actually runs in the browser. It's a build-time dependency only, but many a developer has inadvertently included it in their runtime dependency list.

Confusing these two dependency types can lead to bloated environments containing unneeded code, security risks, or even broken deployments. You want your environments to run with the fewest dependencies possible; being explicit about *when* a dependency is needed is just as important as specifying *which* dependency is needed.

Linux Package Management

Let's take a look at operating system dependency management. On Linux systems, *package management* is the primary way software is installed, upgraded, and removed. Rather than downloading binaries manually or compiling everything from source, Linux distributions provide package managers that handle installation, dependency resolution, version tracking, and removal in a consistent, scriptable way.

From an automation perspective, Linux package managers are foundational building blocks. Almost every provisioning script, container image, and configuration management run relies on them in some form.

What a Linux Package Manager Does

At a minimum, a Linux package manager is responsible for:

- Installing software and required dependencies
- Tracking installed versions
- Upgrading or downgrading packages
- Removing software cleanly

Crucially, package managers understand relationships between packages. When you install one package, the manager determines which additional libraries are required and installs those as well. This dependency resolution is one of the biggest advantages of using package managers.

I remember using package managers on Unix-based systems before the concept ever made it to other operating systems. It seemed like magic, and to be honest, it is a bit magical. No hunting down install scripts or dealing with incompatibilities; the package manager just finds what packages you need, whether direct or transient. It's so nice that when you do come across something you want to install that lacks package manager support, and you're left compiling software from source or even just downloading an RPM file yourself, you feel as though you were just asked to build fire by rubbing two sticks together.

Common Linux Package Managers

Different Linux distributions ship with different package managers, but the concepts are largely the same.

Debian-based systems (Ubuntu, Debian) use a tool called `apt` (and the lower-level `apt-get`). These tools use signed repositories defined in configuration files and are widely used in cloud images and containers.

In these examples, we install, then uninstall `nginx`:

```
sudo apt install nginx
sudo apt remove nginx
```

We can look for and install updates for every package on the system with this command:

```
sudo apt update
```

Red Hat–based systems (RHEL, CentOS, Amazon Linux) use `yum` (legacy) or `dnf`, its modern replacement. Here's an example:

```
sudo dnf install httpd
sudo dnf update
```

The equivalent of the system-wide package update for this command is `dnf update`.

Patching the System

When Linux systems administrators "patch a system," very often their first task is to run a general package manager update command like `sudo dnf update`, letting the system's native patch manager fetch all the newest package versions, patches, and hotfixes of system dependencies.

While there is certainly more to keeping a system updated and secure than just running this command, if you make this (or your OS's equivalent) the first line of your system startup, Dockerfile, or initialization scripts, you'll be taking an excellent step toward keeping your OS-level dependencies patched.

Package Repositories and Trust

Linux package managers pull software from repositories—curated collections of packages that are cryptographically signed. This gives you a level of trust that your package manager is installing software from a secure location. Though it's not out of the question that a malicious package can make its way into a package manager's repository, it's rare. Package managers are built on the idea that they are a consistent, trusted source of software.

Most Linux OS package managers have a default repository where most software resides. Every now and then, you'll encounter a need to enable a secondary repository; a great example is EPEL, or Extra Packages for Linux, a package repository maintained by the Fedora Project that supplies packages not in the standard `yum` repo used by Red Hat Linux–based systems.

To maintain security, be sure to only add trusted repositories to your package manager's configuration.

Versioning and Drift at the OS Level

OS-level packages are still subject to drift. If one system updates packages automatically while another does not, you can end up with subtle differences across machines. For this reason, mature environments control when OS updates happen or constrain versions where necessary. Both OS package managers and language-level package managers give you options to "pin" a package's version to a specific number or range. This is called *version pinning*. For `apt`, the process involves installing a specific version number of `curl` with the equal sign:

```
sudo apt install curl=7.74.0
```

then setting a "hold" with this command:

```
sudo apt-mark hold curl
```

The `unhold` command undoes this version pinning. Other package managers all have equivalents. Be careful with this kind of command; it will prevent this package from ever being upgraded. This can become a security issue if the package has a CVE that goes unaddressed; even worse, it could be a hidden vulnerability if no one realizes the package is not being upgraded during patch cycles. Use this ability sparingly and make sure to document your choices clearly.

Configuration Management Tools

Like any command-line tool, package managers can be scripted and often show up in automations from shell scripts to Dockerfiles and more. However, as we've discussed in previous chapters, this is an imperative approach, and a task that can be easily taken up by configuration management tools.

Don't forget that tools like Ansible, Chef, and Puppet run on top of Linux package managers to let you declare which packages should be present; handle installs, upgrades, and removals; and ensure idempotency.

As an example, in Ansible, you describe desired state:

```
- name: Ensure nginx is installed
  apt:
    name: nginx
    state: present
```

The package manager still does the work, but Ansible decides when and whether that work needs to happen.

Windows Package Management

For a long time, Windows didn't have a first-class tool for package management. Software was installed through installers, setup wizards, and MSI files. Windows users know that installing software as an individual tends to involve graphical interface and clicking Next a lot until the application is installed—not a mode extremely conducive to automation.

The shift toward automation on Windows accelerated as PowerShell matured and Windows began to embrace infrastructure-as-code and configuration management patterns. Lucky for us, Windows now supports scriptable, declarative package management that fits cleanly into DevOps and automation workflows.

Modern Windows Package Managers

Today, there are two primary package management approaches you'll encounter on Windows systems.

Chocolatey

Chocolatey emerged first as a community-driven solution, allowing software to be installed, upgraded, and removed via the command line.

Chocolatey is a high-level interface wrapping NuGet, the native package manager for the .NET ecosystem. (Take a moment to appreciate the multiple layers of puns it took to get from "New Get" (NuGet) to "Chocolatey NuGet." That's programmers for you. Disappointingly, there was no "old" "Get" software, so this pun parfait is only two layers deep.)

NuGet was designed to manage application-level dependencies for .NET projects: libraries referenced at build time and bundled with applications. If you've worked with C# or .NET, you've almost certainly interacted with NuGet through a `.csproj` file or a `packages.config`.

Chocolatey builds on top of NuGet's packaging format and infrastructure but applies it to a different problem space. Instead of managing libraries inside an application, Chocolatey uses NuGet packages as wrappers around system-level software installers like the ones mentioned earlier—MSIs, EXEs, or scripts. Chocolatey standardizes how they are fetched, installed, upgraded, and removed.

Here are a few examples of Chocolatey syntax, starting with an install:

```
choco install git -y
```

The `-y` flag auto-confirms any interactive questions that might come up. The verbs `upgrade` and `uninstall` will update and remove the package, respectively. You can pin a package to a version:

```
choco pin add -n=nodejs
```

And remove the pin as you wish:

```
choco pin remove -n=nodejs
```

Chocolatey packages often contain PowerShell scripts that handle silent installs, configuration, and cleanup. From the user's perspective, though, this complexity disappears behind a consistent command-line interface. Installing Git, Python, or a browser becomes a single, repeatable operation rather than a custom scripting exercise.

winget

In the early 2020s, Microsoft introduced `winget`, the Windows Package Manager. `winget` is now included by default on modern versions of Windows and is Microsoft's official answer to system-level package management. It provides a standardized way to install and manage software from curated sources, with native support for scripting and automation.

One of the interesting things about `winget` is that, like PowerShell, `winget` tries to solve some of the ambiguity that accompanies its Linux equivalents—namely, the random guessing at package names that is sometimes required. In Linux, for every easily guessed package name like `git`, there's something like `httpd` (for the Apache Web Server) that requires a little bit of arcane knowledge. To help, `winget` attempts to formalize package names.

Installing a package in `winget` requires you to specify a fully qualified name of the format `Publisher.Package`. For instance, you might call

```
winget install Microsoft.VisualStudioCode
```

or

```
winget install Git.Git
```

To me, the first one makes a lot of sense, but the latter is less intuitive. If in doubt, run **`winget search`** ***`<package_name>`*** or check the Microsoft-published manifests at `https://github.com/microsoft/winget-pkgs`.

One other helpful set of flags in `winget` automatically accepts license agreements:

```
winget install Microsoft.VisualStudioCode
  --accept-package-agreements
  --accept-source-agreements
```

Both Chocolatey and `winget` solve the same problem: making Windows software installation predictable and automatable.

PowerShell and Automation

Windows package management fits naturally into PowerShell-based automation. PowerShell provides structured error handling, remote execution, and object-based output, which makes it well suited for orchestrating system changes.

When combined with Windows Remote Management (WinRM) or PowerShell remoting, package management scales beyond individual machines. A single command can install or upgrade software across an entire fleet of servers or workstations, without logging in interactively. This is how you start treating Windows systems as cattle rather than pets.

Configuration Management on Windows

Just as tools like Ansible, Chef, and Puppet call `apt` or `dnf` under the hood on Linux, they can invoke Chocolatey, `winget`, or native Windows package providers when managing Windows hosts. Each tool works in a similar way to its Linux counterpart, with the main difference being that push-based tools like Ansible use WinRM instead of SSH to connect to remote machines.

Whether you are working imperatively or with declarative tools like these, Windows now supports a robust ecosystem to allow at-scale management of operating systems and their dependencies.

Managing Programming Language Dependencies

Modern web applications are built on complex webs of language-level dependencies—third-party libraries that fill in functionality not provided by the base programming languages. In fact, most web applications these days are not just built on vanilla programming languages like JavaScript; they are built using frameworks that layer functionality on top of that language. For instance, React, Angular, and VueJS, all very popular JavaScript-based web programming frameworks, require a slew of libraries to be downloaded before they can begin working.

Even Python, with its famous "batteries included" mantra, has not avoided spawning a robust ecosystem of external packages that have become essential for many use cases. Sometimes an external library improves on the baseline in a way that drives adoption; many developers prefer the third-party `requests` package over Python's built-in `http.client` specifically for the ways in which it layers on higher-level functionality. Other times, a package adds new features that would be cumbersome to implement by hand, such as the web-scraping package `BeautifulSoup`. Whatever the case may be, your code depends on these libraries to run—hence the name.

It only gets more complicated. Higher-level dependencies often depend on lower-level libraries, sometimes for many layers. Multiple libraries may have the same underlying dependencies, creating a complicated web of interconnected requirements. What's even more challenging is when two libraries that are required by a project themselves require conflicting dependencies, such as two different versions of the same package. It can all become very confusing, very quickly.

Luckily, we don't have to understand it all ourselves. Package managers are the tools that developers and systems operations engineers use to manage this chaos and get code running; let's learn about how they work.

Python and Scripting Dependencies

Effective Python dependency management is about containment and repeatability—making sure each script runs with exactly the libraries it expects, no more and no less. Virtual environments are a great way to "sandbox" applications and their dependencies.

Virtual Environments

A Python *virtual environment* is an isolated sandbox that contains its own interpreter and set of installed packages. Instead of installing libraries globally on a system, you install them into a project-specific environment.

Assuming you're running Python 3, to create a virtual environment you invoke the `venv` command:

```
python3 -m venv <location to install>
```

This command will create all the necessary folders and files for managing a virtual environment at the location you specify. A common practice is to make this location a hidden folder within your project—hidden, so that it's not automatically picked up by version control. Virtual environment definitions don't typically need to be pushed to Git. To do this, the common idiom is this command:

```
python3 -m venv .venv
```

This creates a hidden folder called `.venv` in your current location. If the naming is too confusing, you can call it whatever you want!

At this point, the virtual environment is created, but not "active." To activate it, run the following on Linux machines (and assuming your folder was called .venv):

```
source .venv/bin/activate
```

or on Windows, execute .\<your_venv_folder>\Scripts\activate. From here, you are in a little pocket universe. To start, python3 will be aliased to python on the command line, which is nice, and any packages you install will only be installed in this sandbox. To get out, simply type **deactivate**.

This isolation solves two practical problems at once. First, it prevents version conflicts between projects that need different versions of the same library. Second, it makes scripts more portable, because the environment definition travels with the project instead of being tied to a particular machine.

From an automation standpoint, virtual environments are essential, as installing global Python packages is a recipe for creating conflicts across applications hosted on the same compute.

Using *requirements.txt*

Virtual environments pair nicely with pip's requirements.txt feature. This file lists the packages a project depends on, often with explicit version constraints. Whether you have one package dependency or two dozen, it's a good idea to list them in a requirements.txt file. The file itself is just a newline-delimited list of packages you want to install, with optional version specifications. For example:

```
flask==2.3.3
requests>=2.31.0
gunicorn~=21.2
pandas
```

In this file, the flask API library must be installed at exactly version 2.3.3 and the requests package must be at 2.31.0 or higher. The tilde syntax defining gunicorn is a *compatible release constraint*, allowing patch-level updates without jumping major versions. Finally, pandas will be installed at the latest version at the moment, with no constraints. Then, pip can install everything with one command:

```
pip install -r requirements.txt
```

This is very convenient, ensuring that you don't forget any dependency you or a developer has installed along the way of building an app, and making sure those dependencies are documented. Be sure this file goes into version control, and your collaborators (or a continuous integration system, or the production server) will have no problem establishing the same runtime environment as the developer.

Lockfiles and Reproducibility

The idea behind lockfiles is simple: Flexibility is useful during development, but once you're trying to deploy software, things need to be predictable. Allowing package managers to resolve "the latest compatible version" can introduce subtle changes that break scripts without any changes to your own code.

Lockfiles capture not only direct dependencies but also transitive ones, specifying the exact versions of packages currently in use on a system. Some languages and tools formalize this more than others. For instance, in Python:

```
pip freeze > requirements-frozen.txt
```

creates a new `requirements-frozen.txt` that specifies the exact versions of packages currently active in your environment (even if they were originally specified with no version constraints). Make sure not to clobber your existing `requirements.txt` accidentally with this command.

Lockfiles in NodeJS

In NodeJS applications, things are a bit more explicit. The command-line tool npm, short for Node Package Manager, plays a role similar to `pip`. However, npm doesn't require you to maintain a `requirements.txt` file, as it updates a file called `packages.json` automatically. Also, because NodeJS projects often have both build-time and runtime dependencies, it lets you divide them up with distinct commands: npm `install --save-dev <package>` installs a package for use at build time, while npm `install --save <package>` ensures the library exists at runtime. Here's a brief, mocked-up example of a `package.json` file:

```
{
  "name": "example-api-client",
  "version": "1.0.0",
  "description": "Simple Node.js app that calls an external API",
  "main": "index.js",
  "scripts": {
    "start": "node index.js",
    "lint": "eslint .",
    "test": "echo \"No tests defined\" && exit 0"
  },
  "dependencies": {
    "axios": "^1.6.0",
    "dotenv": "^16.3.1"
  },
  "devDependencies": {
    "eslint": "^8.56.0"
  }
}
```

The `dependencies` section specifies runtime dependencies (also available at build time), and `devDependencies` specifies those that are only needed at build time.

You can also edit the `package.json` file yourself, treating it like a manually created `requirements.txt` file, and then install everything with a simple `npm install`.

In any case, once your packages are installed, npm creates a file called `package-lock.json` that captures all the direct and transient dependencies of your app. When this file is present, it dictates the versions that will be installed by `npm install`, and those versions stick unless you `npm update` specific packages to upgrade them. This becomes the file that ensures your development, test, and production environments all run with the same exact dependencies, creating the consistency that is so essential to automation.

Opening a `package-lock.json` is also the best way to understand the eye-popping complexity of interconnected dependencies that defines modern web application development. It expands `dependencies` and `devDependencies` with the exact versions present, as shown in this truncated mockup:

```
"packages": {
  "": {
    "name": "my-sample-app",
    "version": "1.0.6",
    "dependencies": {
      "axios": "^1.6.7",
      "core-js": "^3.36.0",
      "dotenv": "^16.4.5",
      "vue": "^3.4.21",
      "vue-router": "^4.3.0"
    },
    "devDependencies": {
      "@types/node": "^20.11.30",
      "eslint": "^8.57.0",
      "eslint-plugin-vue": "^9.23.0",
      "typescript": "^5.4.5",
      "vite": "^5.2.8"
    }
  }
}
```

And it contains a JSON object for each package installed, specifying details like its origin in npm's registry, plus transient dependencies and co-dependencies:

```
    "node_modules/@algolia/client-account": {
      "version": "4.25.2",
      "resolved": "https://registry.npmjs.org/@algolia/
client-account-4.25.2.tgz",
      "integrity": "sha512-IfRGhBxvjli9mGIZS/pl/FuXB7hA0lE5kqOzsQDP6OmGQ==",
      "dependencies": {
        "@algolia/client-common": "4.25.2",
        "@algolia/client-search": "4.25.2",
        "@algolia/transporter": "4.25.2"
      }
    },
```

These files can easily stretch to the tens of thousands of lines. They are there to help `npm` stay on top of all these details so you don't have to!

In automation and CI/CD contexts, deterministic installs are essential. Builds should fail because code changed, not because a dependency behaved differently today than it did yesterday. Flexible version ranges still have their place, but reproducibility should win by default anywhere automation is expected to be reliable.

Container-Based Dependency Management

So far, we've not discussed much about containers. They are a widely used method for deploying applications, and we'll get into them a bit more in the next chapter, "Patterns of Application Deployment," but a comprehensive overview of Docker is outside the scope of this book. For now, our focus will be on how a Dockerfile defines the environment inside a container, and how that specification relates to the environment management we've discussed so far in this chapter.

At a high level, containers package an application together with everything it needs to run: code, libraries, runtime, system dependencies—even the operating system itself. They don't virtualize hardware like traditional virtual machines; instead, they provide isolated user-space environments that share the host kernel. If virtual machines are like self-contained servers inside physical servers, containers are even lower-level and more lightweight, sharing more host machine resources than VMs without breaking isolation.

For this chapter, what matters is how containers change the way dependencies are defined, managed, and deployed.

Writing a Dockerfile for Dependency Control

A *Dockerfile* is the specification for a container image. From a dependency perspective, it plays the same role a lockfile does for a language package manager, but at the system level.

Every Dockerfile starts with a base image:

```
FROM python:3.11-slim
```

This line establishes the operating system and runtime foundation. Choosing a base image is equivalent to choosing an OS and language runtime combination. Official images are generally preferred because they're widely used and regularly patched. For a wide selection, check the world's largest repository of base images, DockerHub, at `https://hub.docker.com`.

Next in the Dockerfile come system-level dependencies, installed using the OS package manager:

```
RUN apt-get update && \
    apt-get install -y --no-install-recommends \
        build-essential \
        curl && \
    rm -rf /var/lib/apt/lists/*
```

This mirrors traditional Linux package management, but now it happens in a controlled build context. Every package installed here becomes part of the image, captured permanently in a layer.

Application-level dependencies follow. For a Python app, that usually means copying in a `requirements.txt` file and installing dependencies with `pip`:

```
WORKDIR /app

COPY requirements.txt .
RUN pip install --no-cache-dir -r requirements.txt
```

This builds directly on the dependency-locking ideas you've already seen. The difference is scope: Instead of shipping a specification of the environment, you're now shipping the environment itself.

Only after dependencies are installed do you copy in the application code:

```
COPY . .

CMD ["python", "app.py"]
```

The result is an immutable container image that includes up-to-date operating system packages, a few additional extra packages, and any Python language dependencies defined by the application's `requirements.txt`.

Layers, Immutability, and Rebuilds

Docker builds images in layers, and layer ordering matters. Each instruction creates a new layer. If something in an early layer changes, all subsequent layers must be rebuilt.

The idea is to start the Dockerfile with the instructions that will change the least and work up toward those that will change more frequently. By installing OS packages and application dependencies *before* copying application code, you get faster rebuilds during development, as well as clean separation between dependencies and application logic. More importantly, this structure reinforces the container mindset that dependencies are fixed at build time and not modified later. When deploying with containers, your deployment scripts would not run (in this example) `pip install`, because the Python libraries would be expected to be part of the container.

When a dependency changes (e.g., because of a security update or version bump) the correct response is to update the Dockerfile and rebuild the image. The running container is disposable. If something goes wrong, rollback just means deploying the previous image. In Docker, you don't make live changes to the runtime environment; you're always building a new image or reverting to an old one.

In this model, container images become versioned, deployable artifacts, just like compiled binaries. You're no longer shipping instructions for how to build an environment. You're shipping the environment itself.

Dependency Management Strategies

Good dependency management leads to structure and consistency. Versions should be constrained and not left to chance, and dependencies should be defined explicitly rather than inferred from whatever happens to be installed. Separating concerns also helps: System packages, language libraries, and application code each live at different layers, whether conceptually in your deployment scripts or explicitly in Docker layers. Clear boundaries make failures easier to diagnose and environments easier to reproduce.

As with configuration management and infrastructure-as-code, rely on declarative tooling and resist the temptation to make live fixes. Capture and version control dependency definitions with whatever methods are available in your stack. With the techniques you've learned in this chapter and the previous ones, you have plenty of tools to make your environments and their dependencies reviewable, testable, and repeatable.

Virtual Network Infrastructure Configuration

Applications don't run in a vacuum. Even the most carefully packaged code still depends on the network it lives in: how traffic reaches it, how it reaches other services, and what is allowed to talk to what. Once the realm of dedicated network professionals only, cloud-based, virtual network infrastructure now allows operations engineers to play a role in defining the network context in which applications run.

In cloud environments, networks are software-defined, versioned, and deployed as code. The same principles you saw earlier with infrastructure-as-code apply here: declarative definitions, repeatable provisioning, and predictable behavior across environments.

Subnets, Route Tables, and Routers

At the most basic level, a virtual network is subdivided into *subnets*, which define address ranges and group resources with similar connectivity or security requirements. Subnets are often used to separate resources based on networking requirements; a common pattern is to create *private subnets* that cannot be accessed from the Internet alongside *public subnets* that can.

Routing determines how traffic moves between those subnets and how traffic may go out. *Route tables* define where packets should go based on destination, controlling whether traffic stays internal, moves between tiers, or exits the network entirely. Figure 7.3 depicts how these components fit together.

From an automation standpoint, these components are rarely configured imperatively. Instead, routes and subnets are declared in IaC templates and applied consistently across environments. The network topology itself becomes part of your deployment.

FIGURE 7.3 Basic network architecture for web applications.

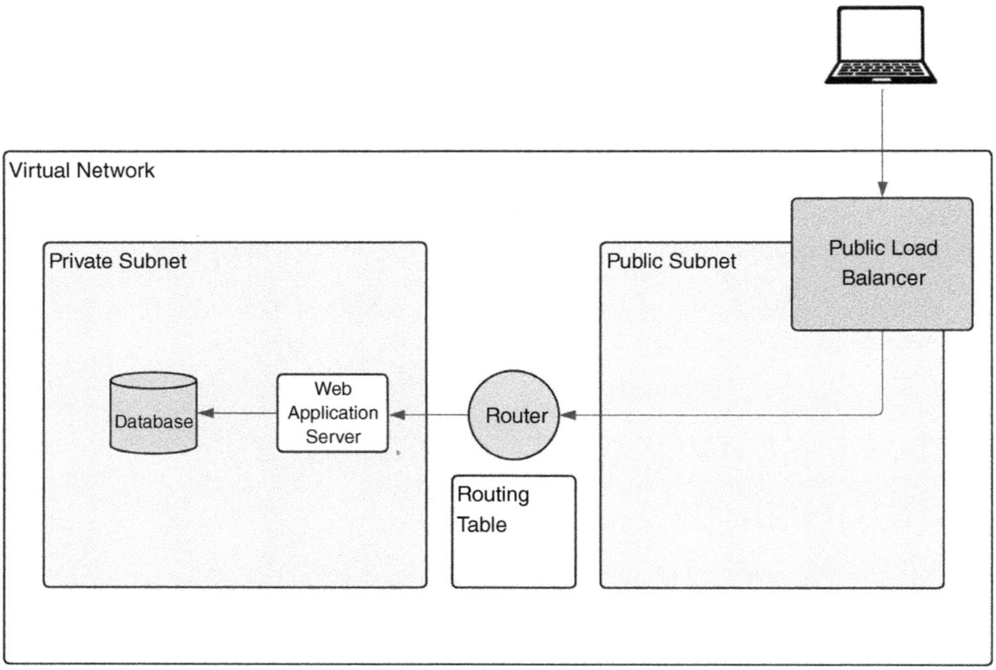

However, as we discussed earlier, some template-defined parts of your environments change more slowly than others. It's a good idea to keep core networking infrastructure in its own IaC template. That way, you don't risk it falling into an inconsistent state because some faster-changing element (virtual machines, container infrastructure, etc.) experienced an error.

Domain Name System (DNS)

Domain Name System (*DNS*) is the connective tissue that allows humans and applications to refer to resources by name instead of IP address. In automated environments, DNS becomes especially important because IPs are often ephemeral. Instances are created, destroyed, and replaced regularly, but service names must remain stable.

Virtual network configurations typically integrate DNS at multiple levels: internal name resolution for services within the network, and external resolution for public-facing endpoints. Automation tools rely heavily on this indirection. Scripts, applications, and configuration files reference hostnames, not addresses, allowing infrastructure to change underneath them without breaking consumers.

In many platforms, such as AWS's Route 53 service, DNS records can be software-defined. Likewise, they can be managed declaratively alongside the rest of the infrastructure (i.e., in CloudFormation templates).

DNS is a distributed system, where many nodes on the Internet work together to answer queries. Each node, and indeed endpoints like your own computer, cache responses to help ensure answers can be returned as fast as possible. The duration of this cache is determined by the record's *Time to Live* (TTL) attribute. TTL determines *propagation time*, or how long it takes a DNS record update to make its way to any node that might query it. Many an operations engineer has cursed TTL and DNS propagation time when trying to make an emergency DNS fix; alas, it is an intrinsic part of how DNS works, and we'd miss it if it were gone.

DNS records come in many flavors; operations professionals need to know about these few.

A Records

An *A record* in DNS is a name that points directly to an IP address. For example, let's say you have a public-facing server with an exposed IP address. First of all, this is not recommended over having a load balancer in front (defined in the next section), and you'd better have a TLS certificate encrypting traffic to this host! An A record would allow you to point a domain name directly to this host, so `myapp.example.com` can route traffic directly to this machine. Figure 7.4 shows how this works.

CNAMEs

CNAME records are the other DNS record type most often used in application automations. Let's say you do have a load balancer in front of your application. Now users out in the world will not connect directly to your host, but to the load balancer—which has its own

FIGURE 7.4 Example of a DNS a record.

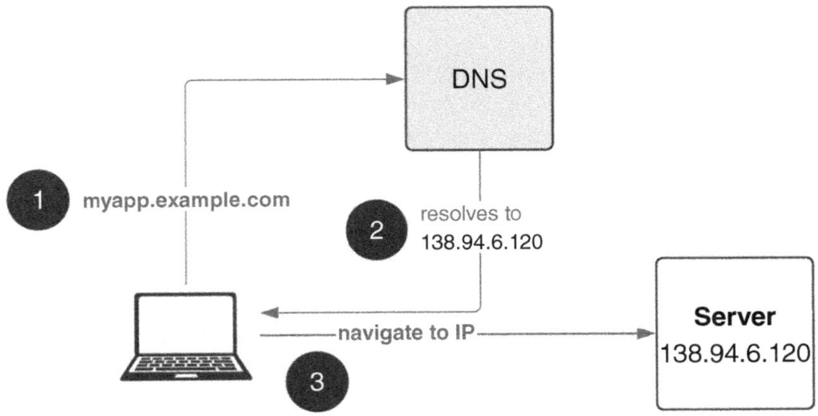

FIGURE 7.5 Example of a DNS CNAME record.

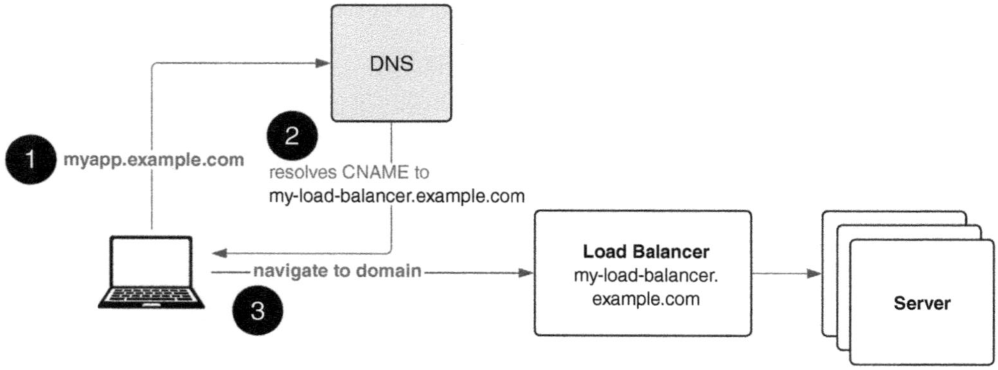

A record. A CNAME lets you route one domain name to another. This is especially helpful because provider-managed, scalable cloud infrastructure is subject to change at runtime or during IaC updates, and while IP addresses might shift, DNS records tend to stay consistent. Figure 7.5 depicts this scenario.

NS

NS records, or Name Server records, are used to tell the world which DNS service manages this domain. These records aren't purely informational; they are essential when defining or switching service providers. For instance, if you were to switch a site's domain management from Hover.com to AWS Route 53 so that you can automate DNS record creation for it, you'd update your NS record to enable the change.

TXT

Finally, the little-used *TXT record*, originally intended just for human-readable metadata, has come into some favor lately with the advent of DNS-based ownership verification. When doing things like changing or creating a TLS certificate for a site, you may need to prove your ownership. One way of doing this is that the TLS provider will direct you to create a TXT record of a certain value. The provider can query DNS for this record, thereby confirming you had the access to make the change. This is a bit like when a financial service makes microdeposits in your bank account to validate your ownership; if you have the access necessary to recite the amounts the service deposited, that entity knows you own the bank account.

Traffic Management: Load Balancers

Getting an application up and running on one server is an accomplishment, but if you want a flexible, scalable, and fault-tolerant architecture, you'll need to introduce another networking component: the *load balancer*. Load balancers sit at key junctions in the

FIGURE 7.6 A load balancer in action.

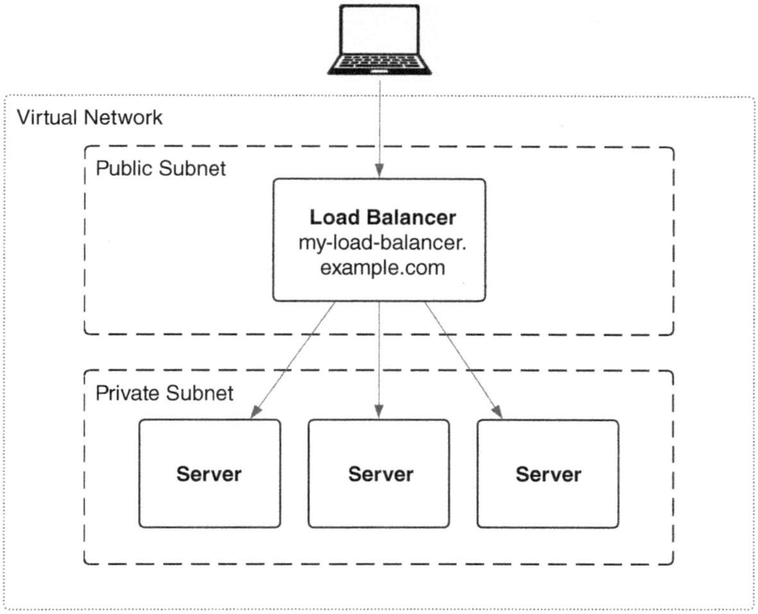

network, distributing incoming traffic across multiple back-end servers (or containers). Figure 7.6 shows a basic load balancer-based web architecture.

For a web application, a load balancer becomes the entry point for user traffic; as such, its configuration determines which ports are open, which protocols are allowed, and which backend targets are considered healthy. In automated deployments, they also become integration points for rolling updates, blue/green deployments, and canary releases—all topics you'll encounter again when we discuss continuous delivery in Chapter 10, "Continuous Delivery." As with other network components, modern load balancers are configured declaratively. Their listeners, routing rules, and target instances can be specified in templates.

Load balancers are essential for scaling your applications and workflows. Also, as we'll learn in a few sections, that they can manage TLS certifications, which makes securing application traffic much easier. Finally, cloud-based load balancers are quite scalable, and can be set up to route traffic not just for one load-balanced application, but for many, making them an invaluable part of any web-based architecture, and one that we'll explore in more detail in the next chapter.

Perimeter Security: Firewalls

Firewalls define the boundaries of what traffic is allowed into, out of, and within a virtual network. In cloud and virtualized environments, these controls are often implemented as software-defined rules rather than physical appliances, but the underlying purpose remains the same.

Firewall rules typically operate at multiple layers: Some control traffic at the network boundary, while others restrict communication between internal components. Like subnets and routes, firewall rules are best managed as code. This allows them to be reviewed, versioned, and audited alongside application and infrastructure changes.

In the past, firewalls were implemented as physical network appliances that operated primarily on IP-based rules. You had to know either specific IPs to allow or deny or you needed to know ranges from which traffic might originate. I've had the experience of working with network engineers to trace down traffic from logs to try to understand which of a dozen different rules might be preventing necessary connections—it got pretty confusing! Today, firewall appliances (virtual or otherwise) still have their place, often at the network border, while most intra-network firewall rules are defined as rules attached to cloud resources.

The Security Group Model

In cloud infrastructure environments, you have the ability to define network security rules as distinct objects that can be reused and attached to resources. As an example, perhaps in your environment, you allow SSH on all web servers—but only from the centralized Ansible server. You might define a rule that looks like this (in pseudocode):

```
ALLOW TCP 22 from <IP of Ansible central server>
```

We can then give this rule (or set of multiple rules) a name like `allow_ansible_management` and attach it to any new virtual machine you create with infrastructure-as-code tools. Then, if the IP address of your Ansible server changes, you only have one place you need to update to enable the SSH configuration management traffic to flow again.

In AWS, such firewall definitions are called *security groups*, and they have one key innovation over traditional firewall rules: You can define a rule as applying not just to an IP or range of IPs, but to any resource having another security group. To explain, consider this scenario: All web servers need to allow traffic on port 80 (HTTP) from a load balancer. The load balancer needs to allow world traffic on port 443 (HTTP). You just need two definitions to allow this:

```
my_load_balancer_security_group (sg-123)
ALLOW TCP 443 from 0.0.0.0 (world)

my_web_server_security_group (sg-456)
ALLOW TCP 80 from sg-123
```

Notice how the second rule doesn't allow traffic from an IP. It allows traffic from another security group—to be precise, from any resource possessing that security group. Figure 7.7 shows this approach in action. Here, web instances possessing `sg-web-server` are allowed to reach the web database, whose own security group allows `sg-web-server`. At the same time, they are not able to reach the sales database, which only allows traffic from resources bearing security group `sg-sales-server`.

FIGURE 7.7 Security groups as role-based firewalls for cloud resources.

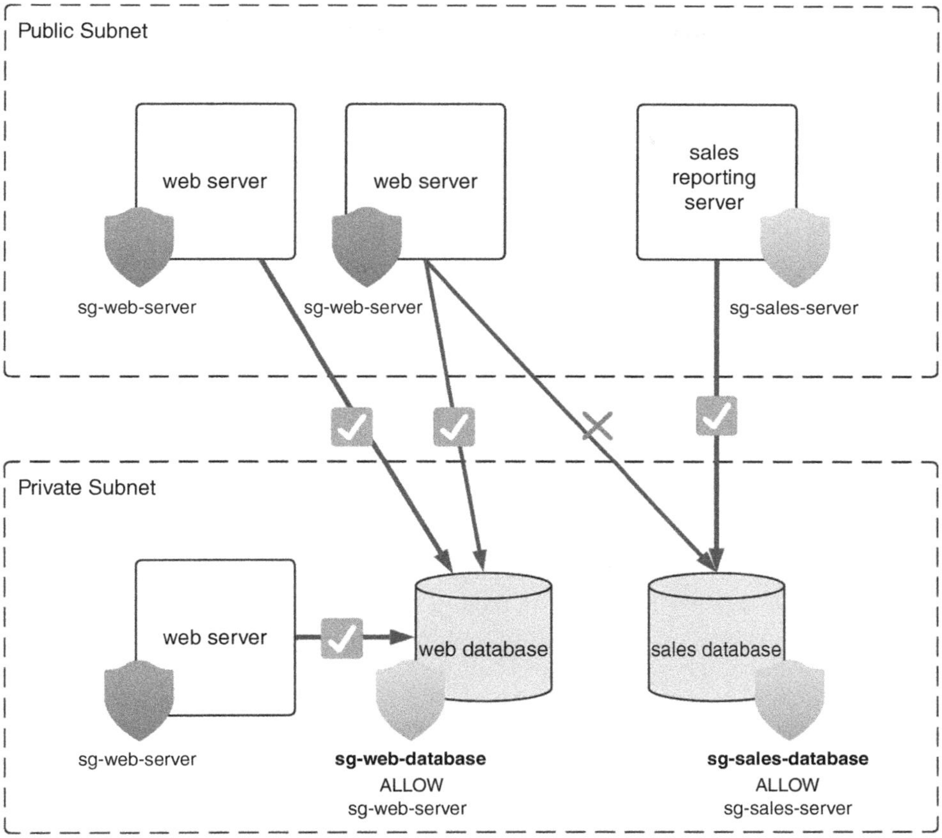

In this architecture, security groups function more like a badge than a firewall; for the web servers, if incoming traffic bears the badge of the load balancer's security group, it's allowed in. Now you're not thinking about IP addresses at all—you're thinking about how to classify resources into roles and defining what roles should talk to each other on what ports.

Workload Configuration and Access Control

Once infrastructure and networking are in place, workloads still need to be configured so they run correctly and securely. Workload configuration sits at the boundary between system setup and application behavior. It includes the settings, permissions, and credentials that determine *how* a service runs and *who* is allowed to interact with it.

In automated environments, these concerns are handled declaratively and repeatably. Configuration is not something applied once and forgotten; it is part of the system's desired state and must be enforced continuously.

Workload Configuration Techniques

Workload configuration covers the runtime-specific details that shape how an application behaves. This includes environment variables, configuration files, feature flags, and runtime parameters. These values are often environment-specific, but the mechanisms used to apply them should not be.

Configuration management tools and infrastructure-as-code templates are typically responsible for injecting these settings at deploy time. This avoids hard-coding values into application binaries and allows the same artifact to be deployed across multiple environments with different behavior. When configuration is externalized and versioned, changes become auditable and reversible, rather than ad hoc.

Access Control Lists (ACLs)

Access control lists define who or what is allowed to access a resource. In virtualized and cloud environments, ACLs are commonly used to control network access, service permissions, and data-layer interactions.

From an automation perspective, ACLs are just another form of configuration—one with security implications. They should be defined explicitly, applied consistently, and reviewed alongside other infrastructure changes. Relying on defaults or manual exceptions introduces risk and makes behavior harder to reason about over time.

Well-designed ACLs follow the principle of least privilege: Grant only the access required for a workload to function, and nothing more. Encoding these rules as part of infrastructure or configuration templates ensures they are enforced uniformly across environments.

Managing Certificates

In information technology, security is everyone's responsibility, because security happens on every layer of the stack. One essential element of security is encryption and knowing when to apply it. You'll often hear security professionals refer to the distinction between encryption "at rest" and encryption "in transit." Encryption at rest means encrypting data on hard drives or other storage locations, whereas encryption in transit is about what happens when data travels between systems over network connections. For our purposes, we are most concerned with encryption in transit, and that means TLS.

Transport Layer Security (TLS) is the successor to Secure Sockets Layer (SSL). Even many nontechnical web users are familiar with the distinction between HTTP and HTTPS, or

HTTP over SSL. Whether they know the acronyms or not, web users understand that the little lock icon associated with HTTPS means their credit card numbers and passwords are not exposed to hackers as they make their way to their banking website.

Even though today's HTTPS is actually HTTP over TLS, the original acronym remains. In practice, implementing this protocol means that web traffic is encrypted and cannot easily be viewed or altered by an attacker. It's an essential part of your understanding as an operations automation expert, and to implement TLS, you need to know about certificates.

Certificates enable encrypted communication and identity verification between systems. One important concept in certificate management is determining when traffic actually stops being encrypted. After all, at some point a system has to actually read the text of the request in order to process it. The boundary at which this occurs is called *TLS termination*, and it not only has implications for when traffic is encrypted, but it also determines the point in your infrastructure at which you must manage TLS certificates. This can happen in several places:

At a **load balancer or reverse proxy**, where incoming HTTPS traffic is decrypted before being forwarded internally

At the **application server itself**, where the workload directly handles TLS

At an **edge service or gateway**, in front of the application

Terminating TLS on the web server itself is definitely "cert management on hard mode." You need to manage a certificate request and update process on every host and stay on top of ever-shrinking validity timelines, because certificates expire.

Managing Cert Expiration

TLS certificates have a predetermined shelf life. When they expire, users get one of the classic error screens, as shown in Figure 7.8.

The website in the screenshot is `https://expired.badssl.com`, a site that maintains an expired certificate to allow clients to test their behavior under this condition.

Even though an expired cert might be easily resolved, having this screen appear to users even once is disproportionately bad; no service provider ever wants to give users reasons to distrust the security of their service. It's the kind of thing that can send users to alternatives or competitors, fast.

The expiration of certificates is done in the name of security. Like passwords, certs can be compromised, and rotating them frequently gives you the best chance at reducing the potential harm. If an attacker is in possession of a legitimate certificate, they can spoof your website and steal users' data. For this reason, it's best if certificates are not long-lived.

Though certs themselves have expiration dates, web clients can choose to treat them as expired even earlier. Google has proposed web security by enforcing limits as low as 90 days in their Chrome browser. This means that it's absolutely essential that you automate the renewal of certificates as much as possible! Luckily, many services exist to help you do just that.

FIGURE 7.8 Chrome warns users of an expired certificate.

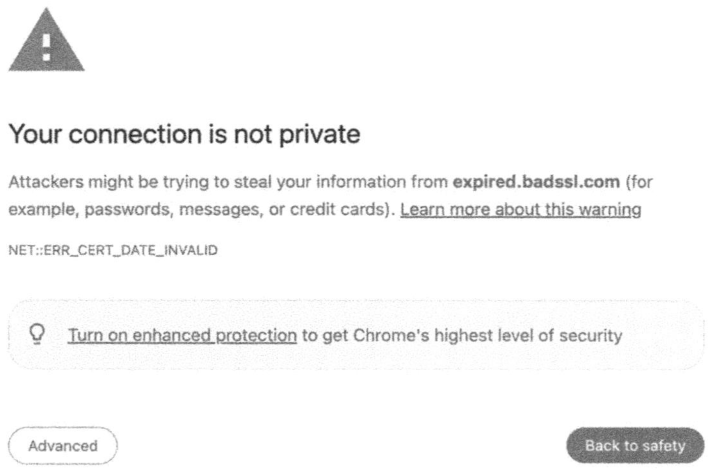

Centralizing Certificate Management

Centralized TLS termination (e.g., at a load balancer) simplifies certificate management significantly over host-based options. In Amazon Web Services, AWS Certificate Manager provides both the provisioning and automatic renewal of TLS certificates. Equivalents exist in the other providers like Azure App Service Certificates or Google Cloud Certificate Manager, which issue and renew certificates automatically for supported services like load balancers and gateways.

For anyone who has ever scrambled like mad to renew a cert in production in the aforementioned expiration scenario, "automatic cert renewal" sounds like a blessing from on high—and it is. Use these services whenever possible.

End-to-end TLS, where traffic remains encrypted all the way to the workload, sounds better on paper. It provides stronger isolation but requires certificates to be managed on every host or container. If your virtual network infrastructure is built correctly, this isn't necessary, because you're routing unencrypted traffic to secure subnets where potentially malicious user traffic cannot reach them directly. In this safe networking zone, unencrypted traffic can flow freely without fear.

Automation fundamentally changes how certificates are handled. Instead of manually generating, installing, and renewing certificates, modern systems integrate certificate management into deployment workflows. Certificates are provisioned, rotated, and revoked automatically, reducing both operational overhead and the risk of outages caused by expired credentials.

Host-Based Certificate Management

If you must manage certificates on an individual endpoint or host, a common approach is to use a reverse proxy like `nginx`. You obtain the certificate—a key file that you must treat like a password and store securely—and configure it as part of your proxy setup. `nginx` or its equivalent handles the TLS termination.

To obtain and manage the cert itself, look into `certbot`, a popular command tool that allows you to more easily automate the provisioning and renewal of certificates yourself using public certificate authorities like Let's Encrypt.

No matter what route you choose, it's important to make sure your users' traffic is always secure and that your infrastructure is set up to actively manage TLS provisioning and renewal.

Secrets Management

Credentials, passwords, tokens, and keys are among the most sensitive inputs in any system, yet in order to do their jobs of connecting applications to APIs, databases, and other systems, they must be accessible in plain text to the application at runtime. This intrinsic tension between the need to secure secrets and the need to use them has led to many solutions that help minimize secrets' exposure both at runtime and at rest. Modern automation assumes secrets are centrally stored, encrypted by default, short-lived where possible, and accessible only to explicitly authorized workloads. Taken together, these practices are known as *secrets management.*

Leveraging Environment Variables

Before we talk about secrets management services, let's take a look at some of the ways you can enhance your secret handling even for more manual/ad hoc deployments.

Let's get the basics out of the way: *never, ever hard-code secrets.* Don't put them in your source code; always refer to variables that you define elsewhere. One of the best ways to do this is to fetch secrets from the environment; that is, the shell environment. We've seen this with shell scripts. If you first `export API_KEY=abc123`, then your shell script can connect to an API like so:

```
response_code=$(curl http://api.example.com/sales \
  -H "Authorization: Bearer $API_KEY"
```

Or in Python, you can use the `os` package to fetch from the environment:

```
import os
import requests

token = os.environ["API_KEY"]
resp = requests.get(
    "https://api.example.com/sales",
    headers={"Authorization": f"Bearer {token}"}
)

print(resp.status_code)
```

To do this, you have to set each variable in your environment before invoking the script, which can get cumbersome. A very common way of doing this is with a *dotenv* file. This is a file, literally called `.env`, that has some tooling around it to import secrets into your environment. Packages exist in multiple languages to handle dotenv files. Here's how it works in Python. First, create a newline-delimited file of key-value pairs and name it `.env`:

```
API_KEY=abc123
API_BASE_URL=https://api.example.com
DATABASE_PASSWORD=foo
```

This file should *never* be committed to a Git repo or pushed to a remote repository! Post-commit hooks and security scans in GitHub can help ensure this doesn't happen, or at least that you are notified quickly if it does. Hackers have tools set up to constantly monitor public GitHub repos for mistakes like this. You'd be amazed how quickly a bad guy can spin up an expensive crypto-mining operation in the cloud account of a hapless developer who accidentally uploaded their keys to a public repo—no doubt using the kind of automation techniques you're learning in this book.

First, add `python-dotenv` to your `requirements.txt` file and run `pip install` (in your virtual environment, right?). Then you can use the dotenv file like so:

```
import os
import requests
from dotenv import load_dotenv

load_dotenv()  # loads variables from .env into the environment

token = os.environ["API_TOKEN"]
resp = requests.get(
    f"{base_url}/sales",
    headers={"Authorization": f"Bearer {token}"}
)

print(resp.status_code)
```

Some language and frameworks even let you bundle secrets with your app, encrypted so that they can be pushed safely to version control. In this case, you still have one secret that must be kept separate and safe: the master key that unlocks the repo-based secrets repository.

Environment variables can also be used when working with Docker; rather than encode them in the Dockerfile or embed a secrets file in the layers of your image, the `docker run` command itself can inject secrets at container deployment time, making sure that your secrets are only ever "active" in the most ephemeral way possible. This secrets injection is an option in the Docker command-line tools as well as cloud container orchestration. In AWS, it can even tie in automatically with the cloud provider's centralized secrets management tool . . . which leads us to the topic of secrets management as a service.

Encrypted Key Vaults

The most robust secrets management approaches use a centralized secrets management tool, a strategy that centers around an encrypted *key vault*. Vaults store sensitive values securely at rest and expose controlled APIs for retrieving them at runtime. Instead of trying to build secure distribution of secrets into your application deployment pipelines, applications request secrets when needed and discard them when finished.

Note that in some cases, this can put more responsibilities on the application layer, as it's now the responsibility of app code to fetch secrets upon startup or even later, at runtime. Other methods exist to fetch secrets in batch from a vault so that they can be injected into the app's runtime upon deployment.

Dynamic Secret Rotation and Leases

As with TLS certificates, application secrets are more potentially dangerous the longer-lived they are. This is why security professionals suggest rotating your passwords regularly. *Dynamic secret rotation* makes this an automatic part of your application's environment by issuing credentials with limited lifetimes and rotating them automatically. Because credentials are often created in the target system (e.g., inside a Postgres database), such dynamic systems involve some degree of integration with other applications. As a result, this feature does not apply to every system, but when it's available, it can be a powerful way to limit the blast radius of compromised credentials.

Some platforms issue secrets on demand and attach *leases* to them. When the lease expires, the secret becomes invalid without requiring manual cleanup. Applications are forced to reauthenticate regularly, which dramatically limits the usefulness of compromised credentials.

This pattern is especially effective in automated environments, where workloads are short-lived and frequently replaced. Keep in mind that for longer-lived workloads, like web applications deployed to virtual machines, your app may easily have uptimes longer than secrets are valid. You must code in safeguards to check for failures due to expired keys and automatically request a reissue. Again, security requires a little more sophistication in both automation and application code.

Edge Cases of Short-Term Credential Renewal

Short-lived credentials significantly reduce risk, but they can also introduce subtle timing issues in production systems. Credential renewal is not always handled in a synchronous manner (i.e. try to perform an operation, then attempt a lease renewal before trying again).

Often, credential renewals are handled asynchronously, either by background threads, sidecars, or shared token managers. Database connection pools, which dole out handles to databases to ensure the database's connection limit is not overwhelmed, are another source of indirection when it comes to handling time-limited credentials. All of these factors can create some interesting (irritating) possibilities for race conditions, where requests fail despite the best intentions of you or your app developers.

Under sustained load, it is possible for some requests to overlap a lease expiration window, resulting in authentication failures even when renewal is functioning correctly. In these cases, applications still often recover automatically by renewing credentials and retrying subsequent requests, but individual requests may fail in the process. This is just a natural consequence of time-bounded authentication in concurrent, distributed environments.

Revocation Strategies

Secret rotation expires keys on an expected schedule; *revocation* is for cases where you know a secret has been compromised, and you need to take action immediately. When this happens, the secret must be invalidated right away, everywhere it is used. Centralized vaults make this possible by acting as the single authority for secret validity.

Because secrets are not copied into code or configuration files, revocation becomes a single operation rather than a scavenger hunt. Once revoked, dependent systems fail safely instead of continuing with compromised access.

Secrets Management Platforms

There are a number of great options for the operations automation professional looking to adopt centralized secrets management. As with infrastructure-as-code, some are tied to certain providers, whereas others are cross-platform.

AWS Secrets Manager and IAM Roles

In AWS environments, AWS Secrets Manager is a common choice for storing sensitive credentials such as database passwords and API keys. Secrets are encrypted at rest and accessed via the AWS API.

A key advantage to AWS's implementation is integration with IAM (Identity and Access Management) roles. Rather than accessing credentials stored locally or even in a vault, compute resources (such as EC2 instances or containers running on Elastic Container Service) assume roles that grant permission to retrieve specific secrets.

For example, a script running on an EC2 instance might retrieve a secret like this:

```
aws secretsmanager get-secret-value \
  --secret-id prod/db/password \
  --query SecretString \
  --output text
```

The script itself contains no credentials—and neither does the server it's running on. Access is granted by the IAM role attached to the instance. This allows permissions to be scoped tightly to a workload's purpose.

HashiCorp Vault

HashiCorp Vault is a widely adopted, cloud-agnostic secrets platform. Vault supports encrypted storage, dynamic secrets, leasing, and fine-grained policies across cloud and on-premises environments.

A simple Vault workflow might look like writing and reading a secret:

```
vault kv put secret/app/db password=supersecret
vault kv get secret/app/db
```

Vault can also generate secrets dynamically—for example, creating short-lived database credentials on demand. When the lease expires, Vault automatically revokes access without relying on human intervention.

Azure Key Vault

In Azure, Azure Key Vault provides encrypted storage for secrets, keys, and certificates. Similar to AWS, applications typically authenticate using managed identities rather than static credentials, allowing access to be scoped per workload.

Google Secret Manager

Google Cloud offers Google Secret Manager, which integrates with GCP IAM and supports identity-based access for workloads running on Compute Engine, GKE, or Cloud Run. As with the other platforms, secrets are retrieved at runtime and never embedded in code.

The tooling differs slightly across providers, but the architectural pattern is the same: identity-based access, centralized storage, and automated life cycle management.

Managing Configuration Values

Sometimes you have values you want to avoid hard-coding because they vary across environments, but they're not considered sensitive, like the base URL of an API. For nonsensitive configuration values like these, you may certainly use secrets management systems, but this can sometimes be overkill.

For both application and automation code, you want to externalize configuration values in much the same way you externalize secrets, hard-coding nothing and relying on pulling in variable values at runtime. Some languages and frameworks have first-class support for this, such as Ruby on Rails' per-environment settings in `config.rb`. For others, third-party packages can assist.

Finally, cloud services can fill the bill here. Google's Firebase platform offers Cloud Functions Configuration (now replaced by the `params` package) that lets you define key-value pairs that are fetchable in your code. Similarly, AWS Systems Manager Parameter Store is a good option that lets you follow the same identity-based access pattern as Secrets Manager. Azure offers Azure App Configuration and GCP allows unencrypted values in its Secrets Manager.

Whatever approach you use, the guiding principle is this: separate secrets and configuration from code, keeping changeable and sensitive values in externally managed stores where they are easy to create, update, delete, and fetch at runtime. This allows you to write and ship one version of code, varying the per-environment behavior through the injection of per-environment configuration.

Principles of Zero Trust

Increasingly, systems architects are adopting the principles of what is somewhat inconveniently named *zero trust*. Although the phrase itself doesn't necessarily sound secure, it implies an increased emphasis on security not just at network boundaries, but at the *identity* boundary.

Essentially, this design philosophy holds that network security rules and firewalls are an insufficient—maybe even unnecessary—method of keeping systems secure, and that the focus should be on those methods described above, including identity- and role-based security that relies on consistent, structured, and protocol-based validation of a caller's identity. As you build automation systems, think about ways to secure your workloads and properly manage access to credentials that would give you confidence even if the secure resource were open to all the traffic on the internet.

Summary

In this chapter, you focused on everything that surrounds automation code and determines whether it succeeds or fails once it leaves a developer's laptop. We began with dependency management, showing how libraries, packages, runtimes, and operating system components form the foundation of the execution environment. We emphasized that dependencies must be clearly defined and versions locked to let us rebuild the same environment predictably across systems.

From there, we explored how different platforms approach dependency management, surveying Linux and Windows package managers and examining how scripting languages like Python isolate and reproduce dependencies using virtual environments. We also looked at containerized workflows, where dependencies are baked directly into immutable images and rebuilt instead of patched, reinforcing many of the same principles we encountered in infrastructure-as-code.

We widened the lens to include virtual network infrastructure and workload configuration, highlighting how subnets, routing, DNS, load balancers, firewalls, access control lists, and certificates determine the connectivity and security of automated systems.

Finally, we closed the chapter by examining secrets management, learning how modern systems use encrypted vaults, dynamic rotation, leasing, revocation, and identity-based access to protect sensitive configuration at scale.

With these pieces in place, you now have a cohesive view of how environments are prepared for reliable automation. In the next chapter, we'll build on these elements as we look at patterns of application architecture, the details of which will directly inform our approach to continuous integration and delivery.

Exam Essentials

Understand dependencies as part of the execution environment. Know that automation depends not just on code, but on the full execution environment, including operating system packages, language runtimes, and third-party libraries. Understand how unmanaged dependencies cause nondeterministic behavior across machines, build systems, and production environments.

Recognize common dependency management approaches. Be familiar with system-level package managers on Linux and Windows, language-level dependency files such as `requirements.txt`, and how containers formalize dependencies through image definitions. Understand the role each layer plays and why separating system, language, and application dependencies improves clarity and troubleshooting.

Understand why reproducibility matters more than convenience. Know why pinning versions, freezing dependencies, and using lockfiles are essential for reliable automation. Be able to explain why using "latest" versions introduces risk and how deterministic installs support automation pipelines and repeatable deployments.

Understand how containers change dependency management. Know that containers bundle dependencies into immutable images and shift dependency management to build time. Understand why containers are rebuilt rather than patched, and how versioned images function as deployable artifacts in automated systems.

Understand workload configuration as a separate concern from code. Know that workload configuration includes runtime settings, environment variables, and parameters that vary by environment. Understand why configuration should be externalized, injected at deploy time, and managed declaratively rather than hard-coded.

Recognize common virtual network infrastructure components. Be able to identify subnets, route tables, routers, DNS, load balancers, and firewalls as foundational infrastructure elements that automation relies on. Understand that these components are commonly defined using infrastructure-as-code and directly influence application reachability and security.

Understand access control mechanisms in automated environments. Know how access control lists (ACLs) and firewall rules enforce boundaries between systems. Understand the principle of least privilege and why access controls should be explicit, versioned, and automated rather than manually adjusted.

Understand the role of certificates in secure automation. Know that certificates enable encrypted communication between systems. Understand why certificate provisioning, rotation, and renewal are commonly automated and treated as part of workload configuration.

Understand modern secrets management patterns. Be familiar with encrypted key vaults, tokenization, secret rotation, leasing, expiration, and revocation. Understand why secrets must be handled differently from general configuration and why static, long-lived credentials undermine automation security.

Recognize common secrets management tools and patterns. Know that platforms such as AWS Secrets Manager, HashiCorp Vault, Azure Key Vault, and Google Secret Manager provide centralized, encrypted secret storage. Understand how identity-based access, such as IAM roles in AWS, allows workloads to retrieve secrets securely without embedding credentials.

Understand how zero trust principles apply to automation. Know that zero trust assumes no implicit trust based on network location. Understand how identity-based access, short-lived credentials, continuous verification, and centralized secrets management support secure automation at scale.

Review Questions

1. You're running a Python automation script locally. It works on your laptop but fails in your continuous integration environment with `ModuleNotFoundError: No module named 'requests'`. What is the most appropriate long-term fix?
   A. Install the missing module manually on the CI runner.
   B. Add the module to a `requirements.txt` file and install dependencies as part of the build.
   C. Copy the `requests` source code into the project repository.
   D. Modify the script to catch the error and continue execution.

2. A Python service works correctly on a developer's laptop but fails on a shared Linux server with a version conflict between two libraries. Multiple automation scripts run on that server for unrelated projects. What is the most appropriate long-term fix?
   A. Install the required library versions globally and document the change.
   B. Copy the working site-packages directory from the laptop to the server.
   C. Use a Python virtual environment per project to isolate dependencies.
   D. Migrate the script to another compute environment.

3. Your team uses Docker images for deployment. A critical OS library vulnerability is discovered. What is the best remediation strategy?
   A. SSH into running containers and patch the library.
   B. Restart containers to apply automatic updates.
   C. Update the Dockerfile and rebuild the image.
   D. Install the patched library using configuration management.

4. An application retrieves a database password from AWS Secrets Manager using the AWS CLI. No credentials are stored in the code. How is access most likely granted?
   A. A hard-coded access key in the container image
   B. A shared IAM user used by all applications
   C. An IAM role attached to the compute resource
   D. A public secrets endpoint

5. Two environments use the same `requirements.txt` file, but deployments behave differently. What is the most likely cause?
   A. Python version mismatch
   B. Network latency differences
   C. Missing environment variables
   D. Dependencies with no lockfile or version constraints

6. A security scan flags a critical vulnerability in a transitive dependency used by your application, even though your code never imports it directly. What is the most accurate interpretation of this result?
   - A. The issue can be ignored because it is not a direct dependency.
   - B. Only the package author is responsible for fixing transitive issues.
   - C. The vulnerability may still impact your application and must be addressed.
   - D. The scan is a false positive caused by dependency graph depth.
7. A team deploys a containerized application that uses short-lived, Vault-issued credentials to authenticate to a backend service. Credential renewal is handled asynchronously, and the backend validates credentials at request execution time. After a rollout, the application intermittently returns authentication errors, but only during periods of sustained high traffic. What is the most likely cause?
   - A. The Vault server is running out of disk space.
   - B. Some requests are executed after the credential lease expires, before renewal takes effect.
   - C. The container image was built with outdated dependencies.
   - D. DNS resolution for the Vault endpoint is unstable.
8. Your organization defines firewall rules, subnets, and route tables using infrastructure-as-code. A manual firewall rule is added in production to "temporarily fix" an outage. What is the most significant long-term risk?
   - A. The firewall rule may be removed automatically by the cloud provider.
   - B. The rule may conflict with DNS resolution.
   - C. The change introduces configuration drift that automation cannot detect.
   - D. The rule increases network latency.
9. You are reviewing a Dockerfile that installs build tools, application libraries, and then copies in source code. Why is it considered best practice to install dependencies *before* copying application code?
   - A. It ensures application code can modify dependency versions at runtime.
   - B. It minimizes container size by merging layers.
   - C. It improves rebuild performance by maximizing layer cache reuse.
   - D. It allows dependency versions to be injected dynamically.
10. A team pins an OS-level package version to avoid breaking a legacy script. Months later, the package is found to have a known CVE. What risk does this version pin introduce?
    - A. The package manager may refuse to install unrelated updates.
    - B. The system may silently miss critical security patches.
    - C. The pinned package will auto-upgrade during reboots.
    - D. Dependency resolution will automatically downgrade other packages.

11. Why are DNS records preferred over hard-coded IP addresses in automated environments?
    A. DNS guarantees lower network latency.
    B. DNS records are encrypted by default.
    C. DNS allows infrastructure to change without breaking consumers.
    D. DNS prevents unauthorized access to services.
12. An application receives HTTPS traffic at a load balancer, which then forwards requests unencrypted to backend servers in private subnets. What is this design an example of?
    A. End-to-end TLS
    B. Host-based certificate management
    C. TLS termination at the load balancer
    D. Insecure transport due to plain text traffic
13. What problem do short-lived credentials with leases primarily solve?
    A. They eliminate the need for authentication.
    B. They reduce the usefulness of stolen secrets.
    C. They simplify application code.
    D. They remove the need for encryption.
14. An application reads API tokens from an ENV file during local development. Why must this file never be committed to version control?
    A. It will break dependency resolution.
    B. It prevents container builds from succeeding.
    C. It may expose secrets to unauthorized parties.
    D. It causes environment variables to override defaults.

Answers to Review Questions

1. B. Option B is correct. Adding the dependency to `requirements.txt` makes it explicit and reproducible across environments. Option A is not scalable or repeatable, especially since continuous integration environments tend to be ephemeral. Option C doesn't work and is essentially the opposite of package management! Option D hides the failure rather than fixing it, and your code just won't work.
2. C. The correct answer is C. Virtual environments isolate language-level dependencies per project, preventing version conflicts between unrelated workloads on the same machine. Option A overwrites the existing global package version, fixing your script but likely breaking others. Option B is brittle and nonreproducible. Option D would work temporarily, but it's not a long-term solution.

3. C. Option C is correct. Containers are immutable, so the correct approach is to update the Dockerfile, rebuild the image, and redeploy. In fact, if your Dockerfile contains a general patching command line `apt update`, you may only need to rebuild, not edit the Dockerfile. Option A is incorrect because containers are ephemeral; you are not intended to update them at runtime. Option B is incorrect because restarting a container does not trigger any of the code inside a Dockerfile; this only occurs when an image is built. Option D is also incorrect; configuration management is meant for long-running compute instances like virtual machines. Plus, unless you rebuild the Docker image, all future containers spawned from it will reflect the old, vulnerable package configuration.

4. C. The correct answer is option C. IAM roles allow workloads to retrieve secrets securely without embedded credentials. Option A is incorrect; do not hard-code secrets! Option B violates practices of least privilege, so it is not the best choice. Option D is incorrect, as this is not how AWS Secrets Manager works, nor would it be secure to expose publicly.

5. D. Option D is correct. If versions are not pinned with a lockfile, and the requirements file contains package directives that allow the package manager to fetch the latest version (or the latest from a range), it's entirely possible that different dependency versions will be resolved over time. Option A is incorrect; the version of Python doesn't impact how packages are fetched. Neither does option B, nor option C.

6. C. The correct answer is option C. Transitive dependencies are part of your runtime environment and can introduce vulnerabilities just as easily as direct dependencies. They are your responsibility to keep up-to-date. Option A is incorrect and a very risky idea. Option B is incorrect; the package author needs to fix the vulnerability, but it's your responsibility to update your app—or to find a replacement if the owner doesn't fix the package. Option D is a poor assumption; don't ignore the signals you get from your security tooling!

7. B. Option B is correct. Vault-issued credentials are time-bound. Under sustained load, requests may still be in flight when a lease expires, and renewal does not retroactively extend to a request in progress. This can result in intermittent authentication failures that correlate with traffic volume. Option C would cause consistent failures, not load-dependent ones. Options A and D could cause problems but do not specifically explain authentication errors tied to system load.

8. C. Option C is correct. Manual changes bypass the declared infrastructure state, creating drift. Future automated deployments may overwrite or depend on incorrect assumptions about network security. Options A, B, and D are either incorrect or secondary effects.

9. C. The correct answer is C. Docker rebuilds layers only when inputs or Dockerfile code changes. Installing dependencies before copying code ensures that code changes don't invalidate cached dependency layers. Option A is inaccurate and contradicts Docker's principles of immutability. Option B is a characteristic of Docker, but not the primary reason to install dependencies first. Option D is not how Docker layering works.

10. B. The correct answer is B. Version pinning can prevent security updates from being applied, leaving known vulnerabilities unpatched. This is why external dependency scanning tools like Dependabot are so important. Option A is unrelated. Option C is not how version pinning

works; the package would never be updated without intervention. Similarly, Option D is not how package managers resolve versions.

11. C. The correct answer is option C. DNS provides stable naming for clients while underlying IPs can change. Option A is not something provided by DNS. Option B is false and doesn't make much sense because DNS records are not secret. Option D is incorrect because DNS does not determine access in any way.

12. C. The correct answer is C. In this pattern, TLS termination occurs at the load balancer, which decrypts traffic before forwarding it internally. Option A is incorrect because it describes an architectural property (traffic remaining encrypted all the way to the application) rather than how certificates are provisioned or managed. Option B is incorrect because it refers to an operational approach in which individual hosts manage their own certificates. Option D ignores the protected network boundary.

13. B. The correct answer is option B. Short-lived credentials limit the blast radius of compromised secrets. Option A is incorrect. Option C is inaccurate, because handling credential renewal often means more application logic is required. Option D is false.

14. C. The correct answer is option C. An ENV file commonly contains secrets that should never be stored in source control. Option A is false. Option B is unrelated. Option D is normal and expected behavior.

Deploying and Operating Software

Chapter 8

Patterns of Automation Architecture

THE AUTOOPS+ EXAM TOPICS COVERED IN THIS CHAPTER MAY INCLUDE, BUT ARE NOT LIMITED TO, THE FOLLOWING:

✔ **1.0: Automation Coding Concepts**

- 1.1. Given a scenario, use code to support automation.

✔ **2.0: System Configuration**

- 2.2. Compare and contrast basic approaches to automation.

✔ **3.0: Continuous Integration**

- 3.2. Explain workflow management concepts in CI.

So far, we have focused on how to automate individual tasks like writing scripts, managing configuration, provisioning infrastructure, and preparing environments to ensure your code works once it leaves your laptop. Your toolbox is filling up with all the tools you'll need to construct complete operations automations!

Each tool or technology we've covered plays a role in moving application code through a journey that enhances quality and stability as updates make their way from developer laptops to production. Now, we're going to begin combining everything into end-to-end pipelines that put all those skills to work.

When you automate operations, you move away from manually kicking off scripts whenever something needs doing. Instead, you build event-driven orchestrations that respond automatically to code changes, completed builds, infrastructure updates, alerts, and even failures. The shift from "run this script" to "respond to this event" is one of the hallmarks of cloud-native automation.

In this chapter, we'll explore event-driven automation patterns. We'll look at polling versus event-driven logic and examine notification-based systems, where signals get sent without expecting a response back, before expanding into queues, cloud functions, and the orchestration patterns that tie these pieces together.

Event-Driven Automation and Cloud Architecture

We've established that cloud computing environments are software-defined places where infrastructure is code and services communicate via APIs. This fundamentally changes how teams work: Developers can participate in operations, while operations professionals get to apply their programming skills in new ways.

Because every infrastructure change happens through code, and because every change can alert other systems and trigger actions, these environments create rich opportunities for integration and automation.

Cloud systems are chatty; they emit events constantly. When a resource changes state, when a job completes, when something fails, or when an alert threshold is crossed, cloud infrastructure takes note and either logs the occurrence or notifies other systems. Automations that listen for these signals tend to be faster, cheaper, and more reliable than those that constantly check whether something happened—an approach known as *polling*.

From Polling to Events

Polling is the most straightforward automation trigger to understand. You write a script that asks a question, waits, and asks again, checking things like:

- Has the build finished yet?
- Is a new file present?
- Did the deployment complete?
- Did the server come back up?

If the answer is "no," the script sleeps for a bit and tries again. Polling is easy to reason about, easy to implement, and easy to debug. It's also rather inefficient at scale.

For one thing, most polling loops spend the majority of their runtime doing nothing, and the interval of your polling determines how reactive your scripts can be. If you poll too frequently, you waste compute cycles, API calls, and, potentially, money. If you poll too infrequently, you introduce latency, delaying actions that could have been executed immediately. Also, because polling schedules are usually fixed, they don't adapt well to bursts of activity or sudden changes in load.

Finally, if the external service you're querying fails silently, your polling script may not have any way to distinguish that failure from an "expected" empty response. Silent failures can be the hardest to debug.

So polling is easy and frequently used but has some drawbacks. Wouldn't it be nice if we could just take action exactly when something happens? Cloud platforms give us that option.

Event-Driven Automation as the Default

In an *event-driven automation* model, systems announce that something happened instead of waiting to be asked.

This brings several benefits. First, your response can be immediate. Automations run when the event happens, not on the next polling interval. Second, overhead is lower. There's no constant checking, no idle loops, and no wasted work. Third, intent is clearer. An event describes *what* happened, not just that something might have changed. Finally, error handling can improve, as your systems react to failure messages just as proactively as success.

Push and Pull in Event-Driven Integrations

Automation integrations can come in both push and pull flavors. There is a clear parallel here to the discussion we had about push versus pull models in the context of configuration management. The same distinction applies here, just at a higher level.

Polling is a pull model. Automation pulls state from another system on a schedule, whether or not anything has changed. Events are a push model. Systems push notifications outward when state changes occur.

Differing Event Payload Design Approaches

Using an event-driven architecture doesn't mean you never query the source system. An event may prompt the consumer to request additional details, such as event details, metadata, or related resources.

To some degree, this is determined by the design philosophy of the system emitting the events. Is it providing a simple payload that alerts you that an event occurred, or is it providing enough context to show a clear picture? Some event sources are best described as *notification systems*, wherein the message payload is lightweight, alerting you only that something happened. Other systems send much larger payloads with additional information.

As an example, GitHub's commit webhooks don't just say "a commit happened"; they give a robust JSON object that tells you many related details of the commit. A differently designed system might require you to make a synchronous API call after receiving an event to gather more details. The former tells you the exact state as of the occurrence of the event, whereas the state of a notification-based system might change between the time you receive an event and the time you ask for more information. The challenge is understanding the assumptions baked into the system behavior so that you are acting on the most accurate representation of the system at a given time.

Pub-Sub Systems

A *publish–subscribe* (often shortened to *pub-sub*) system is an event-driven communication model where producers publish messages to a topic or bus, and consumers subscribe to receive those messages. The key idea is that publishers do not send messages to specific recipients; instead, they emit events and let the platform handle distribution.

The producer emits a message and moves on in a "fire-and-forget" manner. The receiver decides what, if anything, to do with it. The producer doesn't need to know who is listening, how many listeners exist, or what actions they might take.

This is the difference between a "publisher-subscriber" system and a queuing system, which we describe in the next section. With pub-sub, neither producer nor consumer needs to be aware of the other. Figure 8.1 shows the high-level architecture of communication in pub-sub systems.

As you can see, one publisher can serve many subscribers. In AWS, this pattern is served by Simple Notification Service (SNS). In SNS, you create *topics*, which are sources for

FIGURE 8.1 Pub-sub message flow.

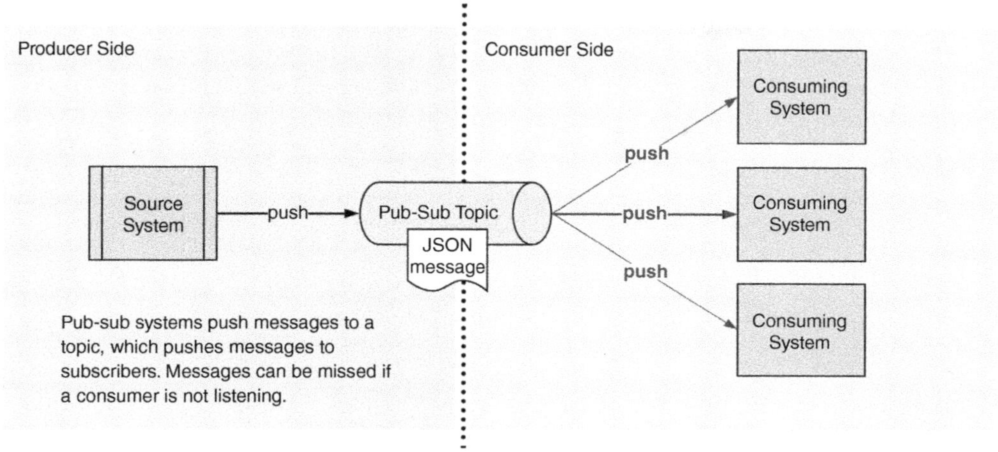

published information. Publishers push event information to a topic. Here's an example of some Python code that pushes information to a topic using the `boto3` AWS library and the `json` library for handling JSON:

```
import boto3
import json

sns = boto3.client("sns", region_name="us-east-1")

response = sns.publish(
    TopicArn="arn:aws:sns:us-east-1:123456789012:build-events",
    Subject="BuildCompleted",
    Message=json.dumps({
        "build_id": "build-1234",
        "status": "SUCCEEDED",
        "commit": "a1b2c3d4",
        "timestamp": "2026-01-18T14:32:00Z"
    })
)

print(response["MessageId"])
```

As you can see, an SNS event message has a target ARN (a unique identifier for the topic), a subject, and then an arbitrary JSON message as its payload. This message might be sent at the end of a build in an automation pipeline.

Once a topic is established, you can create subscriptions that listen for messages on the topic and take some action. A subscription receives the message as pure JSON. Subscriptions can take on many forms, and the way they receive the event differs slightly depending on the destination:

HTTP(S) subscriptions ask SNS to POST the event JSON to a URL of your choosing. If you set up a web API with a POST endpoint, the above event would hit your API with this payload:

```
{
  "Type": "Notification",
  "MessageId": "95df01b4-ee98-5cb9-9903-4c221d41eb5e",
  "TopicArn": "arn:aws:sns:us-east-1:123456789012:build-events",
  "Subject": "BuildCompleted",
  "Message": "{\"build_id\":\"build-
1234\",\"status\":\"SUCCEEDED\",\"commit\":\"a1b2c3d4\",\"timest
amp\":\"2026-01-
18T14:32:00Z\"}",
  "Timestamp": "2026-01-18T14:32:01.123Z",
  "SignatureVersion": "1",
  "Signature": "EXAMPLE",
  "SigningCertURL": "https://sns.us-east-1.amazonaws.com/
SimpleNotificationService.pem",
  "UnsubscribeURL": "https://sns.us-east-1.amazonaws.
com/?Action=Unsubscribe..."
}
```

You can see that you get many metadata fields alongside the `Message` field containing the event JSON itself.

Email (SMTP) subscriptions send the payload to an email address, with the subject as the event's stated subject text. In this case, you receive only the message JSON.

Lambda subscriptions trigger code in the cloud (a powerful concept explored later in this chapter). A Python Lambda function defines a handler that receives two parameters: `event` and `context`. Such a function triggered by the above event would receive this payload in the `event` object:

```
{
  "Records": [
    {
      "EventSource": "aws:sns",
      "EventVersion": "1.0",
      "EventSubscriptionArn": "arn:aws:sns:us-east-1:123456789012:build-event
s:abcd1234",
      "Sns": {
        "MessageId": "95df01b4-ee98-5cb9-9903-4c221d41eb5e",
        "TopicArn": "arn:aws:sns:us-east-1:123456789012:build-events",
        "Subject": "BuildCompleted",
        "Message": "{\"build_id\":\"build-1234\",\"status\":\"SUCCEEDED\",\"com
mit\":\"a1b2c3d4\",\"timestamp\":\"2026-01-18T14:32:00Z\"}",
```

```
        "Timestamp": "2026-01-18T14:32:01.123Z",
        "SignatureVersion": "1",
        "Signature": "EXAMPLE",
        "SigningCertURL": "https://sns.us-east-1.amazonaws.com/
SimpleNotificationService.pem",
        "UnsubscribeURL": "https://sns.us-east-1.amazonaws.
com/?Action=Unsubscribe..."
      }
    }
  ]
}
```


Again, you're given the message, but also plenty of metadata. Your Python could use the `json` library to extract just the message, like so:

```
import json
payload = json.loads(event["Records"][0]["Sns"]["Message"])
```

At this point, you start to get an idea of how pub-sub and event-based systems can provide the glue for advanced automations, as an event in one system can trigger an action via a web API, an email notification for a human reviewer, or another programmatic action in a cloud function.

Event Buses and Cloud Pub-Sub

Modern cloud platforms often implement pub-sub through the concept of an *event bus*. An event bus acts as a central channel where events are published and from which consumers can selectively subscribe based on rules or filters.

A good example is AWS EventBridge. EventBridge allows services, applications, and custom code to publish structured events to a shared bus. Consumers then define rules that match on event attributes such as source, type, or detail fields. When an event matches a rule, it can be configured to be automatically delivered to one or more targets, such as Lambda functions, Step Functions, or HTTP endpoints. Figure 8.2 shows a typical event bus architecture, where multiple producers publish events and multiple consumers react independently.

In an event bus system, there is no topic or queue to provision; every system can be both a contributor to and a consumer of events on the same common event stream. Consumers register themselves with filters specifying attributes of messages they wish to receive, such as the source system or the event type. The event bus system coordinates the delivery of events to any consumer whose filters match the event's attributes.

The important thing to note is that EventBridge is still pub-sub at heart. It puts event notifications on the bus (fire-and-forget style!) and any user of that account can configure a consumer to react. While it adds structure, filtering, and native integration options, it does not fundamentally change the notification-based nature of the model.

FIGURE 8.2 Event bus message flow.

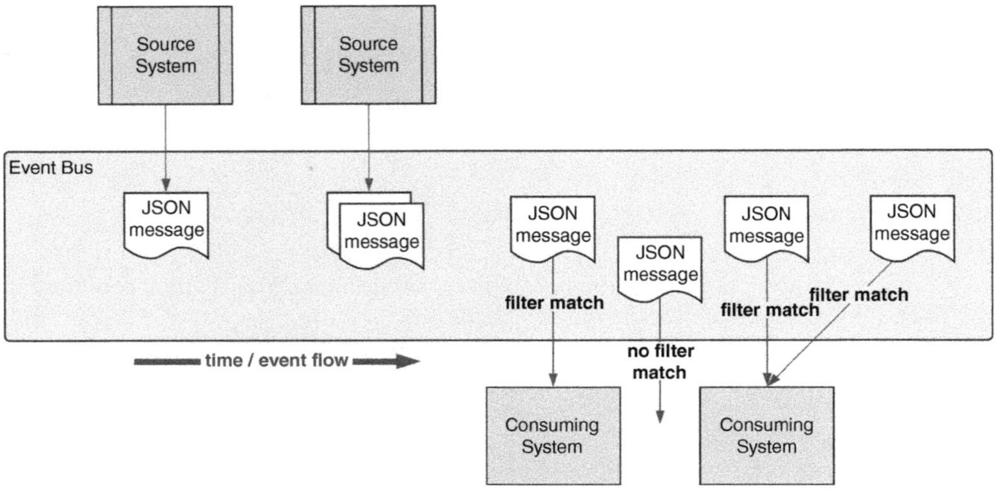

Other Examples of Notification-Based Event Systems

Most modern platforms provide some form of publish–subscribe or event bus service. While the underlying mechanics differ, they all share the same core idea: producers emit events, consumers subscribe, and the platform handles fan-out.

Outside of the AWS services we've just seen, similar service patterns appear in the other cloud services. Azure Event Grid provides event routing for Azure services and custom applications, while Google's Cloud Pub/Sub offers a managed pub-sub service with strong integration across GCP. Open source Apache Kafka (and managed variants like Confluent or Amazon Managed Streaming for Apache Kafka [MSK]) is another well-supported option.

Strengths and Limitations

Notification-based events are simple, scalable, and flexible—but that simplicity comes with trade-offs.

Their strengths are low overhead, loose coupling between systems, easy extensibility, and fast, nonblocking behavior. Their limitations are equally important: There is no built-in state tracking, no guaranteed delivery without additional tooling, and no retries by default.

That makes notification systems excellent for signaling, but less suitable for workflows that require guaranteed processing, ordered handling, or durable storage of events. They tell you that something happened; they do not ensure that something was done.

That distinction becomes increasingly important as automation systems grow more complex. For change-driven architectural patterns that provide some of those features missing from the pub-sub model, you'll want to look at message queues. Spoiler alert: When pub-sub and message queues get together, you can get the best of both worlds.

Message Queues

Message queues are structures that behave very much like the mailbox you might have at your house. A mail carrier (the message or event source) drops mail (the event details) into the mailbox, and it stays there until you pick it up. Your mailbox is yours and yours alone. If you don't check the mail, the mail stays put; no one else is coming to take it. This means that, unlike with subscription-oriented pub-sub services where messages are ephemeral, messages in a message queue are *durable*, a quality that makes them work for use cases where pub-sub alone won't get the job done.

Figure 8.3 shows the message queue pattern. When a consumer retrieves and acknowledges a message, that message disappears from the queue. That's why each downstream system/consumer needs its own dedicated queue in this design. To be clear, a single downstream system can spin up multiple consumers to speed up processing, but that downstream system is responsible for coordinating those consumers and ensuring no events are missed. A completely separate downstream system wouldn't want to share the same queue, since each message can only be processed once. That's why in this image, the source system sends messages to two different queues; there is one for each downstream system.

Take a look at the relationship between source systems and consumers. The source system pushes events, but for consumers, it's a pull-based model.

Queues as Durable Event Buffers

The biggest strength of message queues is that the messages within are persistent: They stay in the queue until a consumer retrieves them. In contrast to pub-sub systems, where it's

FIGURE 8.3 Message queue flow.

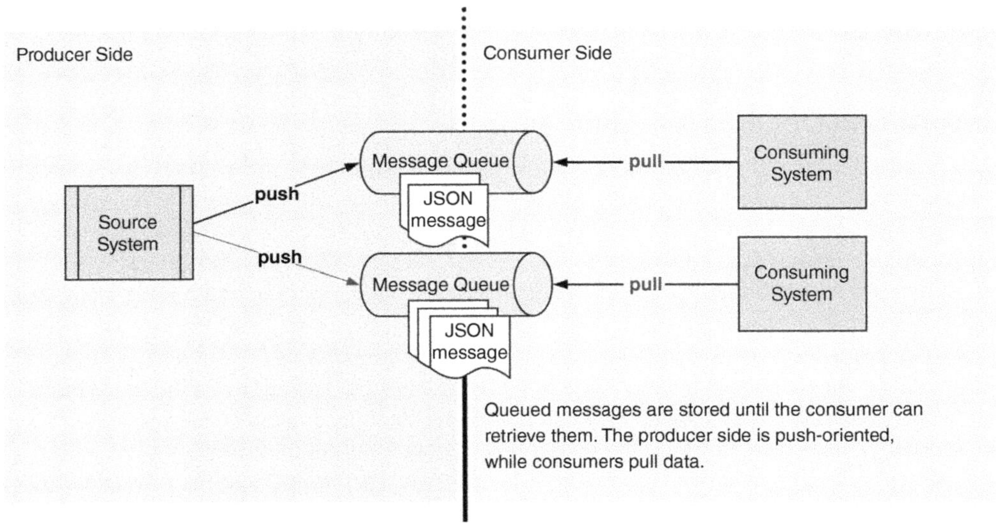

possible to miss an event if a listener is not online when a notification occurs, queues tolerate failure well, because the subscriber can just "pick up the mail" when it comes back online.

This solves the challenge of timing mismatches, where systems do not operate at the same speed or availability. A deployment pipeline may emit events in bursts. A downstream automation might be temporarily offline, throttled, or restarting. With queuing systems, those accumulate and wait until they can be processed.

Acknowledgments Enable Resilience

Queues often also have a requirement that subscribers *acknowledge* the message in some specific way, giving the queue permission to dispose of it. While this might sound like a tedious extra step, it actually plays a role in making event-based systems more robust. Imagine a process that checks for events in a queue before performing some multistep response. If a step in that reaction fails, you don't want to lose that event forever; you want to be able to clean up and attempt to reprocess the event another time. Saving the acknowledgment until the last step of a consumer's processing is successful means that your integrations are more resilient to failure.

Handling Spikes, Retries, and Back Pressure

In real systems, work rarely arrives at a steady pace. Code pushes from developers may cluster around the end of business hours. Monitoring alerts spike during incidents. Batch jobs finish all at once. Queues help downstream systems absorb these bursts by letting them pull events at their own pace.

If consumers can't keep up, the queue length grows without throwing errors. That growth is a signal that tells you that demand temporarily exceeds processing capacity, and indeed it may cause you to rework part of your automation pipeline to avoid bottlenecks. Still, queuing relieves the pressure, so that even in times of heavy load, your response times may stretch but your system will not fail. You can respond to load by scaling consumers, throttling producers, or simply letting the backlog drain naturally.

Retries and Dead-Letter Queues

Queues also enable retry semantics. If a consumer fails while processing a message, the message can be returned to the queue for another attempt or sent to a *dead-letter queue* for later inspection. Dead-letter queues (*DLQs*) are alternate queues where you can send unprocessable messages for debugging or later reprocessing. This is often preferable to endlessly retrying or requeuing the offending message, since it may be impossible to process as is.

A queue's *visibility timeout* defines how long a message remains hidden after a consumer retrieves it; if the consumer fails to acknowledge the message before that window expires, the message becomes visible again and can be retried. Backoff controls how aggressively those retries occur. Instead of immediately reprocessing a failing message in a tight loop, consumers typically implement increasing delays between attempts, usually with linear or exponential backoff defining the wait time between attempts.

Rather than overwhelming downstream systems, queues apply natural resistance. Producers keep producing, consumers keep consuming, and the queue mediates the difference in pace.

Guaranteed Message Ordering

Some queues provide stronger guarantees around ordering and uniqueness by associating messages with identifiers and enforcing first-in, first-out (FIFO) semantics. In *FIFO queues*, messages are processed in the exact order they are received, and message IDs or deduplication keys are used to prevent accidental reprocessing. This is particularly important when the order of operations matters. The trade-off is reduced throughput and parallelism, since strict ordering limits how much work can happen at once.

Examples of Queueing Systems

Most cloud providers offer managed queuing services that implement these patterns.

In AWS, the prime (pun intended!) example is Amazon SQS, or Simple Queue Service. Indeed, SQS was the first of Amazon's "Web Services" to go to market, kicking off the expansive AWS ecosystem we have today. This gives you an idea of how foundational event-driven systems and queuing are to a robust, decoupled architecture!

SQS provides durable message storage and guarantees that messages remain in the queue until they are successfully processed or explicitly discarded. Consumers poll the queue, process messages, and acknowledge completion. If a consumer crashes or times out, the message becomes visible again and can be retried by another worker.

SQS supports multiple queue types. Standard queues prioritize throughput and availability, while FIFO queues enforce strict ordering and exactly once processing semantics. Both reinforce the idea that queues exist to manage *units of work*, not just signals.

Other platforms offer similar services. Azure Queue Storage and Azure Service Bus queues provide managed work queues in the Azure ecosystem. Google Cloud Tasks and Cloud Pub/Sub subscriptions with pull semantics fill similar roles on GCP.

Dedicated message queuing systems like RabbitMQ and ActiveMQ are widely used in self-managed or hybrid environments, as they can be deployed on any infrastructure you own.

Making the Choice Between Queuing and Pub-Sub

When deciding between queuing and pub-sub systems for automation integrations, there are a number of tradeoffs to consider. Table 8.1 has a handy breakdown.

Sometimes, it can be advantageous to combine the two technologies.

Fan Out: Combining Pub-Sub and Queuing

It is possible to achieve the fire-and-forget behavior of pub-sub integrations with the durability and resilience of queuing by combining the two technologies. As Figure 8.4 illustrates, having a pub-sub topic as the event source for a queuing system allows the

TABLE 8.1 Comparison of pub-sub and queuing systems

Aspect	Publish–Subscribe (Pub-Sub)	Queuing Systems
Primary purpose	Broadcast notifications	Distribute units of work
Consumer model	One-to-many	One-to-one (per message)
Producer awareness	No knowledge of consumers	No knowledge of consumers, but expects processing
Delivery expectation	Best-effort by default	Guaranteed (with retries)
Acknowledgments	None	Required
Failure handling	Consumers may fail silently	Retries, visibility timeouts, dead-letter queues
Ordering guarantees	Not guaranteed	Optional (e.g., FIFO queues)
Common use cases	CI/CD triggers, event fan-out, system notifications	Job processing, task orchestration, batch workloads
Example services	AWS SNS, AWS EventBridge	ActiveMQ, AWS SQS, Azure Service Bus queues

FIGURE 8.4 Fan-out configuration.

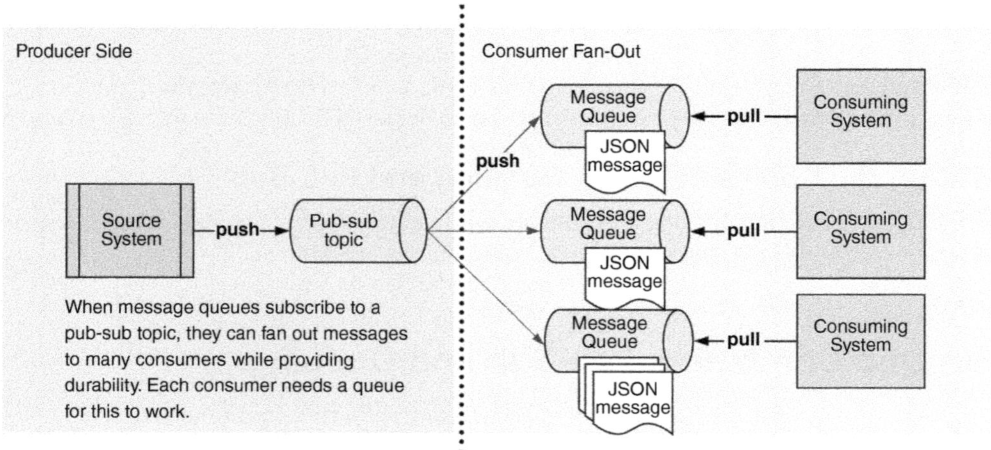

producer side to interact via pub-sub patterns, while consumers pull events on their own schedule from a queue. This is called the *fan-out pattern*, and in this design, it's still necessary to have a queue per consumer.

Some queuing systems allow you to configure patterns like this without the additional overhead; for instance, ActiveMQ's Durable Subscription option acts like a pub-sub with message queuing characteristics. Take a look at the details of your chosen technology stack to see what is possible.

Gotta Go FaaS

At first, the core pitch of cloud computing was around elastic compute, meaning that providers would give you easy ways to spin up (and tear down) virtual machines quickly. You, as the automations engineer, would use all the tools of scripting, image building, configuration management, and infrastructure as a service to leverage this capability into scalable systems. For persistent workloads, this makes sense; for instance, long-lived web application nodes need to stick around to process web traffic at scale. But what about workloads that don't need to live long?

Event-driven architectures are full of elements that need to run some code to react to an occurrence in another system; they get in, do some work, and get out. Runtimes may be very short, but they happen sporadically. Does it really make sense to run an entire virtual machine 24/7 so that a 20-line Python script can occasionally react to an event? Do we really need servers in this situation? Enter the concept of *function as a service (FaaS)*.

Functions as Automation Glue

Function as a service (FaaS) is often described as "serverless" compute, but don't let the name fool you. All code needs compute to run, and servers absolutely exist in FaaS; you just don't ever see or manage them. What matters for automation is not the absence of servers, but the absence of management responsibilities for you.

With FaaS, you don't decide where a function runs, how it scales, or how long it stays alive—you just provide the code. That makes FaaS particularly well suited to integration work, where the goal is not sustained computation but quick reactions.

Most automation functions are small by design. They validate input, transform data, call another API, write a record, trigger a downstream process, or update state somewhere else. They are not business applications in their own right; they are glue.

In that sense, FaaS replaces a whole class of brittle automation scripts that used to live on dedicated utility servers whose sole job was to run `cron` jobs, catch webhooks, or host scripts. Those servers required patching, monitoring, credential management, and capacity planning. Cloud functions remove that overhead almost entirely.

Event → Function → Action

The most common FaaS pattern is simple and repeatable: An event triggers a function, and the function performs an action. This was previewed earlier in the section on pub-sub systems as we saw an AWS Lambda function, a type of FaaS, as a subscriber to a message topic.

Event triggers don't just come from pub-sub sources, though. Operations automations use many event sources and integration code to create complex, powerful orchestrations. For instance, imagine a sequence like this: A developer's code push (or Pull Request merge) in GitHub or GitLab hits a webhook. That webhook runs a function to validate the branch name and starts a build. When the build completes, it triggers another function, which tags an artifact and updates a deployment record. This causes a file to appear in a storage location. From there, a function scans it, transforms it, or routes it elsewhere, and so on, and so on.

This pattern shows up everywhere because it aligns cleanly with how cloud systems already behave. Services emit events, functions consume them, and workflows are born.

Crucially, the function itself does not need to know or care where an event originated, nor does the event source need to know what the function will do. This is loose coupling; event-driven integrations have fewer explicit interdependencies, making it easier to swap out components and scale parts of the system independently. It also allows automation logic to evolve independently of the systems that trigger it.

Stateless by Design

One of the defining characteristics of FaaS is that functions are stateless. Each invocation is independent. If a function needs context, it must either come from the incoming event, or the function must retrieve it from somewhere else, like a database or API.

Although this can feel limiting at times, stateless functions are easier to reason about, easier to retry, and much easier to scale. The cloud provider, behind the scenes, can scale up 1 or 100 different instances of your function, something that can only work because the functions have no dependency on a particular compute instance.

Tradeoffs and Constraints

FaaS is powerful, but there are some possible limitations to consider. Most platforms impose execution time limits. For instance, AWS Lambda functions time out at 15 minutes. Functions are meant to be short-lived, not to run for minutes or hours. This means that FaaS is not necessarily the best choice for workloads like data processing pipelines, which may crunch on large data sources for hours, but they are very well suited for event-oriented tasks like operations automations.

Cold starts are another consideration. When not in use, cloud functions *scale to zero*, meaning that after a period of time, all underlying compute is turned off. In practical terms, behind the scenes, this may mean a container orchestration has scaled down to zero nodes, and your function needs at least one running to respond to events. Because of this, the first invocation after a period of inactivity may incur startup latency. Be aware that there are ways to mitigate this risk, including implementing keep-alive functions that periodically generate "ping" events to fire your functions, and cloud configuration options that help ensure a warm container is available.

Visibility can also be a challenge. Functions don't have shells to log into or processes to inspect. Debugging cloud functions relies heavily on logs, metrics, and traces. This pushes teams toward better observability practices, including robust logging in their code, but it can be frustrating for those accustomed to just being able to SSH into a machine and diagnose an issue. Of course, as you have learned, ephemeral infrastructure practices discourage this sort of manual intervention!

Finally, there is the risk of overuse. Because functions are easy to create, it's tempting to scatter logic across dozens of tiny handlers without clear ownership or structure. At scale, this can lead to sprawl that is hard to trace and hard to track over time. Governance and cataloging are as important with cloud functions as they are with physical or virtual machine infrastructure.

Survey of Cloud Functions

Each cloud platform offers some form of function as a service. As we've already discussed, AWS's cloud functions feature is called AWS Lambda, and the resulting functions are often referred to as *Lambda functions* or even just lambdas. AWS Lambda supports Java, JavaScript (NodeJS), Python, Ruby, C#, and more. You can even provide your own container images to run any language you wish on a container runtime managed through Lambda. Lambda functions can be invoked from many other services within AWS.

In Azure, the Microsoft equivalent is called Azure Functions. Azure Functions supports C#, JavaScript, Python, Java, PowerShell, and other languages, with strong integration into the broader Azure ecosystem. Functions can be triggered by a wide range of events, including HTTP requests, storage changes, message queues, timers, and Event Grid events.

Google Cloud Platform's equivalent service is Google Cloud Functions. Cloud Functions support all the same native runtimes as Azure and AWS, and they are tightly integrated with Google Cloud's event infrastructure, including Pub/Sub, Cloud Storage, and Eventarc. Google also offers Cloud Run as a related option, allowing containerized functions and services to run on the same underlying event-driven, serverless infrastructure with more control over runtime behavior.

Patterns of FaaS Integration

We've already seen how you might use cloud functions as consumers of pub-sub events. Let's take a look at a few of the ways you might use cloud functions in operations integrations.

Schedule

Sometimes notification-driven event designs just aren't available to you and polling is inevitable. Instead of scheduling a script on a persistent virtual machine with `cron`, you can configure a FaaS function to wake up and run on a schedule, check for work, and terminate.

Webhooks

When we discussed webhooks in Chapter 6, "Working with APIs," did you wonder how exactly you're supposed to configure a service that can act as a webhook destination? If

FIGURE 8.5 API gateway plus cloud function as webhook destination.

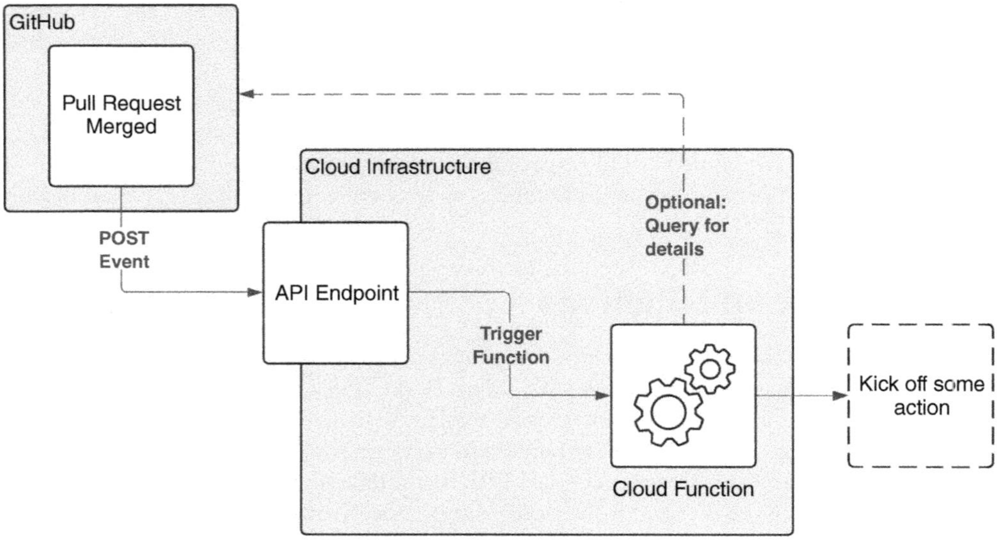

you're a capable developer (or have one handy), you can always spin up a server and host an API with a web framework or an API-dedicated framework like Python's `flask` library.

However, cloud platforms can provide an easier way to host an endpoint where FaaS provides the compute. For instance, in AWS, the API Gateway service offers a way to stand up a `POST` endpoint that routes all traffic directly to a Lambda, giving you a very easy way to get up and running with webhook-based integrations. Figure 8.5 depicts just such a configuration.

Azure and Google Cloud offer similar capabilities. In fact, for simple use cases Azure Functions can be exposed directly over HTTP, allowing a function to act as a webhook endpoint without even requiring a separate API management. For more advanced scenarios, Azure API Management can sit in front of functions to provide routing, authentication, and throttling.

In Google Cloud, Cloud Functions and Cloud Run services can receive HTTP requests directly, commonly fronted by Google's managed HTTPS endpoints, making them well suited for webhook integrations from external systems. Google Firebase suite of developer tools offers Firebase Functions, built on top of GCP Cloud Functions; they also expose HTTP endpoints natively. Writing a quick NodeJS express app to listen for a `POST`, then publishing it via Cloud Functions or Firebase is a great and easy way to get up and running with a webhook.

On each platform, infrastructure-as-code templates can define the API endpoints and their integration with cloud functions. It's all coming together!

FIGURE 8.6 Direct integration between AWS S3 and Lambda.

Direct Integrations

Pub-sub, queues, and webhooks are great for integrating disparate systems into cohesive automation architectures. However, most cloud-based services will also have native, service-to-service integrations that provide an "easy mode" for setting up event-based workflows.

For instance, in AWS an S3 bucket (an object-based storage location) can be configured to directly invoke a Lambda function, which will receive an event parameter with full details of the newly uploaded or updated S3 object. Figure 8.6 shows this pattern.

Likewise, Amazon's continuous integration service, CodeBuild, can be directly configured to trigger deployment services elsewhere in AWS. EventBridge's most compelling features are those that let you build integrations with configuration, not code.

Azure and Google Cloud follow the same pattern. Azure services commonly integrate through Event Grid and Logic Apps, enabling event-driven automation with minimal code, while Google Cloud uses Eventarc and Pub/Sub to connect storage, build, and compute services through managed event flows.

Even better, most of these connections can be configured through your infrastructure-as-code templates. While the names and details differ, the architectural idea is consistent across providers: Use native integrations where possible, fall back to general-purpose pub-sub or queues when flexibility or durability is required, and let configuration do as much of the integration work as it reasonably can.

Orchestration Patterns

Individual automations are part of a larger design. Each event, trigger, or action is a step in a workflow, which may itself be a component of an overall system of business processes. Orchestration is deciding when, in what order, *and* under what conditions each piece runs. As deployment workflows grow beyond a single script, you must consider the structure of task execution to make sure things run smoothly.

Sequential vs. Parallel Execution

One of the simplest, yet most consequential considerations is whether steps should run one after another or at the same time. Sequential and parallel execution solve different problems, and choosing between them affects not just speed, but reliability and debuggability as well.

Linear Pipelines

Sequential pipelines are simple: Do A, then B, then C. Each step depends on the successful execution of the previous, or at least on knowing how the previous step failed. Artifacts, such as compiled code, flow naturally between steps. Failures are easy to locate because only one thing is happening at a time. When a pipeline stops, the point of failure is usually obvious.

Linear workflows may still have conditional steps; for instance, you might branch based on the target environment of the build (dev, test, or production), and of course, no one runs their deployment step when test automation fails.

For many teams, linear execution is more than acceptable, offering clarity and correctness over speed, which is often the right trade-off in deployment automation. However, when you have multiple workloads firing at once, or events are happening with such frequency that performance tuning is a must, you need to look for opportunities to parallelize.

Parallel Execution

Parallelism exists to reduce total runtime. Independent steps, such as linting or running unit tests, don't need to wait for one another. Running them concurrently can significantly shorten feedback loops.

Modern orchestration tools make this easy to express. You define a set of stages that can run at the same time and wait for them all to finish before continuing. When the steps are truly independent, this works well and feels like a free performance win, but be careful, because parallel execution opens up a whole new world of potential failure states.

If multiple steps modify the same environment or resource, you introduce the possibility of a race condition error, that bane of systems automators and developers everywhere. In a *race condition* scenario, you're dealing with subtle and (worst of all) hard-to-reproduce timing conditions where one step updates a resource before it should, leading to, at times, genuinely confusing and difficult-to-fix behavior.

Parallel execution also complicates failure handling. When one step fails while others are still running, orchestration logic must decide whether to cancel, wait, retry, or continue.

Parallelism in operations automations can be a valuable and powerful technique, but understand the trade-offs and be ready for the increased complexity that comes with building a faster pipeline.

Failure Handling

Like any automation or script, your automation pipelines will experience failures. In the loosely coupled, distributed systems described in this chapter, failure can come at multiple stages: It could be in an external system, like your version control system; it could occur in the configuration of a webhook or message queue; it could happen in event processing code in a cloud function, or anywhere in between. Complex systems require robust error handling and logging to make sure that failures are caught early and that they can be diagnosed and fixed quickly.

Building *observability* into each component of your automations is essential. Centralized cloud logging, provided by services such as CloudWatch Logs, Azure Monitor, or Google Cloud Logging, puts logs under one roof and allow you to more easily correlate events and errors across services. In each of these services, most cloud resources emit status messages and updates to the central logging service, or can be made to do so with configuration options; at the same time, developers have the ability to write information to the same centralized logging repository from custom scripts. In this way, a service like CloudWatch becomes a one-stop shop to trace the behavior of cloud services and integration code as they manage the end-to-end processing of key events.

Whether your automation code is running on a virtual machine, a container, or in a FaaS execution environment, you should always write to the cloud provider's central logging. In AWS, the effort necessary to do this differs based on the environment. Custom scripts running on an EC2 instance can always using Python's `boto` to write to the CloudWatch service, provided the script or instance IAM role has permissions to do so. Another common approach is to write logs to the typical `/var/log` locations but use an on-system agent to convey logs written to this location to CloudWatch. Finally, code running in a Lambda automatically, by default, writes to CloudWatch any time output goes to `STDOUT` or `STDERR`.

Robust script-level failure handling should be paired with pipeline-level recovery mechanisms. When a deployment goes wrong, the ability to quickly redeploy a known-good version is essential to restore stability. This capability is known as *rollback*, and it's often configurable in deployment tools. Automated rollback works best when build artifacts are immutable and failures are detected early. Ideally, you would never deploy an application revision to production that wasn't perfect, but even the most thorough test suites, security scans, and linters can't catch everything. Having the ability to quickly jump back to a previous deployment means you may be able to fix your application before real-world users take notice.

Summary

In this chapter, we stepped back from individual tools and scripts to look at automation patterns as a whole. We began by contrasting polling-based automations with event-driven designs, showing why cloud platforms naturally favor events, notifications, and reactions over polling. This pattern is heavily used in modern automation and underpins everything from continuous integration pipelines to infrastructure orchestration.

We then explored the major event-driven building blocks: publish–subscribe systems, event buses, and message queues. You learned how pub-sub excels at broadcasting signals with loose coupling, while queues introduce durability, acknowledgments, and retries for workloads that demand increased reliability.

From there, we went into function-as-a-service offerings and discovered how cloud functions help you glue systems together without the overhead of managing servers. We examined common trigger patterns such as schedules, webhooks, direct service integrations, and native cloud events, along with the trade-offs of stateless execution, cold starts, and observability.

After that, we tied these patterns together with orchestration concepts and failure handling. You saw how sequential and parallel execution affect speed, complexity, and debuggability, and why distributed automation requires deliberate observability through centralized logging. Finally, we introduced the idea of rollbacks as a key recovery capabilities for failed deployments.

In the next chapter, we'll put these integration patterns to use and start automating for real, building the first half of CI/CD automations: continuous integration.

Exam Essentials

Understand the difference between polling and event-driven automation. Know why polling-based automations are simple but inefficient at scale, and why event-driven systems react faster, reduce wasted work, and better align with cloud-native architectures. Be able to identify scenarios where polling is unavoidable versus cases where events provide clearer intent and lower operational overhead.

Recognize push vs. pull models in automation architectures. Understand polling as a pull-based model and events as a push-based model. Know how this distinction affects latency, scalability, and failure modes, and how it relates to similar push/pull concepts in configuration management and deployment workflows.

Understand publish–subscribe systems and their use cases. Know how pub-sub systems decouple producers from consumers by broadcasting notifications without expecting responses. Understand strengths, including fan-out, loose coupling, and low overhead, as well as their limitations, including lack of guaranteed delivery, ordering, and built-in retries.

Differentiate notification-based systems from message queues. Be able to compare pub-sub systems with message queues. Understand acknowledgments, retries, visibility timeouts, dead-letter queues, and how queues help manage spikes and consumer failures.

Know when and how to combine pub-sub and queuing patterns. Understand fan-out architectures that use pub-sub for event distribution and queues for durable processing. Recognize why each consumer typically requires its own queue and how this hybrid approach balances decoupling with reliability.

Understand the role of function as a service (FaaS) in automation. Know why FaaS is well suited for event-driven automation: short-lived execution, automatic scaling, and minimal operational overhead. Understand common use cases such as reacting to events, handling webhooks, and orchestrating integrations between services.

Recognize the stateless nature and constraints of cloud functions. Understand why FaaS functions are stateless by design and how state must be passed via events or external systems. Know common trade-offs, including execution time limits, cold starts, and increased reliance on logging and metrics for debugging.

Understand common event sources and triggers for automation. Be familiar with scheduled triggers, webhooks, direct service integrations, and native cloud events. Know how API gateways and managed services simplify exposing functions over HTTP and reacting to platform-generated events.

Understand orchestration patterns and execution models. Know the difference between sequential and parallel execution, and how each affects speed, reliability, and complexity. Understand risks such as race conditions, partial failures, and coordination challenges introduced by parallel workflows.

Recognize the importance of observability in automation pipelines. Understand why distributed, event-driven systems require centralized logging and monitoring. Know how cloud logging services aggregate logs from scripts, functions, and managed services to support troubleshooting and root-cause analysis.

Review Questions

1. Which statement best describes a polling-based automation trigger?
   - **A.** A script checks a condition repeatedly on a schedule.
   - **B.** A system emits an event only when state changes.
   - **C.** A consumer acknowledges messages to remove them from a queue.
   - **D.** A function runs only when a rule matches on an event bus.
2. In a publish–subscribe (pub-sub) system, what does the publisher typically know about subscribers?
   - **A.** Their IP addresses and port numbers
   - **B.** Exactly how many subscribers exist
   - **C.** Nothing specific; it publishes to a topic or bus.
   - **D.** Which subscriber will process the message first
3. Which feature is most strongly associated with message queues rather than notification-based pub-sub?
   - **A.** Fire-and-forget delivery
   - **B.** Durable storage until consumed
   - **C.** Fan-out to multiple subscribers
   - **D.** Filtering events by attributes
4. Which best describes an "event bus" in cloud automation?
   - **A.** A database table used to store build artifacts
   - **B.** A central channel where services publish events and rules route them to targets
   - **C.** A log aggregator that stores application logs
   - **D.** A system in which a single source system sends events to multiple downstream systems
5. A team polls an external API every 5 seconds to check whether a build finished. At peak hours, they hit rate limits and the poller sometimes gets empty responses. What is the most appropriate architectural improvement?
   - **A.** Poll every second so the build finishes are detected sooner.
   - **B.** Ignore empty responses; they are expected in polling systems.
   - **C.** Add more compute to the polling server so it can retry faster.
   - **D.** Switch to an event-driven callback/webhook so completion is pushed once.

6. You publish `BuildCompleted` notifications to a message topic. Downstream, an automation must always create a deployment record, even if the consumer is temporarily offline. Which change best supports this requirement?
   - A. Add more subscribers to the pub-sub topic.
   - B. Replace the topic with a durable queue or subscribe a queue to the topic.
   - C. Convert the message payload to a larger JSON object.
   - D. Add a second topic for production events.
7. A queue-based consumer processes a message, performs three API calls, then crashes before finishing. What is the best practice for acknowledgment behavior?
   - A. Acknowledge the message immediately after receiving it.
   - B. Acknowledge after each API call so partial work is recorded.
   - C. Acknowledge only after the full processing succeeds.
   - D. Never acknowledge; the queue will remove messages automatically.
8. Your team parallelizes linting, unit tests, and integration tests to speed up a build process. Occasionally, runs fail in inconsistent ways when two steps write to the same temporary directory. What is the most likely issue?
   - A. Drift detection
   - B. Race condition due to shared resource access
   - C. Cold start latency
   - D. Over-encryption at rest
9. A team uses FaaS functions for webhook handling. They complain debugging is harder because there's no server to SSH into when something breaks. What is the most appropriate way to support their needs?
   - A. Implement centralized logging and structured logs with correlation IDs.
   - B. Disable logs to reduce noise.
   - C. Add more CPU to the function runtime.
   - D. Convert the function into a long-running VM so SSH is available.
10. A pipeline triggers two parallel steps: One updates IaC to replace a load balancer, and another runs post-deploy smoke tests against the load balancer DNS name. Some runs fail because tests hit the old load balancer right as DNS changes propagate. What is the most appropriate fix?
    - A. Increase time-to-live so DNS changes propagate more slowly.
    - B. Remove DNS and hard-code the load balancer IP.
    - C. Add explicit step dependencies so smoke tests run only after infrastructure changes are complete, and validate readiness via health checks rather than DNS timing.
    - D. Run smoke tests first; they should pass before any changes.

11. An organization uses FaaS functions triggered by build events. During a postmortem, engineers struggle to reconstruct the full sequence of actions taken for a specific build across multiple services. What is the best preventive improvement?
    - **A.** Increase log retention duration.
    - **B.** Add structured logging with a shared build ID across all events and functions.
    - **C.** Reduce the number of functions involved.
    - **D.** Serialize all actions into a single workflow.

12. A team designs an automation that reacts to a `DeploymentFailed` event by immediately triggering a rollback. Later, they discover some failures are transient and would have resolved on retry without rollback. What is the best refinement to this design?
    - **A.** Add logic to classify failures and attempt limited retries before rollback.
    - **B.** Disable automatic rollback and require manual intervention.
    - **C.** Delay all rollbacks by a fixed amount of time.
    - **D.** Implement a loop back on error that returns to the build step and retries using exponential backoff.

Answers to Review Questions

1. A. The correct answer is A. Polling means repeatedly asking "Did something change yet?" on an interval. Option B describes event-driven push notifications; option C relates to message queues; and option D describes an event-bus rule/target pattern.

2. C. The correct answer is C. Pub-sub is designed for loose coupling: The publisher emits to a topic/bus without needing to know who is listening. Option A would be a tightly coupled integration. Option B is inaccurate, and option D implies work distribution and ordering semantics that pub-sub does not guarantee.

3. B. The correct answer is B. Queues hold messages until a consumer retrieves and processes them. Option A is a pub-sub hallmark. Option C is a common pub-sub pattern (one-to-many). Option D is commonly associated with event buses like EventBridge, which are still pub-sub at heart.

4. B. The correct answer is B. An event bus centralizes events and routes them to consumers based on rules. Option A describes artifact management. Option C is observability tooling. Option D describes a pub-sub pattern, of which event bus is a type but event buses support multiple sources.

5. D. The correct answer is D. A webhook pattern avoids wasteful repeated checks and reduces rate limiting while providing immediate response when completion occurs. Option A makes the rate limit problem worse, and option B just normalizes the failure without fixing it. Option C doesn't fix the root design issue; it just burns more resources.

6. B. The correct answer is B. Queues provide durability so messages aren't lost when consumers are down, and combining pub-sub with per-consumer queues is a common fan-out pattern. Option A increases fan-out but does not guarantee processing. Option C improves context but not durability. With option D, you're not affecting anything in the current environment.

7. C. The correct answer is C. Acknowledging only after success ensures failed processing results in retry rather than message loss. Option A risks losing the message before work completes. Option B still risks losing the message before the overall workflow completes and may create inconsistent partial work. Option D is incorrect; many queue systems require explicit acknowledgment before any message can be purged from the queue.

8. B. The correct answer is B. Parallel execution can cause race conditions when steps share state or resources. Option A is a configuration management concept. Option C applies to FaaS, not local CI job steps. Option D is unrelated.

9. A. The correct answer is A. Serverless debugging relies on logs, metrics, and traces centralized into systems with structured logs. The correlation between log entries and specific event instances makes distributed workflow errors diagnosable. Option B is basically the opposite of good practices. Option C doesn't help, but it might make the errors process faster. Option D throws away the advantages of FaaS to get back to an undesirable debugging habit.

10. C. The correct answer is C. This is a dependency ordering problem. Delay later steps until you can confirm resource health rather than assuming DNS timing. Option A makes the transition window longer, but still leaves you guessing instead of knowing the next step is safe. Option B breaks the decoupling DNS provides; plus, when is the right answer ever "hard-code something"? Option D tests the old state, which is irrelevant.

11. B. The correct answer is B. Embedding unique identifiers in your logs allow those logs, metrics, and traces from distributed components to be tied back to a single build or event, making reconstruction possible. Option A is incorrect; it retains more data but doesn't improve traceability. Option C in incorrect, reducing modularity without improving the logging situation. Option D is even worse than C! You want granularity in your functions and logs to make tracing through incidents possible.

12. A. The correct answer is A. Classifying failures and retrying transient errors reduces unnecessary rollbacks while preserving automated recovery for real faults. Option B removes the critical safety mechanism of rollback entirely. Option C is just arbitrary and doesn't solve the root issue. Option D is wrong because it applies the correct solution for this case to all failure cases, which would cause problems when the build is not going to recover on its own.

PART IV

Building, Testing, and Shipping

Chapter 9

Continuous Integration

THE AUTOOPS+ EXAM TOPICS COVERED IN THIS CHAPTER MAY INCLUDE, BUT ARE NOT LIMITED TO, THE FOLLOWING:

✓ **1.0: Automation Coding Concepts**

- 1.1. Given a scenario, use code to support automation.
- 1.3. Explain concepts related to infrastructure-as-code (IaC).
- 1.4. Given a scenario, troubleshoot common issues with the code life cycle.

✓ **2.0: System Configuration**

- 2.1. Given a scenario, use configuration management techniques to deploy a solution.
- 2.2. Compare and contrast basic approaches to automation.

✓ **3.0: Continuous Integration**

- 3.1. Explain environmental factors related to continuous integration (CI) management.
- 3.2. Explain workflow management concepts in CI.
- 3.3. Given a scenario, analyze configurations to manage basic automation pipelines.

We now arrive at one of the central goals of operations automation: continuous integration. More than simply a stage to run automatic tests, *continuous integration* (CI) is a feedback system whose job it is to evaluate code changes early, verifying that they work, meet quality expectations, and that they are prepared for deployment.

Continuous integration is the place where you discover if the code that works on a developer's machine actually works in a production-like environment, integrated with other developers' changes. It's also the place to validate coding best practices and style, as well as the time to conduct security scans. In short, CI is an automated enforcer of code quality and an invaluable source of feedback for teams. This becomes increasingly important as teams grow, more developers contribute to the same or related code bases, and changes arrive more frequently.

CI is also the place where we will generate any artifacts needed for production deployment, whether that be compiled Java code, transpiled and minified JavaScript, or an application packaged into a Docker container. If your team's code needs to be built before shipping, CI is where you automate, validate, and store that artifact for deployment.

With proper checks in place, CI reduces regression errors, prevents developers from overwriting each other's work, and paves the way to production readiness. Once again, we're shifting away from manual, error-prone processes toward scripted and configurable *pipelines* that provide consistency and speed. CI is definitely about testing, but it's more than that. In this chapter, we'll take a deep dive into CI concepts, starting with the quality-enhancing pipeline steps that help make sure your code is polished and working up to spec.

Building Quality

Let's take a look at some of the most important steps you can perform in a CI pipeline: testing, linting, and security scanning.

Testing

Automated tests are the star of the CI show. If you do nothing else in a continuous integration pipeline, you should be running tests. Unit tests are the first line of defense against regression errors, those failures that pop up to cause trouble in code you thought was working. Any time you make a change—or more pertinently to CI, any time you integrate your changes with others—regression errors may occur. Having a solid suite of automated tests is your guard.

A test validates a small piece of functionality, verifying things like a function returning the expected output, a class method handling edge cases correctly, or an API endpoint responding with the right status code.

When tests pass, you have confidence the code works, or at least the parts that are covered by your tests!

Testing Here, There, and Everywhere

Running tests locally before committing is good practice, and can help you squash bugs and regression errors before you push them (maybe saving you a bit of embarrassment in the process). Some teams practice "test-driven development," wherein devs write tests first, then implement code that makes the tests pass. Most of the time, an application's test suite is both something devs run frequently on their own laptops and part of the CI pipeline, where no one can choose to skip the tests or ignore a finding, and where changes from multiple developers can be evaluated together.

What Makes a Good Unit Test

Automation engineers should be primarily informed about how to execute tests and handle their output, leaving developers to come up with well-constructed test suites. However, these lines can blur, and the spirit of DevOps means that developers and operations engineers need to understand a bit about what happens in each other's worlds.

In general, unit tests should be fast, isolated, and focused on small units of code, like specific functions or request flows. They should have as few dependencies as possible, which often means mocking up data to supply to the code being tested (e.g., mocking up the data backend for a test involving a `GET` API).

Writing comprehensive tests is beyond this book's scope, but understanding their role in automation is critical.

Unit Tests in Practice

Here's an example of a simple unit test. Consider a function that calculates tax:

```
def calculate_tax(amount, rate):
    return amount * rate
```

And another function that tests its behavior:

```
def test_calculate_tax():
    result = calculate_tax(100, 0.08)
    assert result == 8.0
```

The test calls the function with known inputs and verifies the output matches expectations. If someone changes the calculation logic and breaks this behavior, the test will catch it immediately and throw a flag.

Of course, your application code should catch errors, right? Another common test pattern asserts that code emits the proper errors when input is bad:

```
def divide(a, b):
    if b == 0:
        raise ValueError("Cannot divide by zero")
    return a / b

def test_divide_by_zero():
    with pytest.raises(ValueError):
        divide(10, 0)
```

This test verifies that dividing by zero raises an expected exception. If the error handling breaks, the test fails.

Unit tests aren't the only tests CI can run. Integration tests verify that components work together; end-to-end tests simulate user workflows; performance tests measure how the application handles high-request loads.

Speed is important. Unit tests are usually fast enough to run locally on every commit. You might run slower or more complex tests less frequently, perhaps on pull requests or a nightly schedule. Long test suite runtimes are the bane of many projects' existence: You want well-covered code, but the slower the test execution, the more reluctant developers will be to spend time running it. It's critical to find a good balance.

Code Coverage

Your test suite is only as good as its coverage. Many testing tools can give you an indication of *code coverage*, which refers to the amount of code in your repository (usually given in number of the lines) that is executed by your test suite. Coverage isn't the final word on how thorough your tests are; after all, simply knowing some test runs a line of code doesn't mean your test captures the nuance of expected code behavior. But it is a proxy measurement that can help you make your test suite more useful.

Most test utilities offer a way to assess code coverage. For instance, Python's `pytest` can do this when the package `pytest-cov` is installed. The following command returns a failed exit code when the coverage percent falls under the given value of 80:

```
> pytest --cov=app --cov-fail-under=80
_____________ coverage: platform darwin, python 3.14.2-final-0 ______________

Name                  Stmts   Miss  Cover
-----------------------------------------
python-app/app.py        21      2    90%
-----------------------------------------
TOTAL                    21      2    90%
Required test coverage of 80% reached. Total coverage: 90.48%
============================ 4 passed in 0.10s ============================
```

Assessments like these can be used to reject a build if a developer adds more code without corresponding test coverage.

Linting

Linting is the process of analyzing source code to detect potential errors, stylistic inconsistencies, and suspicious patterns without actually executing the program. Although running a linter may feel like a modern concept, the term actually originated with Stephen C. Johnson's original Unix `` `lint` `` tool, created back in 1978 to improve C code. The name means just what it sounds like: Johnson likened the tool to a dryer's lint trap, capturing the little bits of fluff that appear when you tumble-dry clothes. Linters focus on the aesthetics of code, though increasingly they can also find improvements and potential errors. Today, linters exist for virtually every programming language and serve as the first line of defense in code quality enforcement.

Categories of Linting Rules

Linters typically enforce several types of rules. The most common is stylistic warnings, which help ensure consistent writing style across a codebase. For instance, such a rule might flag inconsistent indentation in Python:

```
# Violation: Inconsistent indentation
def calculate(x):
  if x > 0:
      return x * 2  # Mixed 2-space and 4-space indent
  return 0
```

Style rules might catch mixed tabs and spaces, inconsistent double-versus-single quote usage, irregular whitespace, and line length violations. While these don't affect program behavior, they make code harder to read and maintain. Linters can also help you style code in a way that's more idiomatic to the language you're using, as in this example that suggests a more "Pythonic" approach to a comparison:

```
# Violation: Comparison to None should use 'is', not '=='
if value == None:
    handle_empty()
```

Linters can also flag code patterns that are risky or that indicate some oversight or omission on the developers' part. Here are a few examples:

```
try:
    some_risky_operation()
except:
    pass # A linter flags this very broad exception handler that does nothing

def process_data(items):
    result = []  # A linter notes this variable is never used
    return items
```

Findings like these may not be actual bugs, but they indicate ways developers can clean up their code to make it easier for others to follow. Other examples include unused imports and unreachable code. Linters can also identify overly complex patterns, sometimes called "code smells" (but not by me!). These findings flag code that runs contrary to best practices:

```
# This function may be flagged as too complex due to excessive nestin
def validate_input(data, mode, strict, legacy, override):
    if mode == 'A':
        if strict:
            if not legacy:
                if override:
                    return True

# This function has a long argument list, which some linters will flag
def create_user(name, email, age, address, phone, city, state, zip, country):
    pass  # Consider passing a user object instead
```

Some linters include security-focused rules:

```
# Hardcoded passwords are not allowed!
PASSWORD = "admin123"

# This code risks SQL injection since it doesn't sanitize user input used
in SQL
query = "SELECT * FROM users WHERE id = " + user_input

# This use of eval() is potentially dangerous for the same reason
result = eval(user_provided_string)
```

Each of these violations may be caught by a well-configured linter. Most come with good defaults; often you can customize.

Configuring Linters

Most linters are configurable, allowing teams to enable or disable specific rules, customize thresholds, exclude certain files or paths, and configure specific parameters. For instance, you might set a custom line or variable name length, or provide a regex that matches your team's naming convention for function names.

Your linter configuration should be checked into version control alongside the code, ensuring that everyone on the team, plus the CI system, uses identical rules.

Security Scanning

The next step is security scanning. *Static code analysis* tools are specifically designed to recognize code defects and security vulnerabilities.

As with linting, the code is not actually executed; static analysis tools make their determinations from the source code itself. This is a valuable step in improving code quality, but it cannot identify security issues that only appear at runtime. To maximize your information security, pair source code analysis with penetration testing tools that access your running code.

Static analyzers are fairly sophisticated; they can track how data flows through a program, understand which code paths are reachable, and know what values variables might hold at different points.

Consider this example:

```
def process_user(user_id):
    user = database.get_user(user_id)
    if user is None:
        log_error("User not found")

    return user.email  # Potential None
```

A linter might not flag this code—there's no obvious pattern violation. But a static analyzer can trace the control flow and recognize that `user` might equal `None` when you try to access `user.email`, which the code doesn't anticipate.

Types of Static Analysis

Let's take a look at some of the methods a static vulnerability analyzer might use to detect issues in your application code.

Data Flow Analysis

Data flow analysis tracks how values move through a program. It can detect:

```
password = get_user_input()
sanitized = sanitize(password)
log(password)  # Warning: Unsanitized value logged
```

The analyzer recognizes that `password` contains potentially sensitive data and flags its use in a logging context before sanitization occurs.

Control Flow Analysis

Control flow analysis examines all possible execution paths:

```
def calculate_discount(price, customer_type):
    if customer_type == 'premium':
        discount = 0.2
    elif customer_type == 'standard':
        discount = 0.1

    return price * (1 - discount)  # Error: discount may be undefined
```

The analyzer identifies that if `customer_type` is neither "premium" nor "standard," the variable `discount` will be undefined when the code reaches the last line and tries to return it.

Taint Analysis

Taint analysis tracks untrusted data as it flows through a system, throwing up warnings if it reaches sensitive operations without proper validation:

```
# User input comes from an external file and is "tainted" (not validated or
sanitized)
user_input = request.get_parameter('filename')

# Tainted / untrustworthy data used in filesystem operation.
# It's much safer to restrict this input to a set of known file paths.
file_path = '/data/' + user_input
content = open(file_path).read()
```

The analyzer marks `user_input` as tainted and alerts when it's used to construct a file path without validation. This catches injection vulnerabilities that pattern-based linters might miss.

Type Analysis

Type checkers perform static analysis to verify type consistency:

```
def add_numbers(a: int, b: int) -> int:
    return a + b

result = add_numbers("5", "10")  # Type error: expected int, got str
```

Even in dynamically typed languages, type hints enable static verification. Tools like `mypy` (Python) or TypeScript's compiler catch type mismatches before runtime. Linters will often detect this sort of error.

Practical Considerations

Static analysis works well in CI pipelines because it can run stand-alone, requiring no test environment, runtime dependencies, or mocked-up data. They can sometimes run faster than the unit test suite, depending on the latter's size. Static analyzers can also be configured in a variety of ways to tune their scope and execution time.

For instance, `bandit`, the Python tool we'll use later, lets you choose which kinds of tests you want to run via a config file; you can define a smaller-scoped configuration for developers to run locally, reserving the more in-depth (and longer running) scan for CI.

You'll also spend part of your time managing false positives. No static analyzer is perfect. They might flag code that has no real issue, or perhaps they are warning about some vulnerability that you know is mitigated by other circumstances (say, an outside tool ensuring input sanitization before data reaches your app). In this case, you can flag lines as excluded from the scanner or specific tests. This takes time, but it's important to reduce false positives so that your team doesn't become conditioned to ignore the scanner's output.

Shift Left with Pre-Commit Hooks

The concept of "shifting left" in code quality or security means to handle or intercept problems earlier in the development life cycle, closer to the point at which changes are made. This way, issues can be addressed before they ever get far enough to become part of a build or live deployment.

We can set this up for developers using `git` pre-commit hooks. These are commands that you configure to run before certain actions take place on a local `git` repository, meaning they execute on the developer's machine. They can apply certain checks or fixes on code before passing it along to its destination; likewise, they can stop execution of a `git` command if a certain check fails.

Git offers the ability to create hooks before or after many commands: pre-commit, pre-push, and post-update are all examples. To demonstrate, let's look at how a pre-commit hook can be defined to run a linter before any commits can be made.

We'll use the popular Python linter called `ruff`, which will make an appearance later in this chapter as part of a complete CI pipeline example.

Creating a Pre-Commit Hook

We'll start by opening the folder in our repo called `.git/hooks/`. The `.git` folder (very important to note the leading dot) is a hidden folder that gets created any time you create or clone a `git` repository, so if you're working with `git` already, it should exist. In fact, so will the `hooks` folder, and it contains a number of samples for you to peruse, as shown in Figure 9.1.

Each one of these shows some example syntax for creating a hook of that type. If you rename the file to drop the `sample` suffix and make sure to set it executable with `chmod`, it will start to work as a hook. If you forget the latter and run a command that would trigger the hook, you'll see a warning:

```
> git commit -m"added file"
hint: The '.git/hooks/pre-commit' hook was ignored because it's not set as
executable.
hint: You can disable this warning with `git config set advice.ignoredHook
false`.
[branch-name edd3ae3] added file
 1 file changed, 0 insertions(+), 0 deletions(-)
 create mode 100644 my_file
```

FIGURE 9.1 Sample `git` hooks.

```
[./.git/hooks> ls
applypatch-msg.sample        pre-commit.sample          prepare-commit-msg.sample
commit-msg.sample            pre-merge-commit.sample    push-to-checkout.sample
fsmonitor-watchman.sample    pre-push.sample            sendemail-validate.sample
post-update.sample           pre-rebase.sample          update.sample
pre-applypatch.sample        pre-receive.sample
```

Let's set up a hook to run our linter before each commit. We'll create the file `.git/hooks/pre-commit` with the following content:

```
#!/bin/sh
Echo "Pre-commit hook go!"
ruff check .

# If ruff fails, prevent the commit
if [ $? -ne 0 ]; then
    echo "Ruff linting failed. Fix errors before committing."
    exit 1
fi
```

Pretty simple, right? We're just executing the `ruff` command like a developer would do interactively. This command runs a linting analysis on the code and sends its output to the console. The crucial part for the pre-commit hook is the check for `$?` and the line that says `exit 1`. If linting passes, `ruff`'s exit code will be zero, or "all clear." In Bash, the last exit code for a command ends up in the variable called `$?`, so that `if` statement is checking the exit code of `ruff`. If it's non-zero, we take some action (in this case, echoing a message) and call `exit 1`, giving our own non-zero exit code out of the hook script. If the hook exits with anything but zero, the hook prevents the action (i.e., the commit) from succeeding.

Note that this script could just return `exit $?` directly, but the `if` statement allows us to echo out a final message.

Let's set it executable with this command:

```
chmod +x .git/hooks/pre-commit
```

Let's test it with a file that contains some code that will trigger the linter:

```
> git commit -m"dubious code"
Pre-commit hook go!

bad_code.py:1:8: F401 [*] `os` imported but unused
  |
1 | import os
  |        ^^ F401
2 | import sys
3 | import json
  |
  = help: Remove unused import: `os`

bad_code.py:6:5: F841 Local variable `unused_variable` is assigned to but
never used
  |
5 | def badly_formatted_function(x,y,z):
6 |     unused_variable = 42
  |     ^^^^^^^^^^^^^^^ F841
```

```
7 |     very_long_line = "This is an extremely long line that definitely
exceeds the recommended 88 character limit for Python code and will trigger a
line length warning"
8 |     result=x+y+z
  |
  = help: Remove assignment to unused variable `unused_variable`

bad_code.py:7:89: E501 Line too long (167 > 88)
  |
5 | def badly_formatted_function(x,y,z):
6 |     unused_variable = 42
7 |     very_long_line = "This is an extremely long line that definitely
exceeds the recommended 88 character limit for Python code and will trigger a
line length warning"
  |
^^^^^^^^^^^^^^^^^^^^^^^^^^^^^^^^^^^^^^^^^^^^^^^^^^^^^^^^^^^^^^^^^^^^^^^^^^^^^
^^^ E501
8 |     print(very_long_line)
9 |     result=x+y+z
  |

Found 3 errors.
[*] 2 fixable with the `--fix` option (2 hidden fixes can be enabled with the
`--unsafe-fixes` option).
Ruff linting failed. Fix errors before committing.
```

This commit will not succeed until this check passes successfully. Resolve these issues, and the commit will work as expected.

```
> git commit -m"applied fixes"
Pre-commit hook go!
All checks passed!
[branch-name b9147ac] applied fixes
1 file changed, 1 insertion(+), 1 deletion(-)
```

Now, developers get a clear assertion that their latest changes are in compliance with your team standards.

To Commit or Not to Commit?

Because `git` hooks live in the hidden folder `.git`, they are not committed or pushed to remote repositories by default. If your team wants to share hooks, one way is to lift your hook scripts out of this hidden folder into one that is seen by the `git` version control system.

For instance, you might create a new folder called `/hooks` at the root of your project. If you keep your hooks in that folder, you can commit them like any other file, then set the `git` config option `core.hooksPath` to use them:

```
git config core.hooksPath hooks
```

Any new developer cloning your repo would need to run this command to configure `git` to use the hooks in this folder.

For another option, check out the framework called `pre-commit` at `https://pre-commit.com` that is designed to help developers manage repository hooks with a YAML config file.

Finding the Right Balance

If you want to run more checks, just edit them into the `pre-commit` file, but be warned that the longer your pre-commit hook logic, the longer it'll take to commit files. There's always a balance to be struck between speed and the benefits of checks like these. Typically, you want to encourage developers to commit frequently so that their code changes are more isolated and documented with commit messages, so consider carefully the value of any disruptions you place in that process.

Reserve lengthy test suites for continuous integration, letting long-running checks happen asynchronously, off the developer's machine. Use pre-commit hooks for the kinds of things that are most critical, most common, or easiest to resolve when caught early. A great example would be checking for hard-coded values or secrets. If there are quality issues you want to make sure never leave a developer's laptop, a pre-commit hook is a great place for that. Finally, remember that developers have full control over `git` hooks and can always edit or disable them, so any critical checks happening in a hook should be replicated in CI.

With this approach, you can shift quality checks left for your devs and help them fix problems before they ever reach the CI server, improving quality overall and avoiding noisy warnings and errors for the whole team.

Software Bill of Materials (SBOM)

An ever-increasing challenge facing both operations and security professionals is understanding exactly what is going on under the hood of modern applications. As we discussed in Chapter 7, "Preparing the Environment," dependency management reflects the complexity of today's application development, which involves deeply nested hierarchies of both direct and indirect dependencies. It's essential that we have ways to unpack this complexity, both when working to ensure a deployment environment is prepared for runtime and when securing applications.

This complexity has become a source of vulnerability in information security. Back in 2020, a software package called SolarWinds, a widely adopted part of many organizations' networking stacks, became the source of a backdoor attack that affected businesses and other institutions worldwide. The hackers responsible compromised not SolarWinds itself, but a package nested inside the tool's dependencies, in a part of the application that was less-scrutinized because it was not directly created by the company. This incident, called a "supply chain attack," highlighted the growing risk of managing software dependencies and understanding the potential vulnerability at each layer.

What's more, information security professionals know that critical vulnerabilities don't just pop up in the "front-facing" software that people know by name; they are often discovered in obscure OS packages or language libraries. At that point, the race is on to understand where those packages or libraries might be used in an organization's vast array of software.

In short, organizations need detailed inventories of what they are running. A *software bill of materials* (SBOM) is part of the solution to that problem. An SBOM is an inventory of the components that make up a software artifact, listing dependencies, versions, and sometimes their origins. Similar to concepts we've seen before, like package manager lockfiles, SBOMs are often generated by external tools that probe the complete stack of an application to generate a complete picture of dependencies.

Generating an SBOM

There are two major standards when it comes to SBOM formats. CycloneDX was created by the OWASP Foundation, a.k.a. the Open Worldwide Application Security Project; the other is SPDX, built by the Linux Foundation.

Many languages have utilities that will generate SBOMs in these formats. For Python, the OWASP foundation maintains a tool itself to create CycloneDX files. From a Python application folder, try **`pip install cyclonedx-py`**, then run the following:

```
cyclonedx-py environment -o sbom.json
```

This tool scans the current environment and generates a detailed JSON document detailing every software and package dependency it can find. The results are often thousands of lines long, even for simple applications. Here's a heavily truncated snippet of one. You can see the `flask` package dependency described (with parts even of this section trimmed):

```
"components": [
    {
      "bom-ref": "Flask==3.0.0",
      "description": "A simple framework for building complex web
applications.",
      "externalReferences": [
        {
          "comment": "from packaging metadata Project-URL: Chat",
          "type": "chat",
          "url": "https://discord.gg/pallets"
        },
        {
          "comment": "from packaging metadata Project-URL: Documentation",
          "type": "documentation",
          "url": "https://flask.palletsprojects.com/"
        },
      ],
      "licenses": [
```

```
        {
          "license": {
            "acknowledgement": "declared",
            "name": "License :: OSI Approved :: BSD License"
          }
        }
      ],
      "name": "Flask",
      "purl": "pkg:pypi/flask@3.0.0",
      "type": "library",
      "version": "3.0.0"
    },
```

These files are not really meant for human consumption. Rather, they can be used as input for other scanning tools or kept on file for compliance purposes.

Similar tools to `cyclonedx-py` exist for many other languages; they all produce output that adheres to this spec.

Using SBOMs to Drive Security and Compliance

SBOMs play a role in license compliance, regulatory compliance, and security. License compliance was the original motivation behind SPDX, the SBOM standard developed by the Linux Foundation. It helps organizations track and demonstrate that their use of open source software components meets the obligations of each component's license.

On the regulatory and security side, the 2021 executive order on Improving the Nation's Cybersecurity introduces SBOMs as a requirement in federal software procurement. Sector-specific regulations, such as FDA rules for medical devices, have added their own SBOM mandates as well. Increasingly, it's important to be able to depict the full breadth of the code on which your applications depend.

In our Python example, we can use the SBOM as input to another tool that will alert us if our dependencies have security issues associated with them. The most popular tool is called `grype`. See `https://github.com/anchore/grype` for installation instructions, then run it with the SBOM JSON as input:

```
> grype sbom:./sbom.json
 Vulnerability DB                [updated]
 Scanned for vulnerabilities     [3 vulnerability matches]
      by severity: 0 critical, 0 high, 1 medium, 2 low, 0 negligible
      by status:   3 fixed, 0 not-fixed, 0 ignored
NAME      INSTALLED  FIXED IN  TYPE    VULNERABILITY        SEVERITY  EPSS
RISK
Werkzeug  3.1.5      3.1.6     python  GHSA-29vq-49wr-vm6x  Medium    < 0.1%
(18th)   < 0.1
Flask     3.0.0      3.1.3     python  GHSA-68rp-wp8r-4726  Low       < 0.1%
(12th)   < 0.1
pip       25.3       26.0      python  GHSA-6vgw-5pg2-w6jp  Low       < 0.1%
(4th)    < 0.1
```

It looks like our SBOM scan turned up a few low-level vulnerabilities. You can see recommended steps from the output: the `FIXED IN` column shows that we can update each package to a newer version to avoid each issue. And what are these issues? Those strings under the `VULNERABILITY` header are identifiers for CVE (Common Vulnerabilities and Exposures) numbers. These are easy to Google to learn more, letting you make your own assessment as to the severity of each finding and the necessity of taking immediate action.

In a continuous integration context, you'll want to inspect the options of your given tool to see how to trigger failures on certain thresholds. Lacking this option, you can use tools like `grep` or `awk` to check the output of this scan and exit with a non-zero error code if it encounters, say, anything above a Medium severity.

AI-Based Log Analysis

These days, deployment pipelines and distributed systems generate more log data than humans can reasonably inspect. Log analysis systems use patterns like error messages formats, log levels, and structured fields to identify and surface relevant information, and there are powerful (and pricey) tools like Splunk that help you write sophisticated filters, queries, and dashboards around large quantities of logs. Still, the sheer volume of logs can make it challenging to catch everything you need to catch.

Now, AI can help operations professionals scale up their log analysis by identifying anomalies, clustering related log messages, and highlighting patterns that deviate from normal behavior, allowing automation to more readily find the signal in the noise and sound the alert only when it is most appropriate. While individuals can certainly run logs through an LLM to help parse dense text and get answers, this kind of analysis is increasingly built into log-scanning systems, where it can be part of a more integrated experience.

Be warned! Your logs can contain sensitive information. Although it is best practice to avoid logging out secrets, many details about an organization's internal state can be understood from logging, especially by an AI model. You also don't want your logs used to train AI models for other customers. Make sure that any system or service with which you share your logs handles your data appropriately, and that you or your organization are comfortable with the terms of service.

Finally, AI-based log analysis does not replace human judgment. Root-cause analysis, accountability, and design decisions still require domain knowledge and intent that automation cannot always infer. Treat AI log analysis as a supporting tool. It's an assistant that prioritizes evidence and highlights correlations, while humans remain responsible for interpretation, decisions, and corrective action.

The Art of Artifact Management

When we talk about *artifacts* in the context of CI, we mean the tangible outputs produced by a build process. An artifact is the result of turning source code into something that can be run, deployed, or consumed by another system. These might be a file like an SBOM, compiled runtime code, or even an entire Docker image, fully ready to be deployed to production. In any case, such artifacts need to be stored and versioned like code. This process is called *artifact management.*

Common Artifacts

In compiled languages, artifacts are often executables or archives. A Go build produces a single compiled binary. A Java build commonly outputs a JAR or WAR file. In both cases, the artifact is the compiled result of the source code, ready to be run or packaged further.

In interpreted or semi-compiled ecosystems, artifacts are usually packaged distributions. A Python project might produce a wheel (with the extension `.whl`) file. A Node.js library might be bundled and published as a versioned `npm` package. These artifacts aren't meant to be executed directly; they're designed to be installed and consumed by other applications or environments. Although this book mostly looks at automation through the lens of deploying web applications, don't forget that any kind of code build or deployment process can be automated!

In container-based workflows, the container image itself is the artifact. The image includes the application code, runtime, dependencies, and operating system layers. This is the beauty of containers; when the build passes and is complete, you have an artifact that you know will run the exact same way in production.

Web applications sometimes produce static build outputs. A front-end framework might generate a directory of HTML, JavaScript, and CSS files that can be uploaded to a content delivery network (CDN) or object storage service. That directory is the artifact, even though it contains many files.

In each case, an artifact represents a completed build outcome that can move forward in a pipeline without needing to rebuild from source.

Artifact Registries

Once a CI pipeline produces artifacts, those artifacts need to live in some persistent storage location. That is the role of an artifact registry.

An artifact registry is a system designed specifically to store, version, and distribute build outputs. It acts as the handoff between CI and everything that follows, including testing, deployment, and rollback. Downstream systems no longer need to rebuild code from source or guess which output to use. They simply fetch the artifact that was already produced and validated.

Different ecosystems rely on different artifact registries, but they all serve the same purpose: storing and distributing build outputs in a controlled, versioned way.

JFrog Artifactory is a widely used, general-purpose artifact repository that supports many package formats, including Maven (Java), `npm` (Node.js), PyPI (Python), and Docker images. It's often adopted by larger organizations because it can act as a single, unified registry across multiple languages and build systems.

Nexus is another popular binary artifact repository, especially common in Java-heavy environments. Like Artifactory, it supports multiple formats and is frequently used to host internal libraries and proxy public package repositories.

Docker Hub is the largest public registry for container images. It hosts both public and private images and is commonly used for distributing base images and open source projects. As its name suggests, it's a bit like the GitHub of Docker images, and is often the first place you'll look for public base images of popular operating systems and stacks.

Amazon Elastic Container Registry (ECR) is AWS's managed container image registry. It integrates tightly with AWS IAM for authentication and authorization, making it a natural choice for CI pipelines and deployments running in AWS environments.

GitHub Container Registry (GHCR) allows teams to store container images alongside source code in GitHub. It integrates with GitHub's permission model and works well for projects already using GitHub Actions and GitHub-based workflows.

In addition to these tools and services, keep in mind that all the package repositories we described in Chapter 7 are also artifact registries. Centralized public registries such as `npm` for Node.js/JavaScript packages, PyPI for Python, RubyGems for Ruby, and Maven Central for Java artifacts are the primary place from which developers (and their language package managers) retrieve libraries for use in their code. If your team is building libraries or packages, these registries will be your code artifact's final publication destination.

Registry vs. Source Control

Artifact registries and source control systems serve different purposes and should not be used interchangeably. Artifact registries are made for working with larger files, such as compiled binaries; traditional version control is not. Many a developer has felt the pain of accidentally committing a large build artifact to a `git` repository and watching as clone times slow to a crawl. It can take a good bit of high-level `git` repo surgery to remove the artifact. Good luck if it has gone on long enough to have multiple versions committed!

These two things can live alongside each other. You'll see repos on GitHub publishing artifacts (such as zip files) for major milestones under the "Releases" section. GitHub Releases is part of the GitHub platform with its own storage mechanism and is not part of the `git` repo's version control history. And as mentioned earlier, GitHub also has its own container registry, where you can store and version container images. The key is that these kinds of large, unreadable files go in special-purpose repositories, not in the version control where your code lives.

Artifact Versioning

Once you've built your artifacts, you need to tag them so you can distinguish one from another and make use of them further downstream in a CI pipeline.

Just like source control tags, artifact tags should be immutable, so they always refer to the same thing over time. And as with source control, there are two common approaches to versioning artifacts.

Semantic versioning uses structured version numbers such as `1.4.2`, where the digits indicate major, minor, and patch releases. This approach is most common for libraries and packages that will be used by other teams or applications.

In contrast, build-based versions use identifiers tied to the build process itself, such as timestamps, build numbers, or source control commit hashes.

Both approaches can be appropriate; in fact, many systems combine the two, using a semantic version for releases and build identifiers for internal tracking. Later, when we walk through a CI pipeline example, you'll see we tag Docker image in multiple ways. The pipeline applies both human-friendly tags and a tag derived from the commit hash so that a downstream step can use the latter to identify the right image to scan.

That's the goal of our pipeline: secure, high-quality code generating a Docker image artifact that we can ship to production.

Pipelines Automation Triggers

Before we can run any automations in a CI pipeline, something has to kick things off. There are many ways to get the party started.

Trigger Types

CI/CD systems provide multiple mechanisms to initiate pipelines. Some are reactive to events; others are passive. Which you need depends on what type of process you are automating.

Schedule

Scheduled triggers run pipelines at predetermined times. These are useful for running nightly builds, backing up data, or planned off-hours deployments.

Schedule-based triggers typically use `cron` expressions to define execution times, letting you define schedules as simple as "run every 10 minutes" and as complex as "run every other Tuesday at 9 p.m., except in September." You can also layer schedules, say, running compact testing or linting periodically throughout the day, but saving the full (presumably longer-running) test suite for overnight.

Polling

Polling checks your source control system (e.g. GitHub, GitLab) at regular intervals for changes. If the system detects new commits or changes, it automatically starts the pipeline. This approach works well when direct webhooks aren't available or you are unable to expose a listening endpoint to the source control system (i.e., your CI system is internal and can't be reached by cloud version control like GitHub). Polling is also good when you want predictable job scheduling rather than executions driven by developer activities like code pushes or pull request merges.

However, polling can be resource-intensive and may introduce delays compared to webhook-based triggers.

Webhooks

As described in the previous chapters, webhooks allow for very responsive, event-driven integrations. In this pattern, your version control system will have a configuration that asks you to specify a URL. Whenever something happens in the version control system, your URL receives an HTTP request with details. It's then your responsibility to analyze the payload, understand what event just occurred, and start the appropriate process in response. Webhooks take some additional infrastructure and maintenance on your part, since your organization needs to securely host an API endpoint that is accessible to the version control system.

With this approach, you benefit from immediate reaction to code changes without the potential delays of polling, giving your developers faster feedback. Implementing the webhook logic yourself also lets you do more filtering and decision-making about what events to process and when.

Manual

Sometimes you need to run a job yourself. You might manually start a pipeline process after a failed deployment (perhaps rerunning a job that failed due to an external system failure), or you might need to trigger a polling job before its next scheduled execution so you can deploy a hotfix. As long as you are not making changes outside the pipeline definition and creating configuration drift, manually run jobs can be perfectly acceptable.

ChatOps

For teams that live on chat systems such as Slack or Microsoft Teams, tight integration of CI/CD can be very effective. Many automation systems allow you to both post job results directly to a chat channel and to allow team members to react or take action by responding to the system's chat account. Depending on the system and integration, these bots may respond to text commands or even provide simple UI, such as action buttons, embedded directly in the chat. This tight integration of automation pipelines and chat is called *ChatOps*.

For instance, when CI is integrated with chat, you might receive build updates in a `#build` channel and be able to respond to approve a deployment with a `/approve build-123` command. These capabilities are built into some systems (like Microsoft Teams' integration with Azure DevOps) and configurable as extensions to others (like Jenkins' Slack plug-in).

ChatOps is not only very convenient, but it can create some visibility and auditability around your processes, as CI/CD outputs are clearly shown in chat, as are responses. For some teams, having all this co-located where they are already collaborating can reduce context switching and make working with CI systems easier.

Trigger Rules

Once you've chosen a trigger type, you still need to define conditions under which the pipeline should execute. These criteria are trigger rules, and they most commonly revolve around `git` repo structures or events.

Branch

Branch-based rules dictate when pushes to a branch trigger a pipeline action. For example:

- Only `main` branch pushes kick off production deployments.
- All branches trigger test runs.
- The `test` branch triggers CI builds.

This ensures the appropriate workflow runs for each branch.

Tag

Tag-based triggers fire when specific `git` tags are created. Common patterns include:

- Version tags (e.g., `v1.2.3`) trigger production pipelines.
- Release candidate tags (identified by naming convention) trigger staging deployments.
- Hotfix tags (again by naming convention) trigger emergency patches.

Tags are meant to be immutable, therefore providing explicit deployment markers that are easier to track than branch commits. However, you don't want to clutter your tag history, so trigger rules based on tags should be reserved for significant events like production deployments rather than frequent developer changes.

Pull Requests

Another common trigger is the pull request (PR). When a developer creates a PR, they are letting the team know they've got a bug fix or enhancement ready for review. Triggering a CI process on PR creation can give the team valuable feedback about regression errors or code quality issues before they manually review code. This helps streamline the review process, because automated systems have already run to flag issues.

After the team does review, their PR merge action is a common trigger for performing a complete test and build, perhaps initiating a deployment to a staging environment for user acceptance testing by customers.

As you saw in Chapter 8, "Patterns of Automation Architecture," there are many approaches to developer workflows that depend on well-defined branch and tagging strategies. Choose the trigger type and rules that work best with your team's style and goals.

Combining Triggers

Most CI/CD systems allow combining multiple trigger types and rules. Here's an example of how you might combine these approaches:

- Run unit tests on a push to any branch (poll or webhook trigger).
- Deploy to staging only when tags matching `staging-*` are created.
- Run full nightly integration tests on the `test` branch.

CI systems let you layer conditions and apply them to the entire pipeline or to specific stages of the pipeline. This multilayered approach provides flexibility while thoroughly covering repo activities in quality-assuring CI processes.

Build Environments

For CI to do its job of compiling code, running tests, performing other validity checks, and ultimately producing build artifacts, the CI pipeline needs a place where that code can actually run. Throughout this book, we've discussed the many prerequisites and dependencies on which your code relies: the operating system, OS packages, programming language runtimes, and language-level packages. In the context of CI, we'll apply all the lessons for prepping a deployment environment to creating *build environments*.

Build environments are the execution environments where CI jobs actually run. You'll sometimes hear these referred to as *task runners*. To be precise, when a pipeline triggers, a task runner launches a build environment where it checks out the code, installs dependencies, runs build commands, and executes tests. Understanding how these environments are provisioned and configured is essential to building reliable CI pipelines.

Ephemeral by Design

Most CI build environments are ephemeral, built just for the purpose of executing a single CI run, outputting logs and other artifacts before being terminated. The temporary nature of these environments is intentional; it lets you know that your code will execute cleanly in a freshly provisioned environment. This is critical, because otherwise, configuration drift might mean that your code only works (or only breaks) because of a stray package or dependency version that will not be present in the production environment. Starting a new build environment with each CI run means that code that passes build tests will pass every time in a repeatable, consistent way.

Where Do Build Environments Come From?

When CI jobs need a place to run, there are really just a few options. They can run on the same compute as the CI system itself, but this is risky, because you're depending on a shared environment that may have packages and other dependencies that conflict with your code's needs. You need isolation. Languages like Python that support virtual environments can achieve this even on a shared system, but in general, the solution is containers.

Modern CI systems typically provision task runners dynamically via Docker containers. Cloud platforms provide a selection of base images from which to choose, covering a wide array of OS and language combinations. You then provide the scripts necessary to check out your code (if the CI platform doesn't handle that automatically), build the code, and run tests. If necessary, the script should start by provisioning the build environment using any of the techniques we've discussed, such as shell scripting or configuration management.

This approach can be slow; provisioning steps may include downloading and possibly compiling packages in the dozens or more. For this reason, many services allow you to upload your own Docker images. Providing a base image that already has many of the dependencies you need can speed up CI runs significantly. Create a Docker image that has all your app's dependencies preinstalled, keep it up-to-date independently of your app (regularly patching with the OS-level package manager), and you'll always have an environment ready to run CI.

Of course, the concepts of CI predate containers. Before Docker became widespread, CI runners were typically specially provisioned virtual machines or physical servers with build tools preinstalled. The advantage that containers bring is that ephemeral environments are highly resistant to configuration drift, which is one of many reasons you'll see build environments as containers in any modern CI system.

Secrets in the Build Environment

Provisioning a build environment is about more than just installing packages. As described in Chapter 7, a runtime environment often depends on configuration values or secrets, such as database passwords or API keys. To provide these values to your build process, you'll typically use either environment variables or external secrets management—or a combination of both.

Anyone who has used a `docker run` command knows that you can pass along key/value pairs that will end up as part of the container's runtime environment, just as if you'd logged in and run `export my_key=some_value`. Most CI tools will let you customize the `docker run` command that launches the build environment; others give you ways to inject environment variables in the CI tool configuration. Either way, the net effect is the same: You control the environment. That way, you can set `NODE_ENV=test` to let your Node.js application know that it is running in test mode.

Injecting values into the environment is also how you can let your application bootstrap itself once it is running inside the build environment. For instance, perhaps it needs a master key value to access a whole collection of secrets in a HashiCorp Vault. You'd use Docker or CI configuration options to make this value available, then have the build process or app's startup script fetch all the other environment variables needed to run.

Your cloud provider may give you a way to fetch configuration or secret values without even needing a master key; recall that in Amazon Web Services, IAM policies can be attached to compute (like running containers or VMs) that confer privileges to call AWS services like Secrets Manager. In this scenario, your task runner scripts or application code could retrieve secret values without the need for any key injection at all.

Test Mode?

We mentioned setting a value like `NODE_ENV` to `test`. In most applications, the configuration necessary to run tests differs from that of development or production. Often, it means pointing to alternate databases, APIs, or other external services. Sometimes this means things like altering the log level (maybe you want it more verbose—maybe less!—when running in CI). Sometimes it might mean setting certain compiler flags for a compiled language. Whatever it is, it's up to the application developer to make sure a configuration exists that is appropriate for CI.

Incidentally, there's nothing special about an environment name `test`; it's about the configuration choices you make in your application code when test mode is active. You could just as easily call it `NODE_ENV=staging` or `ci` or anything else. The important thing is that this value should be used to conditionally set up the app for running tests.

Build Notifications and Feedback

CI systems are built to provide fast feedback, but that information is useless if no one sees it. *Build notifications* close the feedback loop by alerting teams when builds fail, recover, or require attention. The goal is to balance notification volume, content, and delivery modes to provide only the most relevant information at the right time.

Notification Channels

Email notifications are traditional but effective, especially for build failures. However, they can become noise if not filtered properly.

Chat platforms like Slack and Microsoft Teams offer real-time notifications in team channels. This allows context and discussion around failures.

Version control system (GitHub, GitLab) can integrate status check output into pull requests, showing CI results inline with code review. Some teams automate updates to their README files to place indicating a project's latest test status and code coverage.

Finally, most CI systems provide dashboards—status pages that give high-level status indicators and summary statistics for projects, builds, and outcomes, giving every team member a central location to understand build status.

What to Notify

Tune your alerts to surface significant changes in status, such as a build going green to red or vice versa. Avoid notifying on every successful build if the previous build also succeeded. Focus on:

- Build failures
- Build recovery (green again after red)
- Long-running builds (performance degradation warning)
- Security scan findings
- Deployment completions

Notification Content

Good notifications address:

- Which build failed, and at what stage
- What error occurred
- Who or what triggered the build
- Link to details and logs

Here is an example notification structure:

```
Build #142 FAILED on main branch
Stage: Security Scan
Triggered by: commit a3f2c1d (Jane Doe)
Error: 3 high-severity vulnerabilities found
Logs: https://jenkins.example.com/build/142
```

Notifications like these help your developers take action on failures as quickly as possible.

Introducing the Demo App

In order to demonstrate the ideas behind CI (and later, continuous delivery), we'll be working with a practical example. Our demo app brings together nearly every topic we've covered so far in this book. It's a Python app that uses the `flask` package to present a REST API; there's no UI other than a page of Swagger API docs. It has dependency management that uses `requirements.txt` and a suite of tests that can be run with `pytest`. It can run directly on a VM or be packaged into a Docker container; it's also got a suite of tests we can run with the package `pytest`.

This app is full-featured enough to let us understand essential elements of operations automation like testing, building, and linting, but small enough in scope to be manageable in the pages of a book.

What the Application Does

The app exposes the following endpoints:

- `GET /docs` displays the Swagger UI, with the underlying doc template found in `/openapi.yaml`.
- `GET /health` is a health check endpoint that returns service status.
- `GET /api/greeting` returns a simple message.

The app has no persistence layer (i.e., no database required) and no authentication, keeping things simple.

Here's the complete application code in `app.py`:

```
"""
Simple Flask API for CI/CD demonstration
"""
from flask import Flask, jsonify, send_from_directory
from flask_swagger_ui import get_swaggerui_blueprint

app = Flask(__name__)

# Swagger UI configuration
SWAGGER_URL = '/docs'
API_URL = '/openapi.yaml'

swaggerui_blueprint = get_swaggerui_blueprint(
    SWAGGER_URL,
    API_URL,
    config={
        'app_name': "Python Demo App API"
    }
)

app.register_blueprint(swaggerui_blueprint, url_prefix=SWAGGER_URL)

@app.route('/openapi.yaml')
def serve_openapi_spec():
    """Serve the OpenAPI specification"""
    return send_from_directory('.', 'openapi.yaml')

@app.route('/health')
def health():
    """Health check endpoint"""
    return jsonify({"status": "healthy", "service": "python-demo-app"})
```

```
@app.route('/api/greeting')
def get_greeting():
    """Greeting endpoint"""
    return jsonify({"message": "Hello, World!"})

@app.route('/')
def root():
    """Root endpoint"""
    return jsonify({
        "service": "python-demo-app",
        "version": "1.0.0",
        "documentation": "/docs",
        "endpoints": ["/health", "/api/greeting"]
    })

if __name__ == '__main__':
    app.run(host='0.0.0.0', port=5000)
```

We're using HTTP verbs to act on resources defined by URL paths. The `jsonify()` function returns properly formatted JSON responses, and `flask`'s route decorators (such as `@app.route('/api/greeting')`) map Python functions to routes.

Code Quality Checks

Our demo application includes two essential quality steps: code linting and static security analysis. The former helps ensure that your code's style complies with best practices (or your office's internal standards). The latter looks at your source code to try to identify security issues, such as unsanitized user input that could lead to SQL injection risks. Not every security issue can be recognized by reading the code (whether by a human or a tool), so penetration tests are always recommended, but static code analysis can help flag more obvious vulnerabilities earlier.

Code Linting

`ruff` is a modern Python linter that checks for stylistic issues with your code. It checks for things like unused variables and imports, inconsistent formatting, and naming convention violations.

This tool can be run locally by developers (on the command line or as an IDE plug-in) to flag and fix issues automatically, but in a CI context, we run it in a check-only mode, since we don't want to actually make changes to the code. If violations are detected, the pipeline stops, preventing code with quality issues from moving forward.

`ruff` joins popular Python ecosystem linters like `pylint` and `flake8` in code style and quality checking, but it tends to be much faster than these tools owing to its highly optimized implementation in the Rust language. Many similar options exist for Python or your favorite programming language. Each of these tools allow you to enforce community-defined standards or override configuration files to define your own. Want to make sure every single variable starts with a "t" and is exactly nine characters long? Linters can do that.

Static Code Analysis

bandit is our demo app's package of choice for static code analysis. It's a good first line of defense to check for issues like the aforementioned SQL injection vulnerabilities; it also helps find clear risks like hard-coded secrets. Bandit takes a configuration file to override its default behavior; this can be an INI-style file stored at .bandit or a YAML file whose name you must specify in a parameter value. Bandit also supports another file format we haven't discussed, TOML.

We'll use YAML. Our bandit.yml configuration excludes certain file paths that we don't want analyzed; at the same time, it can constrain the scan to run a specific battery of tests or to skip others. Each test type has a code that is documented on the Bandit websites.

```
exclude_dirs: [.venv, .git, .pytest_cache, __pycache__]

# example: run specific tests
tests: ['B201', 'B301']
# example: skip specific tests
skips: ['B101', 'B601']
```

Running bandit with -h tells you which tests are currently loaded. Here's a snippet of that output:

```
The following tests were discovered and loaded:
-----------------------------------------------
        B101    assert_used
        B102    exec_used
        B103    set_bad_file_permissions
        B104    hardcoded_bind_all_interfaces
        B105    hardcoded_password_string
```

Note B101. By default, bandit complains about assert statements, which can be used inappropriately, but are perfectly normal for pytest tests. Our config file adds this test to the skips array to make sure we don't generate warnings about that usage.

In app.py, there's one bit of code that bandit flags that I'd consider a false positive (or at least a finding I'd ignore for this demo), and that's binding to 0.0.0.0. We suppress the warning with a special comment: # nosec.

```
if __name__ == '__main__':
    # Bind to 0.0.0.0 for Docker container access
    app.run(host='0.0.0.0', port=5000)  # nosec okay within our docker
container
```

The # nosec comment documents that we've reviewed this pattern and accepted it as necessary; the text after it is arbitrary and reminds us why we did this.

Note that while we are demonstrating linting and security scanning as two separate steps with two different tools, these functions can sometimes be found in the same tool. `ruff` claims to have fully implemented `bandit`'s range of security scans; take a closer look to decide for yourself if one tool is enough.

All these quality tools are helpful, but you will always need to spend some time configuring them to work with your style and design choices. If tools like these emit too many errors or warnings, developers and operations staff will learn to ignore them. The path to higher-quality code is not to flag as much as possible, but to flag only those issues that most need addressing.

Managing Dependencies

In Chapter 7, we discussed dependency management. We talked about the importance of explicit dependency specifications, virtual environments, and lockfiles. Our demo app uses `requirements.txt` to specify the packages it needs to run:

```
flask==3.0.0
flask-swagger-ui==4.11.1
pytest==7.4.3
ruff==0.8.4
bandit==1.7.10
```

Flask is a framework that helps Python developers define APIs by handling tasks like route and parameter mapping; you can see this with the @ decorators on each Python function. The package `flask-swagger-ui` lets Python render our OpenAPI YAML docs. Next, `pytest` is a build-time dependency (not runtime!) used for testing. You're already familiar with `ruff` and `bandit`. By pinning everything to specific versions with ==, we ensure reproducibility. Anyone who builds this application later will get the same versions of each package, whether they're working locally, in a CI environment, or deploying to production.

When we run `pip install -r requirements.txt`, `pip` also installs transitive dependencies, the libraries that `flask` and `pytest` themselves depend on. We don't list those explicitly, but they become part of our environment. Tools like `pip freeze` can capture the complete dependency tree if you want that level of control, but for this demo, the direct dependencies are enough.

Testing the Application

The app includes a test suite in `test_app.py`. A full investigation of automated testing is beyond the scope of this book, but let's take a look at a few elements to see what it's doing.

```
"""
Unit tests for the Flask API
"""
import pytest
from app import app
```

```
@pytest.fixture
def client():
    """Create a test client"""
    app.config['TESTING'] = True
    with app.test_client() as client:
        yield client

def test_greet(client):
    """Test greeting endpoint"""
    response = client.get('/api/greeting')
    assert response.status_code == 200
    data = response.get_json()
    assert data['message'] == 'Hello, World!'
```

These are unit tests: small, focused checks that verify individual components work as expected. Each test function focuses on one endpoint and confirms both the HTTP status code and the response payload structure. This is the kind of testing that belongs in a CI pipeline. Tests run quickly, don't require external services or databases, and give clear pass/fail signals.

Pytest's fixture system (`@pytest.fixture`) provides the `client` object, which is a test version of our Flask application. When tests run, they're not making real HTTP requests over the network. They're calling Flask's test client, which simulates requests and returns responses. This makes the test as fast as possible, which is essential for CI; test suites can grow quite large over time, a time-consuming test suite not only slows down developers, but incentivizes them to avoid running full regression tests. In this way, faster tests lead to better code quality, because they can run more frequently.

The assertions are straightforward. We check status codes match the expected `200 OK` and verify the JSON response contains the right keys and values.

Containerization with Docker

Previously, we discussed how containers bundle an application with everything it needs to run: code, runtime, dependencies, even the operating system. Our demo application includes a `Dockerfile` that defines exactly how to build a container image:

```
FROM python:3.11-slim

WORKDIR /app

COPY requirements.txt .
RUN pip install --no-cache-dir -r requirements.txt

COPY app.py .

EXPOSE 5000

CMD ["python", "app.py"]
```

Each instruction here demonstrates a containerization concept.

`FROM python:3.11-slim` starts us with a base image maintained by the Python community. This gives us Python 3.11 and a minimal Debian operating system. With this, we're building on a known-good foundation adopted by many Python practitioners.

`WORKDIR /app` sets the working directory inside the container. All subsequent commands run from `/app`. This is where we'll have Docker put our application code.

`COPY requirements.txt .` Note the dot at the end. Here, we copy just the requirements file into the working directory. This ordering matters for Docker's layer caching. If `app.py` changes but `requirements.txt` doesn't, Docker can reuse the cached layer from this or the next step without reinstalling packages.

`RUN pip install --no-cache-dir -r requirements.txt` installs dependencies. The `--no-cache-dir` flag tells `pip` not to cache downloaded packages inside the container, keeping the image size smaller.

`COPY app.py .` Again, note the dot representing the current directory (`/app` inside the container). This copies in our application code. If our app was more complex than a single file, we'd copy everything in here.

`EXPOSE 5000` tells the container to listen on port 5000. It doesn't actually open the port (that happens when you run the container), but it configures the container to allow this.

`CMD ["python", "app.py"]` runs when the container starts. In this case, we launch our Flask application using `python app.py`, just like we would on localhost.

When we build a container image using this Dockerfile, the result is an immutable artifact. Baked into this image is our app, along with a specific version of Python, specific versions of Flask and its dependencies, and a specific version of our application code. If tests pass on this image, we know the same behavior will occur when we ship the container to production.

The CI Pipeline Process

Now that you understand what our application does and how its pieces fit together, let's talk about what needs to happen when a developer pushes code to version control. A CI pipeline automates the journey from source code to deployable artifact, running the same steps every time to ensure consistency and catch problems early.

Let's consider the steps we'll need in our pipeline. Whether we're using Jenkins, GitHub Actions, GitLab CI, or any other system, the fundamental workflow remains the same.

Stage 1: Source Code Checkout

When a developer pushes changes or merges a pull request, the CI system needs to know, and retrieve that exact version of the source code.

As we've established, this can be done via a push (i.e., a webhook or some other direct invocation of the pipeline) or via pull (i.e., your CI system continuously checks for updates). In either case, everything starts with fetching the code intended for the build.

Stage 2: Environment Provisioning (Install Dependencies)

Once we have the code, we need somewhere to run it. The build environment must match what the application expects: the right operating system, the right version of Python, and isolated space for installing dependencies without conflicts. Most CI tools define environments from which you choose the best fit. Often, this is a container itself, and you can either extend the container environment with some initialization steps (say, installing necessary OS packages with `apt-get`), or providing your own container image already configured for what you need.

Should CI Use Virtual Environments?

We've discussed how, in Python and other languages, you can establish a virtual environment in a folder, effectively sandboxing an app and limiting any packages it installs to just that virtual environment. When building your CI pipeline, the important thing is to have an isolated environment. If you are running in a container, you're on ephemeral compute with no risk of contamination from other running processes, and can typically skip activating a virtual environment. However, if your CI environment (or your ultimate deployment environment) is a shared VM, you'll want to keep that step of your process:

```
python3 -m venv venv
. venv/bin/activate
pip install -r requirements.txt
```

Doing so prevents conflicts with system-level packages or other projects that might be running on the same build machine. Although this is outside the scope of the book, Docker containers are just as useful as local development environments as they are build or deployment environments. To maximize consistency and reduce variables in troubleshooting, it's a good idea to use the same approach in all three places, if possible.

Stage 3: Code Quality Checks and Unit Tests

Once dependencies are installed and the environment is ready, we'll assess quality by first running `ruff`, then `bandit`:

```
ruff check .
bandit -r . -c bandit.yml
```

The latter command tells `bandit` to run recursively on contents of the current working directory (the dot), using a config file specified after the `-c` parameter. Then, we'll run the `pytest` test suite.

```
pytest test_app.py -v --junitxml=test-results.xml
```

Pytest runs the test functions and collects the results. The `-v` flag produces verbose output so we can see exactly which tests ran. The `--junitxml` flag produces test output in the JUnit XML format, providing a standard way to communicate the outcome of tests. Many CI systems can parse these files to show which tests passed, which failed, how long they took, and how results compare to previous runs.

Figure 9.2 shows how Jenkins renders this type of output:

In addition to the detailed breakdown shown here, Jenkins supplies graphs like the one shown in Figure 9.3, which shows a history of test suite outcomes. In this case, we have a spike in failures, followed by some builds that resolve these errors; at the end, a new passing test appears in green. Note that the y-axis does not start at zero, obscuring that three tests continued passing throughout this time period. The graph auto-scales to show notable deltas in the trend line.

This is, literally, the "make-or-break" phase of the automation. If tests fail, the pipeline stops, because there's no point building a container image or deploying code that doesn't work. This is one of the driving principles of CI: catching problems before they become expensive to fix.

We've talked before about sequential and parallel execution. Here's an opportunity: Often, code quality checks and tests can run simultaneously, since the run of one step is not

FIGURE 9.2 Jenkins test output.

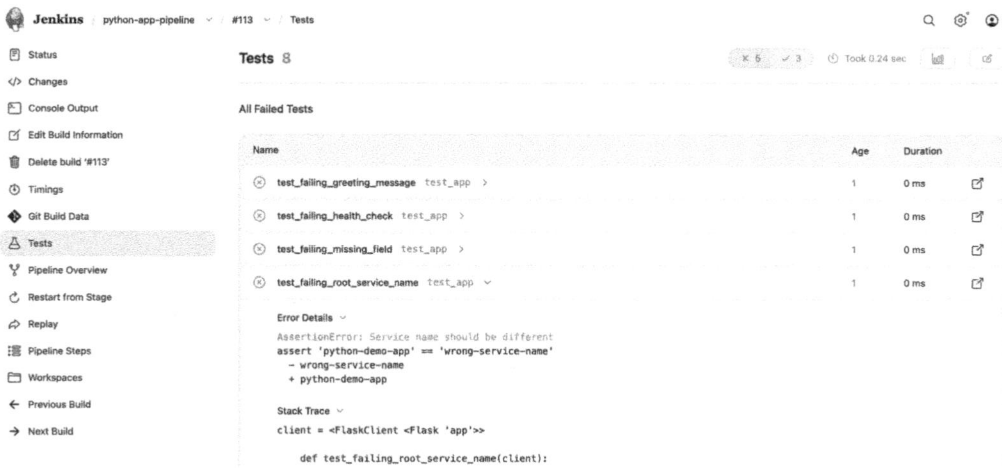

FIGURE 9.3 Jenkins test history graph.

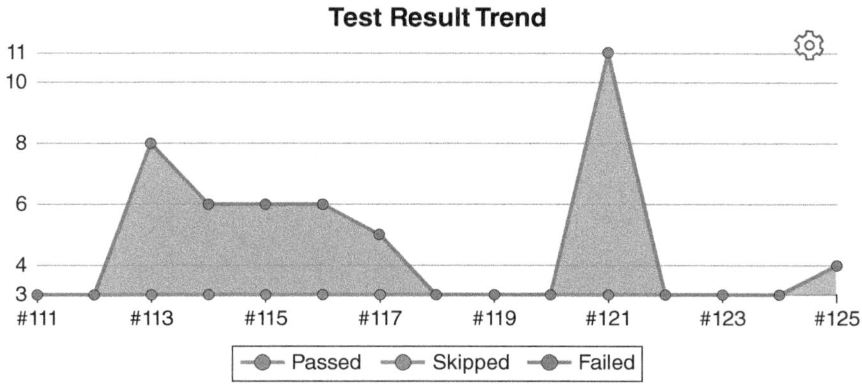

dependent on another. This is supported by most CI tools and can speed up your overall build time.

Stage 4: Building the Artifact

Once tests pass, we build the deployable artifact. For our application, this means creating a Docker container image:

```
docker build -t python-demo-app:${BUILD_NUMBER} .
```

The `docker build` command looks for and reads the Dockerfile in the current directory (referenced via the dot at the end of the command) and executes each instruction, creating layers that stack to form a complete image. The tag includes a build number or commit hash—something that uniquely identifies this specific build. This makes the artifact unique and traceable. If we need to roll back to a previous version, we have a good way to identify which image to deploy.

This is the artifact that actually runs in production. The container image bundles everything: the base OS, Python, application dependencies (like Flask), and our application code. It's completely self-contained. We're creating the entire environment needed to run the code.

This image is the main artifact of our build. It's what we will store in an artifact registry (e.g., a container registry) and eventually deploy to the production environment. Everything downstream depends on this image being built correctly and tagged properly.

Remember, build artifacts can be many things. This might be a Java JAR file; it might be a minified JavaScript package. In some cases, there may not be an artifact at all. The important thing is that CI is where you prep your code for release.

FIGURE 9.4 Our continuous integration workflow.

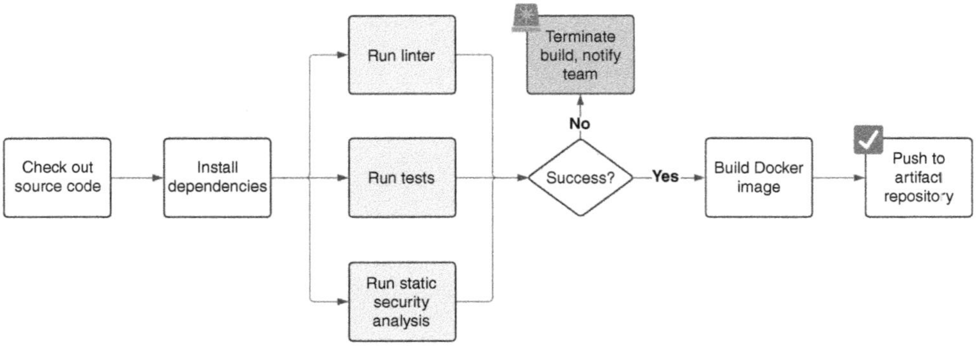

Stage 5: Store the Artifact

In the final stage of our CI pipeline, we'll take the Docker image that was built and tagged in the previous stage and push it to an artifact store—namely, Docker Hub.

The Pipeline Flow

Figure 9.4 illustrates the complete pipeline flow from code checkout through deployment and validation.

The order of these stages is important. You can't test code you haven't checked out or build artifacts from code that hasn't passed tests; still, some stages can run in parallel. For example, linting and security scanning can run alongside tests. They're independent checks that don't depend on each other. But the core flow is checkout, provision/install dependencies, run validations, build, and push artifact. For now, this is where we stop; in the next chapter, we'll push ahead to deploy.

Tying It All Together

Our little demo app is small, but mighty, touching on many aspects of operations automation. In this and the next chapter, we'll see how different CI platforms implement this pipeline, using this app as a lens to understand how different systems use configuration files, provision build environments, handle artifacts, and report results. Whatever your chosen tool, you'll recognize these stages and understand what each one accomplishes.

CI in Action with Jenkins

In this section, we'll see how our conceptual pipeline can be put into practice with Jenkins, one of the oldest and most influential continuous integration tools still in active use today. Long before "CI/CD" became a default expectation and before cloud-hosted build systems were common, Jenkins helped formalize the idea that builds and tests should run automatically, in a central location independent of individual developers' machines. Many of the concepts Jenkins introduced, including pipeline-as-code and stage-based execution, appear in nearly every CI platform that came after it.

Although we'll get into specifics, see screenshots, and look at code, this chapter is not intended to be a complete guide on Jenkins. Instead, you'll gain a general understanding of how CI pipelines are implemented in such a system through the lens of our demo app, preparing you to take a deep dive on your own with whatever tools best suit your needs. In Chapter 10, "Continuous Delivery," we'll look at some other implementations (GitHub Actions and GitLab CI) that provide a different take on the same process.

A Brief History

Jenkins began life in the mid-2000s as Hudson, a Java-based automation server created at Sun Microsystems. Its original purpose was simple: automatically build and test Java projects when code changed. After Oracle acquired Sun in 2010, the community forked the project and, after some kerfuffle about rights to the name "Hudson," renamed it Jenkins, and added a friendly butler mascot to represent the helpful automation that the tool provides. From that point on, Jenkins became a fully open source project with rapid development and a growing ecosystem of plug-ins.

Eventually, CloudBees (that's a company name, not a swarm of angry insects) came along to offer a productized version of Jenkins, offering enterprise features, support, and managed services while also contributing to the open source project. As with many open source products with a similar relationship to a vendor, this partnership has allowed Jenkins to grow, while more enterprise-minded customers have a more robust option than DIY open source deployments.

Jenkins Overview

Understanding Jenkins starts with a few foundational components.

The Jenkins Controller

The Jenkins controller is the central server that coordinates all the automation activities you define. It hosts the web UI, stores configuration, manages credentials, and schedules work. It usually does not run your actual automation jobs, but it's possible to do so, especially if you are starting small and developing your CI pipeline locally. Of course, the challenge of running tasks on the controller node is environment isolation. If you're going this route, I'd recommend you make it temporary, but you can still use local containers or virtual environments to achieve the necessary sandboxing. In any case, you'll soon want to deploy Jenkins on a server, so that it's not dependent on a single laptop, and is accessible to your organization. At that point, you'll want to deploy additional nodes to run tasks. These are agents.

Agents (Build Nodes)

Actual work is performed by agents, sometimes called nodes or workers. They check out code, run commands, execute tests, build containers, and produce artifacts. They are distinct compute from the controller, meaning a VM or container instance, and it's up to you whether they are long-running, persistent machines, or cloud instances/containers that are spun up for a single job before being destroyed.

Agents are what allow Jenkins to scale horizontally; if you have more work to run, you can always configure another agent.

Pipeline-as-Code with Jenkinsfile

Did you really think we'd get this far and not be able to define Jenkins pipelines as code? A Jenkinsfile is a template that describes what should happen when a job runs. It's stored in the root of your repository (or in a subdirectory, if you prefer) and written in a Groovy-based DSL. Don't let the "Groovy" part intimidate you—for declarative pipelines, you're mostly writing YAML-like configuration, not programming.

Here's the complete Jenkinsfile for our demo application:

```
pipeline {
    agent any

    triggers {
        pollSCM('H/5 * * * *')  // Poll GitHub every 5 minutes for changes
    }

    environment {
        APP_NAME = 'python-demo-app'
        APP_PORT = '5001'
        GIT_COMMIT_SHORT = sh(script: "git rev-parse --short HEAD",
returnStdout: true).trim()
        DOCKER_IMAGE = "${APP_NAME}:${GIT_COMMIT_SHORT}"
    }

    stages {
        stage('Checkout') {
            steps {
                echo "Checking out code from GitHub"
                checkout scm
            }
        }

        stage('Install Dependencies') {
            steps {
                sh '''
                    python3 -m venv .venv
                    . .venv/bin/activate
```

```
                pip install -r requirements.txt
            '''
        }
    }

    stage('Run Tests') {
        steps {
            sh '''
                . .venv/bin/activate
                pytest test_app.py -v --junitxml=test-results.xml
            '''
        }
        post {
            always {
                junit 'test-results.xml'
            }
        }
    }

    stage('Run linting with Ruff') {
        steps {
            sh '''
                . .venv/bin/activate
                ruff check .
            '''
        }
    }

    stage('Run security scan with Bandit') {
        steps {
            sh '''
                . .venv/bin/activate
                pwd
                ls -la bandit.yml
                echo "contents of bandit.yml:"
                cat bandit.yml
                bandit -r . -c bandit.yml
            '''
        }
    }

    stage('Build Docker Image') {
        steps {
            sh "docker build -t ${DOCKER_IMAGE} ."
        }
    }

    stage('Push to Registry') {
        steps {
            // Note: This stage requires 'dockerhub-creds' credential in
Jenkins
```

```
                withCredentials([
                    usernamePassword(
                        credentialsId: 'dockerhub-creds',
                        usernameVariable: 'DOCKER_USER',
                        passwordVariable: 'DOCKER_PASS'
                    )
                ]) {
                    sh """
                        echo \${DOCKER_PASS} | docker login -u \${DOCKER_USER}
--password-stdin
                        docker tag ${DOCKER_IMAGE} \${DOCKER_USER}/
python-demo-app:${BUILD_NUMBER}
                        docker tag ${DOCKER_IMAGE} \${DOCKER_USER}/
python-demo-app:${GIT_COMMIT_SHORT}
                        docker tag ${DOCKER_IMAGE} \${DOCKER_USER}/
python-demo-app:latest
                        docker push \${DOCKER_USER}/
python-demo-app:${BUILD_NUMBER}
                        docker push \${DOCKER_USER}/
python-demo-app:${GIT_COMMIT_SHORT}
                        docker push \${DOCKER_USER}/python-demo-app:latest
                    """
                }
            }
            post {
                always {
                    sh 'docker logout'
                }
            }
        }
    }

    post {
        success {
            echo 'Pipeline completed successfully!'
        }
        failure {
            echo 'Pipeline failed!'
        }
        always {
            echo 'Cleaning up...'
            sh 'docker system prune -f'
            cleanWs()
        }
    }
}
```

Let's break this down section by section.

```
pipeline {
    agent any
    // ... rest of pipeline
}
```

Every declarative Jenkins pipeline starts with the `pipeline` block. The `agent any` line tells Jenkins that it can pick any available agent; in production, you can specify certain specific agents or types of agents for different pipelines or individual pipeline steps.

```
    triggers {
        pollSCM('H/5 * * * *')  // Poll GitHub every 5 minutes for changes
    }
```

This section defines a scheduled frequency with which this pipeline will poll GitHub for changes. Keep in mind that you need to run the build manually at least once for this configuration to take effect.

```
    environment {
        APP_NAME = 'python-demo-app'
        APP_PORT = '5001'
        GIT_COMMIT_SHORT = sh(script: "git rev-parse --short HEAD",
returnStdout: true).trim()
        DOCKER_IMAGE = "${APP_NAME}:${GIT_COMMIT_SHORT}"
    }
```

The environment block is where you can define any variables needed by the entire pipeline. We hard-code `APP_NAME` (no harm there), and the `APP_PORT` is a configuration we'll use later in the template.

`GIT_COMMIT_SHORT` calls a command-line command to fetch the latest commit hash from `git`. The `returnStdout` statement lets the response from this command become the value of `GIT_COMMIT_SHORT`.

With this, we construct the string we'll later use to tag the Docker image built by this pipeline. We reference the previous variables in dollar-sign curly braces. This construction means `DOCKER_IMAGE` is a unique string with which we can tag each build, like `python-demo-app:<commit_hash>`.

When using the `git` plug-in, Jenkins defines some useful built-in variables, including `GIT_COMMIT` (the commit hash that triggered the build, but only the long format) and `GIT_BRANCH`, both of which can be used to construct tags or make conditional pipeline decisions. `BUILD_NUMBER` is an auto-incrementing sequence defined by Jenkins for each pipeline run. We'll use this as an alternate tag further in the Jenkinsfile.

Next is the `stages` block, where we get into the actual work. Each stage represents a logical step in the pipeline; note the `parallel` directive, which groups the quality checks into a single block that can all execute at once. Running independent steps simultaneously is a great way to improve pipeline execution times without sacrificing accuracy.

Stage 1: Checkout

```
stage('Checkout') {
    steps {
        echo "Checking out code from GitHub"
        checkout scm
    }
}
```

The `checkout scm` command directs Jenkins to check out/clone the code from whatever source control management (SCM) system is configured for this job—in this case, GitHub. When Jenkins receives a webhook from GitHub or GitLab saying new code was pushed, it knows which repository to check out and which commit to retrieve. This block is technically not necessary for our simple pipeline, because the configuration of the job in the Jenkins UI specifies the target `git` repo. Jenkins clones it automatically as the first step of any pipeline, but having this section makes it explicit and visible.

This stage is our starting point. Everything that follows depends on having the right code checked out in the workspace.

Stage 2: Install Dependencies

```
stage('Install Dependencies') {
    steps {
        sh '''
            python3 -m venv venv
            . venv/bin/activate
            pip install -r requirements.txt
        '''
    }
}
```

Here, we'll run `pip install` to download all the Python dependencies from `requirements.txt`. The `sh` command runs shell commands. The triple-quoted string begins a multiline script that executes in sequence, just like a shell script.

We're creating a Python virtual environment, activating it, and installing dependencies from `requirements.txt`. This is exactly the same process you'd follow locally, now automated and running on a build agent.

Why a virtual environment in CI? Same reason you would on a laptop: isolation. The build agent might run many different jobs. Some might use an older Flask 2.x, others Flask 3.x. Virtual environments ensure each job gets the dependencies it needs without conflicts.

The virtual environment is ephemeral. It gets created fresh for this pipeline run, used, and then discarded (either when the agent cleans up or when the workspace is wiped). This way, every run is clean, provisioned from the ground up.

Stage 3: Run Tests

The next three steps (testing, linting, and security scanning) are done in parallel with the following code:

```
stage('Quality Checks') {
    parallel {
        stage('Run Tests') {
        ...
        stage('Run linting with Ruff') {
        ...
        stage('Run security scan with Bandit') {
    }
}
```

Let's start by looking at the tests:

```
stage('Run Tests') {
    steps {
        dir('python-app') {
            sh '''
                . venv/bin/activate
                pytest test_app.py -v --junitxml=test-results.xml
            '''
        }
    }
    post {
        always {
            junit 'python-app/test-results.xml'
        }
    }
}
```

This stage activates the virtual environment (`. venv/bin/activate`) and runs `pytest`. The `-v` flag gives verbose output, and `--junitxml=test-results.xml` produces machine-readable test results.

The `post` block is new. It runs after the stage steps, regardless of whether those steps succeeded or failed. The `always` condition means "run this no matter what."

The `junit` command is a Jenkins plug-in function that parses JUnit XML files and records test results. This is what lets Jenkins display graphs of test trends, show which tests failed, and track pass/fail rates over time. Even if tests fail (causing the pipeline to stop), the `always` block ensures results get recorded.

Stage 4: Run Linter and Security Scan

```
        stage('Run linting with Ruff') {
            steps {
                sh '''
                    . venv/bin/activate
                    ruff check .
                '''
            }
        }

        stage('Run security scan with Bandit') {
            steps {
                sh '''
                    . venv/bin/activate
                    bandit -r . -c bandit.yml
                '''
            }
        }
```

In these two stages, we run the `ruff` linter and invoke `bandit` for security scanning, making sure to activate the `venv` each time, as each stage launches a fresh shell in the build environment.

Stage 5: Build Docker Image

```
stage('Build Docker Image') {
    steps {
        dir('python-app') {
            sh "docker build -t ${DOCKER_IMAGE} ."
        }
    }
}
```

Here we build the Docker image. Notice we're using double quotes instead of triple single quotes. That's because we need string interpolation—we want `${DOCKER_IMAGE}` to expand to `python-demo-app:abcdef123` (whatever the latest commit SHA is).

The dot at the end of the `docker build` command means "use the current directory as build context." Docker will look for a Dockerfile here and use it to build the image.

This stage only runs if tests passed. Jenkins stops the pipeline at the first failure, so if this stage fails, we never reach the next.

The resulting Docker image gets tagged with our version number and stored in the local build environment. Please note that this requires the Docker executable to be provisioned into your build environment! Later stages can reference the resulting image by its tag(s).

Stage 6: Push to Docker Hub

This stage logs in to Docker Hub and pushes the newly tagged images to that remote repository. Understanding this step requires us to understand secrets management in Jenkins, so let's finish our walkthrough of the script first. If you're just too curious, skip directly to "Managing Secrets in Jenkins," a few sections ahead.

Post-Pipeline Directives

The pipeline-level `post` block runs after all stages complete.

```
post {
    success {
        echo 'Pipeline completed successfully!'
    }
    failure {
        echo 'Pipeline failed!'
    }
    always {
        echo 'Cleaning up...'
        sh 'docker system prune -f'
        cleanWs()
    }
}
```

It has several conditions:

- `success` runs only if the pipeline succeeded.
- `failure` runs only if something failed.
- `always` runs no matter what.

In real pipelines, the `success` block might send a Slack notification, tag the `git commit` as deployed, or update a deployment tracking system. The `failure` block might create a Jira ticket, send an alert, or roll back the deployment.

The `always` block handles cleanup. The command `docker system prune -f` removes unused Docker images and build cache. On busy build agents, the disk can quickly fill with ephemeral Docker images, causing jobs to fail, so it's important to clean up. The `-f` flag skips the confirmation prompt, making it work for our non-interactive pipeline script. `cleanWs()` tells Jenkins to delete the contents of its working directory after a run. If you're working on an ephemeral runner like a Docker container, this may not be necessary, but if not, you'll often want to perform this step to make sure output from a past run can't cause issues in the next.

Sometimes, automation engineers take a more fine-grained approach to cleaning a workspace, leaving some dependencies in place to speed future runs. Whatever your approach, just make sure you understand how the environment changes (or doesn't) from run to run, so you ensure each build is valid.

Declarative vs. Scripted Pipelines

So that's our Jenkinsfile. What CloudFormation and Terraform do for infrastructure, this Jenkinsfile does for our CI pipeline definition, offering a declarative syntax that makes our intentions clear. Jenkins also supports scripted pipelines, which give you full Groovy-language scripting power. Think of these more code-oriented scripts as the CDK equivalent versus CloudFormation.

Declarative pipelines are more restricted but also easier to read and understand. For most CI work, declarative is the way to go. It enforces structure, prevents common mistakes, and avoids more complex logic. Scripted pipelines allow loops, conditionals, and dynamic command generation, but they come with greater risk of creating confusing, hard-to-maintain pipelines. If you see a Jenkinsfile that starts with `node`, that's a scripted pipeline. If it starts with `pipeline`, you're looking at a declarative template.

Setting Up Jenkins

Great! We have a complete Jenkinsfile-defined pipeline. Now, we need Jenkins itself. You can test this pipeline by installing Jenkins on your local machine, but in a real team environment, you'll want a centralized Jenkins server running independent of any developer's machine.

Install Jenkins

Whatever your intended compute environment, be it a Macbook, Windows Server, or Linux system, you'll find a way to install Jenkins at `https://jenkins.io/doc/book/installing`. Jenkins can be installed from source, downloaded via multiple package managers, or run from an official Docker image. Follow the instructions, which include details on how to grab your default administrator password, and you'll be able to access the front door of the Jenkins controller. If you're running this locally, that will be at `http://localhost:8080`. Figure 9.5 shows a successful Jenkins installation's log-in page.

Install Plug-ins

When you first install Jenkins, you'll be offered the chance to install a default set of plug-ins. Plug-ins are extensions of Jenkins' core functionality that make common tasks easier. Make sure to accept the defaults, which include the `pipelines` plug-in, the package that enables us to use a Jenkinsfile.

Create and Configure Job

In Jenkins, select New Item. Give your project a name like **`demo-app`**, choose Pipeline, and click OK.

We'll poll GitHub for our trigger. Select Poll SCM, and in the Schedule box, enter **`H/5 * * * *`**. This schedule will check GitHub for changes every five minutes, as shown in Figure 9.6.

FIGURE 9.5 Jenkins login page.

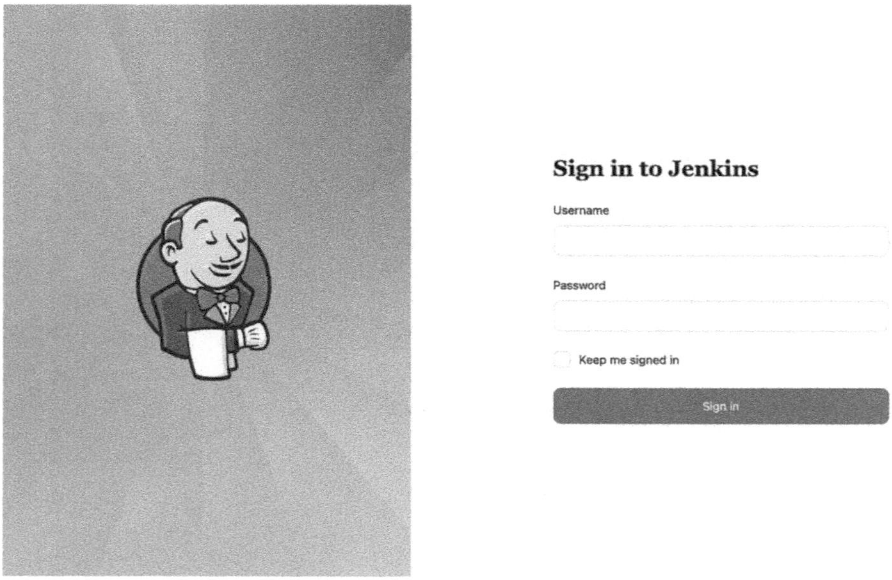

FIGURE 9.6 Configuring SCM polling.

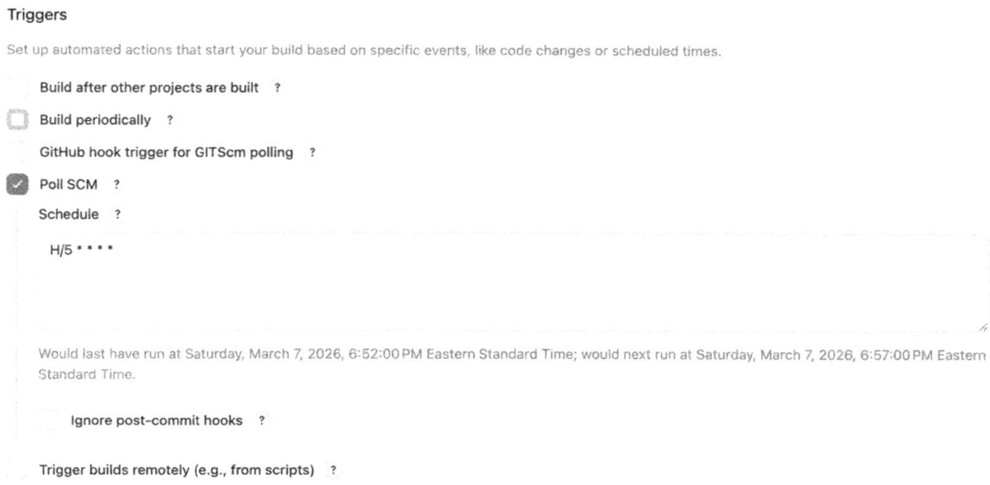

Under Pipeline, find the Definition drop-down and choose Pipeline Script From SCM. This lets us indicate our `git` repo will contain a Jenkinsfile. For SCM choose Git and enter your repository URL. For this demo, I assume you have forked the demo app into a public repo. You can also use a private repo, if you supply credentials using the methods described in the next section.

Set the trigger rule to watch the `main` branch. Under Branch Specifier, enter **`*/main`**.

Click Save. Your pipeline is now ready to execute on the next push of code changes to `main`.

Now, let's get back to the last step of our Jenkinsfile pipeline: pushing our Docker image to Docker Hub. To do this, we'll need to discuss credential management in Jenkins.

Managing Secrets in Jenkins

We've talked about secrets management tools; now, how do we put those secrets to work in our pipeline? Jenkins offers multiple approaches. Its built-in credential store lets you keep secrets natively in the platform, while plug-ins allow you to easily interface with some of the centralized secrets management tools we've seen, like HashiCorp Vault and AWS Secrets Manager. Let's take a quick look at how these options work.

Jenkins-Native Credentials

Jenkins' Credentials feature lets you store secrets in its own encrypted database. You can create credentials in the Jenkins UI (Manage Jenkins ➢ Credentials), assign each an ID, then reference them in your Jenkinsfile. We'll step through this part when we configure Docker Hub credentials in the "Publishing to Docker Hub" section later.

For now, note how we'd use a credential in a pipeline stage. The section `withCredentials` lets you assign a credential into a variable, which you can reference like any other:

```
        stage('Deploy') {
            steps {
                withCredentials([
                    string(credentialsId: 'db-password', variable:
'DB_PASSWORD')
                ]) {
                    sh """
                        docker run -d --name ${APP_NAME} \
                            -p ${APP_PORT}:5000 \
                            -e DB_PASSWORD=${DB_PASSWORD} \
                            ${DOCKER_IMAGE}
                    """
                }
            }
        }
```

Secret values used in this way are only part of the environment while this stage executes, minimizing their potential exposure.

Jenkins also lets you define secrets as explicit username/password pairs. Here's how that looks in code. The one bundled value `database-creds` gets expanded into two variables:

```
withCredentials([
    usernamePassword(
        credentialsId: 'database-creds',
        usernameVariable: 'DB_USER',
        passwordVariable: 'DB_PASS'
    )
]) {
    sh """
        docker run -d --name ${APP_NAME} \
            -e DB_USER=${DB_USER} \
            -e DB_PASS=${DB_PASS} \
            ${DOCKER_IMAGE}
    """
}
```

These options and more make Jenkins secret management very flexible; however, because CI isn't the only place secrets are used, many teams find value in storing them in centralized repositories.

AWS Secrets Manager

One example would be AWS Secrets Manager, which we've discussed before. For this method to work, the instance or container on which your Jenkins tasks run must have AWS IAM permissions to access Secrets Manager.

Here's how Jenkins retrieves secrets from AWS at runtime using `awsSecretValue`:

```
stage('Deploy') {
    steps {
        script {
            def dbPassword = awsSecretValue(
                credentialsId: 'aws-credentials',
                secretId: 'prod/database/password'
            )

            sh """
                docker run -d --name ${APP_NAME} \
                    -e DB_PASSWORD='${dbPassword}' \
                    ${DOCKER_IMAGE}
            """
        }
    }
}
```

The `credentialsId` refers to AWS credentials stored in Jenkins. If Jenkins runs on EC2 with an IAM instance profile, you can skip this parameter and avoid storing local AWS credentials:

```
def dbPassword = awsSecretValue(secretId: 'prod/database/password')
```

As we've discussed, AWS Secrets Manager supports automatic rotation, IAM permissions, CloudTrail audit logs, and direct integration with other AWS services. If you're in another cloud, look for the equivalent in that IaaS provider.

Configuration vs. Secrets

Secrets and configuration should be treated in different ways. Secrets are values like database passwords, API keys, private keys, OAuth secrets, encryption keys, and service credentials. All of these should live in secrets management tools.

Configuration values, on the other hand, are things like port numbers, feature flags, environment names, public endpoints, tool versions, and image names. Rarely changing values can live in the Jenkinsfile; most often, it makes sense to set them as environment variables, so that they can be changed as needed, while keeping the template unaltered.

Publishing to Docker Hub

Our pipeline builds and tests a Docker image, but that image currently exists only on the Jenkins build agent. To make it available for deployment, we need to publish it to an external registry. Although there are many options out there (some of which we discussed previously in "Artifact Registries"), for this example, we'll use Docker Hub.

Docker Hub

Docker Hub is the default public registry for Docker images. It's where images like `python:3.14-slim` or `nginx:latest` come from when you run `docker pull`. You can also push your own images to Docker Hub for free (public repositories) or with a subscription (private repositories).

For our demo application, we'll push to Docker Hub because:

- It's accessible without cloud provider accounts.
- The concepts transfer to any registry.
- It's what most teams use for learning and small projects.

In production environments, teams often use platform-specific registries: AWS ECR for AWS deployments, GitHub Container Registry for GitHub-centric workflows, or self-hosted registries like Harbor for enterprises. The push workflow is identical regardless of which registry you choose.

Creating a Docker Hub Account

Before pushing images, you need a Docker Hub account. Visit `https://hub.docker.com` and sign up with an email address and username. The username becomes part of your image names; if your username is `jdoe`, your images will be `jdoe/`*`image-name`*.

After creating an account, you'll need an access token for authentication. Access tokens are the preferred method over password-based authentication, since they can be revoked or rotated without changing your account password.

To create an access token:

1. Log in to Docker Hub and click your username in the top right.
2. Select Account Settings from the drop-down.
3. Navigate to Personal Access Tokens in the left sidebar, under Settings.
4. Click Generate New Token. The resulting screen is shown in Figure 9.7.
5. Give the token a descriptive name like **`jenkins-ci`**.
6. Set Expiration Date to the shortest possible duration of 30 days. If you will not use the token after this demo, you can delete it sooner.
7. Set permissions to Read, Write, Delete (required for pushing images).
8. Click Generate and copy the token immediately, as you won't be able to see it again.

The token is a long string like `dckr_pat_a1b2c3d4....` Store it securely and treat it like a password. If you lose it, delete the token in Docker Hub and generate a new one.

Storing Credentials in Jenkins

Jenkins needs your Docker Hub credentials to push images. Rather than hardcoding them in the pipeline, we'll store them in Jenkins' credential system.

FIGURE 9.7 Generating a personal access token in Docker Hub.

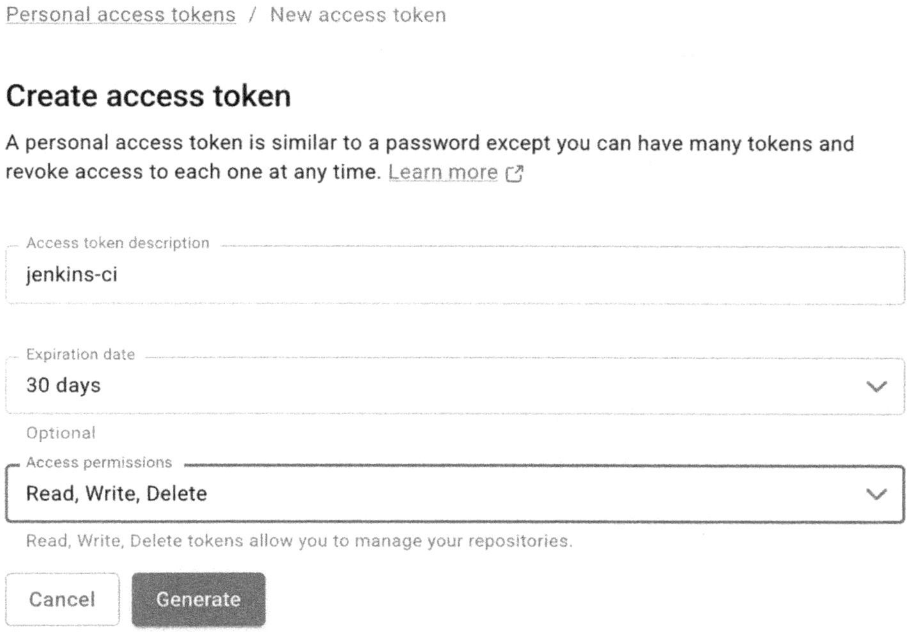

1. In Jenkins, navigate to Manage Jenkins (the gear icon ➢ Credentials).
2. Click (global) under the Stores Scoped To Jenkins section. Secrets can be stored at multiple levels; this is the most permissive, allowing any Jenkins user to make use of the credentials in a pipeline. Credentials can be scoped to different domains, but that topic is beyond the scope of this book.
3. Click the Add Credentials button.
4. Select Username With Password as the credential type.
5. Enter your Docker Hub username in the Username field.
6. Paste your access token (not your password) in the Password field.
7. Set the ID to `dockerhub-creds`, a name we use in the Jenkinsfile to reference the credentials.
8. Add a description like **Docker Hub access token for CI/CD.**
9. Click Create.

See Figure 9.8 for how this looks in Jenkins.

FIGURE 9.8 Configuring the Docker Hub credentials in Jenkins.

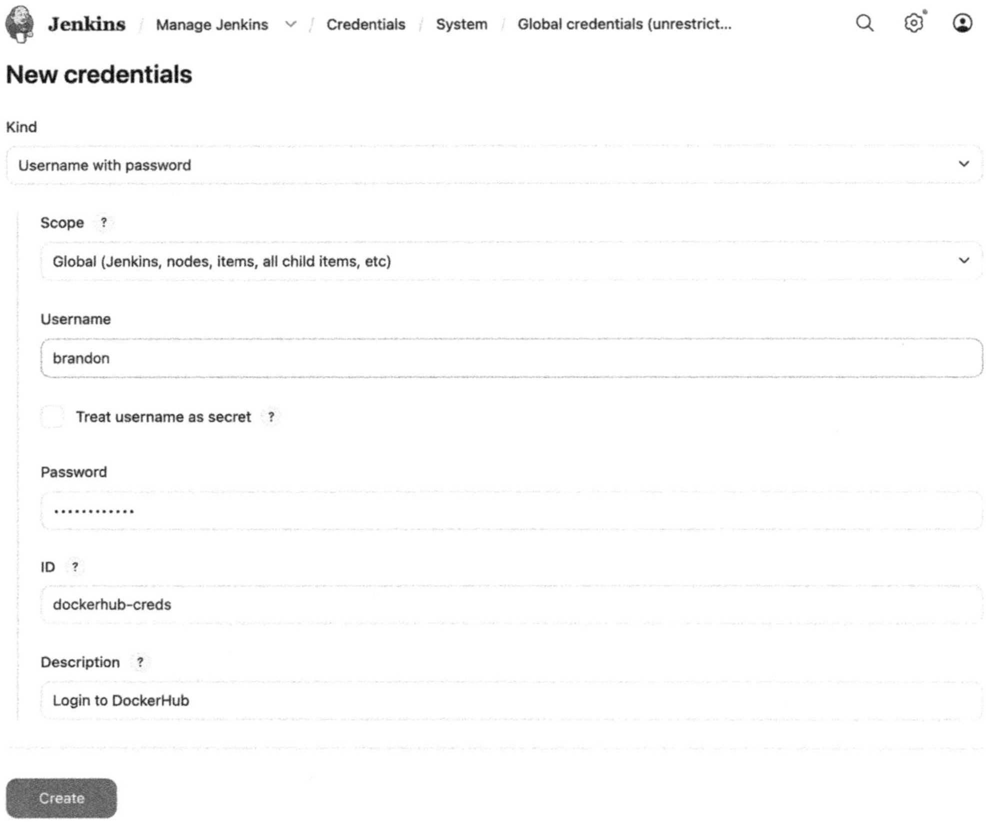

The credential ID `dockerhub-creds` must match the `credentialsId` used in the pipeline's `withCredentials` block. If you choose a different ID, update the Jenkinsfile accordingly.

Once stored, the credentials are encrypted at rest and only exposed to pipeline steps that explicitly request them. The token never appears in logs or build output.

Adding the Push Stage

Our Jenkins pipeline already builds an image tagged as `python-demo-app:${GIT_COMMIT_SHORT}`. Adding a push stage publishes that image to Docker Hub:

```
        stage('Push to Registry') {
            steps {
                // Note: This stage requires 'dockerhub-creds' credential in
Jenkins
```

```
                // For local demo purposes, this stage can be skipped
                withCredentials([
                    usernamePassword(
                        credentialsId: 'dockerhub-creds',
                        usernameVariable: 'DOCKER_USER',
                        passwordVariable: 'DOCKER_PASS'
                    )
                ]) {
                    sh """
                        echo \${DOCKER_PASS} | docker login -u \${DOCKER_USER}
--password-stdin
                        docker tag ${DOCKER_IMAGE} \${DOCKER_USER}/
python-demo-app:${BUILD_NUMBER}
                        docker tag ${DOCKER_IMAGE} \${DOCKER_USER}/
python-demo-app:${GIT_COMMIT_SHORT}
                        docker tag ${DOCKER_IMAGE} \${DOCKER_USER}/
python-demo-app:latest
                        docker push \${DOCKER_USER}/
python-demo-app:${BUILD_NUMBER}
                        docker push \${DOCKER_USER}/
python-demo-app:${GIT_COMMIT_SHORT}
                        docker push \${DOCKER_USER}/python-demo-app:latest
                    """
                }
            }
            post {
                always {
                    sh 'docker logout'
                }
            }
        }
```

The stage authenticates to Docker Hub, tags the image with multiple tags, then pushes them all. The `withCredentials` block retrieves the Docker Hub credentials we just configured and exposes them temporarily as environment variables `DOCKER_USER` and `DOCKER_PASS`.

The `--password-stdin` flag prevents the password from appearing in process listings or shell history. This is a good security practice for any command that accepts credentials. You might be concerned about the `echo` command printing the password to logs, but fortunately, Docker is smart enough to mask values like this:

```
+ echo ****
+ docker login -u johndoe --password-stdin
```

This system precaution is another good reason to use native password-handling capabilities like those offered by Jenkins.

Tagging Strategy

We push three tags for the same image:

Build number tag. Example: `python-demo-app:42`

This lets us trace images to a specific build. This may be helpful if you need to restore a specific build number in the future.

Commit SHA tag. Example: `python-demo-app:2f4553`

With this kind of tag, you can easily determine the version of code running inside an image, and even check out that specific SHA locally if you need to inspect the state of the source code at that point.

Latest tag. Example: `python-demo-app:latest`

Unlike the other two tags, which are never changed (i.e., immutable), the `latest` tag can change—it always points to the most recent build. This is convenient for development environments that always deploy the newest version, but it's not actually best for production, where you should prefer explicit image version numbers to avoid ambiguity about what is deployed.

To be clear, each tag points to the same image, identified by its cryptographic digest, a unique identifier. That digest never changes; tags are just human-readable aliases.

After the Push

Once the image is in Docker Hub, it's accessible from anywhere. The build agent can be destroyed. Deployment systems pull the image by tag. Rollback pulls an older tag. Security scanners can inspect images in the registry without needing access to build agents.

The `post` / `always` section makes sure that after the Docker Hub push, we log out of Docker.

At this point, we've completed the CI workflow: Code is built, tested, scanned, packaged, and published. Our Docker image artifact is ready for deployment, which we'll explore in the next chapter using another set of tools.

Adding Notifications

No build pipeline is complete until it's communicating with the team! Here are two of the best ways to get started with Jenkins notifications.

Email

Among Jenkins' default plug-ins are the Mailer and Email Extension plug-ins. Configuring these features to send mail requires that you bring your own credentials to an SMTP server; this could be a service like Gmail, Office 365, Mailgun, or Amazon SES. Details are beyond the scope of this book, but clicking the plug-in name (under gear icon ➢ Plugins ➢ Installed Plugins) will take you to documentation pages like this one for Email Extension: `https://plugins.jenkins.io/email-ext`.

You can invoke the email feature directly in a pipeline step with this syntax. This directive can be added to the `failure()` block of the Jenkinsfile. Note how you can give HTML in the body and use variable interpolation with the dollar sign/hash mark notation:

```
emailext(
    to: 'recipient@example.com',
    subject: "Build Failed: ${env.JOB_NAME} #${env.BUILD_NUMBER}",
    body: """
        <p>Build failed!</p>
        <p><strong>Job:</strong> ${env.JOB_NAME}</p>
        <p><strong>Build Number:</strong> ${env.BUILD_NUMBER}</p>
        <p><strong>Commit:</strong> ${env.GIT_COMMIT_SHORT}</p>
        <p><strong>Link:</strong> <a href="${env.BUILD_URL}">${env.
BUILD_URL}</a></p>
        <p><strong>Console:</strong> <a href="${env.BUILD_URL}
console">${env.BUILD_URL}console</a></p>
    """,
    mimeType: 'text/html'
)
```

The resulting email is show in Figure 9.9.

The email extension allows you to construct detailed messages for your developers, or even mail lists of teammates defined in Jenkins. Search for information on Jenkins'

FIGURE 9.9 Email notification from Jenkins.

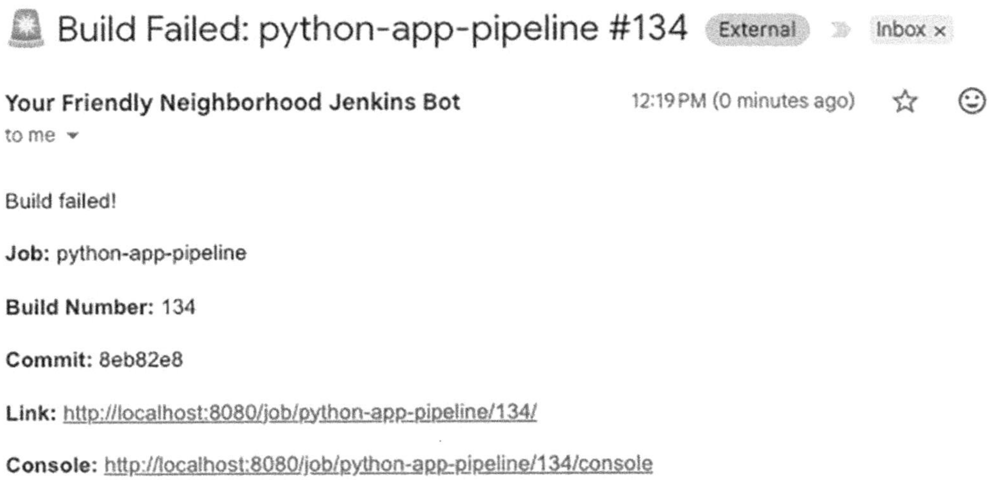

`recipientProviders` to configure that capability. It predefines some email lists based on the context of the current build, including `builderUser`, `developers`, and, hilariously, `culprits` and `brokenTestsSuspects`.

Slack

We can also connect Jenkins to Slack. Again, the configuration is beyond the scope of this book, but check out detailed instructions at `https://plugins.jenkins.io/slack`. You'll need to make changes on both your Jenkins installation and the Slack side. Once configured, you can invoke Slack anywhere in your pipeline, as shown here with the `slackSend` command:

```
        stage('Checkout') {
            steps {
                echo "Checking out code from GitHub"
                checkout scm
                slackSend(
                    channel: '#build',
                    message: "Build started for ${env.JOB_NAME} #${env.BUILD_
NUMBER}\nLink: ${env.BUILD_URL}"
                )
            }
        }
```

The resulting message lands in the `#build` channel of our Slack (along with a previous one declaring the build start), as shown in Figure 9.10.

With that, we're all set to see the output of our build. Let's run the pipeline.

Running the Jenkins Pipeline

Our pipeline is already configured in Jenkins; now, we just need to trigger a job. The pipeline is configured to poll GitHub on a regular basis, but it will only run if it detects changes on the `main` branch. If you're using your own repo, pushing an update to `main` will do the trick.

FIGURE 9.10 Slack notifications from Jenkins.

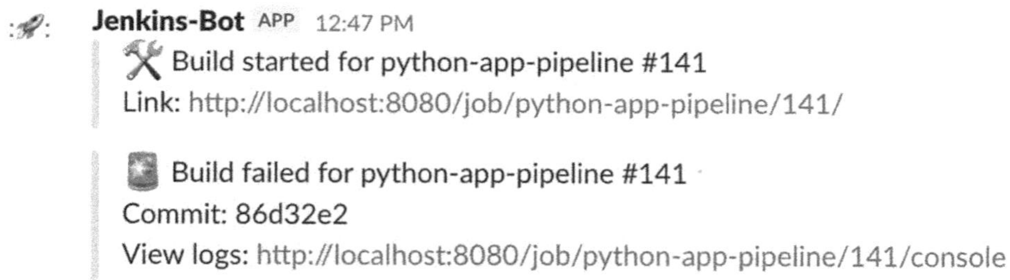

FIGURE 9.11 Jenkins project dashboard.

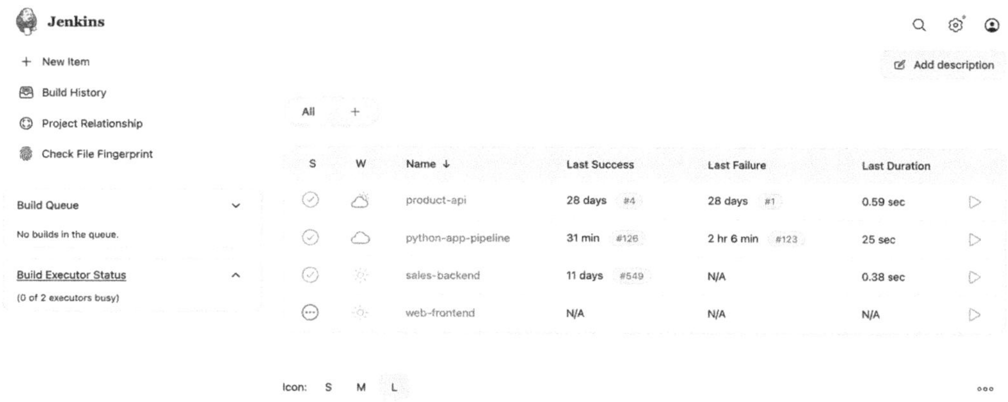

We could also return to the Jenkins project configuration and add a Build Periodically schedule; setting `H/10 * * * *` would make the build run every 10 minutes. Even easier? Navigate to the project and click Build Now.

On the `main` index, Jenkins shows all your projects, along with a summary of its current state, last successful build, and last failed build. Figure 9.11 shows this interface, which features a triangular Build Now button along the right-hand side.

Examining a Job Run

Click the app name to view project details. Here, you can see the result of recent pipeline activities. The JUnit XML output from `pytest` allows Jenkins to render a graph of past test results.

Clicking a build number (found in multiple places) takes you into details of that particular pipeline run. You can view the complete Console output by clicking Console, but perhaps the best overview of the job run is under Pipeline Overview, which offers a nice visual of every part of the pipeline execution, as shown in Figure 9.12.

Here, you can see exactly what parts succeeded and what parts failed, with the console output for each step viewable by clicking that step. In this run, `bandit` is complaining because it was not configured to skip the `.venv` virtual environment folder, which is not part of the application code and whose many triggered reports are thus irrelevant. Resolving this issue yields a successful pipeline run, as shown in Figure 9.13.

Now, we can validate that our Docker artifact was successfully built and pushed to Docker Hub.

Confirming the Build

We can see in the output that our Docker build and push steps ran successfully. To confirm, let's visit Docker Hub in a browser. Figure 9.14 shows the results.

As you can see, the latest Jenkins run pushed all three tags to Docker Hub: `latest`, the commit SHA, and the Jenkins build number.

FIGURE 9.12 Jenkins pipeline overview.

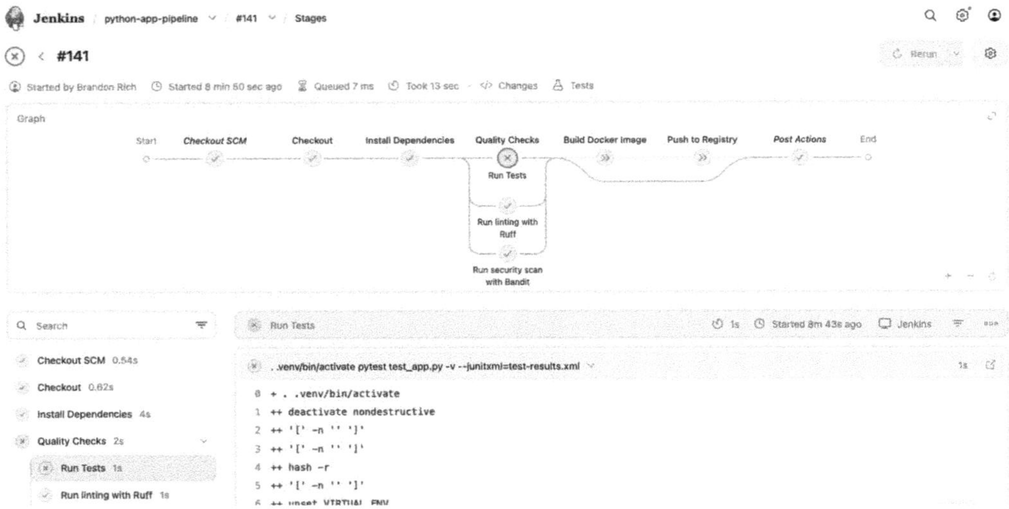

FIGURE 9.13 Jenkins pipeline success.

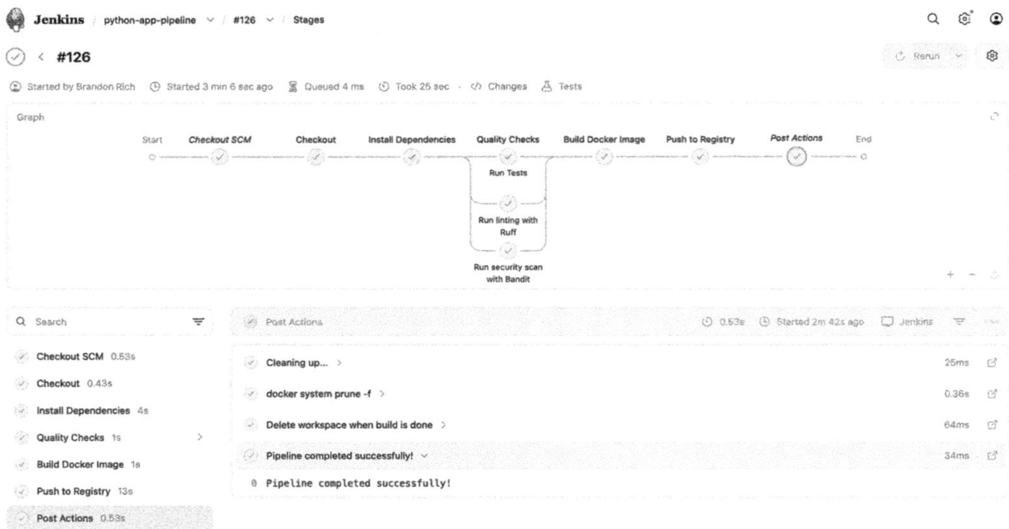

FIGURE 9.14 All tags pushed to Docker Hub.

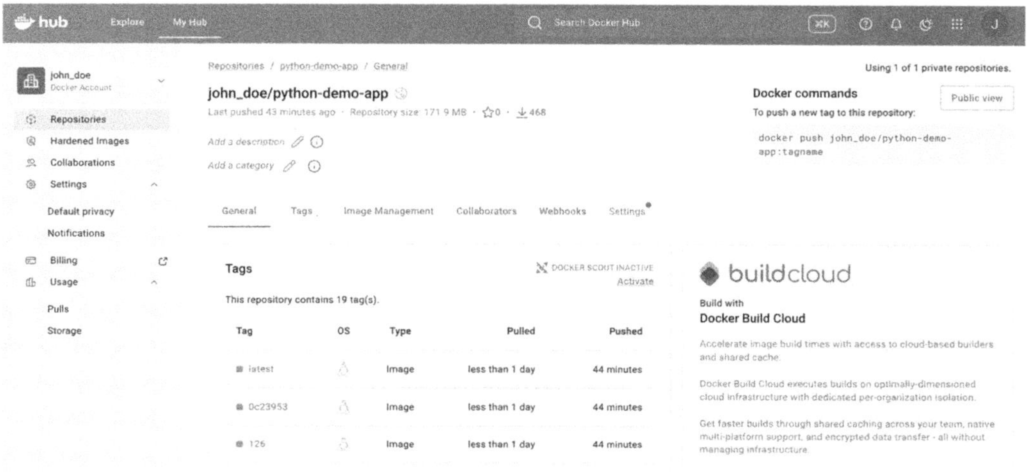

External Build Environments

There is one notable problem with our Jenkins demo: Running builds directly on the Jenkins controller is not a good idea, even if that controller is a central Jenkins server. Why not?

The Jenkins controller serves as the orchestration layer for your entire CI/CD infrastructure. When builds run directly on this machine, they compete for CPU, memory, and disk resources with Jenkins' core responsibilities. A resource-intensive build can slow down or even crash the entire Jenkins instance, blocking anyone from running a pipeline.

Running builds on the controller also creates unnecessary security risks. Build scripts often require elevated permissions to install dependencies, modify system configurations, or interact with external services. When these operations run on the controller, a compromised build script could potentially access Jenkins' configuration, credentials store, or job definitions.

Our demo uses a Python virtual environment, but this doesn't solve the fundamental issues with using the controller instance. A runaway process in a `venv` can still consume all available memory or fill the disk.

Moving Builds to External Environments

To isolate your builds, you want to explore Jenkins "build agents." Start by provisioning your own dedicated build agents as physical machines, VMs, or cloud instances that connect to your controller and accept job assignments. This protects your controller from resource exhaustion and limits the blast radius of build failures.

Jenkins lets you name remote build agents and refer to them in your Jenkins files with `agent { label 'your-build-agent' }` directives. You might organize many agents by OS, associated application or team, language runtimes, or security zones for fine-grained control over your build environment. For best results, use Docker. Because containers are ephemeral, configuration is fresh every time and the runtime is fully isolated.

Jenkins' official documentation covers distributed builds (`www.jenkins.io/doc/book/using/using-agents`) and details how to configure your environments with Docker agents. In the next chapter, we'll see how newer CI/CD services use containers out of the box.

Choosing Jenkins

Jenkins remains a compelling choice in the CI/CD landscape for several reasons. Its plug-in ecosystem and extreme flexibility make it adaptable to virtually any workflow, while its maturity means it has been tested across countless production environments. It can run just about anywhere, and being free and open source with commercial support options makes it accessible to organizations of all sizes and budgets. That said, running Jenkins definitely means more maintenance than the newer cloud-native options we'll explore in the next chapter. Self-hosting means your team must handle scaling, backups, and updates. The Jenkinsfile provides a great template for declarative pipelines with lots of extensibility beyond what we explored, including conditional logic and scripting of reusable functions.

Ultimately, the right tool depends on your context. Teams with existing Jenkins installations, complex requirements, or restricted environments may find Jenkins to be a great choice. Teams starting fresh with access to managed cloud services may find platforms like GitHub Actions offer a simpler path. No matter which tool you choose, concepts like stages, quality gates, and artifact versioning are universal. Learning Jenkins helps build a mental model for CI as a discipline, one that transfers readily to whatever platform you choose.

Summary

In this chapter, we moved from "code that exists" to "code that proves it's ready to move forward." Continuous integration is the system that makes that transition reliable. Rather than trusting that changes work because they worked once on a laptop, CI evaluates every change in a clean, repeatable environment and applies the same standards every time.

We explored CI as a quality gate, not just a testing phase. Automated tests validate correctness, but they're only one part of the story. Linters and static analysis tools enforce consistency and catch risky patterns early. Security scans help surface vulnerabilities before they harden into production incidents. Together, these checks shift failure earlier in the life cycle, where it's cheaper, faster, and far less disruptive to fix.

We also examined how CI pipelines produce and manage artifacts—the concrete outputs of a build. Whether those artifacts are binaries, packages, or container images, CI is responsible for creating them once, versioning them immutably, and storing them in appropriate registries. This separation between source code and build outputs enables repeatable deployments, reliable rollbacks, and clear traceability from running systems back to specific commits.

Workflow management was another key theme. Pipelines are event-driven systems, triggered by pushes, tags, schedules, or human intervention. Hooks, triggers, and pipeline definitions determine *when* automation runs and *what* context it runs with. Understanding these mechanics makes CI predictable instead of mysterious—and debuggable when something goes wrong.

Finally, we looked at build environments themselves. Modern CI relies on ephemeral, isolated execution contexts—often containers—to avoid configuration drift and ensure consistency. Whether you use virtual environments, containerized runners, or cloud-hosted agents, the goal is the same: Every build starts clean, runs deterministically, and leaves behind only logs and artifacts.

By the end of this chapter, you should see CI not as a tool, but as a discipline—one that enforces quality automatically, produces trustworthy artifacts, and provides fast feedback when changes don't behave as expected. In the next chapter, we'll take those validated artifacts and explore how they move safely and deliberately into production through continuous delivery.

Exam Essentials

Understand why dependency management is critical to automation. Know that automation code depends on external libraries, packages, runtimes, and system components. Understand how unmanaged dependencies lead to "works on my machine" failures and why reproducible environments are essential for CI and deployment automation.

Understand the purpose of continuous integration. Know that CI is about early, automated validation of code changes. CI systems verify that code integrates correctly with the existing codebase by running tests, enforcing quality standards, and preparing build artifacts in a consistent environment. CI reduces regression risk and shortens feedback loops.

Recognize CI as a quality gate. Understand that CI pipelines enforce standards automatically. Unit tests, linters, static code analysis, and security scans all serve as gates that prevent known-bad code from progressing. Builds should fail fast when violations occur, rather than allowing problems to surface later in deployment or production.

Know common CI pipeline stages. Be familiar with the typical CI flow: source code checkout, environment provisioning, dependency installation, quality checks, test execution, and artifact creation. Understand which stages are sequential, which can run in parallel, and why ordering matters.

Understand artifact management concepts. Artifacts are the outputs of a CI build, such as binaries, packages, or container images. Know why artifacts should be immutable, versioned, and stored in external artifact registries rather than source control. Understand the role of artifact repositories and why downstream systems reuse build outputs instead of rebuilding from source.

Understand artifact versioning strategies. Know the difference between semantic versioning and build-based versions. Understand tags versus digests, why immutability matters, and how versioned artifacts enable traceability and reliable rollbacks.

Know how a SBOM factors into continuous integration. A software bill of materials (SBOM) describes what an artifact contains, including dependencies and versions. Understand how SBOMs support security, compliance, and vulnerability response as part of modern CI pipelines.

Understand pipeline triggers and hooks. Be familiar with common pipeline triggers such as push-based triggers, manual triggers, scheduled runs, and webhooks. Know how Git metadata (branches, tags, commits) influences pipeline behavior and deployment decisions.

Understand CI build environments and task runners. CI jobs run in build environments provided by task runners, often as ephemeral containers or VMs. Understand why ephemeral environments reduce configuration drift and increase reliability. Know when virtual environments are useful and when containers alone provide sufficient isolation.

Recognize pipeline-enhancing concepts. Understand how containerization, security scanning, code quality scanning, and AI-based log analysis enhance CI pipelines. Know that these tools augment human review but do not replace judgment or accountability.

Understand failure handling in CI. Know that CI pipelines are designed to stop on failure, surface actionable feedback, and prevent invalid artifacts from moving forward. Understand the role of logs, test reports, and standardized output formats (such as JUnit XML) in diagnosing failures quickly.

Review Questions

1. A CI pipeline runs linting, unit tests, and a Docker image build. A developer pushes code that passes all tests but contains a stylistic violation flagged by the linter. The pipeline is configured to fail on quality-check errors. What happens?

   A. The pipeline skips linting and proceeds to build the Docker image since tests passed.

   B. The pipeline fails at the linting stage, and no Docker image is built.

   C. The pipeline completes but marks the build as unstable.

   D. The linter automatically fixes the violation and the pipeline continues.

2. A team stores compiled binaries directly in their Git repository alongside source code. Over time, the repository grows to several gigabytes and clone times become unworkable. What is the correct architectural fix?

   A. Use Git LFS to track the binaries within the repository.

   B. Compress the binaries before committing them.

   C. Publish build artifacts to an artifact registry and remove them from source control.

   D. Split the repository into smaller repositories, one per binary.

3. In an application's Jenkinsfile, the `post` block includes an `always` section that runs `docker system prune -f`. Why is this step included, and why does it run in `always` rather than `success`?

   A. It removes the application container so the next build can redeploy; it runs in `always` because redeployment is needed even after failure.

   B. It removes unused Docker images and build cache to prevent disk exhaustion on build agents; it runs in `always` because cleanup is needed even after failed builds.

   C. It pushes the Docker image to a registry before the agent is freed; it runs in `always` to guarantee delivery.

   D. It restarts the Docker daemon to ensure a clean state; it runs in `always` because the daemon may be in a bad state after failure.

4. A security audit reveals that a CI pipeline logs Docker Hub credentials in plain text during the push stage. Which change best addresses this risk?

   A. Encrypt the credentials in the Jenkinsfile using Base64 encoding.

   B. Use the `withCredentials` block and pass the password via `--password-stdin`.

   C. Store the password in an environment variable defined in the Jenkinsfile's `environment` block.

   D. Add the credentials to the repository's ENV file and read them at runtime.

5. What is the primary purpose of a software bill of materials (SBOM) in a CI pipeline?
   A. To replace the build artifact with a lightweight manifest
   B. To provide a structured inventory of the components, dependencies, and versions that make up an artifact
   C. To encrypt the artifact before publishing it to a registry
   D. To speed up builds by caching dependency metadata
6. A static code analyzer flags the following Python code as potentially dangerous:

```
user_input = request.get_parameter('filename')
file_path = '/data/' + user_input
content = open(file_path).read()
```

   What type of static analysis detected this issue?
   A. Type analysis, because `user_input` might not be a string
   B. Control flow analysis, because `file_path` might be undefined
   C. Taint analysis, because untrusted input flows into a sensitive file system operation without validation
   D. Data flow analysis, because `content` is never used after assignment
7. A team pushes Docker images with only a `latest` tag. After a failed deployment, they attempt to roll back but discover that `latest` now points to the broken build. What versioning practice would have prevented this problem?
   A. Using semantic versioning exclusively (e.g., `v1.2.3`)
   B. Tagging images with immutable, build-specific identifiers (e.g., build numbers) in addition to `latest`
   C. Removing the `latest` tag entirely and using no tags
   D. Signing the image with a cryptographic key before pushing
8. What is the primary advantage of using ephemeral build environments in CI?
   A. They eliminate the risk of configuration drift between builds.
   B. They are faster than persistent build servers.
   C. They reduce the cost of cloud compute.
   D. They allow developers to SSH into the build agent for debugging.
9. A company runs Jenkins with a single controller and multiple agents. A developer notices that the same pipeline produces different test results depending on which build agent runs it. Tests pass on Agent A but fail on Agent B with import errors. The Jenkinsfile creates a virtual environment and installs from `requirements.txt` with pinned versions. What is the most likely root cause?
   A. The `requirements.txt` file uses unpinned versions, so different agents resolve different package versions.
   B. The virtual environment from a previous build on Agent B is contaminating the current build.
   C. The Jenkins controller is caching test results from Agent A and replaying them incorrectly.
   D. Agent B has a different Python version installed, causing compatibility issues with the pinned dependencies.

10. In Jenkins, what is the difference between the controller and an agent?
    A. The controller executes pipeline stages; agents store build artifacts.
    B. The controller coordinates jobs, stores configuration, and hosts the UI; agents execute the actual build work.
    C. The controller handles only scheduled triggers; agents handle webhook triggers.
    D. The controller and agent are interchangeable terms for the same component.

11. A CI pipeline triggers on every push to any branch. The team notices that feature branch builds are consuming significant compute resources and frequently queue behind each other, delaying feedback on the main branch. Builds take 15 minutes each, and the team pushes dozens of feature branch commits per hour. What is the most effective way to balance feedback speed with resource usage?
    A. Increase the number of Jenkins agents to handle the load.
    B. Scope push triggers to meaningful branches and run abbreviated pipelines on feature branches (e.g., tests only, no Docker build).
    C. Switch from push triggers to scheduled triggers that run every 30 minutes.
    D. Disable CI on feature branches and only run pipelines when code is merged to `main`.

12. What does the "shift-left" principle in software development mean in the context of CI pipelines?
    A. Moving production servers to the left side of the network diagram to reduce latency
    B. Detecting and addressing quality issues, security vulnerabilities, and integration problems as early as possible in the development process
    C. Scheduling builds during off-peak hours to reduce infrastructure costs
    D. Storing older build artifacts on slower, cheaper storage tiers

13. A development team wants to enforce code quality standards before code reaches the CI pipeline. They implement a pre-commit hook that runs linting and unit tests. Developers report that the hook significantly slows down their commit workflow. What is the best approach?
    A. Remove the pre-commit hook entirely and rely on CI feedback.
    B. Increase the timeout for the pre-commit hook to allow all checks to complete.
    C. Require developers to use `--no-verify` when committing to skip the hook.
    D. Configure the pre-commit hook to run only fast checks (linting), deferring slower tests to CI.

14. A team builds container images in CI and stores them in a registry. After six months, the registry contains thousands of images consuming significant storage. Many are from experimental feature branches never merged. What is the best artifact retention strategy?
    A. Keep all artifacts indefinitely for complete traceability.
    B. Implement life cycle policies: keep production tags indefinitely, `main` branch builds for 90 days, feature branch builds for 7 days.
    C. Delete all images older than 30 days regardless of tag.
    D. Manually review and delete images quarterly.

15. Two projects on the same Jenkins agent install conflicting versions of a Python library. Project A requires library v2.0, Project B requires v1.5. Builds start failing intermittently depending on which project ran last. What is the root cause and solution?

    A. The projects share a global Python environment; each job should create an isolated virtual environment.

    B. The agent OS is outdated; update the operating system.

    C. The Jenkinsfile syntax is incorrect; use different stage names.

    D. Jenkins agents cannot run multiple projects; provision separate agents per project.

16. A CI pipeline runs a comprehensive test suite that takes 45 minutes to complete. Developers complain about slow feedback, so the team considers these options. Which provides the best balance of speed and quality?

    A. Run only unit tests in CI (2 minutes), run integration tests nightly.

    B. Split tests across parallel agents to reduce wall time to 10 minutes.

    C. Run unit tests on every commit (2 minutes), integration tests on main branch only (15 minutes), full suite nightly.

    D. Increase agent resources to reduce test time to 30 minutes.

Answers to Review Questions

1. B. The correct answer is B. CI pipelines should be configured to fail on quality checks and stop execution. Quality checks like linting and tests can run in parallel, so one may finish successfully while the other fails, but the build will not be reached. This is the quality gate principle in action: preventing known-bad code from progressing further. Option A is incorrect because the pipeline does not skip over failing stages. Option C describes a behavior some CI tools support, but the question specifies the pipeline fails on errors, not warns. Option D is incorrect because in a CI context, linters are run in check-only mode; they detect issues rather than modifying the source code.

2. C. Option C is correct. Artifact registries are purpose-built for storing and versioning build outputs like binaries and container images. Source control systems are designed for text-based files like code, configuration, and pipeline definitions. Options A and B may reduce symptoms but don't address the fundamental misuse of source control for artifact storage. Option D increases complexity without solving the underlying problem.

3. B. Option B is correct. On busy build agents, images and cache from repeated builds can quickly consume disk space. The `always` condition ensures cleanup happens regardless of whether the pipeline succeeded or failed; failed builds can often leave behind images and cache. Option A is incorrect, because `docker system prune` removes unused resources, not specifically the running application container. Option C is incorrect; `prune` does not push images. Option D is incorrect; `prune` does not restart the Docker daemon.

4. B. Option B is correct. The `withCredentials` block retrieves secrets from Jenkins' encrypted credential store and exposes them only for the duration of that block. The `--password-stdin` flag prevents the password from appearing in process listings or shell history. Option A is incorrect; Base64 is encoding, not encryption, and values in the Jenkinsfile are visible in source control. Option C is incorrect; environment variables defined in the Jenkinsfile are visible in the source code. Option D is incorrect; ENV files should never be committed to version control, and this approach exposes secrets in the repository.

5. B. Option B is correct. An SBOM is a structured inventory that describes what an artifact contains, including dependencies and their versions. It supports security auditing, compliance, and vulnerability response. Option A is incorrect because an SBOM describes the artifact but does not replace it. Option C is incorrect; SBOMs are not encryption mechanisms. Option D is incorrect; SBOMs do not affect build performance.

6. C. The correct answer is C. Taint analysis tracks untrusted data as it flows through a system, flagging when it reaches sensitive operations without proper validation. In this case, user input is used directly to construct a file path, creating a path traversal vulnerability. Option A is incorrect; the issue is not about type compatibility. Option B is incorrect, as `file_path` is always defined in this code. Option D describes an unused-variable finding, which is not the vulnerability being flagged.

7. B. Option B is correct. Tagging with immutable build-specific identifiers ensures every build is uniquely referenceable. Rollback becomes explicit: "deploy build 38" rather than hoping `latest` still points to the right image. Option A could also work, but build-based versions are more common for internal deployment pipelines and provide direct links back to the CI run. Option C makes images difficult to reference at all. Option D addresses authenticity, not versioning.

8. A. Option A is correct. Ephemeral environments are created fresh for each build run and destroyed afterward. This ensures every build starts from a known, clean state, eliminating configuration drift caused by leftover artifacts, packages, or state from previous builds. Option B is not necessarily true; provisioning ephemeral environments has overhead. Option C may or may not be true depending on the implementation. Option D contradicts the nature of ephemeral environments, which are destroyed after use.

9. D. Option D is the correct answer. With pinned dependencies and a fresh virtual environment, the most likely remaining variable is the underlying Python runtime. If Agent A runs Python 3.11 and Agent B runs Python 3.9, some packages may not be compatible, causing import errors. This is why it's important that the build environment matches what the application expects. Option A can be ruled out because the question states versions are pinned. Option B is possible but unlikely if the pipeline creates a fresh virtual environment as described. Option C is incorrect; Jenkins does not cache and replay test results across agents.

10. B. Option B is correct. The Jenkins controller is the central server that manages configuration, credentials, scheduling, and the web interface. Agents (also called nodes or workers) are separate compute resources where the actual build work runs: checking out code, running tests, building containers, and producing artifacts. Option A reverses the relationship. Option C incorrectly distinguishes them by trigger type. Option D is incorrect; they are distinct components with different roles.

11. B. Option B is correct. Scoping triggers and tailoring pipeline behavior per branch directly addresses both problems: reducing resource consumption and prioritizing `main` branch builds. Feature branches may only need linting and tests, not a full Docker build and deploy. This aligns CI behavior with the development workflow. Option A addresses capacity but not efficiency; you're still doing unnecessary work. Option C delays feedback significantly and batches unrelated changes. Option D removes the early feedback loop that makes CI valuable, potentially allowing broken code to reach `main`.

12. B. Option B is correct. Shifting left means moving quality checks, testing, and security scanning earlier in the development life cycle, ideally into the CI pipeline where issues can be detected before code reaches production. This reduces the cost and impact of defects by catching them when they're easier and cheaper to fix. Option A is just a joke, of course. Option C relates to scheduling but not quality. Option D relates to data life cycle management, not development practices.

13. D. The correct answer is D. Pre-commit hooks should focus on fast, local checks. Slow tests belong in CI where they run in parallel and don't block developer flow. This balances early feedback with developer productivity. Option A is a potential solution, and some teams conclude that `git` hooks are too cumbersome for regular use; however, in this case, we are looking to optimize the local tests desired by the developers. Option B is incorrect; it does nothing to speed things up, which is the primary goal. Option C has the same issues, but also cultivates bad habits among developers.

14. B. Option B is correct. Retention policies should reflect artifact value and usage patterns. Production artifacts need long retention, main branch moderate retention, transient branches short retention. This balances traceability with cost. Option A is infeasible and ignores cost. Option C risks deleting important production artifacts (don't lose your last known good rollback image!). Option D doesn't scale and makes cleanup take much longer.

15. A. Option A is correct. This demonstrates why isolated virtual environments are critical in CI. Without isolation, system-level or agent-level packages create version conflicts. Each job should provision its own clean environment (`venv`, container, etc.). Option B doesn't address isolation. Option C is irrelevant. Option D is not feasible, nor desirable; other options enable isolation without scaling hardware unnecessarily.

16. C. Option C is correct. Tiered testing strategies balance feedback speed with thoroughness. Fast unit tests on every commit catch obvious breaks quickly. Integration tests on main verify integration before deployment. Full suites periodically catch subtle issues. This matches the risk profile: Feature branches need fast feedback, `main` branch needs thorough validation. Option A defers too much and fails to give sufficiently timely feedback. Option B is not particularly feasible, though parallel-execution options do exist for many test runners, including our example of `pytest`. Option D is costly and still slow for individual developers.

Continuous Delivery

THE AUTOOPS+ EXAM TOPICS COVERED IN THIS CHAPTER MAY INCLUDE, BUT ARE NOT LIMITED TO, THE FOLLOWING:

✔ **1.0: Automation Coding Concepts**

- 1.1. Given a scenario, use code to support automation.
- 1.2. Given a scenario, use source control techniques to version code.

✔ **2.0: System Configuration**

- 2.1. Given a scenario, use configuration management techniques to deploy a solution.
- 2.2. Compare and contrast basic approaches to automation.
- 2.4. Given a scenario, troubleshoot common issues with system configuration.

✔ **3.0: Continuous Integration**

- 3.2. Explain workflow management concepts in CI.
- 3.3. Given a scenario, analyze configurations to manage basic automation pipelines.

✔ **4.0: Continuous Delivery**

- 4.1. Given a scenario, implement techniques of continuous delivery (CD).

In the last chapter, we explored many of the core elements of automation pipelines for application operations and saw how those ideas can be implemented using Jenkins. If the idea of continuous integration (CI) is to fully prepare an application revision for deployment, continuous delivery (CD) is about managing releases, automating success, and handling failures.

In CI, we're performing quality checks, testing, and security analysis before packaging code into an artifact that represents its ready state. That packaging step might mean compiling Java code into a JAR file or transpiling an Angular app into plain and minified JavaScript. In many cases, as in the last chapter, it means building a Docker image.

With continuous delivery, we're automating the movement of code into a live runtime environment. We'll talk about deployment patterns that give you control over the pace of updates, testing that helps confirm your success or failure, and techniques for fixing or rolling back changes, should problems occur.

By focusing on GitHub Actions, you'll see how these steps work in a modern CI/CD platform that offers tight integrations and native cloud-based task runners, letting us automate deployments safely and consistently.

Deployment Options

Before we can deploy, we need to decide where our application should run. There are many deployment targets you might choose, with different architectures, supporting services, and levels of required management.

Deployment to Virtual Machines

One of the most straightforward ways to deploy code is directly on a virtual machine (VM), such as Ubuntu or CentOS Linux servers, or perhaps Windows Server machines.

This style of deployment is common, but it has shortcomings. You are provisioning an entire VM for your application, and scaling means creating more dedicated VMs (often done via cloud autoscaling). You'll decide how much of your stack dependencies you can pre-provision in a golden image and how much to configure at deployment time. How quickly you can scale depends on how long that configuration and startup process takes.

Thus, your application isolation boundary is an entire machine. Although it's possible to run multiple applications on a VM, you'll need to use virtual environments to achieve isolation, and your scaling options become limited, as the applications cannot then be scaled independently. How do you ensure the next instance spinning up to scale has the right version of each application on it? The challenges begin to multiply.

Still, for applications that need an entire VM to themselves or for organizations who are not running containers, using a virtual machine-based infrastructure can be a simple path to production.

Containerization Options

Running your application on containers directly addresses many of the challenges of running on virtual machines. As discussed in previous chapters, containers combine the isolation of dedicated hardware with the fast startup time of image-based VM scaling. With containers, configuration effort happens at build time so that your code is ready to run as soon as it is deployed into a live environment.

Containerized Applications on Virtual Machines

Hosting containers directly on VMs gives you the best of both worlds. You get the isolation and fast startup of containers while still working within familiar VM infrastructure. Just install Docker or your preferred container runtime on each machine and run your containerized apps there. Configuration and provisioning happens in the container image, meaning your code is more portable across environments. Your host environment is still the virtual machine, so you'll still need to handle VM provisioning and scaling, but at least your application dependencies are now packaged consistently. This can be a great intermediate step if you're transitioning from traditional VM deployments toward more modern container orchestration.

Containerized Applications on an Orchestration Platform

If you're running multiple containers across many hosts, orchestration platforms like Kubernetes, Docker Swarm, or Amazon ECS become essential. These platforms handle scheduling containers across your infrastructure, managing failures, scaling up and down based on demand, and routing traffic between services.

As with infrastructure-as-code templates, you declare your desired state to the orchestrator, which implements the changes. This includes how many instances you want, what resources they need, and how they should communicate. Orchestration adds complexity upfront, but once you're managing dozens or hundreds of containers, you'll appreciate the way orchestration lets you scale that management. Most modern cloud-native applications run on orchestration platforms, and they integrate nicely with CI/CD pipelines for automated deployments.

Keep in mind that container orchestration usually means more complex infrastructure as well. Unless you are using a managed compute service like AWS Fargate, part of your responsibility will be maintaining a cluster of virtual machines to act as the compute layer of your container deployment. This comes with additional management and cost implications, but it's often an excellent trade-off for the sophisticated fleet management afforded by container orchestration.

Platform as a Service

If "not managing infrastructure at all" is more your style, platform-as-a-service (PaaS) offerings like Heroku, Google App Engine, or AWS Elastic Beanstalk take that task almost entirely off your plate. You push code, and the platform handles provisioning, scaling, load balancing, and monitoring automatically. There's no VM to configure, no container registry to maintain, no orchestration cluster to manage.

For many applications, especially smaller ones or those with standard requirements, PaaS is the fastest path from code to production. The trade-off is less control and potential vendor lock-in, but if you're focused on shipping features rather than managing infrastructure, PaaS can dramatically reduce operational overhead. You do pay additional costs to the PaaS provider for the privilege, but that money buys time and simplicity.

Function-Based Deployments

We've talked about serverless deployments in the context of automating integrations between cloud components. Services like AWS Lambda, Google Cloud Functions, or Azure Functions let you deploy individual functions that execute in response to events, such as HTTP requests, queue messages, file uploads, or scheduled triggers. Although we often think of deployment automation around "heavier" apps like web applications or APIs, these individual functions must be deployed like any other app, making function as a service (FaaS) a viable target platform for a CI/CD pipeline.

Not only that, but frameworks like serverless exist to deploy much more sophisticated application architectures (such as full web apps) on FaaS-only endpoints; a deployment like this could result in dozens of cloud function updates at once.

Deploying to a cloud function usually means writing scripts that use native cloud SDKs or CLIs to push code to the service. In addition, some FaaS providers let you run containers, meaning the Docker-building patterns seen in the last chapter could work for this target as well.

Cloud functions typically have drawbacks like execution time limits and cold start latency, but for the right workloads, serverless can eliminate almost all infrastructure management while giving you massive automatic scaling.

Static Site Hosting

One of the simplest, cheapest, and easiest-to-maintain options available is static site hosting. If your application runs fully client side (in other words, if it consists purely of HTML, JavaScript, or CSS that can be run exclusively in a browser), you have the option to deploy it to a static hosting service. This could be your entire application or a frontend layer; if it can run on a browser, this is an option. While specifics are outside the scope of this book, consider options like static object storage in a cloud provider (like a Google Storage Bucket or S3 bucket) or a content delivery network like CloudFlare or AWS CloudFront.

Continuous Delivery

The job of continuous delivery is to get code running on your chosen platform. The actual steps will vary depending on your particular application stack and target architecture. Executing those deployment steps can be done in multiple delivery patterns.

When deploying new code to an environment, we want to update the running application as smoothly as possible, minimizing downtime and interruptions for users with the right balance of automation complexity. Your options will depend on your deployment target and the capabilities of your chosen deployment tooling.

Delivery Patterns

Let's look at some of the most common patterns of application deployment.

In-Place Deployments

An *in-place deployment* is exactly what it sounds like: overwriting the existing application in place and restarting the application. This is the simplest deployment pattern, and if your application is running as a single instance in an environment without scaling capabilities, it may be your only option.

In-place deployments do come with notable downsides. First, it is difficult to avoid downtime. However, even apps that live on just one host often run on application servers that allow some parallelism in their execution. For instance, Ruby application servers Unicorn and Puma both offer zero-downtime restarts that work by spawning additional OS-level forked or threaded instances of the app. This lets you achieve zero downtime in-place deployments, even on a single instance. Check your stack components to see what is possible.

Second, there's additional risk of configuration drift or environment provisioning clashes. Even if you're running on a VM that is actively managed by a configuration tool like Ansible, it's possible for an in-place deployment to create some drift. If you aren't isolating your processes well with something like a virtual environment, you could find that your next dependency installation step fails due to a conflicting, existing library or OS package.

Still, in-place deployments can be made to work. If the system is noncritical or part of an integration path that can sustain downtime (say, something that exclusively consumes messages from a queueing system, where the messages will be retained until fetched), in-place deployments may be viable.

Rolling Deployments

From here, the deployment styles assume a horizontally scalable architecture, wherein a load balancer is responsible for distributing incoming traffic across multiple virtual machines, containers, or function instances. In these cases, there are multiple copies of the application running that need to be updated. The goal is to update everything in the fleet while taking advantage of the unique properties of this architecture to avoid downtime and test updates as you go.

In a *rolling deployment*, instead of replacing the application everywhere at once, we update the instances gradually. We take a subset of servers or containers out of service, update them to the new version, and verify them as healthy, before returning them to the load balancer pool.

The load balancer is the key here. When you remove an instance from rotation, the load balancer stops sending new traffic to that host. Existing requests finish, the deployment runs, and once the instance reports healthy again, the load balancer begins routing traffic to it.

In practice, a rolling deployment might look something like this:

1. Remove instance A from the load balancer.
2. Deploy the new application version to A.
3. Wait for health checks to pass.
4. Return A to the load balancer.
5. Repeat the process for instances B, C, and D.

This approach significantly reduces downtime. At any stage of the deployment, some portion of the system stays online and continues to handle user traffic.

However, rolling deployments have their own challenges. During the rollout, multiple versions of the application are running simultaneously. This can cause problems if, for instance, the new version expects a database schema change that older versions cannot handle, or if API dependencies change.

Another risk is partial rollout failure. If an issue appears halfway through the deployment, the system may end up with half the fleet running one version and half running another. Good automation pipelines include rollback procedures that can quickly return all instances to the previous version if something goes wrong.

Because orchestration platforms like Kubernetes and many cloud deployment tools implement rolling deployments automatically, this pattern has become something of a default deployment strategy in modern infrastructure.

Blue-Green Deployments

Blue-green deployments are an excellent way to update an entire application environment successfully without the potentially messy "in-between" states possible in a rolling deployment. At the same time, they are more complex than previous methods.

In a blue-green deployment, you maintain two separate sets of infrastructure per environment and swap between them. One set includes your current production nodes;

the other set has the previously deployed version of the application. When it's time to deploy, you update the code on that nonactive infrastructure, validate the deployment, and swap.

Engineers usually call these alternating environment sets "blue" and "green," though the color choice matters less than the concept: Only one environment receives traffic at a time.

A typical blue-green deployment works like this: while the blue environment runs the current production version:

1. Deploy a new version to the green environment.
2. Validate the running green environment with automated tests or smoke checks.
3. Switch traffic from blue to green.

Most teams implement the traffic switch through a load balancer rule, a DNS update, or some equivalent routing change.

Not only is this a great way to make sure your deployments work before making user-facing changes, blue-green deployments also have significant benefits for rollbacks. If a deployment fails or exhibits errors after it comes online, no rollback is necessary; you just never swap. If you do swap and the new version misbehaves, no problem: just flip the switch back to the previous environment. That kind of rollback usually takes seconds.

Of course, there is a cost to this approach. Blue-green deployments require double the infrastructure, at least temporarily—it's up to you whether the alternate infrastructure is long-lived or spun up for the duration of the deployment. For small services this cost is negligible, but for large fleets it can get expensive.

Canary Deployments

Canary deployments take a more cautious approach to releasing new code. Instead of updating all instances at once or rolling through them systematically, you deploy the new version to just a small subset of your infrastructure—often a single instance or a small percentage of your fleet. This "canary" instance receives a fraction of production traffic while you monitor it closely for problems.

Like the proverbial canary in the coal mine, once traffic starts flowing, you watch those canary instances to see whether they thrive. If the canary deployment has problems, you know not to proceed with the full rollout.

Here's how a typical canary deployment unfolds:

1. Deploy the new version to one or a few instances (the canary).
2. Route a small percentage of traffic to the canary instances.
3. Monitor key metrics: error rates, response times, resource usage.
4. If metrics look good, gradually increase traffic to the canary.
5. Eventually promote the canary version to the entire fleet.

The advantage of a canary deployment is its small blast radius. If something goes wrong, only a tiny fraction of your instances are affected. You can catch issues before they impact your entire user base, which is especially valuable when you're deploying changes that are difficult to validate through preproduction testing alone.

To make this work, you need good observability on your applications and the resources on which they run, and sophisticated enough traffic routing to control what percentage of requests go to which version. Despite the complexity, canary deployments have become increasingly popular. Sometimes, the ability to test new code with real production traffic before going all in is worth the investment in process automation and observability.

Quality Assurance in CD

Many of the steps in our CI automation focus on quality assurance. Linting, static security analysis, and unit tests all help make sure the code we build for production is bug-free and working. Still, quality assurance (QA) doesn't stop at build time. Other pre-deployment quality checks, such as load testing and regression testing, ensure that your application will be responsive under real-world conditions. Then, post-deployment checks let you confirm the update was a success. If it wasn't, you'll need to make some quick decisions about how to respond, and what kind of fix will be most appropriate to the situation. Let's look at each post-build consideration in turn.

Load Testing

Load testing validates that your application can handle expected traffic levels without falling over.

A good load test simulates realistic user behavior at scale. You might send thousands of requests per second to your application, measure response times, and watch for errors or resource exhaustion. The goal is to find breaking points before your users do.

However, you don't usually run load tests on every deployment. They're slow and potentially expensive, as you need infrastructure or an external service to generate the load.

Most teams use load tests as a gate for major releases rather than a per-deployment check. You might run load tests nightly, or before pushing to production, or whenever you make changes that could affect performance. The key is finding the right balance between confidence and speed.

Regression and Integration Testing

Whenever you make a change, there's a risk that change may break something that was previously working. Regression tests help you make sure that doesn't happen. Regression tests are any automated tests you run regularly to ensure quality. Focus regression tests on the most critical paths and the areas most likely to break.

Integration tests verify that your application works correctly with its dependencies, such as databases, external APIs, message queues, authentication services.

Integration tests catch problems that unit tests miss. Unit tests mock out dependencies; integration tests use real ones (or realistic test doubles). This makes them slower and more brittle, but also more valuable for catching real-world issues.

Validation and Remediation

The successful completion of a deployment isn't the end of the story. A few more tests will make sure everything is working correctly. If it isn't, you'll need to take action to preserve your service availability.

Smoke Testing

When a deployment is complete, you want to know right away if things are broken. More complete testing can come *after* you've confirmed that the environment is actually responding. The quick-and-dirty tests that let you know you haven't broken production are called *smoke tests*.

Smoke tests aren't comprehensive. They check that the application is basically alive, responding to requests, and that its critical endpoints are reachable.

These tests usually run immediately after deployment, before traffic is fully routed to the new version. In a blue-green deployment, you'd run smoke tests on the green environment before switching traffic. In a rolling deployment, you'd run them on each instance before adding it back to the load balancer pool.

These tests can be run from the same scripts that manage your deployment, and should complete in only a few seconds, letting you know if it's okay to proceed.

Post-Deployment Testing

No matter how careful you are in managing your deployment environments and avoiding configuration drift, nothing is exactly like production but production. External dependencies, the presence of real and complete data in the database, and real-world traffic patterns are all elements that make your live system unique. Post-deployment tests are more complete than smoke tests; these manual or automated steps give you one last round of testing to confirm that everything went to plan.

If smoke tests or post-deployment tests yield problems, you'll need to consider either a rollback or a *hotfix*. Figure 10.1 gives a simple flowchart for deciding what action to take.

Rollback

Performing a rollback of a deployment means reverting to the last known good state of the app. This might mean deploying the latest successfully deployed tag from version control, or, in container-based scenarios, redeploying the most recent image. On some platforms, this is as simple as flipping a switch. On others, your CI/CD pipeline has to handle it.

When things go wrong in a deployment, rollback should be your first choice. It's usually faster, less risky, and gets you back to a known-good state so you have time to consider what went wrong. If you've designed your deployment strategy well, especially with approaches like blue-green or canary deployments, rolling back should be quick and reliable.

However, a rollback won't always work. One big reason is database changes. If your most recent deployment came with updates to data or database structure that can't easily be unwound, rollback is not an option you can choose. If this or other considerations prevent you from performing a rollback, your team needs to implement a hotfix.

FIGURE 10.1 A decision tree for post-deployment issues.

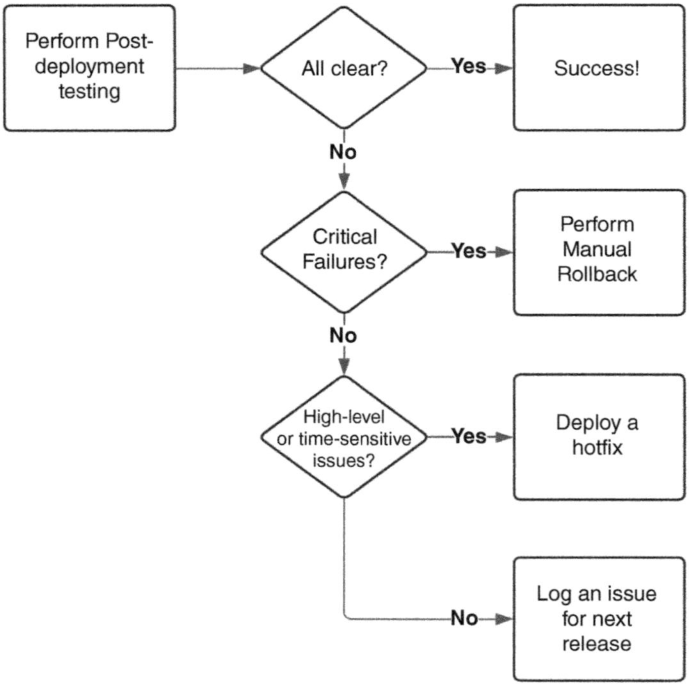

Hotfixes

Hotfixes are code changes that must be done right away. Maybe a critical system is down, costing your company money by the minute, or maybe an error is putting your data at risk. A hotfix is a code update made to resolve situation quickly.

How much this urgency means bypassing your automation is a matter of balancing acceptable risk and speed. Going outside your typical CI/CD practices creates a risk of configuration drift, inconsistency across environments, and untracked, unauditable changes.

If a change must be made in production immediately, one viable strategy is to build a dedicated automation pipeline that deploys hotfix branches. Tie these branches to a documented issue tracked in your ticketing system (e.g., Jira, GitHub Issues). Your CI/CD system can watch for pushes on branches with a name like `hotfix_issue_123` and trigger a production deployment. It's then your responsibility to make sure the associated code changes are propagated back to every nonproduction environment and development branch, lest the critical fix be lost on the next normal deployment.

On the other hand, if your CI/CD automation is sufficiently mature, you may have time to deploy a change through your normal channels. If possible, use your typical change process to preserve traceability and avoid risk of regression errors.

Modern CI/CD Automation with GitHub Actions

Introduced in 2018 as a response to growing developer demand for event-driven automation options, *GitHub Actions* is a CI and automation platform built directly into GitHub, embedded in the same place developers already store code, manage pull requests, and review changes. It's a fully managed service for running build and deployment processes with no infrastructure to run, manage, or patch. It's also designed around modern CI assumptions: ephemeral build environments, configuration as code, and event-driven workflows.

Automation Where Your Code Lives

GitHub Actions has many distinct advantages over our Jenkins example.

First, integration with version control comes out of the box. GitHub Actions' event-driven workflows run in response to events that occur inside GitHub, such as pushes, pull requests, or tag creation. You don't have to set up polling or webhooks; it just works. Plus, because GitHub Actions execute in your GitHub account context, you don't have to set up any additional authentication mechanisms to interact with your `git` repo or push to services like GitHub's container registry.

With GitHub Actions, you define workflows as YAML files stored in the repository under `.github/workflows/`. As with the Jenkinsfile, this declarative template can be versioned alongside the code it builds and tests.

Finally, ephemeral, container-based job runners are the baseline standard, requiring no additional setup from you. GitHub provides a wide selection of hosted runners that execute jobs in clean, temporary environments; just pick your preferred OS or language stack environment and go.

Core Concepts

GitHub Actions workflows are defined in YAML files. Workflows have trigger actions with filter conditions that determine when they execute. Workflows have variables and define jobs, which are composed of steps, each one having details that describe its execution environment and actions.

Like the Jenkinsfile, workflow files are declarative templates, stating exactly what your process will do. Without significant amounts of conditional logic, loops, or other traditional programming constructs, a GitHub Actions workflow is highly readable from beginning to end.

Let's break down our example. As a complete CI/CD pipeline, this code handles not only the quality checks we demonstrated with Jenkins, but also deployment.

Workflows

A workflow has a name:

```
name: CI Pipeline
```

and is triggered by certain events.

The on section defines the conditions that will trigger this pipeline definition will run. A trigger can be repository activity, a clock, a button click, or even an event sent in from outside GitHub. GitHub's documentation groups workflow triggers into repository events, scheduled runs, manual runs, and external events.

Repository Events

These triggers name activities happening in the repo. Because GitHub Actions is built right into the repo, you don't need to poll or set up a webhook, nor establish an authenticated connection to the repo or even specify the repo name. Everything centers around the code you're already working with.

```
on:
  push:
    branches: [ main, github-actions ]
  pull_request:
    branches: [ main ]
```

In this example, we define conditions that trigger this workflow on `push` events to certain branches, or when a pull request is created on branch `main`. Any one of these actions will kick off the jobs specified in the file. You can also target tags:

```
on:
  push:
    tags:
      - 'v*.*.*'
```

As you can see, wildcard patterns allow you to match any tag using semantic versioning, such as `v1.2.3` or `v2.0.0`. You can use the same wildcards to match multiple branches. For instance, if your developers all have branches like `dev-john` and `dev-jane`, a wildcard `dev-*` will define a trigger for any developer that pushes to their personal dev branch.

You can even specify that certain filepaths must be altered before a workflow runs:

```
on:
  push:
    branches: [main]
    paths:
      - 'src/**'
      - '.github/workflows/**'
```

This pattern requires that a push to `main` also include changes under the src directory or a change to the GitHub workflows themselves.

Scheduled Runs

Scheduled runs let you set up good CI practices like nightly builds. These triggers use the familiar `cron` syntax (if you're not familiar, you should be! `https://crontab.guru` is a great resource) to set up recurring jobs. This syntax sets a workflow to run nightly at 3 a.m.:

```
on:
  schedule:
    - cron: '0 3 * * *'
```

You can enter multiple `cron` lines to define complex scheduled tasks.

Manual Runs

By default, you cannot manually invoke a GitHub Actions workflow from the web interface. You can rerun failed jobs, but by default, you can't just trigger a workflow yourself. However, there are certainly situations where this is desirable, and GitHub supports this with workflow_dispatch trigger type.

Taken by itself, the result is an unsophisticated Run Workflow button in the UI, as shown in Figure 10.2.

```
on:
  workflow_dispatch:
```

FIGURE 10.2 A simple Run Workflow button in GitHub Actions.

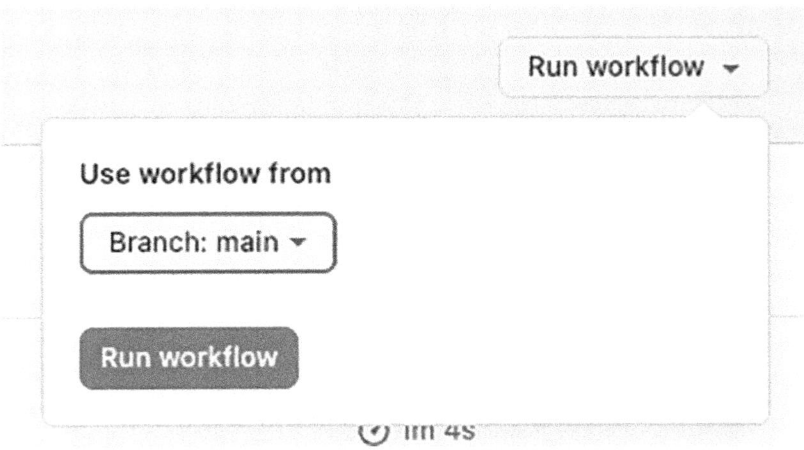

However, with a bit more code, you can define complex inputs that become variables for your workflow. In this example, we define inputs for a rollback procedure. A rollback might be something triggered by failed post-deployment tests, but in many cases, you'll want a human to make the call. A workflow_dispatch trigger lets you do that. In this case, we define a required drop-down selection with two options: which environment do you want to revert? Second, we have a required text input where the user must enter the tag to which to roll back.

```
on:
  workflow_dispatch:
    inputs:
      environment:
        description: 'Environment to rollback'
        required: true
        type: choice
        options:
          - staging
          - production
      previous_tag:
        description: 'Previous working image tag to rollback to'
        required: true
```

This UI ends up looking like Figure 10.3.

With this, you can allow individuals to run jobs in a variety of ways, all auditable in the GitHub Actions history. Just be aware that any user with write access to your repository will see these buttons!

For more ways to manage triggers, see `https://docs.github.com/en/actions/reference/workflows-and-actions/events-that-trigger-workflows`.

Variables

Variables are set up under the env section of the YAML file. As with Jenkins, they can reference built-in values (like `github.repository`) or be hard-coded. These values can be referenced later as `${{ variable-name }}`.

```
env:
  APP_NAME: python-demo-app
  REGISTRY: ghcr.io
  IMAGE_NAME: ${{ github.repository }}
  AWS_REGION: us-east-1
  ECS_CLUSTER: python-demo-cluster
  ECS_SERVICE: python-demo-app
```

For our app, we define a few values. This pipeline will push the built Docker repo both to GitHub's Container registry (hence `ghcr.io`) and Amazon's Elastic Container Registry for deployment to Elastic Container Service (hence references to ECS).

FIGURE 10.3 A more complex Run Workflow interface in GitHub Actions.

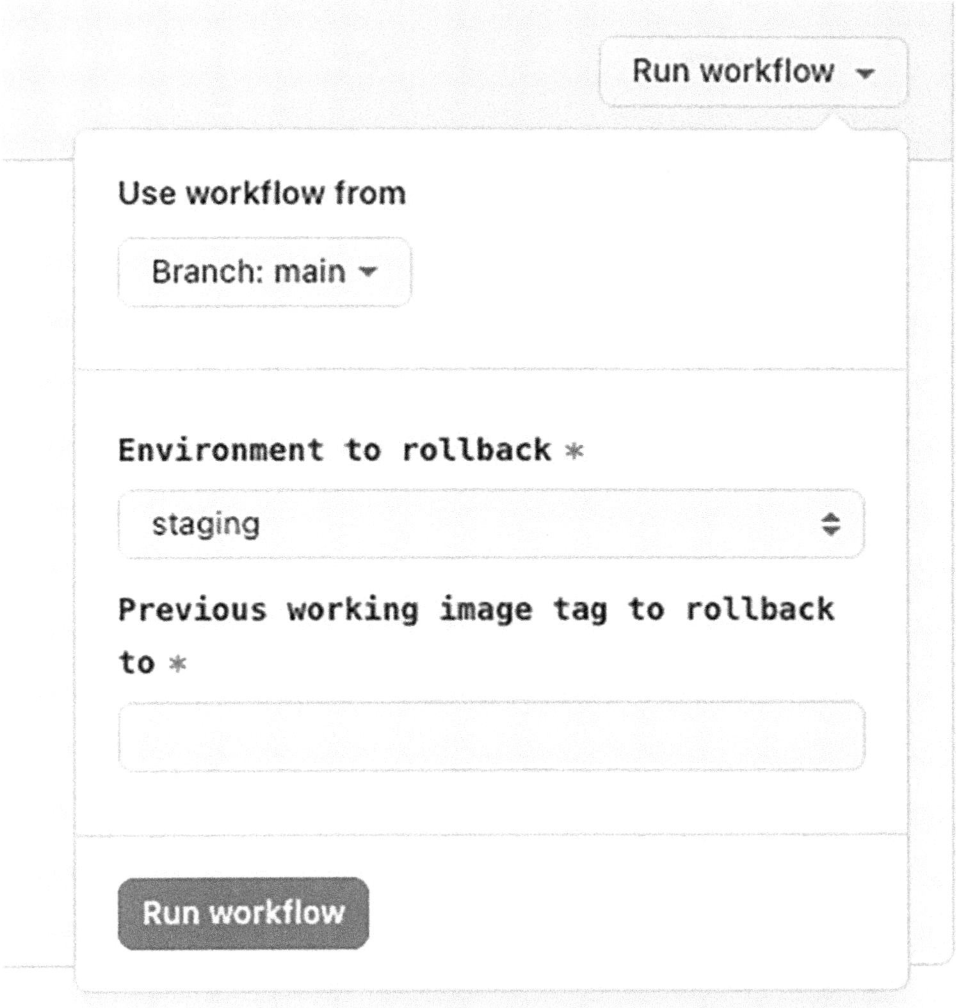

Jobs, Steps, and Actions

Workflows contain jobs, which run independently and can execute in parallel. Each job is made up of steps, which are executed sequentially on the same runner.

This is also where we start to see one of GitHub Actions' unique features: the titular Actions. GitHub Actions are like functions in Python or other languages, encapsulating multiple steps into simple directives. For more on this, see the upcoming section "Reusable Actions."

Here's an example of a job called `build`, whose first step invokes a GitHub-provided action called `actions/checkout@v4`, which clones the code from the repo:

```
jobs:
  build:
    runs-on: ubuntu-latest
    steps:
      - uses: actions/checkout@v4
      - run: npm install
      - run: npm test
```

The `runs-on` line tells GitHub Actions what kind of container environment to run in—back to our principle of isolation in CI/CD steps. The first step runs a reusable action, whereas the next two run shell scripts. In any case, each execution of the above job runs in one ephemeral container.

Here are the first two steps of our CI process, the lint and test steps. This will be a bit long, but it helps make a point:

```
  lint:
    name: Lint (Ruff)
    runs-on: ubuntu-latest
    steps:
      - name: Check out code
        uses: actions/checkout@v4

      - name: Set up Python
        uses: actions/setup-python@v5
        with:
          python-version: '3.13'
          cache: 'pip'

      - name: Install dependencies
        run: |
          python -m pip install --upgrade pip
          pip install -r requirements.txt

      - name: Run linting with Ruff
        run: |
          ruff check .

  security:
    name: Security Scan (Bandit)
    runs-on: ubuntu-latest
    steps:
      - name: Check out code
        uses: actions/checkout@v4

      - name: Set up Python
        uses: actions/setup-python@v5
```

```
        with:
          python-version: '3.13'
          cache: 'pip'

      - name: Install dependencies
        run: |
          python -m pip install --upgrade pip
          pip install -r requirements.txt

      - name: Run security scan with Bandit
        run: |
          bandit -r . -c bandit.yml
```

Note how both the `ruff` and `bandit` steps have some redundancy. They both clone the repo, set up Python, and install dependencies with `pip`. This is necessary because of the ephemeral, isolated nature of GitHub Actions' container-based job runners. Know that each job runs in an entirely new and fresh environment. As a result, you must repeat some steps. If we had not used a local virtual environment with Jenkins, and instead switched to container-based workflows, we'd have done the same in the last chapter.

We could have run each of these steps as steps within a single job, maybe called `lint-test-scan`, and avoided this, but that would mean the steps could not all run in parallel, sacrificing runtime speed.

Still, this redundancy doesn't have to be a time-waster. The line `cache: 'pip'` allows GitHub to store (and later fetch) the files created by `pip install` in a cache, so that subsequent jobs can avoid re-downloading things. In-depth caching behavior is beyond the scope of this book, but you can learn more here: `https://docs.github.com/en/actions/reference/workflows-and-actions/dependency-caching`.

The cache is powerful, but also a potential source of errors. Make sure you read up thoroughly, and be careful that your use of caching preserves sufficient isolation so that each step remains a valid test.

Order of Execution and Parallelism

Like CloudFormation and Terraform, GitHub Actions creates a dependency graph out of the jobs in your workflow file. Figure 10.4 shows how our workflow appears in the GitHub web interface.

The lint, test, security, and Notify Build Start jobs all start immediately. The first three are depicted in a single box, though, because the subsequent step, Build And Push Docker, is explicitly dependent on them via the `needs` directive:

```
  build-and-push:
    name: Build and Push Docker Image
    runs-on: ubuntu-latest
    needs: [lint, security, test]
```

This acts very much like `DependsOn` in CloudFormation. Using this line helps determine which parts of your workflow run in parallel versus those that run in sequence.

FIGURE 10.4 The GitHub Actions CI/CD workflow.

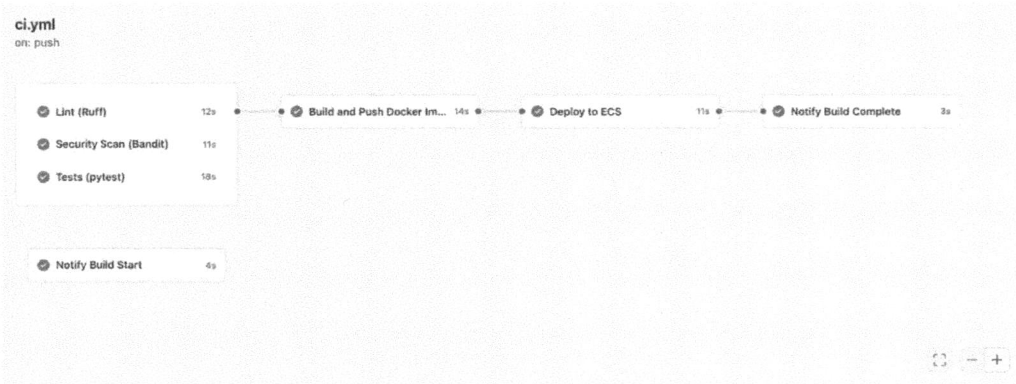

Reusable Actions

GitHub Actions' namesake Actions are one of its defining features. Actions are a bit like packages in other languages, with the key exception that they don't have to be downloaded, installed, or tracked like traditional dependencies. Rather, you can simply refer to an action in your workflow and expect it to work. You can build your own, decomposing complex tasks with function-like encapsulation, or reference Actions built by others, making your workflows easier to both read and write.

GitHub Marketplace is a repository full of these reusable actions: `https://github.com/marketplace?type=actions`.

Actions are referred to by provider, name, and version, such as `docker/build-push-action@v5`. They can accept parameters, which you supply under the `with` keyword:

```
- name: Build and push Docker
  uses: docker/build-push-action@v5
  with:
    variable1: foo
    variable2: foo
```

Actions are a very useful and flexible part of the GitHub Actions ecosystem, and a big part of why the platform is so popular in DevOps practices.

Choose Wisely

Any time you use an Action from the Marketplace, just as when you're downloading language dependencies or installing OS packages, you're trusting code you didn't write. There are a few good ways to evaluate Actions before you use them.

First, look at who wrote the Action. While many Actions are built by GitHub itself, there are plenty out there from third-party creators. GitHub Marketplace lets you toggle your search between Creators and Verified Creators, as shown in Figure 10.5.

FIGURE 10.5 GitHub Marketplace Verified Creators.

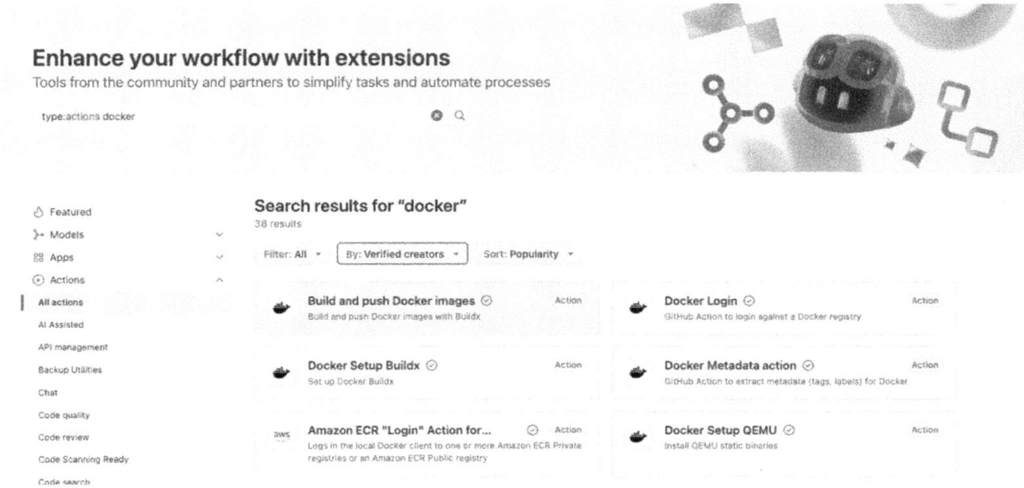

Verified Creators are manually verified by GitHub as an official partner organization. In this case, we're filtering Docker-related actions, and the first results are from the Docker organization. While many popular and reliable Actions are maintained by individuals or open source teams that haven't earned the "verified" tag, using verified Actions is a good way to start.

Second, look at the adoption rate (Popularity), which is the number of times members of the GitHub community have "starred" the Action. The official Docker build action has been starred over 5,000 times, whereas brand-new Actions contributed by an individual may have zero stars. Stars don't equal trustworthiness, but they are a decent proxy.

Finally, inspect the repo. Every GitHub Action links to a GitHub repo you can browse. By reading the documentation, reviewing the code itself, and browsing open issues, you can learn many to help you make an informed decision.

Use Versions

GitHub Actions are versioned. To avoid external updates causing your workflows to behave in unexpected ways, it's a good idea to pin the Actions you use to a specific version, which we have done in our examples (e.g., `docker/build-push-action@v5`). As with package managers we've seen, pinning is flexible with respect to semantic versioning. Referring to `@v5` allows your workflow to fetch the latest version under version 5. One day your workflow may execute `v5.1.2`; the next day, if Docker releases a patch, you'll run on `v5.1.3`. If you want to pin to that specific release, update your code to reference `docker/build-push-action@v5.1.3`.

Just as with language dependencies, it's important to keep an eye on the source repos of any third-party action you use so that if new functionality comes out or a vulnerability gets patched, you're aware and can upgrade—with proper testing, of course.

GitHub Actions Secrets

To securely store secrets for reference in a GitHub Actions workflow, you'll need to enter values in the GitHub web interface. Navigate to Settings ➢ Secrets And Variables ➢ Actions. Here, you'll be able to set repository-level secrets. These may then be referenced like any variable within a workflow using the prefix `secrets`, like so: `${{ secrets.my_secret_value }}`.

Automating Deployment

To demonstrate a full CI/CD pipeline, we need to do some CD by adding a deployment step to our pipeline.

For this example, we'll use an AWS service to run our application via Docker, but whether you are deploying to AWS, GCP, Azure, a local virtual machine, or any other platform, it's up to you to understand the steps necessary to get your app to the running environment. Take time to map out these steps; if necessary, start manually and create local scripts to automate it. Once you have the sequence worked out, tools like GitHub Actions can help you turn it into an event-driven pipeline.

Mapping Out Our Deployment

Figure 10.6 shows the high-level sequence of events that will occur in the deployment part of our GitHub Actions workflow.

As you can see, this workflow handles not only the deployment, but automated rollbacks as well. We save the currently deployed application version before initiating

FIGURE 10.6 ECS architecture.

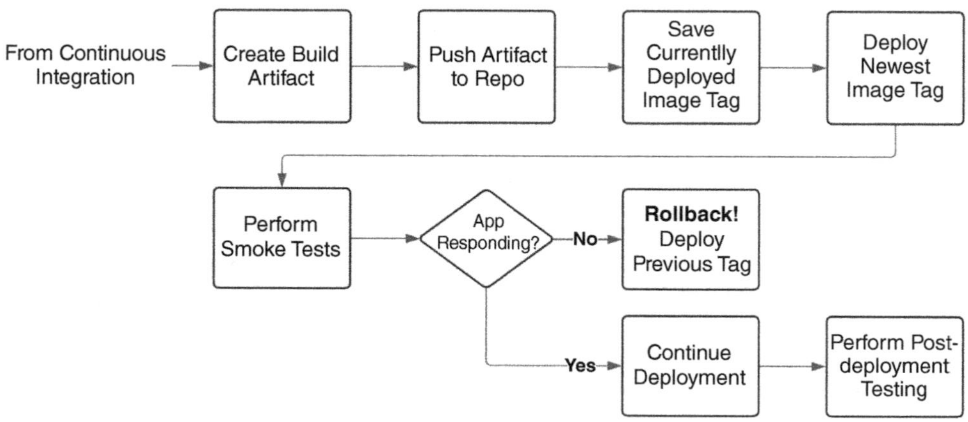

deployment of the new version, and then, if smoke tests fail, we trigger redeployment of the prior version.

This is an all-at-once deployment strategy. For a canary deployment, our smoke tests would concentrate on the canary instances, then proceed with a wider deployment after successful testing. For a blue-green deployment, we'd need additional infrastructure, and our workflow logic would need to accommodate swapping the load balancer from one environment to another. As long as you know the steps to perform and the conditions under which you'll take action, you can automate the pipeline from beginning to end.

Deploy Target

Amazon Web Services' Elastic Container Service (ECS) is an AWS-native container orchestration system that integrates nicely into other AWS services. AWS Fargate abstracts away the compute layer, letting us define a cluster that is fully managed by Amazon.

The infrastructure for this deployment can be created with infrastructure-as-code using CloudFormation. The resulting architecture looks like Figure 10.7.

FIGURE 10.7 ECS architecture.

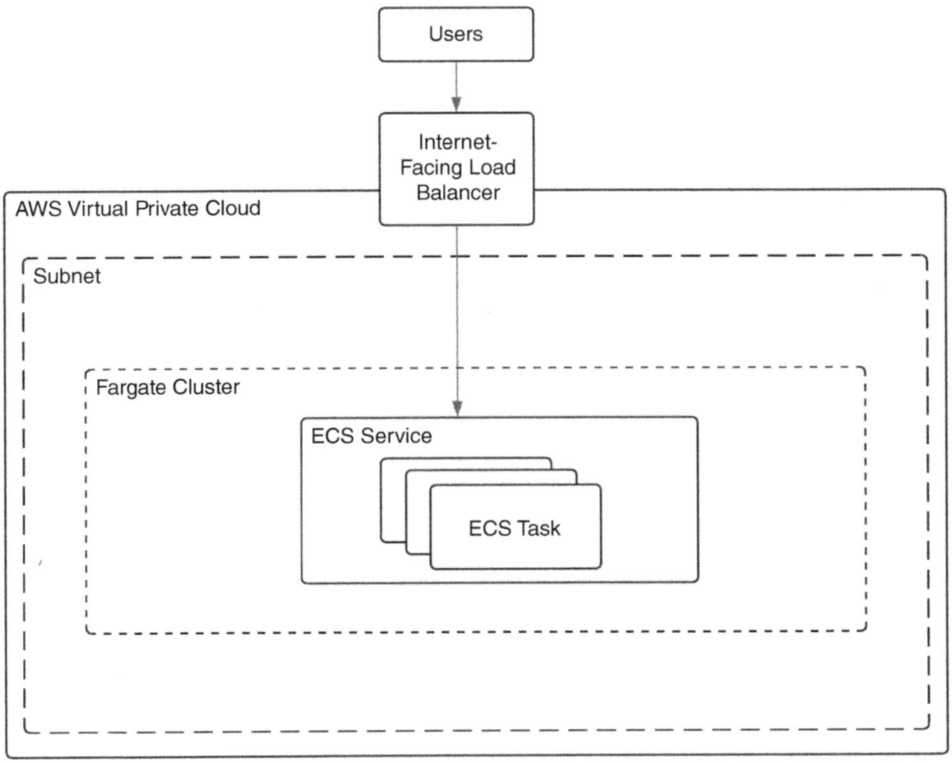

In ECS, a service represents one application or component of an application. Examples of a service might be a web frontend, an API, or a database tier. Inside a service, you run tasks, which are defined by task definitions. Task definitions say what container image should be run, and how widely it should be scaled. Whenever we deploy, we will create an updated task definition that refers to a new version of our container image, which we will store in AWS's container artifact repository, Elastic Container Registry (ECR).

Pushing to ECR

To deploy to ECS, we'll start by pushing our Docker images (with tags) to AWS's ECR with a workflow job we will call `build-and-push`. Like our other jobs, it runs on Ubuntu. Note the `needs` directive, which indicates all the quality checks must precede this step, enforcing which steps are sequential and which can be parallel.

```
build-and-push:
    name: Build and Push Docker Image
    runs-on: ubuntu-latest
    needs: [lint, security, test]
    permissions:
      contents: read
      packages: write
      security-events: write
    outputs:
      image-uri: ${{ steps.set-image-uri.outputs.image-uri }}

    steps:
      - name: Checkout code
        uses: actions/checkout@v4

      - name: Configure AWS credentials
    uses: aws-actions/configure-aws-credentials@v4
      with:
          aws-access-key-id: ${{ secrets.AWS_ACCESS_KEY_ID }}
          aws-secret-access-key: ${{ secrets.AWS_SECRET_ACCESS_KEY }}
          aws-region: ${{ env.AWS_REGION }}
```

To make this section work, we require an IAM account in AWS that has permissions to push to ECR and we must have set its credentials (`AWS_ACCESS_KEY_ID` and `AWS_SECRET_ACCESS_KEY`) as secrets in GitHub.

Please note that managing AWS access keys in this way is not the most secure way to authenticate to AWS; for non-demo purposes, you should use OpenID Connect to let GitHub Actions assume a role in AWS. This avoids the need to store long-lived credentials and is the method recommended by AWS. For more on this, see `https://docs.github.com/en/actions/how-tos/secure-your-work/security-harden-deployments/oidc-in-aws`.

Let's continue.

```
      - name: Login to Amazon ECR
        id: login-ecr
        uses: aws-actions/amazon-ecr-login@v2

      - name: Set up Docker Buildx
        uses: docker/setup-buildx-action@v3

      - name: Build and push Docker image to ECR
        id: build-image
        uses: docker/build-push-action@v5
        with:
          context: .
          push: true
          platforms: linux/amd64
          tags: |
            ${{ steps.login-ecr.outputs.registry }}/python-demo-app:${{ github.
sha }}
            ${{ steps.login-ecr.outputs.registry }}/python-demo-app:latest
          cache-from: type=gha
          cache-to: type=gha,mode=max
```

The next few steps are straightforward: We use AWS-provided actions to log in to ECR and Docker-provided actions to build the image and push to the remote repository with our desired tags.

Passing Information with Outputs

Later in this script, we want to reference the URI of the SHA-based image tag we just pushed. This is a multistep process: First, we output a step-level output; then, we output a job-level output. Here's where we do the former:

```
      - name: Set image URI for deployment
        run: echo "image-uri=${{ steps.login-ecr.outputs.registry }}/
python-demo-app:${{ github.sha }}" >> $GITHUB_OUTPUT
        id: set-image-uri
```

This rather odd-looking syntax is how you set outputs at the step level. First, the step must have an ID (`set-image-uri` in this case). Then, by printing out a key-value pair (`image-uri=XYZ`) and appending it to the special variable `$GITHUB_OUTPUT`, you make the variable `steps.set-image-uri.outputs.image-uri` available elsewhere in the workflow.

By comparison, outputting the job-level output is much more straightforward. It happens in the `outputs` tag, which references the step output. Note that in the workflow, this line actually precedes the line where the step output is set, but that's okay, because GitHub Actions understands the necessary order of operations.

```
build-and-push:
   name: Build and Push Docker Image to ECR
   runs-on: ubuntu-latest
   needs: [lint, security, test]
   outputs:
     image-uri: ${{ steps.set-image-uri.outputs.image-uri }}
```

This makes the `image-uri` available to other jobs that execute later, which we'll see at deploy time.

Deploying to ECS

At this point, we have our image built and tagged, and it's time to move into deployment. First, we need to make sure to save some outputs for rollback purposes:

```
  deploy-to-ecs:
    name: Deploy to ECS
    runs-on: ubuntu-latest
    needs: build-and-push
    permissions: {}
    outputs:
      previous-task-definition-arn: ${{ steps.register-task-def.outputs.
previous-task-definition-arn }}
      task-definition-arn: ${{ steps.register-task-def.outputs.
task-definition-arn }}
      deployed-image-uri: ${{ needs.build-and-push.outputs.image-uri }}
```

With those outputs in place for rollback purposes, we can define the deployment steps themselves. The first step fetches the currently running task definition from ECS and produces an updated version referencing the new container image URI built in the previous job:

```
      - name: Create task definition revision with SHA image
        id: register-task-def
        env:
          IMAGE_URI: ${{ needs.build-and-push.outputs.image-uri }}
        run: |
          set -euo pipefail

          echo "Preparing deployment for image: $IMAGE_URI"

          CURRENT_TASK_DEF_ARN=$(aws ecs describe-services \
            --cluster "${{ env.ECS_CLUSTER }}" \
            --services "${{ env.ECS_SERVICE }}" \
            --region "${{ env.AWS_REGION }}" \
```

```
            --query 'services[0].taskDefinition' \
              --output text)

          aws ecs describe-task-definition \
            --task-definition "$CURRENT_TASK_DEF_ARN" \
            --region "${{ env.AWS_REGION }}" \
            --query 'taskDefinition' > task-definition.json

          jq --arg IMAGE_URI "$IMAGE_URI" --arg CONTAINER_NAME "${{ env.APP_
NAME }}" '
            del(
              .taskDefinitionArn,
              .revision,
              .status,
              .requiresAttributes,
              .compatibilities,
              .registeredAt,
              .registeredBy
            )
            | .containerDefinitions = (
                .containerDefinitions
                | map(if .name == $CONTAINER_NAME then .image = $IMAGE_URI else
. end)
              )
          ' task-definition.json > task-definition-new.json
```

Now, we'll create a new task definition. This step is unique to ECS, but conceptually it's similar to writing an updated Kubernetes manifest Docker Compose service. We're not deploying the app yet; we're writing a new recipe for how it should run.

This code shows a practical use of the `jq` command we covered in previous chapters. We pull down the task's current definition as JSON, delete a few fields, then update the `name` and `image` fields to be associated with our most recently tagged image in ECR. The resulting JSON is used in the next step to create the new task definition:

```
          NEW_TASK_DEF_ARN=$(aws ecs register-task-definition \
            --region "${{ env.AWS_REGION }}" \
            --cli-input-json file://task-definition-new.json \
            --query 'taskDefinition.taskDefinitionArn' \
            --output text)

            echo "task-definition-arn=$NEW_TASK_DEF_ARN" >> "$GITHUB_OUTPUT"
```

Next, we update the service to use this. We've now initiated deployment of our new image.

```
      - name: Update ECS service to new task definition
        run: |
          aws ecs update-service \
            --cluster "${{ env.ECS_CLUSTER }}" \
            --service "${{ env.ECS_SERVICE }}" \
```

```
            --task-definition "${{ steps.register-task-def.outputs.
task-definition-arn }}" \
            --force-new-deployment \
            --region "${{ env.AWS_REGION }}"
```

Now for a smoke test. This command will fail if the ECS service doesn't respond within a certain number of calls. This step uses a native AWS CLI command, but it could just as easily be a series of `curl` commands that probe the main pages or endpoints of our application.

```
      - name: Wait for ECS service stability
        Id: wait-stable
        run: |
          aws ecs wait services-stable \
            --cluster "${{ env.ECS_CLUSTER }}" \
            --services "${{ env.ECS_SERVICE }}" \
            --region "${{ env.AWS_REGION }}"
```

Next, we want to see if it worked. GitHub Actions can conditionally run steps based on the outcome. Note the reference to the `outcome` property of the previous step, which is referred to by its declared ID of `wait-stable`:

```
  - name: Automatic rollback to previous task definition
        if: steps.wait-stable.outcome == 'failure'
```

This step will execute if the smoke test results in a failure. From here, we can roll back by calling another service update to deploy the pre-deployment image tag:

```
      - name: Automatic rollback to previous task definition
        if: steps.wait-stable.outcome == 'failure'
        run: |
          set -euo pipefail

          echo "Deployment failed health checks. Rolling back to: ${{ steps.
register-task-def.outputs.previous-task-definition-arn }}"

          aws ecs update-service \
            --cluster "${{ env.ECS_CLUSTER }}" \
            --service "${{ env.ECS_SERVICE }}" \
              --task-definition "${{ steps.register-task-def.outputs.
previous-task-definition-arn }}" \
            --force-new-deployment \
            --region "${{ env.AWS_REGION }}"

          aws ecs wait services-stable \
            --cluster "${{ env.ECS_CLUSTER }}" \
            --services "${{ env.ECS_SERVICE }}" \
            --region "${{ env.AWS_REGION }}"
```

On the other hand, if the outcome of the smoke test is successful, we are done, and our application is up and running. A quick `curl` test shows our messaging endpoint responsive:

```
> curl http://python-demo-alb-244340651.us-east-1.elb.amazonaws.com/api/
greeting
{"message":"Hello, continuous delivery!"}
```

Meanwhile, Figure 10.8 shows our API documentation accessible through a web browser.

Let's take a moment to appreciate this complete pipeline: Starting with a commit or pull request merge, we perform quality and security checks, package our application into a runnable Docker artifact, tag and push that artifact to a repository, set a rollback point, kick off a deployment, and automatically check for success in case we need to undo it. That's quite a bit of automation from one simple change.

Post-Deployment Checks and Manual Rollbacks

Post-deployment checks help us validate functionality that may not be easy to test until an application is live, especially in production. Sometimes teams will have special user accounts or data records that exist in an environment just to allow these sorts of tests.

Of course, service maintenance is an ongoing endeavor. Once an application is live, the most rigorous testing of all begins: live user traffic! Your application health monitoring, performance monitoring, and of course, user support tickets are all vectors letting you know if you need to take action to resolve an issue.

FIGURE 10.8 OpenAPI (Swagger) docs online.

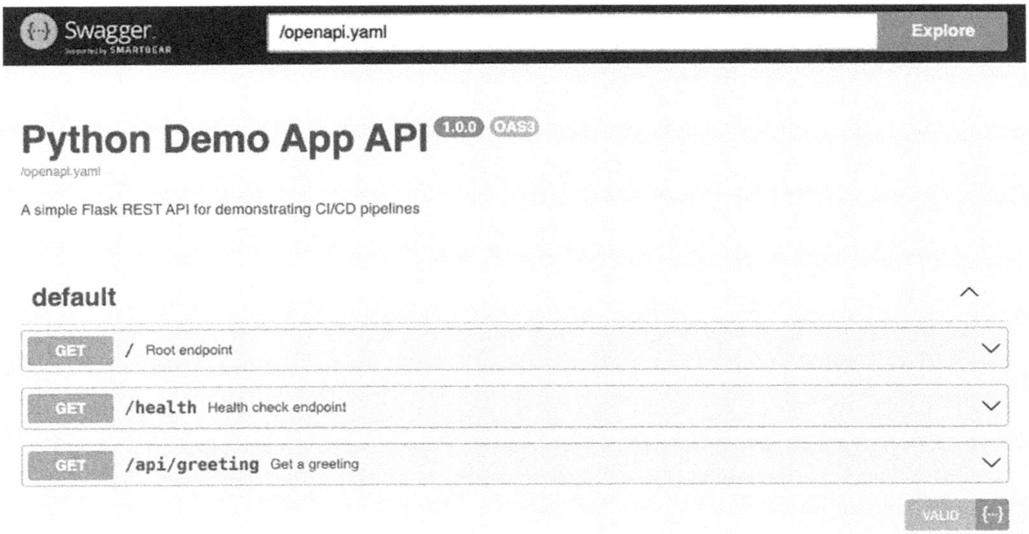

Other CI/CD Platforms

We've explored two quite prominent platforms for operations automations, but there are many more options out there.

GitLab CI

GitLab CI is GitLab's built-in automation platform, offering source control, issue tracking, code review, and CI/CD in one interface—unlike GitHub Actions, which was added later. Pipelines are defined in `.gitlab-ci.yml` files using jobs organized into stages; jobs in the same stage run parallel, stages run sequentially.

The key differentiator is GitLab's runner model. Rather than relying on hosted runners like GitHub, you deploy your own runner agents on-premises, in the cloud, or via GitLab's shared runners. Runners can be shared across projects, scoped to groups, or project-specific, and you tag them to route jobs accordingly. This enables fine-grained control: GPU runners for ML workloads, on-premises runners for compliance, etc.

GitLab CI also features a hierarchical variable system (instance, group, project, and environment levels) that scales well across many projects, built-in container registry integration, and security scanning.

GitLab CI is great for teams who want to run version control themselves. If you're already on GitLab, their CI/CD is a natural fit. If you prefer ready-to-use runners without management overhead, GitHub Actions may be simpler.

Cloud-Based CI Tools

Beyond GitHub Actions and GitLab, every major cloud provider offers its own CI/CD tooling, usually designed to integrate tightly with its ecosystem. AWS provides services like CodeBuild, CodePipeline, and CodeDeploy; Azure offers Azure Pipelines; and Google Cloud includes Cloud Build and related tooling, all of which have managed task runners, integration with their respective security and identity infrastructure, and direct hooks into other cloud services. If your team is well established in one of these cloud environments, working with these tools gives you plenty of automation options, including built-in support for more sophisticated schemes, like blue-green deployments.

Summary

In this chapter, we explored the transition from building code to running it in production environments. We covered deployment architectures, from traditional virtual machines to containerized applications on orchestration platforms, and examined how containers have become the standard deployment primitive by bundling applications with their dependencies into immutable, versioned artifacts.

We looked at CD methods that minimize downtime and risk. In-place deployments are simple but carry risks. Rolling deployments update instances gradually while maintaining availability. Blue-green deployments maintain separate environments for zero-downtime switches. Canary deployments test new code with a small subset of production traffic before full rollout. Each approach has different trade-offs in complexity, cost, and safety.

Quality assurance in CD extends beyond passing tests to validating that code is safe to deploy. Load testing confirms your application can handle production traffic levels. Regression testing ensures new changes don't break existing functionality. Post-deployment monitoring and automated rollback mechanisms provide safety nets when issues arise.

We also surveyed CI/CD platforms beyond GitHub Actions. GitLab CI integrates directly into the GitLab platform with a self-managed runner architecture that gives teams fine-grained control over compute resources and security boundaries. Cloud providers like AWS, Azure, and Google Cloud offer tightly integrated CI/CD services with native hooks into their ecosystems, well suited for teams already invested in those platforms.

The best deployment strategy depends on your application architecture, scaling requirements, tolerance for downtime, and team capabilities. Modern orchestration platforms like Kubernetes and cloud-native tooling have made sophisticated deployment patterns accessible, but the fundamental goal remains the same: getting working code to production with minimal risk and maximum confidence.

Exam Essentials

Compare common deployment strategies. Be able to distinguish between in-place, rolling, blue-green, and canary deployments. Understand the trade-offs between simplicity, downtime, risk, and infrastructure cost, and identify when each approach is appropriate.

Understand how CI and CD responsibilities differ. Recognize that CI focuses on correctness (builds, tests, quality checks), whereas CD focuses on safe deployment into real environments with real dependencies.

Identify key QA practices in a CD pipeline. Understand the purpose of regression tests, integration tests, and load tests, and when each should run. Know that not all tests run on every deployment, and that pipelines balance speed with confidence.

Understand validation steps after deployment. Know the difference between smoke testing and post-deployment testing. Recognize that smoke tests provide fast feedback on basic functionality, whereas deeper validation confirms system behavior under real conditions.

Understand rollback vs. hotfix strategies. Know that rollback is the preferred first response to a failed deployment because it restores a known-good state quickly. Understand that hotfixes are necessary when rollback is not possible, but they should still go through controlled processes.

Understand event-driven pipeline triggers. Recognize common triggers such as code pushes, pull requests, tags, schedules, and manual invocations. Know how pipelines respond to events and automate build and deployment workflows.

Understand pipelines as code. Know that pipeline definitions (e.g., YAML files) are version-controlled alongside application code, making automation reproducible, reviewable, and auditable.

Understand job orchestration concepts. Be able to explain parallel versus sequential execution, dependency management, and conditional execution within pipelines. Recognize how tools determine execution order and handle failures.

Review Questions

1. Which deployment pattern replaces the running version of an application directly on the existing infrastructure without maintaining a parallel environment?

   A. Blue-green deployment

   B. Canary deployment

   C. In-place deployment

   D. Rolling deployment

2. Your team uses a blue-green deployment strategy. After traffic is shifted 100% to the new green environment, monitoring detects elevated error rates. What is the fastest recovery action?

   A. Redeploy the previous build to the green environment.

   B. Switch the load balancer back to the blue environment.

   C. Scale up the green environment to reduce per-instance load.

   D. Restart the green environment's container service.

3. A deployment pipeline sends 10% of production traffic to the new build while 90% continues to hit the current version. After 30 minutes, if error rates are within threshold, the percentage is gradually raised to 100%. Which deployment pattern does this describe?

   A. Rolling deployment

   B. Blue-green deployment

   C. In-place deployment

   D. Canary deployment

4. An API service uses a rolling deployment. During the rollout, 50% of instances run v2 and 50% still run v1. A client request lands on a v1 instance which writes a database record in the v1 schema. A second request lands on a v2 instance which expects the v2 schema. What risk does this illustrate?

   A. Blue-green environment drift

   B. Schema incompatibility during mixed-version operation

   C. Container image tag collision

   D. Load balancer session affinity failure

5. After deploying a new release to a staging environment, the CD pipeline runs a smoke test. What is the primary purpose of this smoke test?

   A. To measure application performance under simulated peak load

   B. To verify that the most critical application paths function after deployment

   C. To confirm that all unit tests pass in the deployed environment

   D. To scan the deployed container image for security vulnerabilities

6. A canary deployment is configured to abort and roll back automatically if the canary error rate exceeds 2% during the observation window. After 15 minutes, the canary reports a 3.4% error rate. Which pipeline action should occur next?
   A. Continue promotion because the rate is below 5%.
   B. Page the on-call engineer and wait for manual approval before continuing.
   C. Automatically roll back traffic to the stable version.
   D. Scale the canary to 50% traffic to gather more data.
7. Which statement best describes why containers on VMs can be an intermediate step between running applications directly on VMs and running them on a fully managed platform?
   A. Containers require a dedicated VM for each running instance.
   B. Containers package application code and dependencies together but still require a host OS and container runtime to run.
   C. Containers eliminate the need for any infrastructure management.
   D. Containers are only suitable for stateless web applications.
8. A GitHub Actions CD pipeline deploys to Amazon ECS. The pipeline includes a step that checks whether the new task definition started successfully. If the health check fails, the pipeline should revert to the previous version. Which GitHub Actions feature enables this conditional rollback?
   A. `on: workflow_dispatch` trigger
   B. `if: failure()` condition on a rollback step
   C. `continue-on-error: true` on the deployment step
   D. `timeout-minutes` on the deployment job
9. Your organization runs blue-green deployments for a cost-sensitive service. After every successful production switch to green, the ops team waits 48 hours before terminating the blue environment. A manager proposes reducing the wait to two hours to save infrastructure costs. What is the primary risk of this change?
   A. The green environment will experience higher latency with blue terminated.
   B. The shortened window may not allow enough time to detect slow-manifesting defects, eliminating the fast-rollback option before issues surface.
   C. Container image layers in the blue environment will be deleted from the container registry.
   D. The load balancer will lose its routing rules when blue is terminated.
10. A GitHub Actions workflow defines four jobs: `lint`, `test`, `security`, and `build-and-push`. The team wants the first three to run simultaneously and `build-and-push` to start only after all three succeed. Which directive should the `build-and-push` job include to enforce this ordering?
   A. Add `depends-on: [lint, test, security]` to the job definition.
   B. Add `needs: [lint, test, security]` to the job definition.
   C. Add `require: [lint, test, security]` to the job definition.
   D. Add `after: [lint, test, security]` to the job definition.

11. A critical bug is found in production. A database migration in the last release makes rollback impossible. The team must patch live immediately. What approach best balances speed with auditability?

A. Push the fix directly to main, bypassing CI checks to deploy as fast as possible.

B. Open a hotfix branch linked to a tracked issue, run it through a dedicated deployment pipeline, then propagate the fix back to all active branches.

C. Redeploy the most recently tagged container image from the registry without rebuilding.

D. Restore the production database from the last known-good backup.

12. A DevOps team needs to deploy a collection of lightweight event processors that respond to queue messages, each completing in under 20 seconds. The team's priority is zero infrastructure management and automatic scaling to handle variable message volume. Which deployment target best fits these requirements?

A. Deploy containerized services on a self-managed Kubernetes cluster.

B. Deploy the processors as a long-running service on a PaaS provider like Heroku.

C. Deploy each processor as a function on a FaaS platform like AWS Lambda.

D. Deploy each processor to a dedicated VM with an autoscaling group.

13. A team's pipeline references a Marketplace action as `some-org/deploy-action@v3`. After the author releases v3.2.0 with a breaking change, the pipeline fails on the next merge. What practice would have prevented this?

A. Pin the action to an exact release tag such as `some-org/deploy-action@v3.1.9`.

B. Remove the version tag entirely so the workflow always pulls the latest release.

C. Copy the action's source into the repository and reference it locally.

D. Replace the action with a shell script that performs the same steps.

14. Smoke tests pass after a new release goes live. The team then runs a second automated suite that validates multi-step user flows against the live database, probes edge-case API paths, and checks third-party integrations. What distinguishes this second suite from the smoke tests?

A. Run the second suite in staging before promoting to production so real data is never at risk.

B. Replace smoke tests with the second suite once the team's test coverage matures.

C. Use the second suite to validate real-environment behavior that smoke tests are too shallow to catch.

D. Limit the second suite to performance benchmarking since smoke tests already cover functional correctness.

15. A team running a large containerized fleet considers switching from rolling to blue-green deployments. The finance team asks for the cost implication. What is the primary trade-off they should communicate?

   A. Blue-green requires more frequent container image builds, raising registry storage costs on every deployment.

   B. Blue-green requires maintaining two full parallel environments simultaneously, which can be significant for large fleets.

   C. Blue-green eliminates load balancer costs because traffic switching is handled entirely by DNS updates.

   D. Blue-green increases compute costs only during smoke testing, then the idle environment scales to zero automatically.

Answers to Review Questions

1. C. Option C is correct. An in-place deployment stops the current version and starts the new version on the same instances or containers, with no parallel environment. Blue-green keeps two full environments. Canary routes a small traffic slice to the new version. Rolling replaces instances incrementally.

2. B. Option B is correct. In a blue-green strategy the old blue environment remains intact after the traffic shift. Switching the load balancer (or DNS) back to blue is an instant rollback requiring no new build or restart. Option A is slow because it requires a build/deploy cycle. Options C and D do not address the underlying code defect.

3. D. Option D is correct. Canary deployment exposes a small subset of users to the new version first and progressively increases the traffic share only after stability is confirmed. Option A, rolling deployment, replaces instances in batches but does not use weighted traffic routing. Blue-green switches all traffic at once after maintaining two full environments. In-place replaces the running version directly.

4. B. Option B is correct. Rolling deployments create a period where multiple versions coexist. If the new version requires a database schema change that is incompatible with the old version, concurrent writes from different instances can corrupt data or cause errors. Backward-compatible schema migrations are important to avoiding this. Option A describes a different problem, whereas Options C and D are not applicable to this scenario.

5. B. Option B is correct. A smoke test is a quick, shallow check that the most important end-to-end flows work; for example, does the service start, key API endpoints return 200, and is the database connection healthy? It catches showstopper regressions fast without the cost of a full test suite. Option A, load testing, along with unit testing (Option C), and security scanning (Option D) are separate pipeline stages.

6. C. Option C is correct. The pipeline has a defined threshold (2%) and the canary has breached it. Automatic rollback is the correct response—it restores the stable version without

human delay. Continuing promotion (Option A) or scaling the canary (Option D) would expose more users to the elevated error rate. Option B, waiting for manual approval, adds latency and defeats the purpose of an automated gate.

7. B. Option B is correct. Containers bundle the application and its dependencies into a portable image, but they still execute on a host operating system via a container runtime such as Docker. This makes them more portable than deploying directly on VMs. Option A is wrong, as many containers can share one VM, as is Option C, because they still require infrastructure management, unlike fully managed PaaS/FaaS offerings. Option D is also incorrect.

8. B. Option B is correct. An `if: failure()` condition on a subsequent step causes that step to run only when a preceding step has failed, making it the correct mechanism for a conditional rollback. `on: workflow_dispatch` (A) triggers manual runs. `continue-on-error: true` (C) suppresses failure and allows the workflow to continue—the opposite of what is needed. `timeout-minutes` (D) cancels a job that runs too long but does not trigger rollback logic.

9. B. Option B is correct. Blue-green's rollback advantage depends on the old environment remaining available. Some defects—memory leaks, date-dependent bugs, rare edge-case failures—only manifest hours or days after deployment. Reducing the retention window from 48 to 2 hours increases the chance that such defects are discovered after rollback is no longer possible. A is incorrect because green operates independently. Option C is incorrect because container registry image life cycle is independently managed. Option D is incorrect because load balancer rules are updated at switch time, not at environment termination.

10. B. The `needs` directive creates an explicit dependency graph in GitHub Actions, holding a downstream job until every listed job succeeds. Option A is incorrect because `depends-on` is a CloudFormation keyword with no meaning in GitHub Actions. Option C is incorrect because `require` is not a valid GitHub Actions job property. Option D is incorrect because `after` does not exist in the GitHub Actions spec; `needs` is the correct directive for sequencing.

11. B. A named hotfix branch tied to an issue ticket preserves a full audit trail and lets a dedicated CD pipeline apply the same quality gates as a normal deployment. Propagating the fix back to all branches ensures the next regular release does not overwrite it. Option A is incorrect because bypassing CI introduces the risk of configuration drift and leaves changes unaudited. Option C is incorrect because redeploying the same image does nothing to fix the code defect. Option D is incorrect because a database restore would discard all data written since the last backup.

12. C. FaaS platforms execute short-lived functions in response to events (such as queue messages), require no infrastructure to provision or maintain, and scale automatically from zero to high concurrency as message volume changes. Option A is incorrect because a self-managed Kubernetes cluster requires managing and maintaining the cluster itself, which contradicts the zero-management goal. Option B is incorrect because PaaS targets long-running processes, not short-lived event-triggered executions, and adds per-instance costs even when idle. Option D is incorrect because dedicated VMs carry ongoing provisioning and operational overhead and scale far more slowly than a serverless platform.

13. A. Pinning to a specific version tag ensures the pipeline runs with a tested, known-good release. An upstream patch or minor update cannot silently change behavior. Option B is incorrect because omitting the version tag makes the workflow vulnerable to any future breaking change the author ships. Option C is incorrect because copying the source into the repo creates a maintenance burden and makes it harder to receive security patches. Option D is incorrect because rewriting the action as a script does not address the root issue of uncontrolled external dependency versions.

14. C. Post-deployment tests exercise real dependencies—production data, live external services, authentic traffic patterns—that pre-deployment checks cannot replicate. Smoke tests confirm the service is alive; post-deployment tests confirm it behaves correctly under real conditions. Option A is incorrect because post-deployment tests by definition run against the deployed environment, not staging. Option B is incorrect because both layers serve different purposes and complement each other. Option D is incorrect because post-deployment tests cover functional correctness, integration, and edge-case behavior, not only performance.

15. B. Blue-green keeps a complete second environment provisioned—ready to receive the next deployment and to serve as an instant rollback target. For small services this overhead is negligible, but for large fleets it can double infrastructure spend for as long as the idle environment is retained. Teams must weigh that cost against the benefits of zero-downtime switches and second-fast rollbacks. Option A is incorrect because deployment strategy does not affect image build frequency. Option C is incorrect because a load balancer (or equivalent routing layer) remains in use; DNS is one traffic-switching mechanism but does not eliminate load balancer infrastructure. Option D is incorrect because the idle environment must stay fully provisioned and healthy throughout the post-deployment observation window, not just for the duration of smoke tests.

Operating in Production

PART V

Chapter 11

Operationalization and Maintenance

THE AUTOOPS+ EXAM TOPICS COVERED IN THIS CHAPTER MAY INCLUDE, BUT ARE NOT LIMITED TO, THE FOLLOWING:

- ✔ 4.0: Continuous Delivery
- ✔ 4.1: Given a scenario, implement techniques of continuous delivery (CD).
- ✔ 4.2: Explain concepts related to application service levels.

By this point, we've automated many processes related to quality assurance (QA), testing, and deployment. We're minimizing risk through security scans, improving collaboration through branching strategies, and integrating tightly with version control. We can detect if a release is successful and reverse it if necessary. We've got live software running, but for operations automation engineers, that's where the fun begins. How do we ensure a high-quality and consistent experience for the service's users, whether they are e-commerce customers out in the world or developers downstream of a critical process component?

This chapter focuses on service levels and reliability metrics, the measurements that tell us whether our continuous delivery (CD) practices are actually delivering value. These aren't just numbers for dashboards. They're the foundation for making intelligent decisions about when to deploy, when to roll back, and when we need to invest in stability.

We'll explore uptime and availability, dive into SLOs and SLAs, examine failure metrics like MTTR and MTBF, and discuss how feedback loops turn all these measurements into actionable improvements. By the end, you'll understand how these concepts work together to support confident, sustainable CD.

Measuring Availability

Availability is perhaps the most critical measure we can make of an application or service. It's a simple binary: Is the service online and taking requests from users, or not? *Availability* measures uptime, the percentage of time a system is operational and accessible. Uptime (and its inverse, downtime) is the baseline for understanding service reliability.

Availability is typically expressed as a percentage:

```
Availability = ((Total Time - Downtime) / Total Time) × 100
```

If your service runs for 30 days (720 hours) and experiences 3.6 hours of downtime, your availability is:

```
Availability = ((720 - 3.6) / 720) × 100 = 99.5%
```

TABLE 11.1 Availability levels and downtime

Availability	Annual downtime	Monthly downtime	Weekly downtime
90% (one nine)	36.5 days	3 days	16.8 hours
99%	3.65 days	7.3 hours	1.68 hours
99.9%	8.77 hours	43.8 minutes	10.1 minutes
99.99%	52.6 minutes	4.4 minutes	1.01 minutes
99.999% (five nines)	5.26 minutes	26.3 seconds	6.05 seconds

Although 99.5 percent sounds pretty good, operations engineers know that numbers that sound high can still mean lots of downtime for users. Let's look at what availability percentages like this translate to in the real world.

Number Nine

Like John Lennon, service operators are obsessed with nines, measuring uptime in "nines" of availability. Each additional nine represents an order of magnitude improvement, plus a corresponding increase in effort and cost. Table 11.1 shows what different availability levels mean in practice.

Notice the difference between 99 percent and 99.9 percent. That extra nine means reducing annual downtime from over three days to under nine hours. Achieving that requires redundancy, automated failover, careful change management, and constant monitoring.

Most web services target somewhere between 99 percent and 99.9 percent. Mission-critical systems might aim for 99.99 percent or higher. The scale is logarithmic; each additional nine stretches the expected time between errors by 10×, and that jump costs roughly 10 times more than the previous level to achieve.

There are many helpful uptime calculators on the web. Try entering a percentage value at `https://uptime.is/` to see how it translates into real-world downtime.

Time-Based vs. Request-Based Availability

There are two main ways to measure availability: by time and by request throughput.

Time-based availability measures the percentage of time the system is up. This is what we've shown above. It's simple to understand and commonly used in SLAs.

Request-based availability, on the other hand, measures the percentage of requests that succeed. This provides a user-centric view:

```
Request Success Rate = (Successful Requests / Total Requests) × 100
```

If you handle 1 million requests in a day and 995,000 succeed, your request-based availability is 99.5 percent, even if the system was technically "up" 100 percent of the time.

Request-based metrics often tell a more accurate story about user experience. A service can be technically "available" but returning errors for a subset of requests due to database connection issues, rate limiting, or partial outages.

Service-Level Objectives

Uptime percentages are a start, but real-world reliability is more nuanced; not all downtime is equal. A two-minute glitch at 3:00 a.m. may affect fewer users than a 30-second outage at peak traffic. Parts of your system may be considered mission critical, while others are dependencies that can sustain some downtime without notice. Your system's shopping cart feature is far more essential to the business than the recommendation engine. We need our reliability measures to reflect what actually impacts users. That's where service-level objectives come in.

What Are SLOs?

Service-level objectives (SLOs) are internal metrics that define reliability in terms of user experience. They are tied to specific outcomes called *service-level indicators* (SLIs). You may have encountered a similar concept in your own work, as SLOs and SLIs are analogous to the "objectives" and "key performance indicators" that many organizations use to set goals for teams and individuals.

An SLI is the actual measurement you track; an SLO is the target for that metric. For example, one service-level indicator might be "Request success rate over the last 30 days," while the corresponding SLO requires that the rate be 99.9 percent.

Choosing Meaningful SLOs

Good SLOs are user-focused, measuring observable things that impact users (e.g., page responsiveness, not CPU load). They should be clearly measurable, with achievable goals. For instance, setting a threshold for acceptable first-load latency at 200 ms is much more measurable and achievable than expecting "fast page loads."

Again, this is not unlike individual goals, which are often encouraged to fit the SMART pattern: specific, measurable, achievable, relevant, and time-bound. Just as this approach helps people set goals, well-defined SLOs help teams know when they're keeping their reliability promises.

Common types of SLOs include:

- **Availability:** "99.9% of requests should return non-error responses"
- **Latency:** "95% of requests should complete within 200 ms"

- **Throughput:** "The system should handle at least 10,000 requests per second"
- **Durability:** "99.999999% of stored objects should remain intact" (common for storage services)

Note the percentile thinking in latency SLOs. You don't commit to making every single request fast. Instead, you target a percentile like 95th or 99th. This acknowledges that some requests will naturally be slower (e.g., complex queries, cold cache loads) while still setting a performance bar.

Thinking in Error Budgets

With this chapter, we're just skimming the surface of a very deep pool. Site reliability engineering is the discipline that thoroughly engages with these topics, and its practitioners define a useful concept: *error budgets*. The idea is to take your service-level objectives and consider how much downtime you are "allowed" to have.

For instance, if your SLO is 99.9 percent availability, that means 0.1 percent unavailability is acceptable. That 0.1 percent becomes your error budget, and it's the wiggle room you have to work with each day, month, or year as you maintain your SLO threshold. In terms of clock time, 99.9 percent availability means you have 43.8 minutes of allowable monthly downtime. This is something you can track over time as your team discusses steps to take that impact the running system.

Error budgets can change the conversation between development and operations teams. When time remains in the error budget, teams can take risks, deploy faster, and experiment. On the other hand, when you're near your SLO thresholds and the error budget is low, teams must slow down, focus on reliability, and potentially defer launches. When the budget is fully depleted, it's time for a code change freeze until the window resets. The name of the game is balancing development velocity with risk avoidance.

This creates a data-driven mechanism for balancing innovation and stability. When considering steps that could impact uptime, the conversation becomes quantitative, asking "What's our error budget status?"

If a risky deployment consumes 20 minutes of your 43.8-minute budget, you have 23.2 minutes left for the rest of the month. Teams can make informed decisions about subsequent changes.

SLO as Code

Let's define a realistic example, and let's do it in code. Throughout this book, we've seen ways to define many things as code: infrastructure, user permissions, automation pipelines, and more. Why stop now?

Many observability platforms let you define your SLOs as code, helping to automate tracking and alerting on these key measures. For instance, DataDog uses JSON, Prometheus allows YAML, and other tools, like Google Monitoring and Grafana, literally use our old friend Terraform.

In DataDog, you might set an availability target like this:

```
{
  "name": "Checkout API availability",
  "type": "monitor",
  "description": "Sets availability targets for the API",
  "thresholds": [
    {
      "timeframe": "30d",
      "target": 99.9,
      "warning": 99.95
    }
  ]
}
```

A definition like this configures the uptime threshold desired by the business, and because the observability tool is already watching key metrics like uptime, it's able to alert you when you approach or breach your set limit. As with all our X-as-code approaches in this book, defining your SLOs as templates lets you track them over time, version control them, and manage large-scale configurations all in one place.

SLO Example

Taking the SLO-as-code (or at least YAML pseudocode) approach, let's imagine a somewhat realistic set of policies for an API service. Your SLOs might combine multiple layers of latency requirements and look like this:

```
service: payment-api
owner: payments-team
window: 30d

slos:
  - name: availability
    target: 99.9
    description: "99.9% of requests return successful HTTP responses"

    sli:
      type: request_ratio
      good_events:
        metric: http_requests_total
        filter: status_code < 500
      total_events:
        metric: http_requests_total

  - name: latency_p95
    target: 200ms
    description: "95% of requests complete within 200 ms"
```

```
    sli:
      type: latency_percentile
      metric: http_request_duration_ms
      percentile: 95

  - name: latency_p99
    target: 500ms
    description: "99% of requests complete within 500 ms"

    sli:
      type: latency_percentile
      metric: http_request_duration_ms
      percentile: 99
```

Every day, you measure actual performance against these targets. If you're consistently hitting 99.95 percent availability, you're doing well and have room for calculated risks. If you're at 99.85 percent, you're burning error budget and should proceed more cautiously.

Setting Realistic Targets

When defining SLOs, don't aim for perfection. Setting a 99.99 percent availability target sounds impressive, but if you can't actually achieve it, the SLO is meaningless.

Instead, start with where you are, and try to make iterative improvements. If your current availability is 99.5 percent, don't jump straight to 99.95 percent. Set an initial SLO at 99.7 percent, achieve it consistently, then keep raising the bar.

Also consider dependencies. If your service relies on a third-party API with 99.5 percent availability, that bottleneck determines your highest possible SLO. Your reliability is bounded by your dependencies.

Service-Level Agreements

While SLOs are internal targets, *service-level agreements* (SLAs) are external promises with consequences. An SLA is a contract between a service provider and customers that specifies the expected service level and remedies if that level isn't met. Even if you aren't steeped in site reliability engineering, you may have encountered SLAs as a consumer. They often come into the conversation when negotiating support contracts with software-as-a-service providers; during any outage, someone will eventually wonder aloud, "What is the SLA on this service?"

SLAs determine a service's promised level of reliability, the response from a service provider during outages, and what recompense customers can expect if any of the above is breached.

The Business Side of Reliability

As with SLOs, SLAs turn reliability from a technical goal into a business commitment with specific and measurable metrics that target a certain value or threshold. In addition, an SLA will often contain some remedy that kicks in if the SLA is breached, giving customers peace of mind and providers incentive to keep their systems performing optimally.

The remedy is what gives an SLA teeth. If you promise 99.9 percent uptime and miss it, customers might receive service credits proportional to the downtime. This creates financial incentive to maintain reliability.

AWS has experienced a few notable outages that triggered SLA payouts to customers. For instance, back in 2017, sites all over the Internet went down due to their dependency on AWS S3 buckets. This multi-hour outage was covered by the SLA and entitled customers to submit requests for compensation. It also sparked more than a few conversations about how SREs should think about avoiding single points of failure, like depending on a single cloud vendor's storage infrastructure. Even the most scalable, robust architecture is only as resilient as its least reliable component.

Because SLAs are customer-facing, they often have very specific language about what aspects of the service they cover and what exclusions may apply, such as planned maintenance outages or outages due to third-party dependencies outside the company's control. They should also include specific remedies or compensation for when breaches occur. A sliding scale is common. For example, you might offer refunds or service credits that escalate depending on the length or severity of the outage.

An SLA is what you promise customers, whereas your SLO is what you promise yourself. Any gap between them is your internal buffer zone for failure or outages.

For example, if your external SLA promises 99.5 percent monthly availability, you can set your internal SLO at 99.9 percent monthly availability; reaching the latter guarantees the former. If you dip to 99.7 percent, you've violated your internal SLO (triggering internal alerts and actions) but haven't breached the customer SLA. This early warning system lets you fix issues before they impact contractual obligations.

Failure Metrics: MTTR and MTBF

While uptime tells you how often an app is available, failure metrics describe pattern of failures when they do occur. Two metrics are most important to learn: mean time between failures (MTBF) and mean time to repair (MTTR).

Mean Time Between Failures

Mean time between failures, or MTBF, measures the average time between system failures. It's calculated as:

```
MTBF = Total Uptime / Number of Failures
```

If your service runs for 720 hours in a month and experiences 4 failures during that period:

```
MTBF = 720 hours / 4 failures = 180 hours
```

On average, you can expect a failure every 180 hours (7.5 days).

MTBF is most useful for:

- Hardware reliability (when will this disk fail?)
- Systems with distinct failure events (database crashes)
- Capacity planning (how often do we need redundancy?)

However, MTBF has limitations in modern software systems. Failures often don't follow neat patterns. A system might run flawlessly for months, then experience multiple failures in a day due to a cascading issue or deployment problem.

MTBF also assumes failures are independent, which isn't always true. If a memory leak causes crashes, subsequent failures aren't independent because they're symptoms of the same underlying issue.

Mean Time to Repair (MTTR)

Mean time to repair, or MTTR, measures how long it takes to restore service after a failure. It's a more actionable metric than MTBF:

```
MTTR = Total Downtime / Number of Failures
```

Using our previous example, if those four failures caused 3.6 hours of total downtime:

```
MTTR = 3.6 hours / 4 failures = 0.9 hours (54 minutes)
```

On average, it takes 54 minutes to restore service after a failure.

Unlike MTBF, MTTR is something you can actively improve. You might not be able to prevent all failures, but you can definitely get better at recovering from them.

What Affects Repair Time?

Several factors influence MTTR:

Detection time. How quickly do you know something's wrong? Automated monitoring can detect issues in seconds; waiting for user complaints might take minutes or hours.

Diagnosis time. Once you know there's a problem, how long does it take to identify the root cause? Good logging, tracing, and observability tools reduce this dramatically.

Remediation time. After diagnosis, how long to implement a fix? Automated rollbacks can happen in seconds; fixing a data corruption issue might take hours.

Verification time. How do you confirm the fix worked and service is fully restored?

Reducing MTTR often means optimizing each of these phases.

Strategies to Reduce MTTR

Many topics covered in this book can directly improve MTTR. First, automated monitoring and alerting help detect failures immediately instead of waiting for reports. Comprehensive logging and tracing help you quickly understand what went wrong and why. Automated rollbacks can undo bad deployments in seconds rather than minutes.

In addition, automation can standardize responses to common issues and reduce troubleshooting times. On-call rotations make sure someone is always ready to respond quickly. Post-incident reviews help teams learn from failures, improving future responses.

Good time to repair metrics can make up for more a less-than-desirable failure rate. A service with frequent small failures but very low MTTR might provide better overall availability than one with rare failures but high MTTR. This is one of the philosophies behind CD: Small changes are easier to diagnose and fix than large ones.

In fact, MTBF and MTTR work together to determine availability:

```
Availability = MTBF / (MTBF + MTTR)
```

If MTBF = 180 hours and MTTR = 0.9 hours:

```
Availability = 180 / (180 + 0.9) = 180 / 180.9 = 99.5%
```

This reveals an important insight: You can improve availability by either increasing MTBF (prevent failures) or decreasing MTTR (recover faster). Often, reducing MTTR is more achievable than preventing failures.

Feedback Loops: Closing the Reliability Circle

All these metrics are only valuable if they drive improvement. This is where feedback loops come in: systems where outputs influence future inputs, creating a cycle of continuous adjustment and improvement.

Types of Feedback Loops

Operational feedback loops exist at multiple levels.

Monitoring and Alerts

The fastest loop comes from your monitoring system: CloudWatch, DataDog, Splunk, or the like. These tools watch both your compute resources and running services, monitoring metrics like uptime and response times, letting you detect SLO violations, trigger alerts, and engage on-call engineers. With properly observability tools, changes can happen within minutes.

Incident Postmortems

Postmortems are after-action meetings where teams gather to discuss and break down the details of an outage, bug, or service interruption. They are an essential step in understanding the root causes of issues in your ecosystem. *Blameless postmortems* are an industry best practice in which teams establish ahead of time that these meetings are not designed to assign blame or dole out punishment for any individual's mistakes or shortcomings. Rather, the goal of the postmortem is to discover opportunities to improve the processes that surround such mistakes. This culture of improvement reduces the intimidation factor around postmortem meetings and creates a healthy culture of continuous improvement.

Postmortems are medium-term feedback loops; they don't give you feedback in the moment, while an incident is occurring, but rather after the fact, when more of the picture can be known. Any resulting changes might be implemented within days or weeks.

Long-Term Performance Data

Analyzing long-term performance data is a great source of feedback, if a longer one. Aggregated performance data reveals patterns; maybe certain features are consistently slow or specific endpoints have high error rates. Often, these patterns can only be discovered after they have been in play in a production system for longer periods of time, making this one of the slower feedback loops in operations engineering.

Customer Feedback

Although it's the slowest and most costly loop (because it usually involves a customer getting annoyed enough to speak up), customer feedback can be a valuable signal for process improvement. Sometimes, it's the only way to catch failure states; developers and operations engineers can't think of every scenario. Channels for this kind of feedback might be support tickets, satisfaction surveys, or even social media posts. All these inputs highlight reliability issues from the customer perspective. Because this input is not automated and may spotlight issues that only arise rarely or after the system has been running for some time, this feedback loop might drive architectural changes over quarters.

A Feedback Loop Example

Let's walk through a concrete example. Monitoring on an API shows that latency for the `/search` endpoint has increased. Latency increased from 180 ms to 350 ms over the past week, violating your 200 ms SLO.

You investigate with observability tools and discover that database query times have increased. You can see that the latency increase correlates with the timing of a recent release, as logged by your CI/CD system. In your source control system, pull request notes, related commit messages, and the code diff itself indicate that this new release added a complex join. You work with database administrators to determine that database performance would improve with a new index on one of the tables involved in the join.

Taking action, you work with the database administrators to add the index and optimize the query.

Back to observation, you can see latency drop back to 150 ms, satisfying your SLO and closing the loop.

That resolves the immediate issue. In your postmortem, you realize that there are process-level challenges that could be improved. New features aren't always being performance-tested adequately, and there's no automated way to flag missing indexes.

Using this feedback, you take additional action, first by adding performance regression tests to the CI pipeline. Second, you introduce query analysis tools to the pipeline. Finally, you update the people process, making sure that code review includes steps to flag potentially complex new database queries.

In this scenario, you see the concentric circles of feedback loops and process improvements. Short-term feedback leads to an immediate fix (adding the index), while the longer-term feedback of the postmortem triggers longer-term improvements through better testing, which should prevent future incidents of this type.

Thinking Through a Deployment Example

Now, let's think about these concepts in relation to CI/CD and deployment events.

Your deployment cycle might look like this: pre-deployment, you verify your error budget. You have 80 percent of your monthly budget remaining, leaving plenty of room for a change. You then execute a canary-style deployment, rolling out new code to 5 percent of your fleet. Post-deployment checks pass, and monitoring shows latency and error rates within SLO bounds, which stipulates 99.9 percent uptime.

With confidence in your testing and monitoring, your team triggers the full rollout of the deployment to your entire fleet.

Over the next hour, you notice that availability remains at 99.95 percent (above your 99.9 percent SLO). Latency increases slightly but remains under your 200 ms SLO threshold.

The slight latency increase triggers investigation. You find some inefficient caching behavior and file a ticket with the dev team to optimize it. That optimization then ships in the next sprint, improving latency even below pre-deployment levels.

This cycle of deployment, measuring, learning, and improving is CD in action. Your service levels provide the measurement framework, while error budgets guide your decision-making. MTTR drives your incident response, and feedback loops drive long-term improvement. Everything you hear from your environment, including errors, resource alarms, uptime monitoring, and user feedback, all contribute to improving your service operation.

Summary

In this chapter, we explored how to measure site reliability through uptime tracking, SLOs, SLAs, failure metrics, and feedback loops that make reliability a measurable, manageable discipline.

These concepts tie directly to CD. They give your team the confidence to deploy frequently because you'll know immediately if something goes wrong, you'll recover quickly when it does, and you'll learn from every incident to prevent repeat mistakes.

Service levels also bridge the gap between technical teams and business stakeholders. When ops teams speak the language of SLOs and error budgets, product managers understand the trade-offs. When engineering demonstrates consistent SLA compliance, your customers gain confidence.

Most importantly, these practices create a framework for continuous improvement. Each deployment gives you real-world data; each incident becomes a learning opportunity. Your metrics and monitoring provide continuous feedback. Over time, your systems become more reliable as your team becomes more effective.

That's the ultimate goal of operations automation—not just to ship code faster, but to ship better code more confidently, maintaining and improving service quality even as your velocity increases. These reliability practices make that possible.

Exam Essentials

Understand why dependency management is critical to automation. Know that automation code depends on external libraries, packages, runtimes, and system components. Understand how unmanaged dependencies lead to "works on my machine" failures and why reproducible environments are essential for CI and deployment automation.

Understand how availability is measured. Know that availability represents the percentage of time a service is operational and accessible. Be familiar with the formula for calculating uptime using total time and downtime, and recognize that even small percentage changes can translate to significant real-world downtime.

Recognize what "nines of availability" represent. Understand that availability targets are commonly expressed in "nines" (99 percent, 99.9 percent, 99.99 percent, etc.). Each additional nine represents an order-of-magnitude reduction in downtime and typically requires increased architectural complexity such as redundancy, monitoring, and automated failover.

Understand time-based vs. request-based availability. Know the difference between measuring availability by uptime versus measuring it by request success rate. Time-based availability tracks whether a system is running, while request-based availability measures whether user requests succeed, often giving a more accurate picture of user experience.

Understand the relationship between SLIs and SLOs. Know that a service-level indicator (SLI) is the metric being measured (such as request latency or success rate), whereas a service-level objective (SLO) defines the target threshold for that metric. SLOs represent internal reliability goals tied to user-facing outcomes.

Understand the concept of error budgets. Recognize that an error budget represents the allowable amount of failure implied by an SLO. For example, a 99.9 percent availability target allows 0.1 percent downtime. Error budgets help teams balance reliability with deployment velocity by providing a quantitative limit on acceptable risk.

Understand the difference between SLOs and SLAs. Know that service-level objectives are internal reliability targets, whereas service-level agreements are external commitments to customers that may include contractual consequences such as service credits if targets are not met. Organizations often set SLOs stricter than their SLAs to maintain a safety buffer.

Recognize the purpose of MTBF and MTTR. Know that mean time between failures (MTBF) measures the average time between system failures, whereas mean time to repair (MTTR) measures how long it takes to restore service after a failure. These metrics help teams understand both system stability and recovery effectiveness.

Understand how MTTR influences availability. Recognize that reducing recovery time can improve overall availability even when failures still occur. Automation, monitoring, observability tooling, and rapid rollback mechanisms are common strategies used to reduce MTTR.

Understand the role of feedback loops in operations. Know that feedback loops transform operational metrics into improvements. Monitoring alerts, incident postmortems, long-term performance analysis, and customer feedback all contribute signals that help teams improve reliability and processes over time.

Recognize how service-level metrics influence deployment decisions. Understand that SLOs, error budgets, and operational metrics guide release decisions in continuous delivery environments. When reliability metrics remain within targets, teams can deploy confidently; when error budgets are depleted, teams should prioritize stability and remediation before introducing further changes.

Review Questions

1. What is the primary difference between an SLO and an SLA?
   A. SLOs are internal targets, whereas SLAs are external commitments with contractual consequences.
   B. SLOs measure availability, whereas SLAs measure latency.
   C. SLOs are set by customers, whereas SLAs are set by engineering teams.
   D. SLOs apply to production, whereas SLAs apply to all environments.
2. A service experienced four failures over 720 hours of operation, with a total accumulated downtime of 3.6 hours. What is the mean time to repair (MTTR)?
   A. 0.9 hours (54 minutes)
   B. 180 hours
   C. 3.6 hours
   D. 720 hours
3. A service runs for 720 hours in a month and experiences exactly four failures. What is its mean time between failures (MTBF)?
   A. 3.6 hours
   B. 180 hours
   C. 0.9 hours
   D. 99.5%
4. A team has a 99.9 percent monthly availability SLO. So far this month they have experienced 35 minutes of downtime. Approximately how much error budget remains?
   A. 8.8 minutes
   B. 43.8 minutes
   C. 35 minutes
   D. 0 minutes (the budget is exhausted)
5. A service targets "five nines" of availability. Approximately how much annual downtime does this permit?
   A. 5.26 minutes
   B. 52.6 minutes
   C. 8.77 hours
   D. 3.65 days

6. Which type of operational feedback loop provides the fastest response to a live service degradation?
   A. Long-term performance data analysis
   B. Automated monitoring and alerting
   C. Customer support tickets
   D. Blameless postmortems
7. What is the primary goal of a blameless postmortem?
   A. To identify and formally discipline the engineer responsible for the outage
   B. To identify systemic process improvements that will prevent similar incidents in the future
   C. To calculate the financial cost of the incident and bill customers accordingly
   D. To update the service-level agreement with stricter uptime targets
8. A service was technically running 100 percent of the time last month, but 0.6 percent of requests returned `HTTP 500` errors due to intermittent database connection failures. Which metric most accurately reflects the user experience?
   A. Time-based availability (100 percent)
   B. Request-based availability (99.4 percent)
   C. Mean time between failures
   D. Mean time to repair
9. A company's external SLA commits to 99.5 percent monthly availability. The engineering team sets an internal SLO of 99.9 percent. What is the primary reason the SLO is stricter than the SLA?
   A. Regulatory requirements mandate that internal targets always exceed external commitments.
   B. The stricter SLO creates a buffer, allowing the team to detect and correct issues before they breach the customer-facing SLA.
   C. SLOs must always be set to the theoretical maximum to keep the team motivated.
   D. The SLA only applies during business hours, so the SLO compensates for the difference.
10. Two services each experience four failures per month and have an MTBF of 180 hours. Service A has an MTTR of 0.9 hours, while Service B has an MTTR of 4.5 hours. Which statement best explains the difference in their availability?
    A. Service A has higher availability because it has fewer failures per month than Service B.
    B. Service A has higher availability because its shorter recovery time reduces total overall downtime.
    C. Service B has higher availability because a longer repair time implies more thorough fixes.
    D. Both services have identical availability because they fail the same number of times.

Answers to Review Questions

1. A. The correct answer is A. Service-level objectives (SLOs) are internal targets that teams set for themselves to guide operational decisions, whereas service-level agreements (SLAs) are formal contracts with customers that include defined remedies (such as service credits) when service levels are not met. Teams typically set SLOs tighter than SLAs to create a buffer for catching issues before they breach customer commitments. Option B is incorrect because both SLOs and SLAs can measure any service-level indicator, including availability, latency, error rates, or throughput. Option C is incorrect because it reverses the actual relationship. Option D is incorrect because both concepts primarily apply to production systems where user-facing service levels matter, though teams may set internal SLOs for any environment.

2. A. Option A is correct. MTTR = Total Downtime / Number of Failures = 3.6 hours / 4 = 0.9 hours (54 minutes). Option B is the MTBF, not the MTTR. Option C is total downtime, not per-failure. Option D would be total uptime.

3. B. Option B is correct. MTBF = Total Uptime / Number of Failures = 720 / 4 = 180 hours. Option A is total downtime; C is mean time to repair. Option D is the resulting availability percentage, not a time value.

4. A. Option A is correct. A 99.9 percent monthly SLO allows 0.1 percent of roughly 43,800 minutes (30 days), which is approximately 43.8 minutes of downtime. With 35 minutes consumed, approximately 8.8 minutes remain. Option B is the full monthly budget before any consumption. Option C is the amount already spent. Option D is incorrect because 35 < 43.8.

5. A. Option A is correct. Five nines (99.999 percent) permits roughly 5.26 minutes of annual downtime. That's an order of magnitude less than four nines (99.99% ≈ 52.6 minutes). Option B represents four nines. Option C is three nines (99.9 percent), and Option D is two nines (99 percent).

6. B. Option B is correct. Automated monitoring and alerting can detect SLO violations and notify on-call engineers within seconds or minutes. Option D, postmortems, occur after the fact. Customer tickets depend on users noticing and reporting issues, which means this channel lags behind automated ones. Option A, long-term analysis, operates over days, weeks, or months.

7. B. Option B is correct. Blameless postmortems deliberately avoid attributing fault to individuals and instead focus on identifying root causes at the process and systems level, fostering a culture of continuous improvement without fear of punishment. Option A contradicts the blameless principle; options C and D are not the primary purpose of a postmortem.

8. B. Option B is correct. Request-based availability measures the percentage of requests that succeed. Even though the service never went fully down, the 0.6 percent error rate means users experienced failures on roughly 1 in 167 requests, a more accurate reflection of their experience than time-based availability. Options C and D, MTBF and MTTR, measure failure frequency and recovery time, not per-request success.

9. B. Option B is correct. Setting the internal SLO higher than the external SLA creates a safety margin. If availability drops to, say, 99.7 percent, your internal SLO is violated and alerts should go off, giving you time to intervene before the situation deteriorates to the 99.5 percent SLA threshold. Option A is not a standard regulatory requirement. Option C is impractical and is not how SLOs are used. Option D is wrong because SLAs are not limited to certain hours.

10. B. Option B is correct. Let's do the math. Availability = MTBF / (MTBF + MTTR). Service A: 180 / 180.9 ≈ 99.5 percent. Service B: 180 / 184.5 ≈ 97.6%. With equal MTBF, Service A's much shorter MTTR is the deciding factor. Option A is wrong, because both services fail equally often. Option C is incorrect; repair time doesn't tell you anything about quality. Option D is incorrect because MTTR, not just failure count, determines availability.

Index

Note: Page numbers in *italics* and **bold** refers to figures and tables respectively.

A

D

E

F

L

M

N

O

P

Q

R

S

Online Test Bank

To help you study for your CompTIA AutoOps+ certification exams, register to gain one year of FREE access after activation to the online interactive test bank—included with your purchase of this book!

To access our learning environment, simply visit `www.wiley.com/go/sybextestprep`, follow the instructions to register your book, and instantly gain one year of FREE access after activation to:

- All of the chapter questions from this book, so you can practice in a timed and graded setting
- A set of 100 flashcards
- A searchable glossary